P9-DHG-238

The United States and South Africa, 1968–1985

E
183.8
.S6
C65
1986

The United States and South Africa, 1968–1985

Constructive Engagement and Its Critics

Christopher Coker

Duke University Press   Durham 1986

© 1986, Duke University Press
All rights reserved
Printed in the United States of America
on acid-free paper ∞
Library of Congress Cataloging in Publication Data
appear on the last printed page of this book.

The purpose of diplomacy is not
to solve problems, but to live with
them unresolved.

Dean Acheson
Present at the Creation (1969)

Competing pressures tempt one
to believe that an issue deferred
is a problem avoided. More often
it is a crisis invited.

Henry Kissinger
The White House Years (1979)

Contents

Preface

Books have many origins. This one began life as an Oxford D. Phil. thesis in 1978 when constructive engagement was already part of the history of American policy toward South Africa. It was finally completed after the policy had been resurrected and applied once again, with indifferent success and amidst great controversy. Oscar Wilde expected to be met at the gates of Heaven by a flustered Saint Peter bearing an armful of his unwritten works. Between the time that the thesis was completed and the book embarked upon, it seemed that this work might be one of the author's phantom pregnancies.

Any book on South Africa must begin with a disclaimer, particularly a book on such a narrow theme. It is still surprising that even at this late date there seem to be an amazing number of books which go over the well-trodden ground of what the West might do to bring peaceful change in South Africa, many of them oblivious to what little leverage for positive change the West still has. This study is intended to suggest that there is little the West can do, that the black community will have to rely largely on its own efforts, that external actors only delude themselves (and others) about the extent of their political influence.

If one is to begin with a disclaimer, one might also add a confession. I have great sympathy for those authors who have argued that the political scene in South Africa must be looked at in its own right before there can be any suggestion that external intervention may be a critical variable. If there is still disagreement as to whether the external factor is or is not to be considered important, or is in any event to be seen more as a response than an initiative, I suspect that the story yet to be recorded of negative sanctions on South Africa may be as unrewarding and full of false promise as the recent history of contact and "constructive engagement."

The story this book has to tell is more disappointing still because engagement enjoyed one great advantage. In the past, one of the key errors of American policy had been to devise a set of tactics in default of a strategy. As George Ball once observed, "We have never thought through the problem of South Africa. Thus we have no clear idea of how we want the story to end."[1] Between the years 1969 to 1974 and 1981 to 1984 the United States had a clear strategy and even a plausible tactical plan; the very fact that it achieved so little might therefore be taken to illustrate the limits of American power, the threshold beyond which external powers can expect to exert little or no influence over events.

In writing this book I have found myself asking many of those questions that seem to be central to the political scientist's claim to a fair hearing from the policymakers, those who are responsible for the policies we criticize without constraint. How does the political scientist choose his theme, or is he in some sense chosen? What real degree of access to the inner thoughts of politicians can he obtain through reading government papers or personal memoirs? What principles of selection of materials does he work on beyond mere hunch and instinctive feeling? What risks does he run, perhaps unconsciously, by identifying with the subject? Above all how does he bring his own present into fruitful relation with that of the past—a problem I encountered for the Nixon years? The last problem is one of the most intractable of all, for if one can have little respect for those who allow themselves to be blinded by hindsight, there is little to be said either for those who decline to ask the questions that hindsight suggests.

How far I have answered such questions remains to be seen. I hope, however, that I shall not incur opprobrium for speaking up for the authors of constructive engagement, for telling something of their aspirations and hopes, and explaining why they acted as they did. If this study is critical of the policy, it is more so in the sense of disappointments shared, of aims that were honorable if elusive, of opportunities that may not have been missed, because they may never have existed. In this sense the present study is a conservative critique of a conservative policy, and I hope none the less worthwhile for that.

In such a confessional mood it is only fair, perhaps, to end by stating the main conclusion of this book, implicit throughout but never stated. What the Nixon and Reagan administrations set out to accomplish bears testimony, at least in the early years, to a seriousness of purpose it is hard to find in the Kennedy or Carter years. Neither administration deserves its bad press. If they erred, they erred on the side of wishful thinking. In a situation as complex and appalling as South Africa's, who would dare cast the first stone against hope?

Biographies of Major Policymakers

Abshire, David Born 1926; executive director, Center for Strategic and International Studies, Georgetown University, 1962–70; assistant secretary of state for congressional relations, 1970–73; presidential appointee, Commission on the Organization of Government for Conduct of Foreign Policy, 1973–75.

Ball, George Born 1909; under secretary of state for economic affairs, 1961; under secretary of state, 1961–66; U.S. permanent representative to the United Nations, 1968.

Blake, James Born 1922; Foreign Affairs Office, Department of Defense, 1961–63; deputy director, Office of North African Affairs, 1963–65, director, 1965–66; country director, Office of North African Affairs, 1963–65; deputy assistant secretary of state for African affairs, 1974–76.

Bowles, Chester Born 1901; special assistant to the secretary-general, United Nations, 1947–48; ambassador to India, 1951–53; member, 86th U.S. Congress; under secretary of state, 1961; president's special representative for Asian, African, and Latin American affairs, 1961; ambassador to India, 1963.

Buffum, William Born 1921; director, Political Affairs Bureau, International Organization Affairs, 1959–67; deputy assistant secretary of state, 1965–67; deputy U.S. representative to United Nations, 1967–70; assistant secretary of state, International Organization Affairs, 1973 —.

Crocker, Chester Born 1941; consultant, Department of State; NSC staff officer for the coordination of policy studies on the Middle East, Africa, and the Indian Ocean, 1970–72; director of African studies program, Georgetown University, 1976–81; assistant secretary of state for African affairs, 1981— .

Easum, Donald   Born 1923; director, Interdependent Group Staff Bureau on Inter-American Affairs, NSC, 1969–71; ambassador to Upper Volta, 1971–74; assistant secretary of state for African affairs, 1974–75.

Fergusson, Clyde   Born 1924; U.S. representative to United Nations, Subcommittee on Discrimination, 1964; special coordinator, relief to civilian victims of the Nigerian civil war, 1969–70; ambassador to Uganda, 1970–72; deputy assistant secretary of state for African affairs, 1972–73.

Finger, Seymour   Born 1915; U.S. Mission to United Nations, 1956–65; counselor of Mission to United Nations, 1965–67; senior adviser to permanent representative, U.S. Mission to United Nations, 1967–71.

Goldberg, Arthur   Born 1908; secretary of labor, 1961–62; associate justice, U.S. Supreme Court, 1962–65; U.S. representative to United Nations, 1965–68.

Kissinger, Henry   Born 1923; professor, Harvard University, 1962–69; professor, Faculty Center for International Affairs, 1960–69; assistant to president, National Security Affairs, 1969–74; secretary of state, 1973–77.

Lord, Winston   Born 1937; member of staff, International Security Affairs, Department of Defense, 1967–69; member of staff, NSC, 1969–73; special assistant to president, National Security Affairs, 1970–73; director, policy planning staff, Department of State, 1973–77.

Mitchell, Clarence   Born 1911; director, NAACP Washington bureau, 1950–78; chairman, Leadership Conference, Civil Rights; U.S. representative, seventh special session, 30th General Assembly, United Nations, 1975.

Morris, Roger   Joined government, 1966; foreign service officer, staff of Secretary Rusk, 1967; special assistant to McGeorge Bundy, 1967; NSC staff, 1968; succeeded Edward Hamilton as senior staff member, African affairs, 1968; senior staff assistant to Kissinger, 1968.

Newsom, David   Born 1918; deputy director, Office of African Affairs, 1962–63, director, 1963–65; U.S. ambassador to Libya, 1965–69; assistant secretary of state for African affairs, 1969–74; special adviser, U.S. delegation, United Nations General Assembly, 1972.

Palmer, Joseph   Born 1914; deputy assistant secretary of state for African affairs, 1956–58; American consul general to Rhodesia and Nyasaland, 1958–60; assistant secretary of state for African affairs, 1966–68.

Phillips, Christopher   Born 1920; U.S. representative to United Nations Economic and Social Council, 1958–61; president, U.S. Council, International Chamber of Commerce, 1965–69; deputy U.S. representative, United Nations, 1970–73.

Rogers, William   Born 1913; attorney general, 1958–61; representative, 20th United Nations General Assembly, 1967; United Nations Ad Hoc Committee on South Africa, 1967; secretary of state, 1969–73.

Rusk, Dean   Born 1909; assistant secretary of state, 1949; deputy under secretary of state, 1949–50; assistant secretary of state for Far Eastern affairs, 1950–51; secretary of state, 1961–68.

Schaufele, William   Born 1923; deputy director, Office of Central African Affairs, 1965–67; country director, Central West African affairs, 1967–69; ambassador to Upper Volta, 1969–71; senior adviser to U.S. representative, United Nations, 1971–73; U.S. deputy representative, UN Security Council, 1973–75; assistant secretary of state for African affairs, 1975–77.

Williams, G. Mennen   Born 1911; governor of Michigan, 1949–60; assistant secretary of state for African affairs, 1961–66.

Wright, Marshall   Born 1926; spokesman, State Department, 1964–66; NSC member, 1967–68; senior NSC member, director of long-range planning, 1970–72; assistant secretary of state for congressional relations, 1972–74.

1 The United States and South Africa, 1960–1968

In the early 1960s Southern Africa became the focus of one of the most divisive of all international problems: that of racial conflict. Although 90 percent of Africa's white population, compared with only 11 percent of its black, lived in the region, the former constituted only 15 percent of the area's total population. This concentration provided the white community with the means of control that had eluded the white settlers of Algeria and Kenya. For a time it appeared that in this region life was strong in political and social structures that elsewhere in the continent had fallen victim to black nationalism. Where the concentration was largest of all—in South Africa—the whites seemed most secure. Apartheid—the mandatory segregation of the races introduced onto the statute book in 1948—provided a philosophy more potent than the defense of group interest or privilege. The South Africans appeared to be better placed than any other white settlers to contain black nationalism, and better equipped to consolidate their own position. Such was the extent of white control that less than a fifth of South Africa's inhabitants owned 88 percent of its land and held no less than two-thirds of its purchasing power.

Although the whites tended to see Southern Africa as a regional subsystem which extended beyond their own sphere of influence to the Zambezi River (one South African writer described the region as "the third Africa" to distinguish it from the rest of sub-Saharan Africa and the Arab north),[1] this study is concerned only with the Republic of South Africa (as the Union became in 1961). J. F. Malan's victory in 1948 heralded a social revolution. In the space of less than seven years his government introduced a series of laws and regulations of a complexity unparalleled in any society outside the communist bloc. Most Western governments failed to recognize the extent of the transformation until it was too late; certainly most failed to appreciate the importance of intervening before apartheid had been institutionally consolidated. If South Africa's racial laws offended against the liberal conscience, few liberals appreciated the implications of National party rule until well into the 1950s. Disapproval of apartheid may well have been widespread and deep-seated; but it was neither deep-seated enough nor voiced unanimously enough to persuade the West to intervene. It was not until the early 1960s that the United States, in the person of Adlai Stevenson, its ambassador to the United Nations, recognized that the race problem in Southern Africa was the result not only of a long historical legacy of social injustice but also of a process of arrested political development in the preceding fifteen years.[2]

It was a story with which the world was soon to become familiar. The 1948 election may have been fought on the issue of apartheid, but the real issue had been Afrikaner unity, which held sufficiently to enable the new government of J. F. Malan to break decisively with the English-speaking "liberalism" which South Africa's former Prime Minister Jan Smuts had represented. The upshot was a radical shift in voting patterns, aided by Malan's program of race legislation: the repeal of the Indian Representation Act (1948) and the award of six new seats to South-West Africa the following year, every one of which were won by Nationalist MPs in the election of 1950. Hopes that the period of National party rule might be brief were dashed in 1953 when Malan increased his majority to thirty-one, despite a massive campaign by the United Democratic Front—an alliance of the United and Labour parties.

Throughout the 1950s the National party defended itself against enemies internal and external alike, in part by creating a formidable security apparatus and subordinating the legal system to the goal of maintaining white supremacy. Because of the decline of municipal and provincial councils the government became increasingly centralized, absorbing one-half million of the one and a quarter million economically active whites into the public service, 26 percent of the white population, the largest percentage outside the communist world. In 1950 the cornerstone of apartheid—the Population Regis-

Table 1 Population Breakdown of Southern Africa
by Country and Race (1969)

Country	Population[1]	White	Black	White as % of black
Angola[2]	5,230,000	270,000	4,975,000	5
Mozambique[2]	7,505,000	160,000	7,445,000	2
South Africa[2]	21,448,000	3,751,000	15,058,000	20
Namibia	500,000	70,000	420,000	14
Rhodesia	5,051,000	228,000	4,823,000	4

SOURCE   National Security Study Memorandum 39 (NSSM 39) Annex I.
1. Not including Portuguese military forces.
2. Figures supplemented by Susan Gitelson, "The transformation of the Southern African state system." *Journal of African Studies* 4:4 (Winter 1977), 369.

tration Act—assigned the entire population to three racial groups: whites, Coloureds, and Africans. The Coloured classification was further subdivided into Asians as well as persons of mixed race. Under another law the Africans were divided into eight major tribal groups. The same year saw the Group Areas Act, which created separate group areas of residence in the main towns and cities (in many of which existing ownership and occupation patterns were permanently fixed).

These measures did not go without resistance, but for the most part it was ineffective. Although more than eight thousand blacks went to jail for defying the segregationist laws in the "Defiance Campaign" of 1952, the movement never came close to sparking the general strike it had hoped for. Repressive laws already on the books, including the sweeping Suppression of Communism Act, soon came into play. New laws further limiting demonstrations were enacted, ensuring that although smaller-scale protest meetings, strikes, and consumer boycotts continued, they did so in a very attenuated form. Otherwise, the government encountered very few setbacks in its clampdown on black dissent. Indeed, it went much further, removing the Coloureds from the common voting roll in 1956 and eliminating African representation by white parties in the National Assembly three years later. Long before Sharpeville, events had borne out the prediction of Smuts's deputy Jan Hofmeyr on the eve of the 1948 general election: that the defeat of the United party would mark not only an electoral upset; it would mark nothing less than the beginning of a major social revolution.[3]

Until 1960 the United States was able to stand on the sidelines as a dispassionate, if not disinterested observer. For most of the period it refused to choose between its economic interests and moral responsibilities and for the most part was not required to do so. During the years that Malan and his successor J. G. Strijdom introduced the political and legislative infrastructure of apartheid, the West largely remained silent. In the first major United Nations debate on apartheid in 1952 the United States took a middle-of-the-road position, in the hope of avoiding "both excess of zeal and timid legalism." Its ambassador saw fit to remind the General Assembly that the role of the United Nations was strictly limited. It could not intervene in matters essentially within the domestic jurisdiction of states; it had "no power to impose standards, but only to proclaim them."[4]

Moreover, if Washington's critics believed the United States had the power to preempt the structuring of South African society on such blatant racial lines, for much of the period the cost of doing so appeared to be disproportionate to the political returns. In an era of containment South Africa's friendship was of more enduring concern than the policy of separate development, or apartheid. In Eisenhower's world picture, and that of his secretary of state, John Foster Dulles, South Africa was one more ally in the struggle against international communism. Shortly before the Sharpeville massacre Joseph Satterthwaite, the first assistant secretary for African affairs, asked the Senate Committee on Foreign Relations whether it was sensible for the United States to express its opposition to National party policies when the government of South Africa offered such unqualified support in the overriding issue of the day: the containment of the Soviet Union.[5]

For many years this was a perception shared by Pretoria. American behavior was so ambiguous, so open to interpretation, that it was possible for South Africa's first foreign minister, Eric Louw, to pass off an adverse American vote in the United Nations in 1959 as an event which did not represent any fundamental change of American policy, to dismiss it as an unfortunate chance result of the fact that the leader of the U.S. delegation happened to be a prominent labor leader well known for his dislike of racial segregation in all its forms.[6]

It was the Sharpeville massacre, in which seventy blacks lost their lives, which changed the terms of the debate overnight. In the days that followed, 120 of the country's magistracies were placed under a state of emergency, the two main nationalist parties—the African National Congress (ANC) and the Pan African Congress (PAC)—were banned, and 1,500 of their members were arrested. Those who were fortunate enough to escape went underground, turning to sabotage and subversion where constitutional opposition had failed. For the first time Washington was haunted by the specter of revolution. The climate of unrest that lasted for several months paralyzed the public services, as well as industry, and produced a serious run on the stock exchange. The flight of foreign capital and the run on the country's foreign reserves continued throughout 1960 and well into the following year. Later the South African writer Lewis Nkosi wrote that what had taken place in the spring and summer of 1960 was "the kind of crisis which all too often makes possible a transfer of power overnight."

Somewhat belatedly the United States came out in support of a rapid transfer of power. The threat of revolutionary unrest forced it to act quickly for fear that any undue delay might be fatal. If Sharpeville had any long-term impact on American thinking, its impact was largely negative. The United States appeared to object less to the nature of the political system than the violence it had provoked. In the months that followed, American officials expressed particular concern that if the nationalist leaders, now in exile, turned to subversion it would only be a matter of time before they succumbed to Marxism's seductively articulate visions of the future. In short, the United States intervened to contain the violence that had broken out, not to preempt it. It was no longer possible to contend as Satterthwaite had done in the immediate run-up to the crisis, that the most America could do was to set an example by pursuing civil rights legislation at home, in the hope of proving conclusively that a pluralistic society could exist once racial discrimination had been removed from the statute books. After 1960 the tenor of American statements changed quite dramatically. Satterthwaite's successor, for one, questioned whether the United States could refrain from intervening if it wished to keep ahead of events, and not be swamped by them.[7]

In April 1960, in keeping with this sense of urgency, Washington agreed to place apartheid permanently on the Security Council's agenda. In November it followed up this initiative by dispatching an aide-mémoire urging South Africa in the strongest terms to abandon a policy and a set of political principles which were so clearly in violation of the UN Charter. When Pretoria refused to comply with the request, President Kennedy felt compelled to apply a selective arms embargo, a year before the United Nations applied its own. Toward the end of 1962, South Africa's Prime Minister Hendrik Verwoerd conceded that the Americans might consider international action against the republic. Although he went on to question whether it would be in their economic or strategic interest to do so, the very fact that he had been forced to deal publicly with such speculation revealed how far along the road to divorce relations between the United States and South Africa had gone.[8] In any event, the arms embargo proved to be a great embarrassment to Washington. By 1963 the crisis had passed. Almost the entire leadership of the ANC fell into police hands at a secret meeting in Rivonia. During the period that followed, which came to be known as the "post-Rivonia stalemate," the Kennedy administration began to suspect that it had misread events completely. Far from being caught up in the "winds of change" that had swept through the continent in the 1950s, South Africa appeared, for the moment at least, to have successfully "ridden the whirlwind."[9]

Two years earlier Kennedy's under secretary of state, Chester Bowles, had written to Secretary of State Dean Rusk: "There are few who doubt that the republic of South Africa will blow up in due course. When this occurs will we be able to say that we took every step or practical measure to prevent or temper the holocaust?"[10] The problem with such forecasts, with their grim vision of the future, was their timing. By the end of 1963 they appeared to be absurdly unrealistic, if not naive. Before leaving for South Africa as America's new ambassador, Joseph Satterthwaite had been told by the State Department to prepare for a black government within eighteen months to five years.[11] Robert Good, the director of the Africa Bureau's department of research and analysis, later admitted that he had been personally responsible for foolishly optimistic forecasts of the rate of political change. By contrast, when Satterthwaite himself appeared before a congressional committee nine years later, he predicted that South Africa would have at least a decade to reform its political system, perhaps much longer: "The fact is that the South African government is presently so strong politically and militarily and the economy of the country is so sound that it would be wishful thinking to expect that the long hoped for breakthrough in racial relations will occur in the near or even foreseeable future in the absence of developments either internal or external that we cannot now anticipate."[12]

The main problem was not that the policymakers had been responsible for tendentious critiques, but that the situation had changed so radically that the hypotheses they had drawn from the critique had lost much of their relevance. No policymaker can escape from his own age with its notions of significance. Policymakers exist to make hypotheses of the future by interpreting future trends in the pattern of their own. But in 1960 the pattern had proved deceptive. By the mid-1960s the situation had stabilized: the whites were once again firmly in control. Writing some years later the South African historian Cornelis de Kiewiet remarked that South Africa provided a bizarre example of "a revolution that had disappeared."[13]

The profound change this gave rise to within government circles can be charted in the academic debate that followed. Writing in 1965, the distinguished social scientist Pierre van den Berghe still felt able to contend that "although the exact course of events is impossible to foresee in any detail, the likelihood of revolution seems high. Mounting internal strains and external pressures doom white supremacy and racial segregation within the near future."[14] Yet even he had to admit that the case of South Africa seemed to challenge the validity and usefulness of most theories of revolution and rebellion. Commenting on van den Berghe's assertion that "South Africa has survived so long in such an acute state of disequilibrium is indeed highly problematic for sociological theory," Diana Russell concluded nine years later that "most of the theories focus on conditions that affect the regime and its agents or the wider structural context of rebellion. That is why they are useless in understanding the South African situation where it is probably not that the push for rebellion is weak, but that the *obstacles* are so enormous [my emphasis]."[15]

The Johnson administration had already come to that conclusion some years before. During a long official review of American policy initiated in 1961 and formally concluded three years later, the State Department had recommended that the United States should concentrate on the encouragement of *achievable* economic and social change in the fields of black labor and education.[16] Since the ANC appeared to be a spent force after the Rivonia trials, the CIA had also asked whether it would not be sensible to encourage change from within by denying support to those groups based outside the country.[17] In the years that followed the U.S. government began to look at some of the ways of dismantling the obstacles to political reform, while minimizing the dangers of internal rebellion. It was a highly elitist response based on Russell's premise that "a rebellion or revolution can succeed only if the regime or elite is disintegrating, or disunited or loses confidence in itself, or stops believing it has the right to keep power." Since Washington wished to preempt a revolution, and since the South African government could hardly be accused of lacking confidence or faith in the future, it seemed sensible to build upon its sense of confidence by persuading or pressuring it to lift some of the obstacles to a political dialogue between the races, that is, to reform itself out of a revolution while it still had time.

If the Johnson administration made remarkably little progress, this was largely because it never resolved in its own mind whether to influence the process through concessions or sanctions. Clearly, the Americans were trapped by the ambiguities of their own position, for they had no wish to see the blacks challenge white supremacy by embarking upon a course of action that would merely invite further repression and render their own noninterventionist posture even more contentious. At the same time Johnson's assistant secretary for African affairs, G. Mennen Williams, publicly conceded that nonintervention on the part of the international community was impossible to defend when the state allowed so little scope for internal discussion of its future.

> It is frequently said that in the last analysis the people of South Africa must work out their own destiny. But how is this to take place when the internal forces for change are so effectively repressed? It is also pointed out that in South Africa economic forces are breaking down segregationist practices and isolationist patterns of thought. But how are such changes to be translated into the political and social fields? How long will it take? And what can outside forces do to accelerate the process?[18]

Williams's predecessors had tended to represent apartheid as a social and economic monstrosity which they felt would be bound to collapse, sooner rather than later, under the weight of its own internal contradictions. Williams managed to transcend such glib analyses by questioning whether any improvement in the economic status of black workers would have any political significance as long as the obstacles to change, especially in the form of legal statutes, remained so severe.

In the past the source of a good deal of false optimism had been argument by analogy. Williams saw no reason to maintain that America's own progress on the civil rights front had demonstrated beyond dispute that fundamental attitudes to race were susceptible to change. The analogy, he recognized, was in fact the main weakness of the argument, for in South Africa the legislative machinery of apartheid ruled out any real possibility of constitutional opposition. If political change turned on what the law allowed, there were few if any lessons to be learned from America's own civil rights campaign. The black community in the United States may have resorted to civil disobedience during the 1950s, but they had done so only after testing the legality of each form of protest in the courts. It was precisely because they had been accepted by the state as legitimate acts of civil disobedience—rather than illegal and illegitimate acts of public disorder—that it had been possible to describe them as a form of "legitimated disobedience."[19] Denied this possibility in South Africa, did the black community have any alternative but violence? If the options were not to be posed in such stark terms, they would have to be given *external* support. Some pressure would have to be applied on the South African government to moderate its response. It was on the question of the form such pressure should take that the debate largely turned after 1966.

Even in the closing days of the Johnson administration American officials began to question whether negative sanctions were a very useful approach. Indecision and indecisiveness tend to generate spontaneous hypocrisy. American policy in South Africa was no exception. The arms embargo of 1962 had proved to be a broken reed. American equipment continued to be exported to the republic throughout the 1960s, with or without the Department of Commerce's knowledge. From the first it had been an expedient to salve Kennedy's conscience, a measure intended to meet the aspirations of the new African states without setting a precedent for sanctions against other states in the future. Writing several years later, Kennedy's speechwriter Arthur Schlesinger recalled how

> the prospect of a total UN embargo troubled the President and the Secretary of State as setting a precedent for collective sanctions which might lead the United Nations down the road imperilling its very existence. Instead, the Department favored a call upon UN states to refrain from supplying arms which could be used to suppress the African population. Then Kennedy, in a brilliant stroke, went further and proposed a unilateral declaration that as a matter of national policy the United States would sell no further arms to South Africa after the first of the year, so long as South Africa practiced apartheid. . . . The action could not long satisfy the insatiable African demand for stronger measures against apartheid; but it preserved the new African faith in American policy.[20]

It may have done so for a time, but it did not do so for very long. According to the text of a memorandum between Kennedy and Tanganyika's new leader, Julius Nyerere, the White House had examined the extent of U.S. arms shipments to South Africa only to find that they totaled less than $2 million. "These quantities," the memorandum concluded, "are not significant to produce a change in South Africa's racial policies." The President said he wished to "consider the matter further."[21] Whatever Kennedy may have had in mind passed into history with his death a few months later.

It is important to note in passing that another memorandum had been penned at about the same time by a junior State Department official, Waldemar Campbell, and had followed quite a different tack. If American arms sales were so small, would it not be more sensible to boost their sale in return for political concessions at home? Would it not be more sensible to continue selling arms to Pretoria to offset its fears about external aggression, and thus bolster any resolve it might one day have toward repealing the pass laws, eliminating petty apartheid, and allowing black workers the right to form trade unions? Only if the whites proved totally obdurate would it be advisable to threaten them with punitive measures, including, Campbell ventured, an official discouragement of any further U.S. investment.[22] Nothing more was to be heard of these arguments until 1969 and the coming of a new administration, by which time their author had moved on to become acting director for Southern African affairs.

As we look back at these arguments twenty years later Campbell's main theme seems incontrovertible, so much so that it is surprising that it was overlooked at the time: that since the situation in Southern Africa was not sufficiently dangerous for an arms embargo to have much effect, and since Washington had no intention of applying further sanctions, it would have been ill-positioned in terms of administrative reach to have met a second crisis if one had come. As it was, the embargo had little effect. In a matter of months the General Assembly began clamoring for tougher measures, including comprehensive economic sanctions and, at the very least, a mandatory ban on the sale of arms. When the United States questioned the efficacy of these proposals it found itself under attack for "racism." As the National Security Council later reported, the measures adopted between 1963 and 1965 were as far as the United States could or would go through the medium of the United Nations.[23]

If this was indeed the case, if in all honesty America felt disinclined to support the forces of radical change, it might have been better to have dropped its call for a peaceful resolution of the conflict. To argue that violence was inevitable was to admit that the United States could do nothing itself to prevail upon the whites to make concessions; to argue otherwise seemed to many rank hypocrisy. As the president of Botswana told an American audience several years later, it had once been customary to describe American policy as disillusioned; perhaps, however, with the passage of time it was more accurate to characterize it as a policy which, beginning with no illusions, had degenerated in the course of time into one of general indifference.[24]

It was clear by 1968 that this posture could not be continued indefinitely. Within the government it came under attack from two sides. Both Arthur Goldberg, President Johnson's ambassador to the UN, and George Ball, his under secretary of state, brought into focus the sharp philosophical differences that divided the Democratic party throughout the 1960s. But for Goldberg's personal lobbying the administration's rhetoric would have been as ambiguous as its actions. As it was, the U.S. mission at the United Nations retained enough autonomy to criticize South Africa more consistently than any other department of state. America's delegation to the UN Commission on Human Rights accused Pretoria of undermining every principle of natural justice, of deliberately violating internationally accepted standards of legal behavior. Later still, however, Nixon's first ambassador, Charles Yost, was prompted to question whether such rhetoric was very useful when the political will to do anything more was so patently absent—whether it might not be more constructive for all sides in the debate to lower their voices in order to better understand each other's position.[25]

By that time Goldberg himself might well have agreed. In fairness, he had pressed for many years for tougher measures. On his retirement he revealed that he had been most preoccupied with the limited nature of sanctions, not whether they could succeed in societies that seemed in all other respects to be impervious to outside influence. Among the measures he had campaigned for without success, two figured prominently: a mandatory arms embargo, despite the risk of bringing the United States into collision with the republic's principal arms supplier, France; and the termination of any future cooperation in the sphere of nuclear energy, regardless of whether the State Department came into conflict with the Department of Commerce.[26] In 1965 Goldberg fought hard to persuade the Commerce Department to discourage further U.S. investment in South Africa, and even to withdraw guarantees on existing investment. Although the State Department did its best to obstruct the policy, Secretary Rusk gave it his support.

By this time, however, even Mennen Williams had begun to question the wisdom of the sanctions approach. During his appearance before the House Committee on Foreign Relations he questioned whether political influence was not contingent upon those very commercial and political links Goldberg wished to sever. By 1966 he had come out strongly against introducing a trade embargo similar to that already in operation against Rhodesia, even though in both cases the objective—majority rule—was the same. Williams remained convinced that the web of interests that bound the United States and South Africa, in particular South Africa's reliance on the West for most of its capital equipment, made comprehensive economic sanctions both unnecessary and inappropriate.[27]

For one reason or another the Johnson administration had begun to rethink its position even before Nixon came to office. Extending the scope of U.S. interests and repealing some of the credit embargoes already in force was not necessarily the only answer to the problem.

It was, however, one answer, and from that a great deal more could follow, especially for those more conservative members of the administration—foremost among them George Ball, who profoundly disagreed with its prevailing liberal ethos. Ball came from a school which doubted whether coercion could ever play a useful role in international politics. As under secretary of state he had opposed the original adoption of the arms embargo in 1962 and continued to remain skeptical that conditions in South Africa would ever permit the government to capitulate under pressure. In the reflections on government service that he published in 1968 he argued that, given South Africa's military strength and industrial self-sufficiency, economic sanctions were unlikely to meet with success: "In the modern world sanctions are not likely to work even when the siege of an economy is enforced by military power. Where military power is not employed and the enforcement of an embargo depends merely on the agreement of nations—whether or not expressed in a UN resolution —the result will more likely be annoyance than hardship."[28]

Nevertheless, Ball went on to draw conclusions that not all would have shared, even those in agreement with his analysis. In so doing he joined with those who had begun to doubt the political objectives the United States had set as well as its methods of achieving them. Majority rule, he believed, would destroy the fabric of the society. Far from leading to the economic liberation of the black worker, it would transform the republic into an "economic slum." Such radical departures from the prevailing consensus were nonetheless held in check by more pressing preoccupations, notably the war in Vietnam, which finally prompted Ball himself to resign from the administration.

Those outside it were more outspoken. In an article a few years later written for the influential American journal *Foreign Affairs*, the veteran political commentator George Kennan, a former director of policy planning in the State Department, criticized successive administrations for minimizing the real changes already under way in South Africa. Real income among the blacks had increased by 4 percent per annum; black skilled workers were being brought into the labor market at the rate of 2.5 percent a year. Educational opportunities were already in some respects far ahead of those existing in the black-ruled countries to the north, and were showing steady improvement at the primary and trade school levels. In the light of these improvements Kennan warned that any sudden and complete removal

of disparities between white and black incomes would only undermine the competitive viability of large sections of South African
industry that had accounted for most of the changes in the pattern of
the black labor market. He concluded: "In general it may be said that
there is a basic conflict between the concepts of separate development that now constitute the official ideology of the regime on the
one hand, and the needs of a successful and rapidly expanding industrial economy on the other; and if the stormy pace of economic
growth is continued this conflict is bound to produce changes and
favorable ones in the position of the non-white portion of the
population."[29]

By the mid-1960s this had become a familiar theme of much of the
criticism of American policy, a theme that merited serious consideration. Whether or not this analysis was realistic is less important
than the fact that part of the "conservative" case against the Johnson
administration could not be faulted. American policy in these years
had indeed reflected "our sense of guilt at home, our desire not to
affront civil rights sentiment and our interest in securing the appro-
bation of the nations of black Africa, particularly by the attitudes we
strike in the UN."[30] Kennedy's methods had failed because they had
been designed to meet a crisis which had never materialized; Johnson had been content to mark time during the war in Vietnam.
Sanctions when adopted had been implemented half-heartedly, or
not at all. The case Ball and others brought against American policy
was not unconvincing, although in the end it obscured rather than
illuminated their main case. For it was above all based on the proposition that negative sanctions had failed when, for the most part,
they had never been applied. And it was on this understanding
that Richard Nixon came to base his own policy of constructive
engagement.

2 National Security Study Memorandum 39

In the circumstances that prevailed when the Nixon administration came into office in 1969, it was not surprising that Southern Africa was one of the first foreign policy issues to come under the scrutiny of Henry Kissinger's revamped National Security Council (NSC). There was reason to suspect that the policymakers in 1962 had had little idea of what they wanted to achieve. The Republicans were not alone in their acute disquiet; many Democrats believed that the State Department had paid too much regard to bureaucratic constituencies and too little to the proper overview of security matters.

Almost immediately on entering office, in February 1969, Kissinger ordered his staff to draw up a series of country program evaluations with the intention of addressing many of the long-term policy objectives that, for one reason or another, had been ignored by other administrations.[1] During the administration's first six months in office national security study memoranda emerged at the rate of eleven a month, the study memorandum on Southern Africa being the thirty-ninth, one of sixty-one comprehensive studies that met Nixon's promise to review all the important foreign policy questions that fell within the area broadly defined as national security. Each was intended to replace policies that Kissinger believed to have been mere trade-offs between competing bureaucratic interests. He was convinced that the validity of a policy should depend on whether it conformed to the facts, not whether it was consistent with past actions. He did not wish to be faced with "agreed papers" for ratification drawn up by bureaucratic agencies more concerned with whether the policy worked for them than whether it worked for the administration as a whole. He did not believe that the different agencies in the government were capable of defining the national interest without regard to their own administrative preoccupations. From the outset he wanted policy decisions to reflect "a well understood national purpose" rather than "the accommodation of different approaches by semi-autonomous departments."[2]

While determined not to treat issues in the light of self-serving bureaucratic interests, Kissinger was not unwilling to listen to independent positions. Indeed, the NSC was reorganized so that all agencies and departments were given a fair hearing before the Interdepartmental Group discussed the different options, and before the Final Review Group, chaired by Kissinger himself, made its final recommendation to the president. All the departments concerned with South Africa, from the Export-Import Bank to the Department of Commerce, played a part in drafting and reviewing NSSM 39. As soon as it was reorganized, however, the new NSC began to generate frictions almost as harmful as those of the old. Its reform had been superficial, not structural. Although it had great potential, its potential could not be realized unless a clear policy line was enforced by the White House. As it happened, it was to work in different, often conflicting, directions.

National Security Study
Memorandum 39 (NSSM 39)

The National Security Council was requested to review the situation in Southern Africa on 10 April 1969. Initially, Kissinger wanted the paper to be completed by the end of the month, but the memorandum did not reach the Review Group until seven months later, in time, though only just, for its recommendations to be included in the president's first "State of the World" message to Congress the following February.

The delay was due almost entirely to the controversy generated by the State Department's initial contribution—a revised version of a national policy paper that had been drafted in the closing months of the Johnson administration for Joseph Palmer's proposed visit to South Africa, the first by an assistant secretary of state for almost eight years. The paper had advised the continued application of negative sanctions—the only hope, it maintained, for "constructive change." It had also proposed two alternatives, neither of which were likely to win much favor: abandoning sanctions altogether, or offering material support to the nationalist movements who had already taken up arms.[3] No mention was made of the specific questions it had been asked to address: whether the arms embargo should be relaxed, and with it the credit limits for whose repeal the Treasury and Department of Commerce had been lobbying for some time.

The NSC was so dissatisfied with this submission that it decided to draft its own. The architect of its eventual report was Roger Morris, a former Soviet analyst who had changed jobs and been made Kissinger's main Africa aide in the Council. His principal objection to the State Department's submission was its alleged failure to recognize that coercion in the past had only stiffened the unity and purpose of the beleaguered white minority and brought little political return.[4]

Morris certainly had a point, even a telling one. As early as 1963 U.S. pressure had begun to erode as political rhetoric became a substitute, and a particularly unconvincing one, for positive action. One official claimed in this period, "We have utilized our diplomatic and consular establishments in South Africa to demonstrate by words and deeds our official disapproval of apartheid," but deeds represented little more than inviting nonwhites for the first time to the July Fourth celebrations at the U.S. embassy.[5] So limited had American influence become that contacts at both the official and unofficial levels had been reduced to a minimum. When the South African ambassador left Washington in 1965 after six years of service, he expressed some dismay that he had never been afforded a private meeting either with John Kennedy or Lyndon Johnson.[6] When Morris, with Kissinger's enthusiastic support, came to review the state of United States–South Africa relations, one conclusion seemed beyond question: that short of comprehensive economic sanctions the whites could never be forced to dismantle the apparatus of white supremacy. From his experience with the Soviet Union, however, Morris did believe that it was possible for two very different countries with two very different sets of values to disagree on the "irreducible differences" that divided them, while continuing to cooperate in other fields.

Kissinger's staff was particularly puzzled by the State Department's insistence on reducing all contacts with South Africa to a minimum, since this was the very attitude of the *verkrampte* (or hard-line)

National party, who feared that if the republic became a more open society it might also become more susceptible to Western influence, more inclined to listen to Western advice. In time, of course, the Nixon administration grew progressively disenchanted at the lack of real contact between the two countries, despite its own best intentions. In time the hope of influencing South Africa by making concessions seemed increasingly remote and unreal. By the mid-1970s the discrepancies between the principle and reality could no longer be systematically ignored—reality began to intrude. But we should not be surprised that in 1969 the NSC believed implicitly that contact would produce change, inasmuch as this was to become the very rationale and justification for detente on the much more vital issue of relations between the United States and the Soviet Union.

Morris's own submission eventually elicited from the State Department a grudging admission that a legitimate middle way *might* exist between collaboration and coercion. Nevertheless, between the international pressures it faced for doing more and South Africa's perennial complaints of unnecessary interference, the State Department negotiated uneasily. Fearing that it might soon lose all room for maneuver, the State Department mounted two rearguard stands: producing, first, an amended version of its original paper on August 15, and then three months later, at the Review Group meeting, a final draft which advocated some accommodation with the white community, provided the United States first canvassed the approval if not the support of the African states traditionally responsive to American influence.[7]

In the eight months which had elapsed since Kissinger's original directive, the Department had contested every thesis which had differed from its own, while at the same time trying to trim its sails to the prevailing political wind. To Henry Kissinger the whole episode seemed an example of bureaucratic brokering at its worst—of unparalleled "intellectual squalor."[8] In the circumstances, the memorandum that finally emerged was not as disappointing as it might have been. It contained, to begin with, a number of critical observations about the mistakes of the past and the reasons that explained them. On first reading, the reader is left with the impression that its authors were not only critical of the direction in which American policy had been going but also were quite prepared, even eager, to approach it from a completely different perspective. It was therefore all the more regrettable that the final determination of American policy lay less with the arguments of the bureaucrats, whether rationally or irrationally reached, than with the willingness of the White House to implement their decisions and its capacity to understand the premises on which those decisions had been made.

In all, five options were submitted for discussion at the final NSC meeting on South Africa in December 1969:

> Option 1: Closer association with the white regime in order to better protect America's economic and strategic interests. It assumed that the United States could have no significant impact on events in South Africa, and that the political costs of underwriting the status quo would not be excessive.

> Option 2: Closer association with Pretoria in an effort to persuade it to reform the political system. It assumed that black violence would be unavailing, even counterproductive. Constructive change could only be brought about by the acquiescence of the whites themselves.

> Option 3: Strictly limited cooperation with South Africa in an attempt to safeguard its interests while at the same time adopting a posture acceptable to world opinion. Such a posture need not entail giving up its material interests.

> Option 4: Dissociation from South Africa and closer relations with the black nationalists. Since the interests of the United States were not vital, this seemed a reasonable price to pay.

> Option 5: Dissociation from both sides in an attempt to limit American involvement. The racial conflict in Southern Africa was unmanageable and potentially dangerous and would grow worse despite any efforts the West might make.

Despite their differences, all five options agreed that black nationalism would be successfully contained. Nothing was more striking about NSSM 39 than the general agreement on this point, from which everything else followed. In this respect the memorandum aptly reflected the concern of the President of Botswana, Seretse Khama, that although the United States appeared to be more informed than ever about events in Southern Africa it had never appeared more pessimistic about the future.[9]

This pessimism gave rise to both personal and political uncertainty. It also gave rise to very different interpretations about the best course the United States could profitably pursue. Morris's own preference for constructive engagement, the policy which eventually carried the day, was embodied in the second of the five options. Beginning with the premise that "the whites are here to stay and the only way that constructive change can come about is through them," Morris went on to argue that, given this situation, the United States had a particularly vital role to play: "We can by selective relaxation of our stance towards the white regime encourage some modification of their current racial and colonial policies . . . , help draw the two groups together and exert some influence on both for peaceful change. Our tangible interests form a basis for our contacts in the region."[10] If the first premise provided a rationale for constructive engagement, the second suggested the means: the use of America's still considerable commercial interests in South Africa. In drafting Option 2 Morris was not concerned that the United States would endanger its interests by interfering in South Africa's domestic affairs; he was considerably more concerned that it might well surrender the political initiative by failing to make effective use of trade ties.

By comparison Option 1 concluded that America could do very little. Six years earlier Adlai Stevenson had pledged that his country would not shrink when the time came for putting its hopes to the test if the arms embargo should fail. Many State Department officials were in a more chastened mood in 1969, doubtful whether it would be wise to put America's power to the test for fear it might be found wanting. "In these circumstances" they concluded, "our economic, scientific and strategic interests in the region . . . are worth preserving and expanding."[11]

The thesis that America's interests were too important to jeopardize was entirely at variance with the opinion that their importance would keep the situation from getting out of hand. To this extent the claim that Option 1 was rational (in its naked pursuit of self-interest) was belied by the irrational nature of its argument and by its very clear message that none of America's interests were actually "vital." The supply of minerals, for example, was accorded no special priority in its classification of economic interests. The only commodity specifically mentioned, gold, was considered important only because its orderly marketing was central to the two-tier International Monetary Fund (IMF) system, which had been negotiated the previous year.[12]

The State Department was from the outset most consistent in its opposition to constructive engagement. Its preferred option, Option 3, began, as did each of the five, with a general premise: "The situation in the region is not likely to change appreciably in the foreseeable future and in any event we cannot influence it." It proposed accordingly nothing more than a codification of existing policy, continuing, in other words, its opposition to South Africa's racial policies without indulging in the hollow rhetoric that had been used so often to censure those policies in the past.

Morris subsequently criticized the proposals for their deliberate equivocation: for neither encouraging nor discouraging American investment; for recommending that naval visits to South Africa should be resumed provided the South Africans gave some assurance that black American naval personnel on shore leave would not be governed by the country's race legislation; for denying American companies Eximbank loans but allowing them to apply for government export credits. Morris accused the State Department of recommending face-saving formulae that offered no immediate prospect of political change.

In its defense the Department was the first to agree that its policy might appear expedient; and that the United States would still be exposed to pressures for more decisive measures since the problem in all essential respects would be left unresolved.[13] But this was not the main reason for the NSC's criticism. It was the conclusion which the State Department drew from its analysis that explained Morris's objections. Its desire to reduce America's commitments to a minimum in the hope that Washington would be able to respond more easily to future events was hardly likely to commend itself to an administration that was convinced that the country's tendency to react to events rather than shape them largely accounted for the dilemmas that it now faced.

Since the last two options were considerably briefer, one can deduce that they were never intended to be taken seriously—that both were straw options drafted to throw into greater relief the contending arguments of the first three, not to promote discussion of more radical alternatives. Both postulated that the situation in Southern Africa was "unmanageable," although Option 4 recommended severing contacts with the whites only, while Option 5 enjoined against identify-

ing too closely with either side. If, as seemed likely, violence continued to escalate, the United States would be well advised to make
clear at the earliest stage that it had no intention of intervening in a
struggle in which the nationalists could not hope to prevail without
support from Moscow, and the whites could not hope to survive
without support from the West. Only by opting out of the conflict
completely would the United States be able to signal its intentions
clearly and thus preempt either side from thinking that they could
count on its assistance on the final day of reckoning. In the words of
Option 5, it was a policy best described as one of "constructive
disengagement."[14]

Neither option advocated disinvesting from South Africa or repealing the arms embargo. Since Option 4 did not consider that the
measures would have much effect anyway, there seemed no need to
antagonize African opinion. Keeping both sides at arms length
required neither further sanctions, nor assistance, material or
otherwise, to the movements of national liberation. Option 4 recommended at most "sympathy for the aspirations of the African insur-
gent groups short of material support."[15]

This greatly exaggerated view of the ease with which the United
States could disengage if it had wished to found no support either in
the State Department or the NSC. Neither intruded into the discussion of the final security memorandum. The role that the NSC had
been given in planning had created an entirely new political situation in Washington at a moment when Kissinger felt most free to
exploit it to his own advantage. It was not an opportunity he would
lightly pass up. Above all, the credibility of both options largely
turned on their main support for disengagement: that it would remove
"the inherent equivocation—tangible interests versus political credibility in present policy."[16] Since nearly all those who met to discuss
the memorandum in December 1969 felt that disengagement was
neither possible nor desirable, they had no alternative but to look to
American interests as the instrumentation, as well as the justification,
for bringing America's influence to bear in a situation of great
complexity.

In view of this discussion it was not altogether surprising that
constructive engagement won more support within the administration than any of the alternatives. Of the alternatives to Option 2,
three were more or less academic; the first, politically unrealistic;

the last two unacceptable since they were both accompanied by a somewhat gratuitous warning that their implementation would jeopardize an agreement on the orderly marketing of gold. This left only Options 2 and 3, and it was around the choice between them that the final discussion revolved.

To begin with, neither the State Department nor the NSC believed that the United States could *morally* remain uncommitted (the opposite of the conclusion reached by the authors of Option 1). It is a point which needs to be underlined, for contrary to popular perception, the Nixon administration took the ethical argument very seriously.

The grievances of other people in the world might have been far worse than those of the black community in South Africa. Minority rule might exist elsewhere, often in much the same form. In Latin America, for example, the United States continued to support societies in which violence was endemic to the social order, in which political power was largely exercised by elites who were not altogether unlike the settler societies of Southern Africa: externally dependent on Western capital and uncompromisingly opposed to change.[17] In Southern Africa, however, Washington did not believe it could allow the grievances of the blacks to go unheeded. As Chester Bowles once noted, America's record in the region was more consistent than in any other area of the developing world.[18] As a member of the Kennedy administration Bowles had firsthand experience of American intervention against revolutionary movements in the name of anticommunism. Only in Southern Africa, as Kissinger later reminded the Senate, had the United States attempted to preempt the threat of communism, "not by truculently throwing our weight around but by identifying with principles which America has always stood for and which the world still looks to the United States to foster and defend."[19]

When asked whether the United States intended pursuing the recommendations of the Rockefeller Report for Latin America, Secretary of State William Rogers went out of his way to set his critics' minds at rest. Rockefeller had returned from Latin America depressed by the fact that the rising frustration with poverty might lead an increasingly large number of countries to seek Marxist solutions to their socioeconomic problems. Concluding that there was little the United States could do to alleviate the peasants' wretched conditions, he suggested that the only alternative was to promote even larger arms transfers to its Latin American allies in the struggle against Communist "subversion." In Southern Africa the Americans were inclined to find these cosmetic solutions unconvincing. Where political instability arose from racial segregation they saw no option but to solve the root cause of the problem. In pursuing constructive engagement, Rogers maintained, the United States had at least derived instruction from its experience in Latin America.[20]

Yet sympathy with the plight of South Africa's black people was not in itself explanation enough for why the United States intervened. Nor was America's interest in maintaining its commercial and strategic interests. The latter were only one part, and not the most important part, of a general interest in the future of the region. The fact that those interests were extensive was important, but not overridingly so. Indeed, there is some reason to doubt whether they were always as much to the forefront of policymakers' minds as some of the administration's critics later imagined. By understanding why this was not the case we may better appreciate why the arguments of Option 1 had such little appeal even to conservatives.

There was no doubt that the United States attached a great deal of importance to the Cape route along which oil tankers from the Persian Gulf and a great variety of merchant shipping passed en route to North America and Europe every day. Without access to South Africa's ship repair and refueling facilities the West's commerce could not move freely; without access in time of war to the naval base at Simonstown some admirals feared the United States Navy might not be able to operate at all. At the end of the 1950s naval exercises with the South African navy had begun, and were continued for several years. American observers were even invited to the series of defense talks between Britain and South Africa which were held between 1956 and 1959. Yet in 1967 visits by the U.S. Navy were suspended, never to be resumed. As soon as the political costs of military collaboration between the two countries began to offset the strategic returns, the United States began to disassociate itself from its former partner.

One of the few South African politicians who predicted this outcome in the 1950s had been the foreign minister, Eric Louw, who had been less than enthusiastic about defense ties with Washington. Indeed, for years he continued to caution his countrymen that the U.S. Navy should be invited to use Simonstown only "with the utmost caution and concern."[21] Even in the era of greatest Afrikaner self-confidence Louw had appreciated that were the West ever to conclude that South Africa was incapable of securing the Cape route because of political unrest at home it might prove unrelenting in its opposition to the existing political order. The only surety against intervention, Louw believed, would be to play down the Cape's importance, and with it that of the Simonstown naval base, rather than raise unnecessary and deeply embarrassing questions about the National party's ability to defend Western interests.

America's interests, of course, existed at many different levels of importance. Its economic interests were again important, but not decisively so. American investment, although significant for South Africa, was fairly minimal for the United States. South Africa might well be America's fifteenth largest capital market, but it accounted for only 2 percent of its total overseas earnings. Although the inflow of U.S. capital, measured as a percentage of capital transfers, continued to increase in the 1960s, it did so only to fall in the first years of the following decade. The fact that the thirteen largest companies in the United States owned 25 percent of American investment in South Africa and that all but three of the fifteen largest companies on the *Fortune* index had substantial investment portfolios would suggest that the opinions of American businessmen carried some weight in Washington. Their influence does not, however, appear to have been decisive.[22]

In addition to capital earnings, South Africa accounted for six of America's thirty-five most important commodity imports: the ferrochrome metals manganese, chromium, and vanadium, the non-ferrous metal fluorspar, and the vital platinum group. Given the country's increasing dependence on imported raw materials, it might have seemed all the more necessary to avert racial conflict so that funds could continue to be invested in technological innovations that would make possible the extraction of reserves which through previous inaccessibility had defied classification as resources. Future capital injections were unlikely if the republic dissolved into political anarchy.

But the need to assure commodity imports does not appear to have been a compelling argument for American intervention. After all, although successive administrations conceded that America's national interest made it necessary to maintain access to South Africa's resources,[23] one government official revealed as late as 1976 that the United States had never had a separate policy for the resource sector.[24] At no stage in the 1960s did the United States, contrary to the advice it received from many quarters, conclude that the prevailing political order needed to be underwritten. Little evidence if any can be produced to substantiate the suspicions often entertained by America's critics that her dependence on raw materials offered no alternative but compliance with the status quo and recognition of "responsible" governments.[25]

It is no doubt unexceptional to detect in political actions apparent confirmation of the primacy of economic interests, and to cite the latter as an explanation of the conservative policies governments pursue. Had the United States considered itself to be vulnerable, doubtless it would have found it difficult to reconcile its public support for majority rule with the need for a stable political order. But South Africa was likely to remain dependent on the West almost indefinitely for export revenue and capital investment. This was also likely to be true, perhaps more so, of a country under Marxist rule. By 1970 the mining sector contributed on average 25 percent of its GDP, employed about a fifth of the country's labor force, and accounted for no less than three quarters of its foreign exchange. A Marxist-Leninist republic committed to large social welfare programs would probably rely on mineral exports much more.

It was because South Africa herself was so dependent on the West that its governments believed they had little to fear from majority rule itself—only the manner of its coming. What the Nixon administration feared most was not a transfer of power as such but the sort of drawn-out political upheaval that would discourage the mining houses from investing in new plant and equipment. The fact that the United States depended to the extent that it did on South Africa was indicative not of the scarcity of world reserves but the qualms that many multinational corporations were beginning to entertain about investing in Third World markets. By 1970 Congress's National Commission on Material Policy found very little evidence of political stability in any of the major world producers except for the former British dominions—Canada, Australia, and South Africa.[26] As the U.S. Council on Economic Policy noted with alarm, all three countries accounted for over 80 percent of all new capital investment in exploration. The United States as a country could not afford to be overly sanguine about such telling statistics. For the rush to invest in South Africa was not an answer at all to its own long-term need for resources, given that political unrest on a major scale might one day break out. It was in the hope of precluding such a situation that the Nixon administration intervened when it did, despite the advice of Option 1. Moreover, it was because it believed that America's interests *were* important that it chose to dismiss out of hand the arguments for disengagement that had been set out with great clarity in Option 4 of the memorandum.

As for the *form* of American intervention, the White House had no truck at all for punitive measures, and little enthusiasm for maintaining existing sanctions; hence its opposition to Option 3. Kissinger and his staff were convinced that negative sanctions had proved worthless as an instrument of political influence. Instead of breaking the political impasse in South Africa they had merely stiffened white resistance, and provided the government with a spurious legitimacy for its own actions. Because they concluded that sanctions had been agreed upon for no other reason than the need, perceived or real, not to jeopardize America's relations with sub-Saharan Africa, Morris and his colleagues went on to argue that their evident lack of success had already discredited the coercive approach in the eyes of all but the most liberal critics of white rule.

Only the U.S. mission at the United Nations ventured to suggest that sanctions had been imposed so half-heartedly by the Johnson administration that it would be ridiculous to maintain that the strategy had failed. Perhaps the mission felt the implications of constructive engagement too keenly to appreciate its finer arguments, or to weigh the alternative options in the balance. Nixon's first ambassador Charles Yost broke ranks with the administration by arguing for those who cared to listen that the lackluster implementation of sanctions in the 1960s had only convinced South Africa that most of the countries who ritually voted for these measures would be unwilling to endorse, if not entirely oppose, any attempt to provide the UN with the authority or power to apply harsher measures.[27]

Yost later went on to accuse the Western powers of undermining the strategy from the outset by doing the bare minimum to appease African opinion without seriously inconveniencing the South African government. After retiring from politics in 1971, he expressed some of his fears for the future: "Someday Southern Africa will be shockingly and hideously on the front pages of the world press. Then the Western powers will ask themselves why they did not, with all their non-military resources at their command, push and drive South Africa . . . into the modern world while there was still time."[28] Yost answered his own question in the light of his limited understanding of the administration's intentions. It later transpired that he had never been informed of the Final Review Group's recommendations, or the president's decision to authorize constructive engagement two months later. By the time of his resignation he had still not been told why the White House had opted for the policy in the first place.[29]

There was of course an elegance and simplicity about Morris's view of United States–South Africa relations that, had it been communicated to New York, might even have drawn some of Yost's criticism. In their dealings with the Soviet Union successive U.S. administrations had reiterated the need to break down barriers to communication, to strengthen trading links, and to trade freely in ideas and information. Against such a background Morris's thesis had an elegance and simplicity that made it immediately attractive if a little too neat. Neat arguments rarely lose their appeal until they have been tried and tested, with what results we shall see in the following chapters.

3 Negative and Positive Sanctions

At this point it seems useful to discuss the *theoretical* premises on which constructive engagement was based, both with regard to the administration's explicit rejection of negative sanctions and its endorsement of the positive alternative. It was almost a point of law, an *idée reçue*, among American officials and academics alike in the 1960s that sanctions could not work. Most believed there could be no direct linkage between economic deprivation and political change. Where sanctions had actually been applied, as they had in the case of Rhodesia, they were deemed to have shown that, while it was possible to have punishment without compliance, or compliance without punishment, punishment on its own could not guarantee compliance.[1]

Three academic conclusions can be taken as representative of the great body of opinion in this period:

Peter Wallenstein (1968)

"The general picture is that economic sanctions have been unsuccessful as a means of influence in the international system."[2]

Margaret Doxey (1972)

"Summing up the analysis of the UN and Southern Africa one must concede that the deterrent and the coercive force of sanctions is weak on almost every count."[3]

Klaus Knorr (1973)

"In principle collective trade sanctions should be more effective
than economic reprisals by one state or a few, since they would
be based in an internationally cumulative degree of monopolis-
tic and monopsonist control over the world market. . . . In
practise, however, collective trade and other economic sanctions
have proved abortive. . . . In the light of recent history the value
of threatening economic reprisals cannot be considered high.
What has made the threat value low is the sharpened sensitivity
of poor and weak states to any attempt at coercion. For this
reason the value of economic threats at present seems at least
subject to secular depreciation."[4]

One of the central reasons why sanctions elicited so little academic support was the distortion that often arose in the attitude of
the receiving nation. If academic critics were agreed on anything it
was that sanctions and economic warfare, while entirely different
acts, could not always be distinguished. To Margaret Doxey, of course,
clearly the object of the latter was "to hasten the enemy's defeat, to
reduce or eliminate its capacity to wage war, to undermine morale
and generally to make life for its citizens as difficult as possible.
When economic measures are used as sanctions the object is to deter
or dissuade states from pursuing policies which do not conform to
accepted norms of international conduct. Sanctions are penalties
which relate specifically to acts which the international body
condemns."[5] In describing sanctions as "conformity-defending
instruments" Doxey was making the point that it was the recipient,
not the sender, who was entirely responsible for their adoption. It is
the recipient who brings upon himself the obloquy of international
opinion.

Unfortunately, past experience had shown that sanctions were
rarely, if ever, believed to be legitimate by public opinion in the
recipient country; that threats to people's incomes tended to be no
less alienating than threats on their lives; that for the most part
economic pressure merely reinforced the moral authority of offending governments at home. Margaret Doxey concluded that a siege
psychosis once engendered could be a powerful factor in sustaining
the will to resist, and a useful support for governments intent on
such unpopular measures as rationing consumer goods and increas-

ing taxes.[6] The more cohesive a society, of course, the more likely a government would be able to draw on previously dormant or unsuspected reserves of strength.[7]

In South Africa's case there was always a very real fear that a society so manifestly under siege, so embattled and beleaguered that it was already described by some as a garrison state, might be able to resist all but the harshest economic measures. If the white community were to retreat any further into the *laager*, South Africa might be impervious to everything but economic warfare. An even closer alliance between English-speaking and Afrikaner opinion was hardly the most desirable end. Many like George Ball already believed that "the psychology of the besieged is too perverse and complex to make such sanctions more than a blunt instrument."[8] To add to the problem might have seemed more perverse still.

If sanctions had been applied, the chances of success would not have been very high. Among the four objectives set out by Ball for American sanctions against Cuba, three might have been germane to South Africa:

— to reduce the will and ability of the Cuban regime to export subversion and violence

— to make plain to the Cuban people and sections within the regime that a policy of revolution could not serve their interests

— to demonstrate to the whole American continent that Communism had no future in the Western hemisphere.[9]

In the case of South Africa the aims would have been equally diverse, and equally diffuse—to reduce Pretoria's interest and willingness to sustain white rule in Rhodesia and the neighboring Portuguese territories; to make plain to the white electorate and the *verligtes* within the administration that apartheid was not in their own best interests; and to demonstrate to the rest of Africa that white supremacy had little or no future in Southern Africa, thereby winning the hearts and minds of the newly independent African nations.

In James Barber's schema these different objectives can be grouped into three separate categories—primary objectives concerned with the actions and behavior of regimes against whom sanctions are initially directed; secondary objectives relating to the behavior and expectations of the government imposing sanctions; and tertiary objectives concerned with broader international considerations concerning the structure and operation of the international system.[10] Examples of all three can be found in the case in question.

It was the primary objective of the United States in the 1960s to prevent any further extension of apartheid, and if possible to set it in reverse. In itself this was not an unreasonable objective, since the most restrictive legislation of all did not come onto the statute book until 1963–66, that is, after Sharpeville and the Pondoland revolt, neither of which elicited a decisive international response. Once it became clear that the ANC was totally unable to mobilize the black workforce and paralyze the economy, after the ANC itself had been forced underground, the authorities in South Africa felt free to introduce legislation that had been the subject of long-drawn-out and often tentative hearings by commissions of inquiry who had felt far from confident about their own powers.

In the climate of opinion that prevailed after 1963 nothing less than this primary objective of seeing the destruction of apartheid could have justified the adoption of sanctions. Given the fact that South Africa's economy was thirty times larger than Cuba's, sanctions would have had to have been considerable in order to ensure success. Again, only the largest considerations would have justified the expense. Lyndon Johnson's reluctance to pursue such ends was dictated by the recognition, real or merely perceived, that, even if unlimited in scope, they were unlikely to achieve the desired result. On this question there was a striking consensus within the administration, reinforced by an equally striking unanimity of opinion among academic observers. A common thread which ran through much of the writing of the period was that sanctions could not succeed unless they formed part of a broader effort. This would include military pressure (internal or external) and diplomatic isolation, steps that in Margaret Doxey's opinion would actually have reduced the chances of an eventual settlement by limiting the channels of communication and narrowing the scope of political dialogue within South Africa itself.[11] Writing many years later, Robin Remnick was to conclude that nations pursue at their own risk the demonstrably untrue supposition "that it would prove possible to deter aggression or otherwise to change fundamentally the political conduct of states by the threat of economic penalties alone."[12]

However, it was not the primary but the secondary objectives which were the principal determinant of American actions from 1960 on. The arms embargo after all had been little more than a public relations exercise to demonstrate American resolve without actually threatening its economic interests. The main argument put forward by Kennedy's critics on the left of the political spectrum was that the failure to press ahead with more radical measures had manifestly demonstrated America's indifference to African opinion, despite the manifestation of especially acute racial tension at home.

Looked at in this light, the arms embargo seemed to conform rather well with Johann Galtung's minimalist justification for sanctions which faute de mieux could but remain limited in scope:

> There is the value of at least doing something, of having the illusion of being instrumental, of being busy in time of crisis. When military action is impossible for one reason or another and when doing nothing is seen as tantamount to complicity, then something has to be done to express morality, something that at least serves as a clear signal to everyone that what the receiving nation has done is disapproved of. If the sanctions do not serve instrumental purposes they can have *expressive* functions.[13]

There is a limit, however, to the price nations are prepared to pay for symbolic gestures. The 1962 embargo may have salved Kennedy's conscience and rescued his new Africa policy by which he hoped the United States would be judged by the emerging Third World nations, but it achieved little else. The very suspicion that further *economic* sanctions would have been equally symbolic ensured that the embargo would be one of the last positive steps the Americans would actually take in the belated attempt to reverse apartheid. In terms of cost alone Kennedy would have had great difficulty justifying them. The fact that the African states were still "emerging" meant that their influence in Washington was fairly minimal—or put another way, the Africa Bureau would have met with almost no success in carrying the battle against the Defense Department or the Department of Commerce, even assuming that the State Department would have been willing to throw its own authority behind the call for more coercive measures.

If the prospects were grim on this front, the supporters of sanctions against South Africa carried even less weight in the matter of possible tertiary objectives, however broadly defined. At various times apartheid's critics urged the United Nations to impose by force the norms of behavior enshrined in the Charter on Human Rights, to discipline a country whose errant behavior constituted a threat to international peace, even a threat to the fragile basis of cooperation between Africans of the North and the South.

Unfortunately, whether South Africa should have been treated as a criminal outcast beyond the pale of civilized conduct, it did not fit the category of post-UDI Rhodesia. Its government might have been reprehensible, but it was not illegal, nor was it illegitimate in the eyes of those privileged to vote for it. The racial equality norm was not sufficiently established in the United States itself, let alone the international system, to have justified international sanctions against South Africa; only a limited degree of ostracism and moral disapproval, which is precisely what the arms embargo and suspended port calls by the U.S. Navy were intended to enforce, would seem to have been justified. In short, the state of interracial bargaining in the republic was not seen either at the time or thereafter to be tantamount to "a racial revolution with a class base which [had] grown into an international war."[14]

Indeed, looked at in a rather different light, sanctions might have resulted in far greater disequilibrium and economic chaos if they had ever been adopted. The loss of South African gold sales alone would have undermined the two-tier international monetary order that had only recently been agreed upon in 1968. The suspension of mineral sales might have gone a long way toward undermining the viability of many Western economies, or so it was argued by most of the world's leading economists. In terms of tertiary objectives, the case for not applying sanctions against South Africa was in many respects more telling than the case in favor of pressing ahead.

It was for this reason that in the first instance a trade embargo would have had to have been selective rather than comprehensive, voluntary rather than mandatory, and sensitive to the liabilities likely to be suffered by the major trading nations. But selective sanctions tend to be even more difficult to apply than most others. They tend to be more complex and difficult to operate, giving rise to serious difficulties of interpretation both within and between governments as to what trade is permissible and what is not. Their effectiveness usually depends on the extent to which they are concentrated on particularly vulnerable export products, those for which alternative sources of supply are not readily available or those in areas such as high technology in which embargoed items are already subject to stringent national export controls.

Beyond these strictly analytical considerations, other factors discouraged the administration from pursuing the matter too far. Sanctions, particularly negative sanctions, are merely one form of power relationship and by no means the most convincing one. Power capabilities or "potential power," as Harold and Margaret Sprout remind us, must be set in a "policy contingent" framework.[15] The power sufficient to punish Rhodesia may not have been sufficient to penalize South Africa; in neither case might it have been adequate to achieve America's stated objectives.

The "paradox of unrealized power" results in most instances from the mistaken belief that the power resources useful in one policy contingent framework will be equally telling in the next. This is rarely the case. Sanctions against a small, agrarian economy like Rhodesia with its one or two staple crops and a highly restrictive consumer economy may be unavailing against a developed or semideveloped industrial economy like South Africa. Or, then again, they may be more successful still. It is largely a matter of interpretation.

There were some authorities who maintained, as did William Gutteridge in 1964, that "the self-sufficient, largely agricultural economy of South Africa fifty years ago could have survived in isolation for a long period. The industrialised state of today in which a substantial proportion of the African population is involved could not long withstand the shock of shortages."[16] On the other hand, the country's remarkable advances in synthetic fuels (for example the oil-from-shale program) and its interest in nuclear energy already revealed by 1970 how creative the South African economy had become merely as a result of the *threat* of sanctions. In the Second World War the German economy had responded to a much sharper economic siege with remarkable success, pioneering some of the most significant breakthroughs in synthetic fuels and the use of ferro-alloys in reinforcing steel. Twenty-five years later Rhodesia, from a much weaker technical base, witnessed a dramatic expansion in the production of ferro-chrome for refined steel products and consumer goods. Selective sanctions intended largely to demonstrate international disquiet with apartheid, not to bring the South African economy crashing down, might only have had the entirely opposite effect of pushing the country into much greater self-sufficiency. In short, confusion abounded in government circles, hardly inspiring anyone with the confidence that negative sanctions could succeed. Success lay in the sphere of speculation, not fact; estimates of likely economic damage were built on hypotheses not facts. In the final analysis, it was impossible to quantify the damage that the American economy might incur, and it was on this latter assessment that everything else largely turned.

In this respect the analogy with Rhodesia was hardly a telling one. The relationship between the United States and Pretoria was very different, the opportunity costs of applying pressure much more complex and daunting. In the last resort South Africa could influence the United States (and thus the form sanctions might take) to a disconcertingly high degree. As Oran Young has pointed out, the level of interdependence between two countries increases both the costs and opportunities of exercising power.[17] An embargo against an agricultural, semideveloped state such as Rhodesia was one thing; the enforced ostracism of a leading mineral producer quite another. No Western country could contemplate with equanimity the denial of gold and semiprocessed metals in which South Africa and the Soviet Union between them led the world. South Africa was the world's preeminent producer of manganese, vanadium, chrome, and the incalculably valuable platinum group metals. It was also the most important producer of uranium. Its share of known resources of chrome and platinum was greater than its share of total production. Elsewhere deposits of the latter were often low-grade and potentially costly. For most of the 1970s recycling was not a realizable option.

The implications of this were not at all reassuring. As David Baldwin argues, the relevant opportunity costs in any given relationship between two or more countries are not those involved in carrying out a transaction but those involved in forgoing it.[18] The true measure of a country's dependency on imported oil is not what it has to give up in order to pay a higher price but what it might have to give up to go without it. In matters of international trade the relationship between international political power and the world's trading structure has long been analyzed in terms of the relative opportunity costs of closure for the respective partners; the higher the relative cost of closure, the weaker the political position of each state.[19] The foregoing argument is rendered even more convincing by the knowledge that embargoes on imports have tended to be more effective than prohibitions on exports, given the intense competition for export markets. Embargoes on exports to Rhodesia were largely ineffective but the prohibition of imports from Rhodesia did substantially reduce its capacity to earn the foreign exchange needed to finance imports of manufacturing equipment.[20] Unfortunately, this would hardly have been of much comfort in the case of South Africa. Heavily dependent on imports of metals, semiprecious or otherwise, the United States believed itself to be in no position to cut back on imports. Even in the case of Rhodesia the U.S. Congress insisted in 1971 on passing the Byrd Amendment to allow the import of over seventy-two different minerals, of which by far the most important was chrome.

In these circumstances it is perhaps not remarkable or unexpected that the Nixon administration should have turned its mind in 1969 toward less coercive and more normative forms of eliciting compliance with its wishes. At about the same time a number of scholars began to dwell on the fact that the secular trend in most Western societies was in the same direction. In the modern world, as power had become less absolute, countries had been persuaded to act more "responsibly," as well as to abstain from some of the more traditional coercive methods.[21] In short, they had begun to look at the power of positive sanctions.

All sanctions are in effect social punishments or rewards for the fulfillment or nonfulfilment of certain desired behavior, employed to increase the probability that certain actions will be performed or refrained from. In *Usage and Abusage* Eric Partridge claims that "*sanction* has four main senses: two that are antithetic—'reward' and 'punishment'; a neutral sense—'authority, (official) permission'; and a political sense, this being a specialization of the 'punishment penalty' sense." He explains that this last had in the main issued from its League of Nations usage.[22] More explicitly in the words of another author, "Sanctions can be mild or severe; formal or informal, negative or positive. Imprisonment is a severe and formal sanction that discourages criminal behaviour . . . tax deductions for contributions to charity are positive legal sanctions for what is considered worthy behaviour."[23] Yet with few exceptions positive sanctions have been ignored in international relations literature.[24] Social scientists have often confused negative and positive sanctions altogether by talking of negative and positive coercion when, like David Easton and Robert Dahl, they have not rejected the distinction entirely.[25] In his seminal study of power Felix Oppenheim merely mentions in a passing footnote that "the promise of a reward is another type of influence."[26]

Thus, although punishments in international politics have become less extravagant and often less severe, and although techniques of influence have become more sophisticated and often less manifest, most political scientists have shown a peculiar reluctance to discuss the power of rewards. Their reluctance may arise, in part, from the fact that the two concepts of negative and positive sanctions are difficult to compartmentalize precisely. Dahl offers a definition of power in terms of the severe penalties which are frequently incurred when a weaker country refuses to comply with the demands of a stronger one, before conceding that substantial rewards "can be made to operate" like severe penalties.[27] Obviously, in certain circumstances the cost of refusing a reward can be almost as great as the cost of ignoring a threat; both courses of action might well provoke negative sanctions. Secondly, regardless of the costs of compliance for the country applying sanctions—the fact that it may be even more expensive to honor a reward once it has been accepted than to threaten a country with appropriate punishment if it fails to comply with its demands—for the recipient the opportunity costs of noncompliance may on both occasions be exactly the same.

Nevertheless, Dahl's view of sanctions is far too restrictive. The provision of incentives or rewards can affect a country's behavior in a way quite incidental to any implicit threat for noncompliance; often it may be quite independent of any punishment that may be incurred if the offer should be refused. Clearly, it is easier to distinguish rewards from punishments than to distinguish promises from threats. The possibility that witholding a reward may itself constitute a punishment has persuaded many political scientists to regard threats and promises as two sides of the same coin. But ultimately there is no logical reason why witholding a reward need always constitute a punishment any more than witholding a punishment need always be seen as a reward. Conditional commitments in the absence of compliance need not necessarily be threats. Threatening not to reward a country for failing to comply with a request can only constitute a threat to punish if the recipient had a prior expectation of receiving a reward.[28]

In fact, the expectations or perceptions of the recipient are usually far more important than the intentions of the sender, a fact that can be usefully illustrated by looking at America's attempt to use foreign aid programs for overtly *political* purposes. Many foreign aid programs are geared to producing what James Rosenau calls "adaptive behavior"—a favorable response by governments to external requests.[29] Most also operate through economic dependence, a condition that to quote David Vital, is "funded on the exploitation of economic vulnerability, and sanctions need not be put into effect or even spelled out explicitly in diplomatic contacts for the desired result to be produced."[30] Obviously, some governments are more exploitable than others, but quite often foreign aid in some Third World countries amounts to 20 percent of government budgets, even if it represents only a fraction of their GNP.

Unfortunately, when aid is tied to political ends which go well beyond mere questions of economic development, it is often too insubstantial to elicit a positive response. In the autumn of 1961 the United States made $14 million available from its foreign aid contingency fund to keep the reformist government of Prime Minister Ali Amini in power in Iran. Yet only six months later Amini resigned from office, blaming insufficient American aid for his failure to close the budget gap and warning the Shah that he would be ill-advised to continue with his reform program without the proper economic support.[31] In Brazil, where foreign assistance was used effectively to bolster the military government in 1964, the promise of further funds failed to dissuade the government from closing the Brazilian Congress four years later. In retrospect the reasons are fairly obvious. U.S. aid was largely directed toward education and agriculture, two sectors that did not rate very highly among the concerns of the military government. As Samuel Huntington argues, it is quite understandable that many Third World governments will be more concerned with how their economies develop (with all the political ramifications that follow from this) than with how fast they develop. Aid from foreign countries always involves some costs. In this case the government of Brazil thought it dangerous for its own survival to introduce democratic principles simply for the sake of faster growth.[32]

That is one answer, perhaps, to Henry Cabot Lodge's despairing conclusion in September 1963 that finding a way to reform a Third World government "would be one of the greatest discoveries since the enactment of the Marshall Plan—because as far as I know the United States has never yet been able to control any of the very unsatisfactory governments through which we have had to work."[33] Through the Marshall Plan the United States managed to resuscitate the war-torn European economies at comparatively little expense largely because its aid program exploited an already existing mood of national renewal. It is doubtful whether it would have succeeded if the Europeans had set themselves different priorities.

Money, in a word, often tells us almost as much about the limitations of power as it does about its possibilities. It also explains why countries like the United States, despite their enormous resources, are often unwilling to incur the expense of positive sanctions. In Latin America the Alliance for Progress was intended in Kennedy's own words "to transform the 1960s into a historic decade of democratic progress."[34] But, from the first, Washington was not prepared to invest vast sums in economic support programs of doubtful value. As Baldwin argues, promises cost more when they succeed, threats when they fail. The larger a promise, the higher the probability of success; the higher the probability of success, the higher the probability of having to honor one's promise, and the more expensive, of course, it is to make large promises. The exact opposite is true of negative sanctions, where the probability of success may be high but where accordingly a country is unlikely to have to implement them.[35] Too big a threat, Schelling reminds us, is likely to be superfluous rather than too costly.[36]

A paradoxical result of this is that the country applying positive sanctions may be worse off when it is successful, as the United States found in 1970 when as part payment for the Azores base it advanced $400 million in Eximbank loans to finance development in Portugal. This provision, which exceeded all loans to Africa over the past twenty-five years, not to mention all previous allocations to Lisbon, represented no less than 10 percent of the bank's annual grants since 1965. Since the loans were explicitly restricted to the metropole, many contemporary observers suspected that the Nixon administration still hoped even at this late stage to develop the country's domestic economy and by decentralizing the international escudo zone to provide an infusion of development dollars which would enable it to survive the passing of its empire.[37] Others saw it as a vote of confidence in those members of the Portuguese government who wished to speed the country's integration into Europe so that it would be better placed to survive the loss of captive markets overseas.[38] Large though it was, however, it is doubtful whether even double or treble the amount provided by the Azores package would have helped "to drag Portugal into the twentieth century," to quote one member of Lisbon's negotiating team.[39] Such an endeavor was simply beyond the capacity of one nation, even a country as rich as the United States.

A completely different question arises from the willingness of countries to be persuaded (or bribed). For, although a reward, like an argument, can often reveal an interest, it can rarely create one. Countries normally succeed in influencing others when the latter are already thinking along the same lines. External assistance in itself, however, is most unlikely to persuade a government to reassess its goals and the costs of realizing them, and in the process persuade it to work toward a different outcome.[40]

Indeed, success or failure is normally contingent not only on the methods or the amount of power applied but, perhaps more to the point, the likelihood of the outcome. It is in this context that Karl Deutsch speaks of the "autonomous probability of events": "The outcome which is already moderately improbable, can be made highly improbable by the application of even a relatively limited amount of power. In such circumstances the change in the probability of this particular outcome will seem quite drastic, and this limited amount of power will seem to have changed considerable uncertainty into near uncertainty and thus to have produced spectacular results. The same degree of power produces far less impressive results when it is applied to promoting an outcome which is already fairly improbable in the first place."[41] All things being equal, a country's prospects of success are worse when it tries to promote improbable outcomes than when it tries to promote highly probable ones, which may still, of course, require an underwritten promise or threat. The threat of nuclear retaliation in an age of nuclear parity is more likely to deter than the threat of military force in a nonnuclear confrontation.

Before proceeding with the argument, however, it is worth pointing out that positive sanctions are also an implicit part of deterrence and that promises as well as threats can, in principle, deter equally effectively. In 1960 the United States, having failed to deter Fidel Castro from nationalizing the assets of its own corporations, implemented sanctions of its own. Had Washington understood some of the reasons for Castro's actions, a more positive approach might have served its interests much better. Fortified by the knowledge that U.S. corporations had often been the agency of American intervention in Latin America, most recently in Guatemala (1954), Castro hoped to preempt, rather than provoke American intervention. Through the sudden nationalization of the private sector he hoped to break the bureaucratic-military nexus between the United States and Cuba before carrying out his revolutionary program. This "revolution within a revolution" as Regis Debray calls it, was intended to prevent the confrontation it unwittingly provoked by making it impossible for the United States to intervene.[42] Had Castro's intentions been clear from the outset, the United States might have attempted to reassure him by agreeing to raise the sugar quota so that the Cuban government could have paid higher compensation to the companies that were eventually nationalized. That would have meant, of course, paying for the privilege of not being provoked, a bitter price for a superpower to swallow, especially one so assiduous in maintaining the Monroe Doctrine. In the light of subsequent events, however, it could hardly have been more humiliating than the eventual outcome: the Bay of Pigs.

Despite doubts whether assurance has any role to play in deterrence,[43] a number of writers believe that deterrence can be used to challenge as well as threaten[44]; to expose the possibilities as well as the limitations of power; to test a country's potential to act, as well as its will to resist. Unlike a threat, a challenge can produce a happier balance between initiating change, responding to it, and resisting it altogether. In principle, it should be able to make a target state more changeable, as well as engendering change.[45]

In arriving at this conclusion James Lieberman recognizes that a positive approach to deterrence is much more problematic when an opponent is weak, embittered, divided, or paranoid. In such circumstances a challenge is likely to be perceived as an attack. This would almost certainly have been true of South Africa if the West had expressed any interest in deterring it from introducing apartheid in the 1950s by positive rather than negative means. Throughout the period the government saw itself as politically weak and reliant (until 1956) on slim majorities in the National Assembly, which tellingly exposed the divisions within the white community. Often the legislation it introduced was delayed for years while it was the subject of endless commissions of inquiry, many of which did not deliver their judgments until after Sharpeville, when it became clear that black opposition no longer posed a real threat.[46] It was Sharpeville that finally gave the Nationalist party the confidence to enact the most repressive security legislation of its entire time in office between 1963 and 1966, by which time the West faced the problem not of deterring the government from its avowed course, but of prevailing upon it to retreat. By that time it was less paranoid, but even less receptive. Security produced confidence, but it also bred complacency.

Let us conclude by looking at three other problems raised by the use of positive sanctions that have forced governments back on a negative approach. Negative sanctions often tend to be applied for purely domestic reasons—to reassure domestic lobbies or pressure groups (as well as international opinion) that a government intends to stand by its principles, and not abandon them in pursuit of national interest or commercial gain. In the case of Rhodesia sanctions were applied to legitimize Britain's decision not to use force. The British derived some credibility from imposing punitive economic measures, although in time it began to appear that they put more emphasis on punishment than compliance, being more concerned with going with the grain of international opinion than necessarily trying through more unorthodox methods to realize their initial objectives.

In short, negative sanctions are useful in *demonstrating* a power relationship. For nonpower relationships they are not useful. Positive sanctions usually succeed, after all, when the ability to get the recipient to respond increases simultaneously with the recipient's ability to persuade the donor to offer an incentive or reward. The problem is compounded by the fact that in many cases one regime is asking another to comply with its demands. In the case of South Africa there was very limited scope for rewarding a regime that lived by a set of social and political principles which were anathema to Western values. In South Africa's case, the object of attack was more than just its regime—in David Easton's definition "a constitutional order which comprises values, norms and the structure of authority of a political community." It was the political community itself—"a group of persons bound together by a political division of labor."[47] In these circumstances there were not many rewards the Nixon administration could have provided South Africa and it is not surprising that the few incentives it found, the selective relaxation of the arms embargo and controls on Eximbank loans, were not considered to be very significant by the South Africans themselves.

The same problem obtained in Rhodesia, particularly in the early days of UDI. In the November 1965 debate in the House of Commons only one MP suggested the possibility of using rewards—"We should start thinking about offering a little carrot to the Rhodesians who may defect from Mr. Smith as well as merely talking about the stick."[48] In an article published in 1967 Johann Galtung cited a scheme proposed by another MP which called for a capital injection by Britain of £200 million—£50 million on education, another £50 million to boost economic growth, with the remainder being spent equally on other projects which might improve the standing of the black community in the eyes of the white minority. As Galtung added, although the scheme reflected the paternalist "education for maturity" approach, it also offered a way out of the impasse, provided, of course, the transfer of funds was explicitly tied to creating "steps towards majority rule."[49]

Such proposals, however, were profoundly unrealistic. If adopted, they would have meant channeling funds through a regime that had been mandated by its own electorate to oppose majority rule, and that might at any point in the intervening period appeal to the electorate again. But, equally serious, what would have happened if the African nationalists had contracted out of the agreement halfway through and turned to armed struggle? As a third party to the agreement, the costs of entering into an open-ended guarantee would have been excessively high for the United Kingdom. What action would it have taken if it had been broken by either party? In the case of Ian Smith it might have applied negative sanctions to bring it back into line, but in the case of the nationalists would it really have been prepared to step up arms supplies to the government? The thought suspended belief. Here too, negative sanctions were not only simpler, but also cheaper.

So far we have looked at the cost of implementing sanctions and the economic cost of providing significant and, therefore, credible rewards. We cannot conclude this discussion without looking at three other sets of cost: (a) the cost of communicating a promise; (b) the cost of making it; (c) the cost of monitoring the target state's response.[50] For if the cost of implementing a promise is contingent on its acceptance, the initiating party may incur the other three regardless of the second party's compliance.

The cost of communicating with a "pariah state" like South Africa was a high one for the Nixon administration even in the preparatory stage, for it meant sending out exploratory missions to evaluate the situation, as well as establishing formal or informal channels of communication at the highest level. It was because of Nixon's concern that America's credibility might be compromised by overt contacts between Washington and Pretoria that communications were severely circumscribed. This strategy was one of the main reasons for the policy's eventual failure, since messages that were sent to Pretoria were disguised in policy statements and newspaper leaks which the South Africans failed to decipher. The new South African ambassador arrived in Washington in 1971 without ever having heard of constructive engagement.[51] In communicating with South Africa the United States also ran the risk of cutting itself off from contact with nonstate actors. The British had found during *The Tiger* and *Fearless* talks concerning Rhodesia that when they considered a range of positive sanctions for securing a commitment in principle to majority rule, the African states found it necessary to remind them of "the forgotten element in Rhodesian politics"—the black nationalists.[52] Unfortunately, once it became impossible after 1974 to ignore the nationalists it became equally difficult to establish close relations with the government in Salisbury.

It is one matter to communicate, to engage another state in open or closed debate; quite another to offer to trade with it more extensively, or lift existing trade restrictions, even to provide oneself with sanctions either immediately or in the future. The main point of including costs in the concept of power is to reveal that the latter is not exclusively a matter of effectiveness; power must be conceived and measured in terms of cost as well.[53] For John Harsanyi the cost of sanctions depends in the final analysis not on their success or failure but the risks a government must run in applying them. Possibly, Nixon ran no immediate risk in pursuing constructive engagement given the public preoccupation with the Vietnam War and the fact that support for disengagement and disinvestment was largely confined to shareholders' meetings and university campuses. But if this was true it was not a perception shared by all. The State Department, for one, was continually preoccupied by the fear of alienating African opinion and black political lobbies at home. During discussion of NSSM 39 it produced a score of telegrams allegedly from African governments urging the United States not to change direction on South Africa. Many were later found to be of its own invention—an example of special pleading at its worst.

As for the third set of costs, William Gamson suggests that the choice of threats or promises largely determines whether a target state's activities need to be monitored. In his opinion positive sanctions do not require such action.[54] It is highly doubtful whether this is right. After all, a recipient country may well falsify the evidence of its compliance, or attempt to pass off cosmetic reforms as fundamental ones, a conclusion which Washington eventually reached by the time the first episode of constructive engagement had run its course. In order to spare itself embarrassment at a later stage, and to remove more immediate doubts about its intentions, a sensible government needs to monitor a target state's activities very closely.

Unfortunately, the costs of surveillance, whether in the form of departmental overview or congressional hearings, proved too high for the Nixon administration. It was in an attempt to minimize both sets of cost that it applied excessive secrecy to its own relations, which ruled out both congressional monitoring and open departmental discussion, particularly in the form of interagency reviews. To have permitted the latter would have meant transferring the initiative from the National Security Council to Foggy Bottom, which would have run against the grain of Kissinger's priorities. Congressional monitoring would have led to public discussion of constructive engagement and thus threatened the whole experiment from the first.

In short, power is a very fluid concept, and even in situations strictly peripheral to U.S. interests or in a situation in which Washington for once recognizes the limits of its own influence the costs of applying positive sanctions can be high. It is for that reason that Deutsch maintains that the inclusion of costs in our concept of power must lead us to conclude that there "are not two states of power for an actor—adequate or inadequate—but three: (1) comfortable; (2) partly over-committed; and (3) bankrupt."[55] One can only conclude that if the United States had applied positive sanctions in the early 1970s other than in the fitful manner it did, it might have discovered that its nonpower influence approximated more the third of Deutsch's three categories rather than the first.

The final question is why so few countries who find themselves in the position of recipients find the prospect of positive sanctions appealing. To begin with, many states find it much easier to deter governments from applying negative sanctions, either by inviting violence or amplifying their own negative response. After 1960 the South Africans were able to paint a grim picture of mass unemployment and economic chaos which would follow any attempt by the international community to follow the policies pursued against Rhodesia. They also communicated with a great measure of success the likelihood that in the event of such action the white community would become much less divided.

There was no doubt that the West feared the breakdown of political authority in South Africa much more than it deplored the continuance of white supremacy. It was to persuade the whites to act while there was still time and thus to preempt social disorder that limited sanctions were first adopted in the early 1960s. It was the government through which the West chose to work and it was its freedom of maneuver, its ability to control the pace of change, that had at all costs to be preserved. The Western powers were not interested in political decapitation. Put quite simply, since South Africa could not hope to punish the international community if deterrence failed (something which both superpowers could have done had nuclear deterrence failed, though at the cost of mutual annihilation), it was forced to engage in the Gandhian tactic of amplifying the threat of violence against it; to use Gandhi's own expression "to stir sluggish consciences"; to pose questions about its own fate which many in the West found deeply disturbing.

A second reason for resistance to positive sanctions is that a recipient, putative or actual, is only likely to be persuaded by the offer of rewards if the rewards in question, or the outcome that may follow upon acceptance of them, clearly and demonstrably offset what it is being asked to give up. In short, the recipient will have to be convinced that the course of action it is being asked to pursue —its alternative future, if you like—offers a better future than the present. In a sense this is what Britain attempted to offer the whites in Rhodesia—in the hope that they would recognize that a return to legal rule (*not* majority rule) would bring with it greater security. Unfortunately, status quo powers like the United States are not always in the best position to support a transformation, as opposed merely to a reformation of the existing political order. The sanctions it may apply are mostly value increments or decrements, not values as such. All it can promise is merely a change of income, not a change of values.[56] To that extent, the United States had very little to offer in critical situations calling for radical political solutions. In Vietnam it financed massive land reform programs only to find itself outflanked by the Vietcong, who promised not just an increment of wealth and income, but a new society in which there would be a general redistribution of land and wealth (and with it status and power).[57]

In Latin America Eisenhower's adviser Adolf Berle wished to make free elections the precondition of future economic assistance; others wanted to use the foreign aid budget as an instrument to persuade Latin American regimes to abide by the electoral process. In both cases Washington gave its support to governments who were interested, at most, only in increasing income. But this factor was of little consequence in Cuba, where the government after 1959 did not wish to be diverted from its radical economic programs by sterile electoral quarrels over patronage of the type that had characterized all previous Cuban elections.[58] In that situation what could the United States offer? Indeed, would it have recognized Castro's programs as reforms or, *pace* Kennedy, a betrayal of the revolution?

Finally, not even the weakest states are likely to be influenced by extensive economic packages if their sovereignty is brought into question. In a domestic context often it is the recipient who requests positive sanctions, making the exchange conditional on its own behavior. But this approach, while frequently successful at home, is fraught with dangers on an interstate level. Take for example the position of an occupied power. Galtung reminds us that there are a number of responses to occupation, varying from nonviolent resistance to urban terrorism, both of which call for large occupying forces at some cost to the adversary. But an occupied people may also acquiesce in their occupation by paying taxes or selling their labor; or they may even seek to subsume their occupied status by offering their cooperation at a price, refusing to accept that they are an occupied power, or more to the point, refusing to *act* like one.[59]

In principle the possibilities are endless, even though in practice the scope for such action is not always great. But the behavior which is realistic for a defeated power is hardly possible for an independent state. It was long a complaint of the Diem government in South Vietnam that Washington often treated it like an occupied state and that if it agreed to institute the political reforms the Americans demanded it would indeed conform to the Vietcong stereotype of a *My-Viet* administration, an American-controlled puppet. But the Diem government also saw (mistakenly as it turned out) U.S. incentives for reform as a form of appeasement, a sign of flagging endeavor, an encouragement to hold out a little longer until Washington lost interest in the struggle. Several authorities have discovered that promises often convey the impression that the initiator is impotent or weak.[60] And if the putative recipient concludes that this is indeed the case, it may well increase its level of aspiration and bargain that much harder. This appears to be especially true when promises are not backed up by threats.[61]

One writer has surmised that the credibility of contingent promises (i.e., the proportion of times that the source actually gives a promised reward to the number of opportunities for giving it) tends to be greater in the conditions of reward and coercive power than the conditions of reward power alone. The carrot may well be offered regardless of whether a country intends to use a stick, but the carrot will only change hands if the stick is in evidence.[62] Unfortunately, American policy toward South Africa after 1960 was punctuated by approaches that combined the stick (Kennedy, Carter) or the carrot (Nixon, Reagan), but rarely both.

The fact that there are few instances of the successful use of positive sanctions should not, however, detract from the general principle that whether such relationships are labeled "power," "influence," or "nonpower influence," power in its generic sense includes all such labels including the use of positive sanctions. The theory of power may not explain very precisely the relationship between the latter and political influence, but politicians would be unwise to ignore it completely. As the Vietnam War entered its last phase the need seemed particularly urgent, as the Nixon administration knew well. If the war destroyed some of America's ambitions it kept the need for less intrusive and less coercive influence very much alive.

The Past as Prologue: The Case of Portugal
(1961 – 1963)

The Nixon administration's public attitude to negative sanctions was stated explicitly for the first time in a speech by the assistant secretary of state for Africa, David Newsom, in September 1971. Sanctions, he contended to a far from disbelieving audience, could never be effective against countries that enjoyed a large measure of economic self-sufficiency. In South Africa they had not helped the nonwhite majority to help itself. By cutting it off from contact with the outside world, and the outside world from contact with South Africa, they had denied the blacks a chance to improve their economic and political position in a period of unprecedented economic expansion.[63] The alternative—seeking compliance through rewards —had been discussed, if at all, only infrequently in the 1960s. Positive sanctions had been discussed only twice—first, in a paper prepared by Waldemar Campbell and, second, in a series of papers that formed the basis of a discussion of Portugal's continued colonial presence in Southern Africa. Before looking at constructive engagement in any detail, it is worth examining why this earlier initiative failed, for upon the answer a great deal should have turned.

The Portuguese themselves could not have been more surprised or less prepared for the crisis which hit them in 1961 and gave rise to the most protracted of all colonial wars in the postwar period. By the late 1960s, after the revolt in Angola, followed shortly afterward by that of Mozambique, nearly a hundred thousand Portuguese soldiers found themselves engaged on three separate fronts, at a cost to the metropolitan power of 3 percent of its GNP and nearly 20 percent of all public expenditure. Nevertheless, it was a conflict which for the most part sustained rather than undermined Lisbon's resolve. In part this was because the issue was very different from that which had informed public opinion elsewhere in Western Europe with the passing of the British, French, and Belgian empires in the late 1950s. Colonial rule might well have been repressive, but it was scarcely more so than Salazar's forty-year rule in Portugal itself. There was no great public constituency to begin with for decolonization.

The onset of the war in Angola found the United States largely divided and uncertain in its response. Stirred into action, a State Department's working group on Angola submitted a report on July 4,

1961, which proposed an unequivocally negative approach, recommending in particular the following steps: the United States should send a special emissary to Salazar to indicate that the United States would consider acceptable progress; if still unsatisfied, the United States should take the lead in the UN in proposing resolutions against Portugal, and should recognize Roberto's provisional government; if these actions provoked a change in government in Portugal, the United States should be prepared to deal with the new government on fair terms; the United States should deny Portugal arms, help refugees from Angola, and establish a program for educating Portuguese Africans in the United States. The group concluded that these pressures could have several consequences: Portugal could concede the reforms, but be incapable of restoring order in Angola; the unrest could spread to other territories; Salazar could lose control and anarchy could develop in the metropole; Portugal could refuse to implement the reforms and then pull out of Africa precipitously, leaving the territories to their fate. In any of these cases the United States should be prepared to finance its share of the costs of the long-term development of the Angolan economy. The cost was estimated at about $30 million, not including the cost of providing food or the cost of "a military intervention."[64] On the part of one faction in the state department there was a willingness to pay the price of negative sanctions however high.

There was another faction, however, which came increasingly to the fore in the years that followed. Among its members there was a much greater faith in conciliation rather than coercion and a preference for paying the price of positive sanctions. By the time of the Mueda massacre in 1961, which sparked off the nationalist struggle in Angola, many Americans had begun to lose their enthusiasm for rapid decolonization. The Belgian Congo was the turning point. It was not long before the American ambassador began to advise the UN that the political content of independence was just as important as "its hollow and sterile image" and that practical knowledge and ability were as much part of self-determination as the appearance of self rule.[65] Former secretary of state Dean Acheson was not alone in suspecting that many of the fledgling members of the UN had "human and material resources . . . varying from none at all to too little,"[66] but he had been one of the few observers to be privately briefed that in lending its support in the General Assembly to resolutions criti-

cal of Portuguese colonialism the United States hoped only to persuade Lisbon to introduce a measure of self-determination, not to
effect immediate self-rule.[67]

If there was a philosophy behind constructive decolonization, other
than the simple and perceived necessity of ensuring where possible a
nonviolent transfer of power, it was that the transfer when it came
should not be allowed to undermine the traditional ties of language,
education, and business that helped link Africa and Europe, that
were the reality behind the concept of *Eurafrique*. It was never
America's intention that Lisbon should sever all links; only that it
should translate formal rule (in the words of the Lusaka Manifesto
"the pretence that Portugal exists in Africa") into informal influence.
Indeed, the lesson could not have been spelled out more clearly than
it was by Adlai Stevenson during a Security Council debate in 1963:
"Portugal's role in Africa will be ended only if it refuses to collaborate in the great and inevitable changes which are taking place. If it
does collaborate, its continuing role is assured."[68] By then it was
already clear that the sympathy which Kennedy had personally shown
for the liberation movements that had taken up arms against Portuguese rule had not survived his death. Among those disappointed
was his deputy national security adviser Walt Rostow, who had at
one time hoped to translate the president's sympathy for the aspirations of black nationalism into more open support for their struggle
for self-rule.[69]

By 1963 the State Department's main concern was that Lisbon
would alienate black opinion, perhaps permanently, by refusing to
decolonize in time. Its main hope was that the more moderate nationalist leaders might still be co-opted if invited to participate in a
transitional government while the development of the overseas provinces proceeded at a rapid rate, subsidized in part by American money.
In reality, the differences between the Americans and Portuguese
were debated upon a singularly narrow front that took little account
of the military struggle beyond it. For with every year that passed the
nationalist leaders became more radical, less inclined to entertain
the prospect of a lengthy transitional period to independence, and
even more impatient of the likely terms.

For their part, the Portuguese remained largely deaf to the urgings
of their American allies. They did not welcome American interference in the country any more than they had in the 1950s. Nor did

they accept that such intervention could make a substantial difference. In the circumstances, this was hardly surprising. In applying an arms embargo in 1963 at the UN's behest the Johnson administration had displayed neither energy nor steadfastness of purpose. The sanctions themselves lacked direction and definition. The Americans only once succeeded in defining what they wanted, or even the terms of the dialogue, which might have been played out according to a different set of rules from those which had obtained since the early 1960s. The Johnson administration's one significant initiative has come down to us by the name of the Anderson Plan, although Anderson himself was only one among many who opened up the entirely new possibility of using rewards rather than punishments as a foreign policy instrument.

The Anderson Plan had its genesis in three key documents. The first was an aide-mémoire drafted by Anderson's predecessor Burke Elbrich in March 1961, in which the United States had offered "to extend important bilateral assistance to Portugal and the overseas territories, and in addition to explore the possibilities of multilateral aid programs with selected NATO countries in order to minimize the economic consequences for Portugal."[70] The offer was allowed to lapse. It was not followed up until mounting international criticism prompted the United States to look at the matter again. In January 1963 Chester Bowles wrote a detailed and convincing report for the secretary of state setting out in detail what positive sanctions might be applied:

1. The participation of NATO allies in efforts to strengthen metropolitan Portugal economically and politically;

2. a comprehensive study leading to the creation under the OECD's Development Assistance Committee of a capital and technical assistance package designed to modernize the Portuguese economy without threatening political stability in the metropole, which program would require up to $1 billion in financing over five years, one half to be provided by the United States; and

3. following the start of an economic modernization in the metropole, a five-year transition period leading to self-determination in the African territories and requiring recognition of African leaders inside and outside the Portuguese territories.[71]

The sanctions discussed in Bowles's memorandum were more detailed than any to be found during the Nixon administration. The initiative was imaginative, and a brave attempt to escape from the logic of coercion. As the political counselor in Lisbon cabled shortly afterward, "The basic principle involved is that of establishing for the effective exercise of self-determination a timetable which would be acceptable to non-extremist Africans and which at the same time may be so sweetened with political guarantees and economic inducements as to diminish beforehand the standard inducements regularly voiced by the Portuguese."[72]

It was against this background that President Johnson dispatched George Anderson, Kennedy's former ambassador to Lisbon, on a fact-finding tour of Mozambique. Anderson returned in 1964 convinced that independence for the colonies would be premature. Portugal had done far less than the other European powers to develop its overseas possessions. It suffered from the same poverty of resources. But he also believed that Lisbon was mistaken to imagine that it could both develop the colonies (to sustain the ever-increasing cost of military operations) and fight the war at the same time. Anderson proposed that the United States should invite the nationalists to join the Portuguese in a transitional government for a period of ten years, at the end of which a national plebiscite would be held to determine whether the people of Portuguese Africa would prefer to opt for continued association with Lisbon, or complete independence. As a guarantor of the agreement the United States would offer appropriate guarantees, including economic assistance to Portugal, so that if the vote went against her she would be better placed to survive the loss of closed markets and colonial tariffs.

Anderson proposed that both sides should try to take part in an interim administration; to abide by the result of an internationally supervised plebiscite and to accept third-party guarantees if the nationalists agreed to end hostilities before negotiations opened and if Lisbon was prepared to trade colonial preferences and tariffs for an economic package funded by its principal allies. For their part, the nationalists would be assured of participating in the administration of the colonies during the run-up to independence, with the assurance of the United States that the terms and conditions of the arrangement would be strictly observed.[73]

In any event, the plan proved unacceptable to the Portuguese government. In Anderson's discussion with Foreign Minister Franco Nogueira objections were raised to the role the Americans proposed giving the nationalists in the transitional government and the extent of the proposed amnesty for the guerrilla leaders.[74] Salazar did not consider that Portugal's position was so hopeless that he needed to make any concessions at all. And in this Anderson concurred. Until events forced the Portuguese to reassess their position it seemed advisable to set the issue aside rather than precipitate a breach with a valued NATO partner: "Without abandoning our principles looking towards government by consent of the governed, a free choice with all opinions and continued political, economic, and social progress, I see no purpose to be gained by unnecessarily precipitating irritations in U.S.–Portuguese relations."[75] In addition, the costs of entering into such open-ended guarantees would have been excessively high. Portugal's reluctance to get involved was doubtless reinforced by a realistic appreciation of the risks. If the United States had given both sides an assurance that the agreement would be honored, what action could the United States have taken if it had been broken by either party? In the case of Portugal it might have applied negative sanctions; but in the case of the nationalists would it really have been prepared to step up arms sales to the Portuguese? The prospect seemed somewhat remote.

In a letter to George Ball penned in February 1964, Salazar concluded that the independence of Portugal's overseas territories would neither guarantee the progress of their people nor assure the continuance of a Portuguese "presence, influence, and interest" in Africa (the language Ball himself had used in a letter the previous October). The government had considered an intermediate preparatory period but did not consider such a program feasible, not only because of the violence to which the nationalist movements appeared wedded but because of the inevitable intervention of "interests foreign to the African continent itself." After all, Salazar added, it was the violent elements that gave the orders, and he had not observed the Great Powers opposing them.[76]

Anderson's advice to await events was consistent with the course of American policy throughout the 1960s. He recommended the same course of action after visiting Mozambique again in 1969, when he found that the guerrilla war was not critical enough to call for far-reaching political reforms on the part of the colonial authorities.

The danger, however, of letting the "pot simmer on the back burner until some significant event [made] a new approach advisable" was that a situation might arise in the future which would render the use of positive sanctions impossible.

> [We] should recognize that Portugal is an ally of the United States and is trying within her own capabilities to do what she believes is right. . . . If we could stop the guerrilla war being waged against Portugal, the Portuguese would then have more of their own funds available to spend in accelerating the introduction of new schools, facilities, work projects and so forth for their African citizens. . . . The mistake that the United States has been making, and the United Nations has been making for so many years, is that we have been putting over-emphasis on political progress when the people themselves have not been ready for political progress. . . . I believe that if we get the economic development in its broadest sense . . . moving along well and at the same time that we do have education and social progress, that when the boys and girls [of Portuguese Africa] graduate from high school . . . then they will have jobs to satisfy their appetites and at that time they will be able to satisfy maturely and wisely the political advantages to which they should be entitled.[77]

Anderson then concluded,

> I think this [Portuguese policy] is far better than the alternative of turning loose prematurely and politically a group of people who are not ready to provide the instruments of government which go far beyond the question . . . of providing ambassadors, ministers, higher officials, but do not have the capability of providing all the things that go to make up a country and provide for the health and welfare and the happiness of the people who live in [the country].[78]

Immediately after visiting Africa Anderson had the following exchange with Salazar:

> "You know, Admiral, you Americans seem to think you can make changes in a matter of years, and we in Portugal know it takes centuries."

"Well, Mr. President, perhaps with good will on the part of all and a good deal of effort, it might be someplace in between."[79]

The Portuguese episode was a brief one in the history of American policy in the 1960s, but it was important for all that. The same objectives were under discussion in 1969; the same mistakes were made. In both periods the opportunity for applying positive sanctions was not especially auspicious; it may even have been beyond America's grasp. The failure to act decisively in the 1970s was not only the result of a lack of intelligence, and a failure of political will. The reasons, as we shall see, ran much deeper.

4 The Nixon Administration and South Africa, 1969–1974

The Vortreker monument, which dominates the approach to Pretoria, symbolized for many the determination of the Afrikaner nation to maintain its national identity. On the eve of Malan's victory in 1948 he had insisted that the question of cultural survival had been elevated in the intervening years to the status of an "irresistible life force and a veritable obsession." Since then the South Africans had been seen in the West as a nation of bigots, ruthless in their will to maintain racial exclusiveness, indifferent to international opinion, and imbued with a deep sense of inborn racial superiority that precluded any serious and sustained process of political debate.

At the outset of the Nixon administration's review of American policy, Roger Morris and his colleagues in the NSC hoped that constructive engagement would test two major premises: that the eras of greatest progress in Southern Africa had been the periods of most open contact with the outside world and that only through maintaining contact with both sides to the South African problem could Washington hope to mediate between them.[1] In this respect constructive engagement offered more of a political analysis than a program of action, even though at times it gave rise to hopes that could only have been met by a program that had been clearly thought out and consistently pursued.

For the most part, moreover, its analysis was at best highly superficial. Take, for example, William Rogers's claim that the only hope for peaceful change in the region would be to encourage "the constructive interplay of political, economic, and social forces."[2] It was a familiar theme, voiced often in the speeches of David Newsom:

In South Africa . . . change is a central theme of discussion; there
is a psychological and intellectual ferment within the Afrikaner
community; there have been isolated instances of acceptance of
multiracial activities; there is a growing realism among businessmen that Africans are important to them as skilled workers
and as a market. . . . We cannot expect change to come quickly
or easily. Our hope is that it will come peacefully.[3]

Unfortunately, there was no evidence of this central theme, a theme
on which so much turned: that as a result of the psychological and
social ferment within South African society the white community
had already begun to question whether apartheid was still in its best
interests. Indeed, there was no evidence of any *fundamental* self-
questioning at all. Newsom found no sign of it during a visit in 1970.
Although he reminded Congress that there was nothing to be gained
from penalizing those who were already opposed to the regime by
"throwing a curtain around them and their country," he had to concede that he had discovered only nine students at Stellenbosch
University, the traditional training ground of National party leaders,
who had actually read the Lusaka Manifesto.[4] Later the critics of
constructive engagement would maintain that the South Africans
had played for time with pretended concessions. Eventually in 1976
the Ford administration had to admit that for most of the period the
United States had mistaken cosmetic changes for substantial and
serious reforms.[5] By that stage it was rather a belated confession.

Despairing of the situation in South Africa, it was natural that
Henry Kissinger and his colleagues should have seized on every
and any sign of political progress. Their doubts, if not silenced,
were effectively held in check until it was too late to voice them.
This was perhaps owing in part to the fact that many of those
who expressed support for constructive engagement including Kissinger himself, Roger Morris, Winston Lord (the director of policy
planning), and Marshall Wright (the director of long-range planning in the State Department) had little or no past experience of
Southern Africa. Their support for the new policy was intelligible
only in terms of the parallel they drew with U.S.–Soviet relations, a parallel which could only with difficulty be squared
with the main conclusion of NSSM 39 that white attitudes to
race were "not amenable to the kinds of influence one nation

exerts upon another through peaceful international relations."

Wedded to the theme that change was already a feature of the public debate was a second: that for the first time in recent memory the United States had an opportunity to make contact with that part of the black community that had most to gain from a peaceful transfer of power. In a confidential telex in February 1974 the U.S. embassy wired from Cape Town: "The Embassy should give direct priority to the labor field. There is still a considerable need to upgrade the political skills—of those who can play a significant role in community organization and sociopolitical awareness."[6] No group seemed more likely to gain from the South African economy's spiraling economic growth than the industrial work force. No issue came under more discussion in Washington than the putative impact of the "internal contradictions" of the republic's economy—the labor regulations and labor codes which starved the labor market of skilled black workers and appeared to offer the government the grim alternative of reforming the political system or settling for lower economic growth.[7]

Mennen Williams, to whom this option had been clear in the mid-1960s, had gone on to question, nevertheless, whether the mere improvement in the economic status of the black workers would ever materially improve their political condition. Two years later South Africa's Prime Minister John Vorster confirmed his worse fears: "It is true that there are blacks working for us. They will continue to work for us for generations. In spite of the ideal we have to separate them completely . . . the fact of the matter is we need them . . . but the fact that they work for us can never entitle them to claim political rights, not now, nor in the future."[8] Even Morris had to concede that while the blacks had recently increased their participation in the country's economic life, the economic regulations of apartheid had actually grown more oppressive.[9] Quite simply, the United States needed a more critical understanding of the political system than Morris's initial analysis offered. Inevitably, his lack of experience told against him. In extrapolating to South Africa his views of the Soviet Union, he obscured the central dilemmas of political change in the first country and distorted the recent history of the second.

Four Target Areas

Once constructive engagement had been agreed upon, it was left to the State Department to draw up an agenda of change; to identify the areas in which progress was most likely and to which the United States could make a significant contribution. In the administration's second year in office David Newsom visited South Africa on a fact-finding mission. He returned to Washington with a list of four areas in which he expected some progress over the next ten years:

> There are really four areas to look for to determine whether the present leadership is really going to permit change or not. . . . The first . . . is what is referred to as petty apartheid —all the frequently absurd division of facilities . . . into white and non-white areas.
>
> The second is the whole attitude of the government toward the rule of law and the courts, something that many among the white South Africans dislike and oppose.
>
> The third . . . is the whole question of the urban African and the Coloureds and the Indians. I was struck by the degree to which these groups in a sense represent the heart of the problem. In that they are more educated, they are more sensitive to what they can't do, than perhaps the rural African. Perhaps, it is in this area that some ultimate accommodation is going to be most necessary. . . .
>
> The fourth . . . is even if one accepts that they go ahead with the so-called development philosophy, then it is what they do with the so-called Bantustans. . . .
>
> . . . these are the four areas where it seems to me one must watch to see whether there is any general movement. What happens in ten years I think will depend in part on what happens in these areas.[10]

Since Newsom never communicated his conclusions to South Africa directly, and positive sanctions were never applied to overcome some of the hurdles to progress in any of the four areas mentioned, it is not altogether surprising that by 1974 there were few examples, if any, of substantial change in any of them.

The rights of the urban black (particularly those relating to security of tenure) were not discussed at all. In agreeing to introduce a lease-hold system to benefit those with ten years or more residence, Vorster merely agreed to restore what had been withdrawn arbitrarily eight years earlier. The homelands program was accelerated after 1971, it is true. Within three years six new legislative assemblies came into existence.[11] Government service advisory committees also began training blacks in public administration. But the early 1970s were remarkable for the change in the political attitudes of the black community. The homeland experiment lost favor with a large body of blacks who found in membership of the Black Consciousness Movement self-respect within the bounds of a *national* black culture.

In the law progress was even slower. The first nonwhite senior counsel (an Indian) was not appointed until 1974. The blacks had to be content with their own law courts in the homelands. And even here progress was painfully slow. The first black high court was established in the Transkei in 1973; the first in Bophuthatswana, not until independence in 1977. As for South Africa proper, its security legislation was if anything tightened during this period. The law continued to offer no redress against government repression.

In the sphere of petty apartheid, progress seemed to be most apparent, but was in fact less significant. As of April 1974 South Africa could point to the desegregation of sixteen hotels and most public libraries and parks, limited multiracialism in sport, and the first attempt to open skilled positions to black workers.

Of all these measures the most significant was the growing consultation between the two communities—including regular meetings between the cabinet and homeland leaders and between the prime minister and representatives of the Coloured and Indian communities on government or quasi-government bodies such as the prime minister's Economic Advisory Council. Otherwise, the easing of petty apartheid in 1973 amounted to very little.

It is also worth pointing out that the initiative for desegregating public facilities came from the municipal authorities in the cities, not from the central government. The United States could claim no credit. And it is worth remembering that South Africa did not publicly condemn discrimination on the grounds of color until September 1974—four months after the collapse of the Caetano government in Lisbon, which precipitated the collapse of the Portuguese empire in Southern Africa.

The most important rider of all came from Julius Nyerere, who undoubtedly spoke for many Africans when he criticized these and other measures for being twelfth-hour reforms.[12] To the outside world the reform of petty apartheid meant nothing at all; to the blacks very little; to the whites, of course, a great deal. It followed that if petty apartheid was one of America's main objectives, constructive engagement was an ameliorative exercise at most. In recompensing the whites for concessions which for most of the time meant very little to the nonwhite community, Washington became the victim of its own wishful thinking. Constructive engagement failed because for most of the time the United States had no clear conception of what to aim for. If new possibilities were glimpsed, new lines of advance were not prepared. This was particularly apparent in the first item on Newsom's agenda.

The Problem of Legal Discrimination

For the better part of the 1960s only a very small group of Foreign Service officers in the Africa Bureau kept abreast of the changes in South Africa's security legislation. The number of people outside the State Department who continued to monitor these legal measures was even smaller. In his report to Congress in 1972 William Rogers briefly alluded to "the indiscriminate application of harsh security legislation which detracts from . . . the promising indications of progress "that he had identified in other areas, including that of petty apartheid.[13] But an analysis of how its application restricted the opportunities and increased the costs of black participation was never forthcoming. As a result of Newsom's four-point program, legal discrimination became a major focus of attention, but not, unfortunately, a fixed one during the first years of the Nixon administration.

To begin with, the Americans had little understanding that South African political life operated at several levels in which the government played a major part. The only members of the black community who were able to participate in the political system without legal restraint were the homeland leaders, or those community groups who were members of government or quasi-government organizations such as the Wage and Unemployment Insurance Boards.[14] The writer Colin Legum recognized as early as 1973 whereas movements such as the ANC "had little effective grassroots support in the reserves and only a precarious base in the urban areas, they [African homeland politicians] now operate legally from substantial political bases within a constitutional framework; the leaders can now legally be deprived of their right to act as spokesmen for their designated constituencies only by an abrogation of the laws designed to establish separate development."[15]

The great majority of blacks, however, operated at a level at which political activity was proscribed. This applied to those in whom the United States began to place so much hope: the industrial labor force, but the fact was not always fully appreciated in Washington. As late as 1972 Beverley Carter still held firm to the belief that "participation" in political life, short of the vote with its attendant electoral systems, constitutional guarantees, and protection of civil liberties was still a practicable goal in a country where the legal system restricted participation to those playing a role prescribed by the government.[16] Few references can be found in the speeches or press statements of the period to the totalitarian character of a legal system that severely restricted the scope for individual action, let alone collective action including strikes, demonstrations, and consumer boycotts.

The question in fact was addressed only once—by the veteran civil rights activist Clarence Mitchell, America's representative on the Political Committee of the Security Council. In a speech in October 1975 Mitchell declared that his country could never condone a political system which denied the majority of its citizens any role in political life, including the right to address the government and be listened to: "The United States deplores the detention of persons whose only act is outspoken opposition to the system of apartheid. The South African government is courting disaster when such repressive measures have the effect of closing off all avenues of peaceful change."[17]

Mitchell's critique went to the heart of the matter. Was there any point in discussing political rights without first discussing an end to legal restrictions? What did the United States mean when it talked of "political participation"? At the very minimum there surely had to be some scope for public debate. Once the United States had ruled out any immediate prospect of majority rule it was surely all the more urgent to ensure that the traditional barriers to communication were quickly removed. Mitchell's speech offered a serious and important critique of the situation. Several years later Daniel

Moynihan, America's ambassador at the time, wrote that it was the first time that a presentation of this kind had been delivered at the United Nations, setting a standard of argument far higher than usual.[18]

Political participation can of course take many forms, not all of which in the early stages require representative institutions. The NSC recognized this when it accepted that "the modification of apartheid" might stop short of majority rule. The cabinet meetings between the government and the homeland leaders, which became a regular feature of political life after 1971, confirmed Morris in his original opinion that constitutional reform was not immediately important. Nevertheless, Mitchell was quite right to argue that without substantial legal changes a dialogue would never get off the ground. The law, after all, prescribed the parameters of political protest, and unless the law was changed the great majority of blacks would never be given a voice to express the principles for which they stood and the future they would accept. There was no point hoping for black participation when those among the participants who were factory workers would not be able to participate in the only way that meant anything to them: collective bargaining. Many black workers with no other means of political expression obviously hoped to use their bargaining power on the factory floor to fight their political battles as well as voice their industrial demands.

Mitchell's criticism of South Africa must be seen in the context of the questions which Newsom left unanswered. The republic's six thousand laws and four thousand regulations, not to mention its sixty public security statutes, had created not only a system of political repression, but also a system of legal detention. Not only had they stifled political expression, they had created a political environment in which participation could have had no meaning for the participants other than the role-playing in which the government liked to indulge.

In support of his case Mitchell produced a six-thousand-word draft, with a three-page annex listing the names of white and nonwhite prisoners in detention. It was a closely reasoned, carefully documented argument which maintained that what was legal in South Africa was clearly not the case according to the standards of an open society, standards by which the South Africans insisted on being judged: "The South African system of detention and repression is built into the legal structure itself. There is a system of political laws which are designed to stifle and intimidate political opposition, laws which make criminal acts which are not criminal in any free society. . . . Acts which form the rough give-and-take that is the life-blood of democracy are considered criminal in South Africa."[19] Mitchell went on to catalog the totalitarian aspects of the law: the 4 million blacks who had been arrested under the pass laws since 1969 (almost half the total population of "white" South Africa); the fact that persons subject to banning were restricted without process of law; and that banning orders were normally imposed on political activists whom the state wished to silence but against whom it did not have enough evidence to proceed.

In principle, South Africa denied she had any political prisoners; in practice those convicted of criminal offenses that might be no more serious than membership in a banned organization were denied rights the state afforded other prisoners, including remission of sentence for good behavior. The law to which Mitchell drew special attention was the most far-reaching: the Terrorism Act of 1967, which defined terrorism so broadly that the use of violence was not actually specified. Acts for which individuals were liable to prosecution ranged from "embarrassing" the state to encouraging "the achievement of any political aim or social or economic change." Those charged under the act were presumed to have acted with intent unless they could prove otherwise.

As Mitchell reminded the Special Committee, the Terrorism Act made illegal every expression of political discontent. It not only denied the black community political institutions through which to press for change, it also denied it the right to political life. The annex to Government Notice 2130 (Part 2, para. 2) even allowed the government to prohibit any organization "which in any manner, propagates, defends, attacks, criticises or discusses . . . any policy of the government." The law, in short, confronted the blacks with a simple choice: of being banned, or ignored; of suffering prosecution for seeking to change a system through which many wanted to work, or joining the ranks of those who wished to overthrow it.

In effect, there was little scope for peaceful civil disobedience. Whatever might be the implications of civil disobedience, the government's response rather than the workers' intentions determined whether such actions were negative or not. In the late 1950s the blacks in the American South had boycotted white companies and small businesses responsible for imposing discriminatory conditions of employment. In Philadelphia three hundred firms had been boycotted on a selective patronage basis—one of a number of measures which had been applied without challenging the political system. Diverse though these actions may have been, all had been within the law. In South Africa the marketplace did not offer an avenue for nonviolent protest. The courts defined trade boycotts as negative (i.e., violent) acts of civil disobedience. In South Africa the black worker was hedged in with countless provisions and procedures. The state continued to harass and intimidate workers using the banning and detention measures of the Terrorism Act, in particular Section 2(2), which permitted the arrest of any person or group responsible for carrying out or even proposing to carry out an act prejudicial to the state. The Internal Security Amendment Act prohibited any action which was designed to bring about "political, industrial, social or economic change through disturbance or disorder." The General Law Amendment Act (1962) went much further by banning any measure which had as its objective social or economic change. White unions were specifically exempt from its provisions; black unions were not.

The Act did more than create a political crime for one race which was not a crime for the other. It served the more general purpose of discouraging participation in the political system: "The system of apartheid has created a system of detention which has made peaceful change not only criminal . . . but next to impossible." Despite his hopes for progress on the legal front, Newsom never really addressed this problem. He was far more concerned to remonstrate with the government about individual prison sentences, which had little immediate bearing on political life.

If Mitchell was right to believe that "the South African system of laws is designed and administered so as to prevent [the] majority from taking effective action to alter [their] condition of fundamental deprivation,"[20] then there was not much point in arguing the usefulness of participation "short of majority rule" until the offending legislation had been repealed. There was not much point either in putting one's faith in collective action when it would inevitably elicit a negative response; when the law continued to define the withdrawal of labor as industrial sabotage whatever the workers' *intentions*.

The situation, nevertheless, need not have been totally discouraging. Because of the scope of ministerial intervention in the South African legal system, a channel did exist for prevailing upon the government to repeal some of the most important statutes which placed political participation beyond the reach of most black leaders. At most, the legal system enforced procedural rights, including the laws of evidence in civil and criminal cases, rather than substantive rights, including freedom from arbitrary arrest. The law required a man on trial to be treated fairly; it could not, however, ensure that a man was brought to trial at all. In the light of this situation the United States' most obvious option was to prevent substantive rights from being eroded any further. But this it failed to do. In 1974, to cite one example, the Riotous Assemblies Act was amended to allow the minister of justice to prohibit political gatherings without fear of judicial review.

A second option was to secure the repeal of statutes which went further than most in setting aside substantive procedures. Two pieces of legislation might have been looked at in particular: Section 6(5) of the Terrorism Act (1967), which expressly removed the right of the courts to review the validity of any action undertaken by the minister of justice in its name (including unlimited detention on suspicion); and Act 44 of the Internal Security Act (1950), which empowered the minister to detain anyone on suspicion of committing an offense against the state, subject only to review by a committee presided over by a judge, to whose recommendations he was not obliged to give effect, and on which the courts were not allowed to pronounce.[21]

It was precisely because ministerial discretion was so extensive that South Africa was vulnerable to external persuasion. The government could hardly hide behind the law; in many instances of banning, the courts were not involved at all. But the Nixon administration remained surprisingly unaware of the opportunity for intervention. Beverley Carter regretted, for example, that the courts in South Africa were not allowed to interpret statutes, only to reach judgments on the basis of parliamentary legislation. He also found the attitude of most lawyers quite depressing: "There is not a great deal that I think one can look for from the South African judiciary in terms of courageous view taking that would help to correct the situation."[22] The judges themselves, however, could hardly be in the van of political change while their freedom of action was so circumscribed by executive privilege.

For the most part, the State Department restricted its intervention not to advocating changes in the law, but to raising court judgments with senior South African officials. Such remonstrances were usually ineffective. After 1972 even complaints at the embassy level became increasingly infrequent at the very time that the Black Consciousness Movement found itself increasingly harassed by the police. Not a single member of the executive committee of the South African Students Organisation (saso) completed a full term in office. Most were either banned, detained, or forced into exile. But there is no evidence that the administration ever tried to persuade the South African government to act with more circumspection; or even to accept the judgment of the courts in the many instances in which the accused were rearrested on being acquitted.[23]

The United States and the Homelands

The Nixon administration spoke frequently of its hopes and objectives during this period, but what it actually meant varied considerably with the situation. We must not be misled into thinking that its support for an end as vague as "the modification of apartheid" was intended to be deliberately misleading. Often the obliqueness of its public statements revealed confusion in the administration's own mind. Its guarded response to the homeland program must be seen in this context. In pursuing "racial justice" the United States implicitly believed in keeping open as many options as possible.[24] As a classic portmanteau term, *racial justice* was sufficiently vague to encompass everything from partition to a qualified franchise, and sufficiently noncommittal to allow the United States to endorse anything the South Africans themselves might have in mind.

In this connection, the Nixon administration was not inclined to look upon the Bantustan (or homeland) program with complete disfavor. Any other attitude would have been difficult to justify given Vorster's determination after 1968 to pursue separate development with increased vigor. Separate development was the code word for the division of South Africa into separate and independent states for its different tribal "nations." The program was regarded as a means of conferring black majority rule on the 8 million residents of the homelands, while denying the urban blacks in "white" South Africa any rights at all. Far from threatening white supremacy, the homeland experiment actually reinforced it. By giving the blacks a voice in their respective states, the rest of the country would be left under white control. To its critics abroad the government retorted that majority rule would indeed be implemented, albeit separately for each tribal group; to its critics at home on the far right of the National party, it could claim that its principles remained the same. By reconciling both elements the government hoped to become all things to all men—a progressive force in the eyes of the international community; the defender of white supremacy in the eyes of its supporters at home.

The only problem with this strategy was that none of the homelands looked very convincing on paper. Eighty-five percent of the population of South Africa was to be crowded into only thirteen percent of the land, the amount originally reserved by statute in 1936. All but three of the homelands—the Transkei, Basotho-Qwaqwa, and South Ndebele—were fragmented entities, with their constituent parts separated in some cases by several hundred miles. To add to the confusion none appeared capable of grappling successfully with the economic problems arising from demographic pressures on the land. As a State Department paper noted, 20,000 jobs a year would need to be created simply to keep pace with population growth. The entire program, it commented wryly, although intended to be the showpiece of apartheid, lagged behind white South Africa in every respect but segregation.[25]

The economic realities of the homeland program were apparent even to the least critical observer, even though it would be difficult to show that the South Africans themselves were any more realistic in outlook at the end of the period than they were at the beginning. After touring KwaZulu, Newsom became more convinced than ever that Verwoerd's experiment might conform with the National party's dogma, but met very few of the criteria of self-determination. Later he told the House subcommittee on Africa: "It was apparent to us that in the continued application of apartheid, in the largely rural nature of these enclaves and in the continuing tight control from Pretoria these areas are yet far from being embryonic free African states."[26] The committee was also reminded by Beverley Carter that Verwoerd's original conception had changed so often in the intervening years both with regard to the number and name of the so-called "national units" that the United States could not be blamed for

Table 2 Size of the Homeland Areas in 1972

Homeland	Total Area (sq. miles)
Transkei	14,178
Ciskei	3,547
KwaZulu	12,141
Lebowa	8,549
Venda	2,333
Gazankulu	2,576
Bophuthatswana	14,494
BasothoQwaqwa	177
Swazi	818

SOURCE *The African homelands of South Africa* (Johannesburg: South African Institute of Race Relations, 1973), 5.

suspecting that the retribalization of the African people was being cynically pursued in the name of self-determination.[27]

On the other hand, at this stage the State Department was not prepared to rule out the program completely. Many Africans had chosen to come to terms with separate development because no other course seemed open to them. In such circumstances Newsom believed it would be quite wrong to penalize the homeland leaders by cutting them off from contact with the international community. In an interview in 1972 he confessed that he was more interested in testing whether the homeland chiefs accurately reflected the interests of South Africa's nonwhite citizens than in adding the State Department's voice to the many already urging the government to think again.[28]

At one time, indeed, the United States seemed to be quite prepared to apply positive sanctions in order to make the experiment more credible. Although skeptical of the homelands as they were constituted, the State Department was not entirely hostile to separate development as a political principle. Its main criticism of the policy centered on its economic viability. When the Five Year Development Plan (1966–1971) for the homelands was set back by inflation and substantial delays in funding, the homeland leaders began to look to foreign investment to redress the shortfall in capital injections. Since the NSC doubted whether the unequal distribution of land would be critical "if South Africa were willing to make a major investment in the Bantustans to make them economically productive,"[29] there seemed to be a genuine argument for American assistance.

With this in mind the State Department sent out a team in 1972 made up of four members of its own African Advisory Council to ascertain whether official endorsement of American investment was still undesirable, or whether its position should be reconsidered.[30] In South Africa the team met two homeland leaders: Gatscha Buthelezi and Kaiser Matanzima, as well as officials from the Xhosa Development Corporation. Their final report challenged the views of those in the Africa Bureau who had not wanted the debate to be reopened at all. The question of the economic development of the homelands, they maintained, had been grossly misrepresented. While acknowledging that economic problems were severe, they did not accept that they were insurmountable. Indeed, they pointed to a number of programs in which the United States could invest, including agricultural schools in the Transkei and KwaZulu, and special training grants for black civil servants.

It was not an extensive program, in part because the authors recognized that direct government assistance might raise a storm of protest in both countries. For, whatever was decided, the problems of the urban black would still remain: "For the moment whatever encouragement or aid we may be in a position to extend to the homelands should be handled in such a way as not to sanction or give recognition to separate development in South Africa."[31] Even so, the State Department did not discourage the government of KwaZulu from sending a member of its executive council to study American community development projects the following summer. One of the authors of the 1972 report even recommended using Eximbank credits for specific development programs in the evidence he gave to a congressional committee some years later.[32] Each of the report's recommendations, moreover, were discussed beforehand with the Xhosa Development Corporation. The failure to discuss the use of sanctions seems all the more remarkable in view of the fact that the administration had for once discussed the report with the South African government. Consultation between the two countries on any aspect of constructive engagement was rare enough.

Although American companies continued to invest in the homelands, they did so, therefore, without official encouragement from their own government. Newsom's failure to win general acceptance for the report served as a partial alibi for the administration's clear lack of interest. It also explains the confusion within government circles—with the Department of Labor, on the one hand, advising against investment, and the State Department, on the other, urging American business to take advantage of the fact that South Africa's restrictive labor legislation did not apply to KwaZulu and Bophuthatswana.[33] Since the United States continued to maintain that the self-governing territories were still part of South Africa, it was hardly in a position to draw up investment guidelines radically different from those that already applied to the republic.[34]

Nevertheless, the development issue could not be divorced altogether from its political context. Until 1971 Kaiser Matanzima, the chief minister of the Transkei, continued to place the main emphasis on development rather than separation. It had long been an article of faith that self-determination would be meaningless if the homelands continued to rely on South Africa for their economic well-being. But when the Transkei's development plans began to lag behind the increase in population, Matanzima quickly reversed his stand. Instead of insisting on economic independence first, and political autonomy second, he began to talk of escaping from the political trammels which were responsible for the Transkei's economic dependence. From then on it was only a matter of time before he opted for complete independence.

It was equally possible, of course, to construct a quite different and more plausible model of the role which homeland leaders like Gatscha Buthelezi, KwaZulu's leader, might play in the republic. Buthelezi was much more interested in becoming the spokesman of the urban blacks than the representative of his own Zulu constituency. Like Matanzima, he recognized that economic self-determination would have to be the first prerequisite; that once this had been achieved everything else would follow. But he preferred to capture control of the South African economy by using the platform the government had given him. He preferred, in short, to make common cause with industrial labor rather than opt for an independent KwaZulu.

In 1971 Buthelezi visited the United States, where he found a sympathetic hearing. For their part the Americans found a man deeply committed to a dialogue with the whites, but deeply concerned that his own freedom of maneuver was severely circumscribed. Since South Africa had set him in the context of its own political initiatives,

he had been able to opt out of the discussions about KwaZulu's
independence, as he was later to withdraw from the government-
sponsored committees on which the homeland leaders and the cabinet first sat in 1971. The only power of which the blacks had not
been deprived, he maintained, was the option not to cooperate in any
initiatives detrimental to their own interests. But noncooperation
was not a viable option. The blacks, he contended, must themselves
be responsible for new initiatives to which the government would be
forced to respond. In using the platform the government had given
him to move from the politics of protest to the politics of power,
Buthelezi proposed to adopt a strategy in which noncooperation would
become a matter of tactics rather than a question of principle.

Some of the more important questions raised in his discussions
with the State Department still remain a matter of conjecture. But
we know that when Matanzima visited Washington on a six-week
leadership grant the following summer the United States did its best
to reconcile him to Buthelezi's thinking, especially his strategy of
merging KwaZulu and the other homelands into a single federation.[35]
Matanzima had arrived in Washington expecting to find the Americans unsympathetic to the homeland leaders, and strongly support-
ive of values he dismissed as "universalistic," such as one man, one
vote. To his surprise he found that many who had taken strong positions on the issue two years earlier were now much more willing to
consider some of the alternatives. Indeed, Newsom urged him to
discuss the federation proposal with the other homeland leaders so
that they might deal with South Africa from a much stronger position than they ever could on their own.

On his return Matanzima announced his intention of rejecting
"second class citizenship" and falling in with Buthelezi's program.[36]
Within months, all but two of the homeland leaders had agreed to
attend a summit meeting at Umtata to open up the matter to much
wider discussion. At Umtata formal agreement was reached to press
ahead with a federation—a goal that was now acknowledged (in the
words of the final communiqué) to be "vital to the unity of the black
people."

In March 1973 Buthelezi wrote to Vorster urging him to accept the
federation scheme. At this stage he was much more concerned with
the strength of the blacks' position in a dialogue with the government than with the form such a dialogue should take:

A federal formula of the kind that raises the whole issue of power at the centre should be avoided. . . . It should be possible to establish a common machinery for certain matters without raising the hardy annual of demand for control of a central Parliament. The issues which bedevil any mutual understanding and mutual confidence could, at least, be postponed for several generations. During that time mutual confidence could grow to a point where agreement could be reached at the centre as well.[37]

It is idle to speculate what might have happened if Vorster had been receptive to these proposals, if the Americans had prevailed upon the government to consider the scheme dispassionately, and persuaded Matanzima to keep in line. As it happened, the second summit meeting scheduled for December did not convene until November 1974, by which time Matanzima had changed his position and chosen to opt for complete independence.

Perhaps Buthelezi's proposals were what the United States had in mind when it talked of encouraging the government to modify apartheid "short of majority rule." Its own attitude to the homelands became much more constructive at the end of this period than at the very beginning. These early years mark a unique period in U.S.–South Africa relations—a period in which black initiatives (however limited in scope) actually shaped (if they did not transform) American thinking. Those officials who were sympathetic to the homeland program, although not enthusiastic in their support, set out to trace the impact it might have on South African institutions, on the South African economy, and Afrikaner thought. This was an ambitious undertaking requiring for the most part far greater knowledge of the program and the country than most officials possessed, or would admit to. But it remains the first serious attempt in the years after Sharpeville to mold American policy to initiatives that directly encompassed black political society. As such it deserved two marks for imagination—if not, regrettably, three marks for success.

A case in point was the report that was commissioned in 1975 by the State Department's Office of External Research, a study of the two largest Bantustans: KwaZulu and Bophuthatswana. Based on discussions with their respective leaders Buthelezi and Lucas Mangope, the Bantu Investment Corporation, and the Bureau of

Economic Research for Bantu Development, the final report endorsed Buthelezi's contention that the homeland program could be used to advance claims that Verwoerd had never envisaged. It maintained that separate development had given the homeland governments a chance to win popular support on a national level, and argued that separate development had given them an institutional base and a political platform as well as access to black constituencies in the cities for the first time. It offered the first real opportunity to take the initiative since the collapse of noncooperation in the late 1950s:

> Africans have for a long time been governed by hierarchical administrations controlled by whites and assisted by traditional authorities whose powers of initiation and opposition were extremely limited. Recent developments have created modern political roles in legislative and executive bodies that make no pretense of being traditional. Limited though the powers and resources of these bodies are, they are not merely part of a hierarchy down which orders can be transmitted. . . . Africans are now able to influence decisions of importance to their white rulers, and, at the very least, raise the price of making them.[38]

In addition, if the future depended on the strength of their bargaining position, then the situation was not entirely without hope: "A continued willingness to work within the institutions of the homelands and to accept limited, possible cumulative concessions—is a major political challenge facing Vorster's government. How vigorously the homeland leaders put their demands and what sanctions they threaten to support those demands may condition how generous a response they receive from the government."[39]

The government's response might also have been conditioned by the sanctions the United States itself was prepared to apply, and the extent to which it was prepared to support the homeland conception, in a federated form. The complexity of the situation was such that one can only hypothesize, of course, what might have happened had the Nixon administration taken these arguments to their logical conclusion, or the conclusion that was logical in the context of constructive engagement. The meetings between the cabinet and homeland leaders did, after all, produce some *national* results, including a promise in 1974 to look at the implementation of the pass laws more closely, and to appoint a tax committee to investigate the fairness of African tax contributions.

It was true that the homeland leaders still continued to petition the government for redress of grievances instead of negotiating with it in the true sense of the term, but it was, at least, a beginning. In August 1972 the minister for Bantu administration grudgingly conceded that he could not prevent Buthelezi or the other leaders from making common cause with the urban blacks, or speaking on their behalf as their national spokesmen.[40] Whether the position could have been exploited had the United States applied positive sanctions more effectively, or whether at this particular juncture such a strategy would have proved unavailing, is open to question. As a "might have been" it may have no particular merit; but it is in the history of lost opportunities that the fascination of the story lies.

Collective Bargaining, the United States, and the Corporate Sector

Throughout the 1960s American investment in South Africa met with criticism from several different schools of thought. Some questioned whether it had contributed to the country's prosperity at the expense of black labor; others questioned whether in such a corporatist state the role of multinational capital could not be other than collusive. Even at the time these conflicting interpretations presented quite formidable problems of explanation for a government that remained convinced that foreign capital had a constructive role to play. The Nixon administration shared that philosophy completely. As David Newsom observed in 1973, "U.S. private interests are involved in a complex and controversial area in Southern Africa. The U.S. government recognizes this and within the limits of its authority seeks to make that involvement constructive."[41]

Indeed, the administration never questioned its belief that an improvement in the contractual status of the black worker would improve his political status as well. For all the subtlety of these arguments there was some danger in such an excessively mechanical interpretation of political actions as a kind of Pavlovian response to economic pressures, some of them very short-term in character. Since so much followed from it, we would be well-advised to look at the economic philosophy in greater detail.

There was no disagreement between the White House and the State Department, as there was on most other issues, about the undesirability of disinvestment. The chairman of the House subcommittee on Africa was informed that the United States could not afford to incur the losses that would follow even if it could be certain that the South Africans would honor their repatriation guarantees.[42] It was most doubtful whether American companies would be allowed to withdraw depreciation allowances or dividends in lieu of profits. If they wished to remove capital, as well as profits, a State Department paper concluded, they would have to sell their South African affiliates, together with "goodwill" stocks and physical assets, and invest for five years or more in South African government securities.[43]

Disinvestment therefore would have been a hazardous undertaking. There were also those who doubted whether it would be effective. American investment was significant in only three sectors of the economy which were particularly important for long-range growth: automobiles (40 percent), petroleum (50 percent), and computers (70 percent).[44] Dollar investment accounted for less than 2 percent of total investment from domestic and foreign sources. And while the companies in control of those particular sectors increased their assets by over 40 percent between 1970 and 1972, for most of the period the rate of investment from the United States actually fell.

An early speech by Robert Smith, the deputy assistant secretary for African affairs, typified the government's attitude to the question. Although he concluded that American investment "provides revenues, increases productive capacity, stimulates the economy, constitutes foreign involvement and cooperation with the system and is a psychologically significant symbol of outside acceptance,"[45] he maintained, nevertheless, that it had brought more nonwhite workers into the labor force and provided a unique opportunity for multinational corporations to introduce more enlightened conditions of employment. In the United Nations the U.S., representative on the Committee of Three argued that disinvestment would drastically curtail the number of blacks entering the market for skilled labor.[46] Later the State Department reminded Congressman Charles Diggs that if American companies pulled out of South Africa the field would be left open to other companies whose employment standards might be less exacting.[47]

Perhaps enough has been said to illustrate that the government's objections to disinvestment were not entirely cynical, though in many respects its attitudes were undoubtedly self-serving. Its public pronouncements carried an implicit conviction that investment would help the blacks to improve their economic status. Newsom singled out new economic opportunities as the most important engine of political change. "We do . . . see an evolution under the impact of growing economic opportunities bringing increased political consciousness to the majority populations of the area."[48]

Few of Newsom's colleagues found much to quibble with in the belief of South Africa's most prominent businessman Harry Oppenheimer that the reform of the political system would follow on automatically once the "economic contradictions" of apartheid had been resolved: "Rapid progress with what we call African advancement would do more than raise material standards for all sections of the population. It would help powerfully to harmonise the natural and reasonable aspirations of the people with the structures of the economy and the stability of the state."[49] Nixon and Kissinger both knew of Oppenheimer's thesis from an article which had appeared in *The Economist* in 1968, in which its author, Norman Macrae, had not only expressed confidence that the South African economy would continue to grow but had also contended that encouraging foreign investment made sound common sense: "Richer and securer generally means lefter which is one reason why efforts to make it less rightist by boycotting it into greater insecurity and poverty would not seem to make any very evident sort of progressive sense."[50]

In his defense Macrae went on to cite the arguments of one of Oppenheimer's own colleagues, Michael O'Dowd. Taking as his framework Rostow's model of the three stages of economic growth, O'Dowd had placed the South African economy in the second, or developing stage, explaining the depressed status of the proletariat (the blacks) in economic rather than political terms. On this understanding a change in their political status could not be expected until their economic condition had substantially improved. According to O'Dowd's model an expanding economy would stimulate living standards and would enable consumers as well as producers to dispense with racial discrimination in a marketplace that was essentially color-blind.[51]

It is not surprising that the economic contradictions of apartheid became the main focus of interest in the years that followed. Nixon reported to Congress in 1972: "There is an imbalance between the needs of South Africa's active economy and her adherence to racial problems which deprive her of the growing pool of human talent which that economy requires. There is some hope in that anomaly."[52] When Newsom visited South Africa in 1970 he found the American business community battling against labor codes which prevented it from drafting blacks into the skilled labor force, despite a critical shortage of white skilled labor. He returned impressed by the determination of many companies to oppose what they considered to be unreasonable obstacles to further growth. One of the largest firms —General Motors—had been granted permission to promote eight hundred of its black employees to positions formerly reserved for white workers. Mobil continued to lobby the South African Chamber of Industries for similar concessions.

Yet Newsom was the first to admit that his description did not do justice to the actual complexity of the situation. South Africa might not be able to defer for much longer a decision whether to pursue economic growth by relaxing its restrictions on skilled labor, or to opt instead for lower growth, but there was no evidence that the attitude of American corporations was likely to prove decisive. General Motors was very much the exception. The manager of one American subsidiary informed him that his company had reached the limits of what could be done by political lobbying.[53] It was now up to the government to make further moves in the right direction.

Possibly because it had no great faith in its own position, the Nixon administration tended to sidestep the issue, neither encouraging nor discouraging investment in South Africa, although even here it was not always consistent.[54] One instance was its complete failure to explain how changes in the contractual status of the black worker would improve his political status. Possibly the question would have remained unanswered but for the Polaroid experiment in the autumn of 1970 when the company's black employees in Boston formed an action group to protest at its involvement in the production and processing of photographic material for South Africa's pass books. In response, the management decided to defuse further criticism by sending out a fact-finding mission to investigate the complaints. The report that it produced advised against disinvestment, but recommended a series of measures to improve the company's conditions of employment. At the end of the six-month probationary period, the management announced its complete satisfaction with the progress that had been made. The response of other companies to Polaroid's initiative was swift. By January 1972 General Motors, Chrysler, and American Metal Climax had adopted similar programs of their own.[55] Many executives were only too ready to introduce programs that, though limited to their subsidiaries, looked forward to the eventual repeal of most of the economic regulations of apartheid: in particular job reservation and the pass law system which placed severe restrictions on labor mobility.[56]

Within the administration, the possibility of building upon the Polaroid experiment became the subject of intense debate. Its proponents did not claim that the measures adopted by Polaroid, Mobil, and others in the months that followed were in themselves far-reaching; but they did claim that foreign investment might become a catalyst of political change. Robert Smith claimed that Polaroid's actions had proved once and for all that change was possible "even within the system."[57] It was significant that the vice-president of the company was the first witness to be summoned by the House subcommittee on Africa when it embarked upon the most extensive set of hearings ever to be devoted to American investment in Southern Africa, spanning three years. David Newsom fully endorsed the company's program, although he declined to take any public posture at such an early stage for fear that Polaroid might fall foul of the South African government.[58]

By the end of 1971 the administration was much less reticent. In an oblique reference in one of its fortnightly publications, the Department of Commerce advised American businessmen to ensure that their conditions of employment were "consistent with American expectations." Where legal restrictions made it impossible to maintain "American standards," they were encouraged to consider compensatory programs including training schemes and educational grants.[59] A list of recommended reforms published shortly afterward by the U.S. Consulate-General in Johannesburg appeared to have been largely influenced by Polaroid's program with its emphasis on equal terms of contract, equal pay, and equal opportunities for promotion. Later still, the U.S. representative on the UN Committee of Three informed its members that since the experiment had first begun seventeen corporations had promoted blacks to their board of directors, and that many more had intimated that they would follow suit.[60]

Yet the Polaroid experiment obscured rather than illuminated the central issue: the administration's role. Officials from the deputy assistant secretary of state to John Fletcher at the United Nations asserted the importance of foreign investment, without apparently resolving in their own minds what the United States government could, or should, do to assist its own corporations. For most of the time the government relied on voluntary decisions by the corporations concerned. It had had no wish to push them into conflict with the South African government. When it acted at all, it preferred to do so behind the scenes, through contacts with the Business Council for International Understanding and the African-American Chamber of Commerce.[61] It even managed to persuade Congressman Diggs to come out in support of Polaroid during a tour of South Africa in 1971. Diggs had initially been a committed advocate of disinvestment; he appears to have changed his mind after an unscheduled four-hour briefing at the American embassy shortly before he was due to attend a press conference to report his impressions.[62]

Nevertheless, the corporate measures introduced between 1972 and 1974 did not go very far. The most restrictive legislation in the sphere of labor relations remained in force. Roger Morris, who had resigned from the NSC in 1970, believed that the administration should have thrown its full support behind the Polaroid experiment, even at the risk of challenging the law.[63] Instead, the State Department advised against any initiative that might force South Africa's hand. It was completely opposed to a mandatory code of conduct that would have compelled all American subsidiaries to adopt specific employment practices. Any attempt to introduce one, it warned, might force many companies to disinvest at precisely the time that their presence was most needed.[64]

Instead of providing a lead, the administration did nothing. Although Newsom informed the African-American Chamber of Commerce that the government hoped all companies would eventually subscribe to the Polaroid experiment, he insisted that it would be quite improper for the administration to intervene in a matter which involved the relationship between employer and employee. If consulted, it would be prepared to advise American businessmen what could be done within the letter of the law, but it would not encourage them to break it. It would feel bound to discourage any initiative that threatened to dislodge American business from its position "in the forefront of peaceful change."[65]

If remaining in the forefront meant refraining from challenging the law, then most companies were unlikely to remain there for long. Exactly what the future might hold became apparent for the first time when the workers in Natal went on strike in 1973. With a white labor force that had always looked to the government rather than labor organizations to entrench its privileges, South Africa had no real tradition of labor unrest since 1948. It came as all the more surprising, therefore, when 67,000 workers organized 246 separate, sudden, and extremely effective stoppages in support of their claim to higher wages. Although the United States tended to pay most attention to the wage issue, the disparity in wages between white and nonwhite labor came to be linked in the minds of the strikers with restricted job opportunities, inadequate training, and the government's persistent refusal to recognize the principle of free collective bargaining.

These matters were brought to a head by the massive labor unrest in Natal which, following the breakdown of the consultative machinery that had been set up twenty years earlier by the Bantu Labour Settlement of Disputes Act, provided a focal point for initiatives specifically aimed at improving communication between white employers and black workers. In the absence of trade unions the workers' interests had been looked after by regional labor committees appointed by the minister of labor. The 1973 strikes finally alerted the government to the ineffectiveness of the Central Bantu Labour Board in negotiating higher wages. The government decided that it was in its own interests to open the door wide enough for black members of the regional committees to negotiate on their own behalf at future meetings of the Industrial Conciliation Council. Even though this concession was partly offset by the fact that they were not allowed to vote, membership did, at least, provide them with an opportunity to deal with the government directly.

The Natal strikes raised the question whether any initiative would be constructive unless the blacks could negotiate from a position of strength. In the labor field, communication was likely to take the form of collective bargaining. Yet any attempt by American companies to recognize black unions would be in breach of the law. It was understandable, though hardly excusable, for the Nixon administration to find shelter behind such an argument that defied refutation yet begged the obvious question: why, if this was indeed the case, the United States itself did not intervene; why, in this field at least, it had failed to consider whether sanctions might be usefully applied. Although the State Department acknowledged after 1973 that changes in the contractual status of black labor could well prove a catalyst for change,[66] it did not come out in favor of black trade unions until 1974 when the American labor attaché addressed the South African Trade Union Congress. Even then, when it came to the point of drafting a new set of guidelines for businessmen, collective bargaining was conspicuously absent.

Although clearly consistent with the ideas which had gained ground in the administration since 1971, the guidelines tackled none of the questions that had emerged during the strikes of 1973. Employers were only asked to engage in direct negotiations with their black employees "if, as and when unions come into existence." Until then they were advised to use "all available channels of communication," hardly the most useful advice. The blacks themselves continued to argue that until they obtained the right to bargain with their employers directly, improvements in working conditions would never be of great significance.

The administration's reluctance to press South Africa on this issue robbed its qualified support of corporate initiatives of ultimate meaning. It is true that the United States' 375 subsidiaries employed less than 100,000 workers out of a total labor force of 5.5 million. In the manufacturing sector, which offered the greatest scope for union organization, they employed less than 30,000 workers in all.[67] General Motors, which ranked eleventh in terms of the total assets held by foreign companies in South Africa, ranked only thirty-fourth in terms of the work force employed. ITT was one of the few American corporations to increase its proportion of black employees to 50 percent of the labor force.

Yet even allowing for the fact that American companies may not have been favorably placed to have changed the contractual status of non-white labor decisively if at all, in the manufacturing sector they owned $4 out of every $5 of their investment. Since directly held investment provided the parent companies in New York with a degree of control which was unique among foreign investors, and since twenty-five of the largest firms employed all but 10 percent of non-white labor employed by American companies, a mandatory code of practice might well have had some influence out of all proportion to the actual size of investment.

It is true, of course, that if the United States had pressed ahead with such a code, other countries might not have followed its example. When Newsom visited Europe in March 1972 he found both the British and West German governments were particularly unwilling to entertain the idea of a coordinated strategy toward South Africa. Of the republic's three major investors, only the United States made any determined effort in this period to improve labor conditions. Only after the Natal strikes brought allegations of unfair treatment to the attention of a Parliamentary Select Committee did the British government feel bound to introduce a code of practice. Nevertheless, the administration does not appear to have worked out a coherent policy with its European allies. In March 1973 Newsom told Congressman Diggs's committee that the United States had tried to persuade the British and German governments to upgrade the wages paid by their own companies. Yet only a month later he admitted before the same committee that "severe competition from others" had forced the United States to relax restrictions on the commercial sale of aircraft.[68] The administration, in short, appeared somewhat unsure of its priorities.

One other point needs to be made. The industrial unrest which paralyzed Natal in 1973 enabled Buthelezi for the first time to make direct contact with Zulu workers in Durban. Although the Department of Bantu Administration rejected the right of the government of KwaZulu to negotiate with employers on their behalf and to intervene to ensure that the Natal Chamber of Industries put a stop to the intervention of homeland ministers in labor disputes,[69] it seemed clear to Harry Oppenheimer that "far from bringing about a real separation between black and white, [separate development] was simply bringing about a situation in which tribal authorities would play an increasingly powerful role in relation to industry in the white-controlled urban areas."[70]

Newsom had returned to Washington in 1970 with the hope that progress might be forthcoming on at least two fronts—an improvement in the conditions of black workers and increased scope for the role of the homeland leaders. By 1973 separate development did appear to have progressed, though not in the direction Verwoerd had foreseen. No longer was the role of the homeland governments restricted entirely to the rural reserves. Both Buthelezi and the leader of Bophuthatswana, Lucas Mangope (who had rallied to the support of the Tswana workers in 1973) seemed intent on capturing economic power in the major cities, particularly Durban. The homeland leaders had discovered that they could operate legally from the platform the government had given them, and that the government could not prevent them from acting as the spokesmen for black workers without repealing the laws that continued to underpin separate development.

Unfortunately, the Nixon administration remained largely unaware of these developments, let alone their significance. By 1974 it was still preoccupied with whether foreign investment could act as a catalyst for economic growth and help narrow the income inequalities between black and white labor. It had only just begun to consider whether the black labor force might be able to negotiate with the government directly without the intercession of an external power. In this area, as in so many others, the promise of constructive engagement remained largely unfulfilled.

Conclusion

The discussion of constructive engagement was the first occasion of its kind when the United States looked at the question of black political participation as part of the process of change, rather than in terms of the end result of that process. The State Department was requested after all to address an intermediate stage "short of majority rule" in which black organizations could play a decisive role in planning the last stage: participation in the electoral system.

Through constructive engagement the NSC hoped to strengthen the resolve of the whites to reform their political structures, and to exploit the "ferment" within Afrikaner society to which reference was frequently made throughout this period. Because the State Department had to implement the policy, it tended to insist on more specific reforms and to look for a more specific timetable. As we have seen, David Newsom returned from South Africa in 1970 with four concrete proposals for the reform of the political system. Aware of the constraints under which he himself had to work, he was often impatient of the constraints to which the South Africans often appealed. The State Department was wary, nevertheless, of putting itself at the center of a dialogue, for fear that the white and black communities might never communicate with one another. At most it wished to play the role of an intermediary, a role that went beyond that of an interlocutor, a role that allowed the Nixon administration to turn its attention to the role of nonstate actors.

Between 1970 and 1972 we find a constant series of public pronouncements recognizing the role that the black community would be called upon to play if constructive engagement were to meet with success, however limited. In December 1970 Newsom contended that engagement might ensure "that each side knows better what the other is talking about. It could mean that greater hope could be given to both whites and blacks in South Africa who seek another way."[71] Three years later he took up this theme again in a speech in London. Constructive engagement had to be seen not in terms of the answers it had to the problem, but the questions it raised about the dynamics of internal change: "The influence of any nation, however powerful, in the internal affairs of another is severely limited. The idea that the United States . . . could bring about *fundamental* change in another society is without foundation. We certainly cannot do it in Southern Africa. If change comes, it must come primarily from within."[72] Later that year he admitted that the administration had discovered that its influence "whether through exhortation or diplomatic efforts, or economic pressures" was far more limited than it had originally thought: "History would suggest that, while outside pressures may have played a part, the ultimate decisions in the case of each of the colonial powers to relinquish the territories were decisions that they made on the basis of their internal determination that this was the thing to do."[73]

The problem with the administration's analysis was that it presupposed that a dialogue could be conducted while the machinery of repression was still in place. It did not recognize that the machinery itself prevented a dialogue from being conducted. The United States failed to recognize that participation in the political system required not only that the government respond to black demands at a variety of political levels but also that it dismantle many of the institutional constraints which prevented it from responding at all. With the exception of Clarence Mitchell, few administration officials appreciated the importance of changes in the law.

The problem of these institutional barriers was critically important.

During the discussion of the Foreign Assistance Act, which it was hoped would facilitate political participation as well as economic development in the Third World, the government had commissioned an independent study of what was meant by the term *participation*. The final report might have served as a textbook definition: "more than the political right to vote in elections. It includes, for example, the right of a people to speak to a bureaucracy *which is responsive and the ability to form voluntary organizations to pursue group interests*" (my emphasis).[74] The report raised two important questions: how governments could respond to the claims of nonstate actors while the law continued to proscribe such claims; and how nonstate actors could form organizations when to do so would bring them into conflict with the state.

These questions were never answered directly. Nor had they been answered by the critics of the Johnson administration. George Ball, for example, had laid particular emphasis on "the encouragement of internal change reflecting the impact of fresh ideas, brought about through free interplay with the outside world, *resulting in the lifting of repressive measures and the creation of a climate of frank debate*" (my emphasis).[75] Unfortunately, a climate of frank debate was hardly likely to flourish while freedom of assembly, free speech, and even expressions of support for political change continued to be proscribed. Washington's main objective should have been the repeal of legislation which had hitherto prevented a dialogue from being opened except on terms unacceptable to black opinion.

In the mid-1960s G. Mennen Williams had been alive enough to the situation in Portuguese Africa, where blacks had been prevented from working through the political system and had been forced to take up arms to overthrow it. How, he asked, could they "organize an effective, resourceful, secret underground network; . . . undertake strikes and other public demonstrations in the face of the ubiquitous and ruthless Portuguese secret police; [and] . . . obtain widespread public support in the face of fear of retaliation against the civilian population?"[76] In Portuguese Africa the situation was compounded by the absence of an industrial sector that might have provided them in other circumstances with channels through which to bring pressure on the government. In Mozambique 88 percent of all Africans practiced subsistence farming. Less than 10 percent worked in the wage economy (and half of these were migrant laborers). The wage economy grew only slowly during the 1960s. By the end of the decade there were only 75,000 workers in the commercial sector. Even if the Portuguese had not stamped out opposition whenever they found it, the workers would have been ill-organized to have entered into a constructive dialogue with the colonial government.

In South Africa, of course, the situation was quite different. Here there *was* a large labor force and a significant industrial sector. In principle, industrial stoppages lent themselves particularly well to political action. The mobilization of labor on a large scale invariably increases a community's sense of self-reliance by reducing its dependence on support from outside its own ranks. Indeed, such support is normally unnecessary since strikes are more likely than economic sanctions to inflict sustained economic damage on a country. However vulnerable an economy may be to fluctuations in international trade, the domestic sector is far more vulnerable to internal sabotage or disruption.

Yet the situation in South Africa was hardly conducive to such action. Writing at a time when there seemed to be no possibility that industrial labor would ever again be able to use industrial stoppages as a political weapon, A. S. Mathews had described how the threat of criminal prosecution inhibited industrial workers from using the withdrawal of labor to secure an improvement in their contractual status. Strikes by black workers had profound political implications: "There will necessarily be a confusion between attempts to introduce political change and assaults against the basic order when the government is committed to securing the interests of a group and to a policy of blocking social change. Such a government is bound to regard pressure for change as an attack upon society as well as a challenge to its own policies."[77]

Although many American companies began to attach great importance to collective bargaining—to the readiness of their black workers to bargain with the government on their own behalf and the extent to which investment codes, voluntarily entered into, might remove some of the constraints which had previously prevented the government from responding to the demands of organized labor—such action was hardly likely to succeed as long as strikes continued to be illegal. In short, the law needed to be rewritten if the workers were to play any role. In that respect, had America's own positive sanctions been used to induce the South Africans to repeal their most repressive labor statutes, the precise relationship between external intervention and the internal dynamics of change on which it placed so much emphasis might not have remained so obscure.

Constructive engagement raised two additional questions: with whom was contact to be made among the nonstate actors, and what channels could be used by Washington without breaching South African sovereignty? As Roger Morris later revealed, the administration started off with the intention of making its contacts with black groups more open and comprehensive.[78] The task was not easy. On the one hand, the Americans had to establish closer links with the black community; on the other, they had to make sure that in doing so they did not alienate the white community upon whose goodwill they depended.

Since balancing these competing claims proved so difficult, the identity of the nonstate actors with whom they would deal was obviously important. There were, of course, the nationalist movements in exile, principally the ANC. But by resorting to force they had already ruled themselves out. The problem was compounded by the fact that in South Africa the political process did not include black political parties. Although the first political party since the banning of the two congresses in 1960—the Black Peoples Convention (BPC)—was indeed launched during the lifetime of constructive engagement, at Pietermaritzburg in the summer of 1972, it survived only a few months. In September its leadership was broken up and its vice-president and secretary-general arrested. By then the government realized the movement was more of a threat to its own favored lobby—the homeland leaders—than an aid in polarizing black and white opinion.

Since political institutions were not permitted, it was difficult to think in terms of a dialogue with the black community. Indeed, there was no environment in which such a discussion would have had much meaning. There was no political society in the accepted sense of the term in which opposition parties could have defined their aims and the ruling party could have defined its own position in response to them. Even the National party itself still remained what it had been before its election victory in 1948: a *volksbewegung* or "people's movement" rather than a political party in the sense understood by the United States.

Since the homeland leaders, however, had been provided with an international platform by the government itself, contact between them and the United States could be quite open. They were after all putative leaders of independent states, although the Transkei did not achieve independence until 1976. As we have seen, the leader of KwaZulu was invited for a two-month tour of the United States in 1971. Kaiser Matanzima traveled from the Transkei to Washington under an American Leadership Grant the following year.

Unfortunately, the United States was so concerned not to alienate Pretoria that it was often only too willing to work through constituencies which had been created in the explicit hope of dividing the black community—groups that had emerged from a political process that they themselves had had no part in shaping. One such person was David Tebehali, who served on the government-created Urban Bantu Council in Soweto and was invited to the United States in 1972 as a guest of the State Department. Tebehali, while associating himself with the Black Consciousness Movement, objected to the BPC's refusal to collaborate with Pretoria and disassociated himself from its hostility to capitalism.

The second problem was that, once constructive engagement had been adopted, the responsibility for its implementation, particularly contact with the black constituencies, was clearly intended to devolve on black Foreign Service officers, many of whom received appointments to South Africa for the first time in this period. Kissinger believed that the United States was the only country in the West which could speak to both sides; that the black members of its foreign policy apparat could make contact with the nationalists without bringing the State Department into conflict with South Africa. Kissinger hoped that the Foreign Service could use its black officers to establish contact with nonstate actors in the countries in which they served.[79]

Unfortunately, nothing came of the matter. A black officer was appointed to the embassy in South Africa (despite the protests of the ambassador, John Hurd) with responsibility for economic matters particularly in the labor field, where he had informal, but infrequent, contact with labor leaders. Beverley Carter was the first black to be appointed deputy assistant secretary for African affairs, John Reinhart the first to be short-listed to head the bureau itself after Newsom's departure. But, for the most part, black Foreign Service officers showed very little interest in Southern Africa for much the same reason they had opposed Mennen Williams's plan in the early 1960s to draft them en bloc into the Africa Bureau. Their fear was that once consigned to the backwaters of African policy they would be effectively removed from the mainstream of decision making. Although their numbers increased after 1969, their appointment to the Foreign Service did not represent "a new dimension" to American policy as the civil rights activist Clarence Mitchell had originally hoped.[80]

The situation was not without irony. In the late 1960s the black community had begun to be absorbed and accepted. In material terms it had gained much; in intellectual terms, possibly much less. Between the civil rights movement and the coming of the Nixon administration most black Americans discovered something about American society and a good deal more about themselves. Ironically the impact of this discovery was blunted by the extent and completeness of their success at home. Their integration ministered to the vanity of the melting pot society which placed a high premium on social conformity. Most blacks in government (as opposed to many outside it) were reluctant to show themselves unduly receptive to impressions and experiences from Africa. In other words they too bore some responsibility for the Nixon administration's policy of "benign neglect."

5 Two Case Studies of Positive Sanctions

Although both the State Department and the NSC had initially developed two quite different strategies, both of which had been debated with vigor in the months prior to the Review Group's meeting, they had, at least, attempted to focus on the purpose at hand. The final discussion did not. The application of rewards and incentives had been proposed by Roger Morris exclusively in the context of political reform. Kissinger's staff had not expected that executive approval for Option 2 would, or should, constitute approval for any specific reward on the part of the United States. Morris had even argued that it would be foolish to offer any incentive without some political quid pro quo—some progress toward political participation by the non-white population within at least five years.

The rewards in question ranged from permitting the sale of dual-purpose military equipment to removing some of the constraints on Eximbank facilities for trade between the two countries. Both were cited in a summary of the review which Nixon received on 2 January 1970. Nevertheless, by falsely describing constructive engagement as "a general posture of partial relations," without further mention of its general context, and by arbitrarily divorcing the operational recommendations from the thesis that had won approval, Kissinger betrayed those who had fought so hard to get the policy adopted. Certain decisions close to the president's heart, including the sale of light aircraft, were adopted at once. Others, such as the removal of restrictions on the terms of Eximbank loans, were introduced several months later. It was not an auspicious beginning.

The result was predictable: both measures were taken to constitute

"business as normal." Both were taken to be concrete evidence of
of the administration's tacit acceptance of the status quo. Not surprisingly, an article in the *Washington Post* in November 1970 concluded that the White House appeared "to be opting . . . where useful
[for] small but increasing accommodation with white minority
governments."[1] What follows is a brief attempt to explain why positive sanctions were never applied as the NSC had intended. The
two examples which are cited illustrate why constructive engagement was likely to fail, though neither can demonstrate that it was
bound to. As far as the administration was concerned, the general
proposition of Option 2 still stood. Why the proposition itself was at
fault will be explained in another chapter.

Export-Import Bank (Eximbank) Loans

In April 1966 President Johnson had imposed restrictions on all
further lines of credit to South Africa. Together with the arms embargo
the measures enjoyed ever diminishing importance as events in Vietnam came to overshadow everything else. Possibly this also explains
why the rules restricting future export credits to five-year maturities
were never made public. The move was unpopular in business circles,
and in 1969, quite independently of the administration's own review,
Eximbank asked the NSC to reconsider whether the measure might
be dropped.

In a memorandum to the president, the secretary for commerce,
Maurice Stans, asked that the commercial argument should be given
a fair hearing. He was convinced that American corporations required
Eximbank financing more than ever, since the South African government had begun encouraging its own businessmen to negotiate
extended repayment terms instead of paying for imports entirely in
cash. In the interim many American businessmen had been prevented from financing foreign purchases in the South African market.
To remain competitive with their overseas competitors, Stans argued,
American companies needed to seek out opportunities wherever they
could be found. Stans, it should be remembered, had actually been
present at the Final Review Group meeting the previous December
in which the principle of using Eximbank loans as a political incentive had been accepted. Obviously, he had not been reconciled to the
principle. "Political objectives," he insisted, "may not always accom-

modate important economic interests."[2] From here it was only a short step to arguing that many of the mistakes of the past had been compounded by the misuse of economic measures for questionable political ends.

The case for retaining the restrictions on export credits remained essentially political. In a memorandum to Kissinger the State Department contended that the United States had been able to resist international and domestic pressures for more comprehensive economic sanctions only by keeping official contacts with South Africa (in the shape of government credit guarantees) to an absolute minimum.[3] Moreover, it maintained that, even if the most pessimistic estimates of current export losses were accurate, which it doubted, Eximbank restrictions could only be partially blamed for the country's growing trade deficit with South Africa.[4]

The case for revoking these restrictions was couched in terms most likely to appeal to Nixon: that they had gravely disadvantaged American exporters. Eximbank's vice-president referred scathingly to the "unfair discrimination" that American business had faced from a most unlikely quarter: its own government. Its financial problems would multiply if it found itself unable to finance South African goods with local capital.[5] Added to this the Bank put forward an argument that was likely to appeal to the State Department, even more than to the Department of Commerce. It had no doubt that if the South Africans were forced to cut back on imports because of Eximbank's refusal to provide medium-term government assistance to U.S. corporations, they would in all likelihood be hit by a major recession, from which the black community would suffer most.[6]

Both sides found themselves in general agreement. Neither wanted government interference when its implications were so clearly political. The State Department did not wish Eximbank loans to be used as a positive sanction because it wished to restrict the scope of American involvement; the Bank wanted to lift the restrictions to prevent the further loss of export orders. Under instruction from the White House, the State Department extended repayment terms from five years to ten, bringing Eximbank's credit limits into line with existing commercial practice. It also agreed to discount loans up to a maximum value of $2 million for all transactions except those requiring direct lines of credit. These measures were never made public.[7] Even the State Department was not informed that the White

House had given formal approval to both measures in January 1970. Kissinger's staff declined to reveal his final letter of recommendation to the president because of its persistent fear of public disclosure. This was shadowboxing at its most absurd. In its preoccupation with secrecy the NSC advised Kissinger to allow the State Department to move "on its own steam" now that its own policy conformed in all essential respects to what had been agreed at the Final Review Group meeting twelve months earlier.[8]

Such an approach was entirely at odds with the principle Kissinger had insisted upon in 1969: the need to reach an agreed position between the contending departments of government. Once the different agencies were allowed to move under their own steam, the repeal of the existing restrictions might well appear to have been determined by naked commercial interests. It is as well to bear this in mind when following the story through to its end. Bureaucratic obfuscation goes a long way toward explaining occasional lapses from the policy agreed upon in December 1969. In Washington, government worked on a consensus basis that produced enough lethargy to stifle the most imaginative initiatives unless they commanded fairly widespread interdepartmental support.

Despite its ban on direct loans to South African buyers, the Bank agreed to discount four loans between October 1969 and February 1971, although two were subsequently canceled by the borrowers. In principle, all transactions were subject to review by the National Advisory Council on International Monetary and Financial Policies, an interdepartmental group whose members included the secretaries of Commerce, Treasury, and State, the president of Eximbank, and the chairman of the Federal Reserve. In addition, all business deals exceeding $60 million had to be submitted to Congress for final ratification.

Despite these safeguards, and largely because of the administration's failure to communicate its intention in rescinding the earlier restrictions on government credits, its critics soon claimed that commercial relations with South Africa were being normalized. In the summer of 1971 Congressman Diggs drew his colleagues' attention to the services that Eximbank now offered American businessmen, including short- and medium-term insurance through the Foreign Credit Insurance Association (FCIA), medium-term loan guarantees for the payment of South African goods, discount loans for South

African buyers, and loan guarantees to help them defray the costs of American purchases.[9] However, by the time the list was published, some of these services were no longer on offer. Diggs was also in error in suggesting that Eximbank normally approved high-risk transactions, or provided South African businessmen with loans during periods of dollar shortfall. Only two medium-term credits were ever approved for high-risk ventures (in 1971 and 1973 respectively).[10]

Because the Bank's new services were so limited, it is doubtful whether these new measures would have been extensive enough either in scope or in volume to have impressed the South African government. It is doubtful, in other words, that if they had been used as Morris had initially intended — as positive sanctions — they would have been very effective. At a time when South Africa was concerned that many foreign companies were beginning to fight shy of high-risk projects, it might have been more impressed by an undertaking to discount loans of more than $2 million, or to provide the government itself with loans in periods when foreign exchange was in short supply. Because at this stage the United States was not prepared to enter into such an undertaking, it lost out on both fronts. The decision to repeal credit restrictions failed to have much impact in South Africa; its impact at home, nevertheless, was quite out of proportion to the financial figures. Despite its oversight system, Eximbank's role in South Africa did appear to the outside observer more nakedly commercial than ever. In 1971 the Bank's executive vice-president informed the House subcommittee on Africa that its investment in the republic amounted to a little under $22 million. Within five years its exposure had risen to $265 million, of which insurance and guarantees were divided in almost equal proportion.[11] In the same period the United States increased its percentage of the market from 16.3 percent to 17.6 percent. By authorizing 134 discount loans with American banks valued collectively at $205 million, it significantly increased the financial assistance it had already extended to South African business.[12]

These were not the only areas of activity that aroused public disquiet. It was difficult to explain away the credit lines which Eximbank extended to the Private Export Funding Corporation (PEFCO), a private consortium, not a government agency, which provided American corporations with a similar range of facilities on stricter financial terms. Its main attraction was that it offered a service to those com-

Table 3   Eximbank Exposure in South Africa

	June 1971	June 1972	June 1973	June 1974
Short term	$ 4,434	$ 6,978	$11,204	$ 22,772
Medium term	10,609	13,136	21,054	19,674
Guarantees	18,770	40,858	53,919	66,977
Total	33,813	60,972	86,177	109,423

SOURCE   *Resource development in South Africa and U.S. policy*, Hearings before the Committee on International Resources, Food, and Energy, House of Representatives, 94th Congress, 2nd Session, May 1976, 254.

panies which, for one reason or another, were not able to take advantage of the government scheme.

In practice, its independent status was less real than it first appeared. Ninety million dollars worth of loans to companies operating in South Africa were, in fact, guaranteed by Eximbank. Unlike the Bank's, its own loans were limited neither by sum nor receipt. A loan to South African Railways, which Eximbank was not allowed to extend, fell just short of $50 million.[13] By entering into second-party arrangements of this nature the administration put itself in breach of its own regulations which forbade the direct funding of the South African government, or its agencies, including the large public-sector corporations which had begun to proliferate in the early 1960s.

These regulations once again might or might not have constituted a political hurdle if Eximbank loans had been used as a positive sanction. We may take as one example General Electric's application in 1976 for a government credit to finance the sale and delivery of a nuclear reactor, a sale that became the subject of intense debate within the administration. Although the Nuclear Regulatory Commission approved the necessary export licenses and did not require South Africa either to sign the Non-Proliferation Treaty or accept the safeguards of the International Atomic Energy Agency as a condition of the sale, the White House delayed ratifying the proposal. In the end its prevarication lost the company the contract.

The Ford administration obviously considered it impossible to agree to such a politically contentious sale. Yet there was no doubt that South Africa attached much more importance to Eximbank in this context than any other; and there is also no doubt that its political ramifications were such as to merit the most careful evaluation of whether to fund the sale or not. The State Department actually went on record that the delivery of a nuclear reactor would provide the United States with leverage over the future development of South Africa's nuclear program at the most critical juncture in the nineteen years of cooperation between the two countries.[14] South Africa had already agreed to allow the United States to review the design of its nuclear facilities, to draw up regular progress reports, and to send inspectors to monitor its nuclear plant at Koeberg.[15] Although the Africa Bureau refused to be drawn on the question of whether the sale of the reactors could be used as a positive sanction, it left Congress in no doubt that the scope for such application did exist.[16]

Surprisingly, the only attempt to employ Eximbank loans for an overtly political end originated *outside* the administration when in 1975 sixteen senators signed a petition in support of a request by the American company FLUOR for a long-term credit guarantee to enable it to successfully tender for a coal gassification plant. On the NSC's advice the White House blocked the sale.[17] No administration could have provided a loan for a South African public corporation, in this instance SASOL 2, whose first priority was to ensure the republic was self-sufficient in energy and thus able to defy future UN sanctions. Added to this the administration was not confident enough about the country's political future to underwrite a commitment of over fifteen years.

Nevertheless, the episode rather curiously illustrates how far the NSC had lost touch with the original rationale for constructive engagement. In a letter to the president the senators had argued that detente with the Soviet Union had been based on the reciprocity of commercial relations between the two countries "despite serious differences over matters of domestic policy."[18] Indeed, detente had been defended on the grounds that such contacts might eventually reduce some of the differences which divided the two societies. If FLUOR was denied support, the senators went on to argue, the decision "would tend to limit our influence in Southern Africa. We would strongly urge . . . a re-examination of American policy towards South Africa so that the United States might play a constructive role."[19] Surprisingly, the administration took little note of this thesis. The NSC dismissed the senators in question as a group obstinately attached to the same fixed views, principles, and prejudices. They may indeed have been more interested in the commercial principle involved, and largely indifferent to its political ramifications. But for its part the NSC was peculiarly unresponsive to their central thesis about "a constructive role." To the uninformed observer coming to the discussions in 1976 for the first time, the use of positive sanctions might never have been debated.

The Arms Embargo

When the United States voted for the UN arms embargo in 1963 it did so under the terms sketched by the director of the Export/Import Control Office during testimony before Congressman Diggs's subcommittee in 1973:

> The U.S. arms embargo policy is administered by the export control authorities of both the Departments of State and Commerce. Materials and equipment which are strictly military in nature are controlled by the State Department, while related or multipurpose items fall within the responsibility of the Department of Commerce. Pursuant to this policy . . . Commerce maintains controls over certain multipurpose items (for example, civil aircraft and airborne communications equipment) and does not authorize their export to South Africa if there is likely to be a military use.[20]

The measures adopted by the United States were in accordance with the costs and commitments the Kennedy administration felt it could afford. It was never in favor of a mandatory ban, which would have been difficult if not impossible to enforce.

In 1970 the United States specifically voted against a proposal which would have extended the embargo to all supplies and equipment and required all licenses for the manufacture of arms to be revoked. In its defense, it drew the General Assembly's attention to its failure to enforce the provisions that had already been enacted. By that time, of course, the administration had already resolved to relax some of the provisions itself.

It was not until 1973 that extensive discrepancies first came to light in the implementation of the arms embargo. As Charles Diggs stated in his summing up of the congressional hearings he had just conducted, "We find that there has been what we consider to be a massive erosion of the principles established during the 1960s with significant sales of equipment [and] aircraft . . . to South African military and civilian users who are likely to be connected with the military, especially in an emergency."[21] Confronted with evidence that the implementation of the embargo had been less than whole-hearted, Newsom at first denied the existence of any "hidden areas of policy."[22] His denial, however, seemed particularly unconvincing in the light of the State Department's refusal to release the text of the new guidelines, to whose existence he admitted only under close questioning.[23]

The guidelines in question had been authorized by the White House in 1970. In all it approved four different memoranda on amendments to the arms embargo, of which by far the most important was National Security Decision Memorandum 81 (NSDM 81), which addressed quite specifically the question of "gray area" export licenses for items which fell uneasily into either category of civilian or military use. It was eventually decided that dual-purpose aircraft "preponderantly employed for civilian use" which had not been manufactured to military specification would now be licensed for export. Similarly, dual-purpose items that were already in the armory of some military forces but which, nevertheless, had no specific military application could now be sold to the South African Defence Force, providing prior approval was obtained from the Department of State. However, dual-purpose items "with a clear and direct application to combat or internal security operations" would not be licensed at all, even to civilian buyers, except on the administration's explicit recommen-dation.[24] NSDM 81 did not receive the president's imprimatur until the cabinet had been assured that none of these provisions would place the United States in contravention of its own regulations, or in conflict with its responsibilities to the UN.

For better or worse, the United States agreed to stand by the arms embargo of 1963. Its enforcement had become a matter of great impor-tance to the Afro-Asian bloc in the General Assembly. Their interest in the sale of arms to South Africa was greater than in any other anti-apartheid issue. Proper standards and procedures may not have been established in 1963: the Security Council had relied in large measure on the integrity of individual governments to translate the general terms of Resolution 381 into specific commercial prohibitions. But the United States had not consciously exploited the loopholes which had inevitably arisen. Nor did it choose in 1970 to invoke the one right which it had reserved seven years earlier—the right to review its position should the international situation change for the worse. That it chose not to do so revealed the extent of its indifference to some of the strategic arguments peddled by the Pentagon in this period.

Despite the arguments of its own strategists, the United States responded with great restraint to the appearance of the Soviet navy in the Indian Ocean in 1968. It was aware that the South Africans would claim that the new situation demanded new measures: perhaps even cooperation with the South African Navy (SAN). The NSC actually warned the White House that South Africa might offer to support the West's interests in the region in return for a tacit understanding that it would go to its aid if attacked.[25] The White House, however, never accepted that the South African Navy could play more than a marginal role in defending the Cape route, or the 2,300 ships which passed the Cape every month. Much to the surprise of Chester Crocker, the NSC's Africa coordinator, South Africa was entirely omitted from the discussion of the defense options in the Indian Ocean, which later emerged in the form of two separate NSC reports in 1970 and 1971.[26] Several years later Kissinger warned the House Armed Services Committee that it would be disastrous if the U.S. Navy ever found itself in Simonstown when the conflict in Southern Africa erupted into open violence.[27]

In the light of these far from dogmatic responses to the security threat to the region, it is not altogether surprising that the United States and Great Britain "agreed to disagree" over the question of renewing arms sales to South Africa.[28] The cost of replacing many of the SAN's aged and aging vessels, many of which would face obsolescence in the 1980s, threatened to be embarrassingly high. Nixon actually upheld President Johnson's ban of 1965 on the sale of Orion Pc3 naval reconnaissance aircraft despite persistent South African requests for the replacement of its old and frequently grounded Shackleton IIIs. In short, the administration did not choose to cite a real or imaginary strategic need as an excuse for the sale of dual-purpose equipment. If constructive engagement achieved little, its failure owed little to special pleading by the admirals. Indeed, so concerned was the administration that the South Africans might draw the wrong conclusions from the new guidelines, that it decided to classify NSDM 81 and to conceal its main recommendations from the public. This was one of the rare occasions on which the White House appreciated the danger of misleading signals.

If the sale of "gray area" items was to constitute a positive sanction, however, secrecy was equally undesirable. In its preoccupation with leaks within the State Department, the administration denied itself effective channels of communication. After NSDM 81 had been sanctioned, Newsom chose to communicate its recommendations in a public speech in Chicago in September 1970. Public announcement of the decision was intended to alert South Africa to a change of policy without revealing its actual content.[29] Unfortunately, the decision to license the sale of executive civilian aircraft was not seen as a major policy departure, largely because there had always been such sales, if not on such a scale.

There was another problem about sidestepping the State Department. The White House had to rely for the implementation of the new guidelines almost exclusively on the Department of Commerce. The fact that the latter was empowered to decide whether an aircraft had a military use or not offered no assurance that Morris's original intention would be adhered to. For several years the American aerospace industry had lobbied successive administrations for permission to sell more civil aircraft than allowed under the existing regulations. Its last appeal had been refused by Lyndon Johnson. When Lockheed and Boeing renewed the request, they found Richard Nixon considerably more responsive to their arguments. Much later Newsom admitted that the administration had felt compelled to reconsider its position in the light of a deteriorating balance on its current account, compounded by a domestic crisis in the aerospace industry. That he was not entirely convinced of the wisdom of the decision may be deduced from his apparent willingness to reveal the pressures which the administration had had to face, especially from commercial lobbies in Congress.[30] He did acknowledge, however, that in the current economic crisis no government could have continued to apply the existing guidelines intact.

Yet it would be wrong to conclude that the administration treated the embargo with total indifference. In October 1970 the Commerce Department overruled a license that had been given by the Department of State for the sale of automobile parts to the South African army.[31] Far from following the naked commercialism of which it was

Table 4   Aircraft Sales to South Africa, 1965 – 1972

1965	235	1969	284
1966	208	1970	180
1967	333	1971	135
1968	300	1972	144
	1076		743

SOURCE   *Implementation of the U.S. arms embargo,* Hearings before the Committee on Foreign Affairs, Subcommittee on Africa, House of Representatives, 93rd Congress, 1st Session, April 1973, 52.

so often accused by its critics, the government refused to allow $9 million worth of helicopter sales in 1972 alone.[32] There was no deliberate collusion by any department or special lobby. Indeed, aircraft sales to South Africa actually fell in Nixon's first term compared with Johnson's last.

On the other hand, the nature of the aircraft sold, if not the volume of sales, suggest that the United States may have circumvented the embargo. The question is not only whether civil aircraft such as the Cessna should have been sold, but whether their sale actually contravened the administration's own guidelines. This would appear to have been the case on a strict interpretation of NSDM 81: "Whether preponderantly employed for civilian or military use, dual-purpose items with a clear and direct application to combat or to internal security operations . . . will not be licensed to military buyers."[33] Light aircraft, nevertheless, were extensively deployed in counterinsurgency operations or exercises such as that in KwaZulu in 1974. South Africa's paramilitary forces kept twelve air commando squadrons of civilian aircraft on permanent standby, with one permanently assigned to the South African army.[34] On many occasions they were used for general border duties in Namibia, including military reconnaissances.

Some American companies also classified their aircraft as civilian in design when the description was patently untrue. The Lockheed commercial Hercules, for example, was almost an exact copy of the C-130 flown by the U.S. Air Force (USAF). The Arms Control and Disarmament Agency listed the United States as South Africa's third largest military supplier in the period 1961 – 1971 because of its commitment to supply spare parts for the existing Lockheed C-130 contract.[35] The White House compounded the case by allowing Lockheed to supply South Africa's state airline, SAFAIR, with ten commercial Hercules planes despite NSDM 81's explicit recommendation that troop transports should on no account be sold. Both the L-100 and C-130 could carry nearly 100 troops, or 40,000 pounds of equipment. Other than the C-130's slightly superior range and payload, there was little to distinguish the two models. Between 1970 and 1973 these ostensibly civilian aircraft flew supplies to South African forces in Namibia and Rhodesia, a practice which ceased only after receipt of a personal demarche from the American government.[36]

Dual-purpose aircraft appear to have represented only the tip of the iceberg. The Stockholm International Peace Research Institute (SIPRI) discovered evidence of much more extensive collusion. The evidence is complicated by the discrepancy between SIPRI's figures and those of the International Institute for Strategic Studies, whose main publication *The Military Balance* failed to reveal a large number of separate items which were sold to South Africa in the early 1970s, including M-47 tanks, Commodore V-150 and M-113AI armored personnel carriers, M-109 155mm self-propelled guns, and 205A Iroquois helicopters. On SIPRI's findings, all these weapons entered service after 1970.[37] *The Military Balance*, which makes no mention of any of them, does record, however, that single-engined Cessna 185s rather than Cessna 401/402s were deployed both by the air force and the reserves despite the fact that NSDM 81 had banned the sale of the first, while authorizing purchase of the second.[38]

On balance, SIPRI's findings appear to be more authoritative. Investigations by the U.S. Justice Department in 1978 revealed that at least 178 of South Africa's 578 military aircraft had been purchased from the United States since 1963 and that of those purchased after 1972 some were clearly military craft. The Beechcraft Bonanza A-36s had been sold to the Mexican and Iranian air forces, while Helio Super Couriers had been used by the USAF itself in combat operations in Vietnam. Together with the twin-engined Rockwell turbocommandos, all three models were sold in the early 1970s with the aid of loans provided by Eximbank.[39]

For much of the time the Nixon administration was probably unaware of these breaches. Officials who served under President Johnson were quite ignorant of the quantity of arms that had slipped through the loopholes and were surprised when it was brought to their attention.[40] The government did not authorize the sale of military equipment directly but did so by the indirect route of licensed production. In principle, the Office of Munitions Control (OMC) should have foreclosed the route by which American corporations allowed foreign manufacturers to produce American weapons under license for reexport to South Africa. Most of the items mentioned by name in the 1962 embargo were included on the munitions list, including such diverse items as the technical equipment required by civilian aircraft for geophysical surveys. But the task of detecting evasions was made more difficult in 1970 when the OMC removed certain items from the validated list and began to grant export licenses for items that were still under validated licensing.[41] Most of these measures were taken for reasons of administrative convenience.

In retrospect, the administration's behavior was neither collusive nor quixotic, simply unwise. In a paper circulated at the Commonwealth Prime Minister's Conference in 1970 Julius Nyerere had taken Britain to task for renewing arms sales to South Africa: "Whatever restrictions or limits are placed on a sale, the sale of arms is a declaration of support—an implied alliance of a kind. You can trade with people you dislike—you can have diplomatic relations with governments you disapprove of; you can sit in conference with those nations whose policies you abhor. But you . . . do not sell arms without saying in effect . . . that in the last resort we will be on their side in the case of any conflict."[42] Nyerere believed that the arms embargo would never be fully effective until it was made mandatory. Yet the United States opposed every attempt to extend it—for reasons that were quite understandable, of course, in the light of constructive engagement, but not in the light of the policy it actually pursued between 1970 and 1973. The United States even abstained from voting for a resolution in July 1970 which merely sought to tighten up the existing loopholes. When Zambia's President Kenneth Kaunda visited New York to take part in the UN debate, Nixon declined to see him on the grounds that the issue did not justify rescheduling his timetable.

These unwise decisions might not have mattered had positive sanctions been applied; but they were not. Nor would it have mattered much if the sale of arms had not been of great value. Unfortunately, this was not the case. Arms imports accounted for two-thirds of

Table 5   Major U.S. Weapon Systems Delivered
to South Africa after 1970

Item	Approx. date of delivery
Lockheed F-104G FGA/Interceptor	1973
Lockheed L-100 transport[1]	post 1971
Augusta Bell 205A helicopter	post 1970
M-47 Patton I tank	1971
M-113AI armored personnel carrier	1973–74
V-150/200 Commando personnel carrier	post 1971
M-109 155mm self-propelled gun	1972–73

SOURCE   *U.S. arms transfers to South Africa in violation of the U.N. voluntary arms embargo*, UN Center Against Apartheid, Notes and Documents 27/78, September 1978.
1. Although this was the civilian version of the Lockheed C-130 Hercules, it was listed in *The Military Balance 1977–78* as part of the equipment of the South African air force.

South Africa's defense budget in the mid-1970s.[43] In the field of counterinsurgency, imports from the United States were undoubtedly significant, especially helicopters (one of the most important dual-purpose items that South Africa did not yet manufacture in any large numbers).[44] The sale of arms was used only once as a positive sanction in 1976, when in return for the promise to bring Rhodesia to the conference table the United States secretly released $1 million worth of aircraft support equipment as well as an unspecified number of Merlin 4A aircraft, which were later deployed at the South African air force base at Zwartkopf in Namibia.[45] Otherwise, the story of the early 1970s is a depressing one of missed opportunities occasioned, in part, by the secrecy in which the Nixon administration conducted its affairs; but there was also a reluctance to come to terms with its own bureaucratic shortcomings.

Conclusion

Of the many faults with American policy which manifested themselves in 1970, one of the most serious was the gap between ends and means, between the political reforms the United States wished to see introduced and the rewards it was prepared to offer. In the main, positive sanctions were not only insubstantial but largely irrelevant in the context in which they were applied. It was extremely unwise, for example, to have divorced its principal concessions from its principal objectives. Although Morris drew up a shopping list of sanctions, none for the most part were actually related to specific reforms. The administration's objectives, though fixed, were not defined. It was one matter to insist that final decisions must be the responsibility of local actors, quite another to expect that sanctions could be post-dated on a blank check left for South Africa to complete.

The lifting of restrictions on Eximbank loans might have been linked directly to the improvement in labor relations in American-owned companies, or even to union registration of their black employees. One member of the Africa Bureau's advisory committee actually recommended tying Eximbank loans to development programs in the homelands. But in the main no such connection was made. South Africa was expected to agree to changes across the entire spectrum of apartheid in spheres in which economic measures had no immediate bearing.

By the administration's refusal to outline the reforms it had in mind, or even to discuss the question with the South Africans directly, every reward was made to appear of little significance in the overall scheme of things. The administration might have spurred South Africa into pressing ahead with granting independence to the homelands had it promised diplomatic recognition; nothing less would have sufficed. By the time Kissinger considered doing so in 1976, it was already too late. Similarly, if it had wished to make the homelands economically viable, it might have offered more generous investment guarantees to its own companies. Nothing was to be gained by offering concessions so indiscriminately that Pretoria had no idea of what was being asked of it. When specific objectives were drawn up, they were not related to specific sanctions. Demands for changes in the legal system were perfectly intelligible in the context of Mitchell's argument that the repeal of the most restrictive security statutes would provide the blacks with an opportunity for political expression, but the United States never satisfactorily explained why such sanctions should have prompted the whites to give serious consideration to the suggestion. As long as the means and the ends remained unrelated, the government was bound to interpret the removal of restrictions on Eximbank loans or the conduct of "gray-area" arms sales as a sign that the United States had lost interest in pursuing a policy which had so demonstrably failed.

This was all the more likely to be true since the administration remained attached to the notion that the repeal of a negative sanction would in itself represent a positive sanction. This was extremely doubtful. The signals it conveyed were bound to misrepresent the administration's intentions. South Africa quite simply misread them. This was not altogether surprising, since constructive engagement had been adopted on the specific understanding that isolation had failed, that negative sanctions had embarrassed the sanctioner far more than the sanctioned. As time passed the whites were more inclined than ever to attribute the administration's actions to the pressures it faced from various interest groups and domestic lobbies, most of whom had a vested interest in the restrictions being lifted. In drafting Option 2 Morris had recognized that "the relaxation of the U.S. stance . . . could be taken by the whites as a vindication of their policies"—which in the end is precisely what came to pass.[46]

Salutary as it might have been to have recognized this from the outset, it would still have left unresolved the problem of how best to proceed. South Africa requested the repeal of only two measures in the whole period: the restrictions on capital exports and the arms embargo.[47] The first of these measures had been introduced in 1967 not specifically with South Africa in mind, but in an attempt to reduce America's growing balance-of-payments deficit. As it happened, South Africa had been hit particularly severely. Twelve times as much capital had been repatriated as invested for every year the measure had been enforced. Its eventual repeal, however, was carried out with little regard for Pretoria's representations and certainly not with constructive engagement in mind.

Even with regard to South Africa's second objective, the arms embargo, it must be doubted whether its repeal would have been all that important. The South Africans were clearly happy with the decision to sell items that did not appear in major inventories, including helicopters and computers, for which they were almost entirely reliant on imports from overseas. But much had changed since 1962 both in relation to the republic's position in the world and the threats it faced, as well as its capacity to meet them. Its security position presented much less cause for concern than it had at the time of the UN embargo. In the intervening years Pretoria had turned to other suppliers, notably France and Italy; licensed planes under contract with a number of aerospace corporations; and developed its own light-arms industry, which by 1973 already met 80 percent of its needs.[48]

Inevitably, the absolute value of the embargo's repeal and the relative value that South Africa attached to items which it couldn't produce itself had changed significantly. The United States also found itself confronted with a basic dilemma. The items that were of most interest to South Africa were also the most useful for counterinsurgency operations. But the fact that the country was not yet faced with such operations reduced the absolute value of such weapons. Whether Washington could have promised to supply dual-purpose equipment at all had such a conflict been in progress was another matter entirely. In 1975 an official spokesman eventually admitted that the United States would never be prepared to resupply Pretoria with arms during a conflict in which American forces were not themselves involved,[49] an argument that though irrefutable was bound to reduce the value of constructive engagement in South Africa's eyes, not only at the time but also in the future.

6 Constructive Engagement:
A Case Study in Bureaucratic Politics

One of the most extraordinary aspects of American policy in the early 1970s was that, although the administration was aware of the questionable premises on which constructive engagement was based, for most of the time it was strikingly oblivious to the difficulties of implementation. With few exceptions Kissinger and Morris showed little interest in the complexities of bureaucratic politics within the Africa Bureau or the problem of monitoring so complex a program. It seems that this was partly because the policy failed to conform to the typical problems which were the staple of most foreign policy issues, and partly because the difficulties of implementing such an involved program were in themselves difficult to grasp.

It was only by slow degrees that the Nixon administration woke up to the hostility to which constructive engagement had given rise, not least within the higher reaches of the State Department. In the early months the administration tended to assume that the problems of implementation were few, the possibilities of success more real than those of failure. Having spent so much energy debating the pros and cons of engagement, how are we to explain this lack of interest in carrying it out, in communicating it to the South Africans as well as to the public at home, and explaining it to Congress? How are we to explain the indifference of Henry Kissinger, whose interest in reforming the NSC system had been determined by a lifetime interest in the academic model propagated by Samuel Huntington, Graham Allison, and Morton Halperin—that of bureaucratic politics? It was as if once the policy had been decided upon, the Oval office had lost interest in it; as with so many policies in such fields as arms control and détente, effort suddenly became too much.

There is nothing particularly novel about such an outcome. An administration wrestling with problems that Kissinger and Nixon considered more important, of which an expeditious withdrawal from Vietnam was merely one, was far too preoccupied with other matters to devote more than fitful attention to problems on the periphery of its interests. It was probably too much to expect either man to have found time for Southern Africa when neither could find time for the Middle East—one of the few areas that was left almost exclusively in the hands of William Rogers, until the outbreak of the 1973 Arab-Israeli war.

In the absence of such interest at the highest reaches of government, constructive engagement was left largely to the Africa Bureau, which for the most part proved a spent force in the administration. Too often Newsom could count on little support from Congress; too often he was reliant on the support of senior State Department officials who had no understanding of what Morris wished to achieve. Denied such support, the bureau retreated into a world made familiar by its own prejudices and invincible preconceptions, and within a year it had begun to challenge the new policy it was supposed to conduct. The dream was not that of its members and had little connection with some of the cruder political realities in Washington. As reality began to impinge at an increasing number of points, so the dream faded.

In June 1972 David Newsom chose to take issue with the administration's critics for interpreting every government initiative as a fundamental change of course, or "tilt" toward the whites.[1] Unfortunately, the administration's policy *was* inconsistent—a fact for which the State Department itself was partly to blame. For its part, the NSC quite erroneously imagined that once a final decision had been agreed on it would automatically be carried out. In fact, the administration's critics recognized what was happening before the policymakers did. The administration tended to treat each of the issues on the agenda separately, with the result that its policy lacked overall direction and became a classic example of bureaucratic muddle.

Writing about constructive engagement several years later, Morris admitted that it had never had much chance of being carried out: "Its greatest single flaw was the assumption that it could be conducted, that any reasonably consistent, purposeful and occasionally even subtle policy could be conducted by the largely chaotic and incompetent bureaucracy which runs our African affairs."[2] It was, of course, natural to blame particular individuals or interest groups for its failure. It would have been more honest to have recognized the very real difficulties the State Department faced in implementing a strategy in which the chance of failure was *implicitly* greater than the chance of success. As Paul O'Neil, director of the Office of Southern African Affairs, confessed in 1974, throughout its first term the administration had had to balance conflicting national interests and competing bureaucratic claims.[3]

The case studies we have examined reveal that the bureaucracy had only a limited capacity for preemptive planning or noncrisis management. Consequently, its initiatives rarely elicited a coherent political response. Morris and his colleagues set themselves certain objectives but gave very little thought to the institutions responsible for implementing them. The priorities that the policymakers set, the role they played, the measures for which they lobbied seem to have varied from one department to the next. Constructive engagement never reflected a well-understood national purpose, upon which Kissinger had placed great emphasis on coming into office.

This is perhaps the main explanation why positive sanctions were never applied. Was the White House always aware of this? To an extent that is not always easy to determine, the NSC did maintain a degree of presidential overview by setting off different agencies against each other. In 1970 the White House was able to engineer the sale of "gray area" items by playing off the State Department, which opposed the decision, against the Department of Commerce, which did not. Eventually the president was called upon to resolve the dispute that divided them: whether the sale of equipment which might have military application would infringe the arms embargo or not. The decision to sell Hercules aircraft actually originated in the Oval office.[4]

Similarly, the control that the NSC managed to establish at the lower levels of the bureaucracy enabled it to redefine the "gray areas" in the first place.[5] In the past, whenever the State Department had been forced to defer to the White House, it had often prevented decisions from being implemented. Where the NSC believed that constructive engagement was directly under threat from the initiatives of other departments, it was often able to intervene directly. In 1970 Colonel Alexander Haig, one of the more prominent members of Kissinger's staff, was able to forestall Eximbank from extending insurance to Westinghouse by visiting the office himself.[6] But such instances of monitoring were rare. On the whole, the State Department and the Department of Commerce, although both were represented at the Final Review Group meeting in 1969, were left very largely to their own devices.

When this was not the case, policy was not carried out at all. With its preoccupation with secrecy, the NSC chose to conceal many of the details of constructive engagement from other government departments. Kissinger himself had once written that one of the problems of government was that "some of the key decisions are kept to a very small circle while the bureaucracy happily continues working away in ignorance of the fact that decisions are being made, or the fact that a decision is being made in a particular area."[7] The NSC deliberately kept the State Department in the dark to prevent the details of constructive engagement from being leaked to the press. Marshall Wright discovered to his astonishment that the department had never been told of the president's decision to reauthorize Eximbank loans to South Africa. In the end, the department came to expect decisions would be taken over its head.

Competition between the White House and the State Department became a fact of life which went unchallenged and largely unremarked. As Kissinger records in his memoirs, William Rogers was completely excluded from Nixon's private exchanges with Ho Chi Minh in 1969, from his talks with Brezhnev in May 1971, and his China initiative two months later, even though, on each occasion, the machinery of interagency consultation formed the actual basis of the discussions. On each occasion Rogers had assumed that the options were purely hypothetical. As Kissinger noted, "These studies told us the range of options and what could find support within the government. We were then able to put departmental ideas into practice outside of formal channels."[8]

Such a method of conducting policy, successful though it may have proved over China, was wholly impracticable for a policy such as constructive engagement. It was impracticable, in the first instance, because positive sanctions could only be applied through formal channels; in the second, because in the opinion of the State Department the strategy presented far more difficulties than opportunities. "Strange as it may seem," wrote Kissinger, "I never negotiated without a major departmental contribution even when the departments did not know what I was doing."[9] In fact, the practice, while deplorable, was not surprising at all. It was quite in keeping with his own style of government. Nonetheless, it made complete nonsense of a policy that demanded a large measure of continuity if it was to have any hope of success.

In keeping the State Department in the dark, the NSC paid two penalties. First, since the policy could not be communicated through normal diplomatic channels, the South Africans received conflicting signals. The annual report to Congress drawn up by the State Department differed markedly in tone from the restrained and even accommodating comments of Richard Nixon in his own State of the World addresses. After the publication of one such State Department report, the *Star* concluded that "in the harshness of much of its language, in emphasis and even in the description of American goals," it appeared much *less* conciliatory than similar reports by the Johnson administration.[10] In these circumstances it was not at all surprising that the South Africans were confused throughout this period. This extraordinary failure of communication stemmed almost entirely from Kissinger's penchant for channeling all decisions through the NSC and in time through a committee system that transformed secrecy from a personal predilection into an institutional necessity. As he had warned some years earlier, bureaucracies often become autonomous organizations in which the internal problems of decision making compound the problems which they were initially set up to solve.[11]

John Chettle, the director of The South Africa Foundation's Washington office and one of the men consulted by Roger Morris in the initial planning stages of constructive engagement, could find no evidence that the policy had been communicated to South Africa through the American embassy in Pretoria. "It is small wonder," he wrote, "that a high policymaker of the Nixon administration was reported to have said that the ambition of the administration's Southern Africa policy was to cover itself so thickly with grease that nobody could get hold of any part of it."[12] It was Senetse Khama, the most moderate of the Front Line presidents, who warned that unless those called upon to apply positive sanctions were prepared to "spell out what they hope to achieve by those means . . . , unless a positive strategy is developed, then communication will slip into acceptance and . . . moral pressure will be reduced to mere rhetoric."[13] Khama did not question whether "a combination of contact and moral pressure" would succeed; but he did question whether the United States as a country, or the Nixon administration as a government, would ever have the political will to pursue constructive engagement over a long period.

Writing in the *New York Times* twelve months later, the journalist William Sulzberger felt able to conclude that the administration had obviously decided not to allow disagreement over South Africa's racial policies to stand in the way of normal commercial and political exchanges.[14] It had, of course, decided nothing of the sort. Sulzberger's analysis parodied the government's policy as well as its intentions. Yet the fact that so well-informed a journalist should have come to this conclusion on the basis of the available evidence helps explain South Africa's confusion as well. For the danger lay not only in alienating public opinion, but in creating a fatal ambiguity in the minds of many South Africans. No country can respond to the policy of another without some knowledge of the other's intentions, some sense of its purpose, of the objectives it has set itself, of what counts most with it in terms of success or failure. Stated more precisely, the United States needed to communicate its intentions. The point is so obvious that it is often overlooked. If constructive engagement were to be followed through to the letter, if Eximbank loans were to be extended not to boost business but to encourage the government to introduce essential reforms, the South Africans needed to be told what was expected of them. The policy, after all, was entirely contingent on the intentions and actions of the second party. In principle, positive sanctions could not be applied until the whites had communicated what they themselves most wanted, and the incentives they considered important and attractive enough to make them rethink their position. Since there was nothing in the notion that was original or profound, there should have been no reason for misunderstanding.

When the Kennedy administration had introduced negative sanctions in the early 1960s, it had never spelled out what it had expected of South Africa either, except in terms so general as to be meaningless. Vorster had not been entirely disingenuous when he complained in

1968 that he had no idea what the United States wanted: "If only I knew what it is. Candidly, we don't know what it is. However, the little we know about U.S. policy we don't understand at all."[15] It was all the more surprising, therefore, that the Nixon administration should have committed the same mistake in 1969. At no stage in the discussion of Option 2 was South Africa consulted about the sanctions most likely to elicit a response. After the Final Review Group meeting, Pretoria was not even informed about the final decision. Vorster's government was briefed neither by the State Department nor the American embassy in Pretoria.

In large part this was because the NSC had no confidence in the integrity of the State Department. It suspected, not without reason, that any private discussions would be leaked to the press. Since the department's own officers were not allowed to communicate the Final Review Group's decision through normal diplomatic channels, Kissinger had to entrust the task to Roger Morris. Morris chose for the occasion Ken Owen, the Washington correspondent of South Africa's leading English-speaking newspaper, the Johannesburg *Star*.[16] Owen duly published a full account of NSSM 39 in three weekly installments. Unfortunately, the South African government failed to decode the signals. Most government ministers did not read the English-speaking press. Even John Botha, the head of the North American Department, arrived in Washington in 1971 as South Africa's new ambassador completely unaware of Owen's extraordinary journalistic scoop. Although Owen broke the news of constructive engagement several years before the American press first learned of it, his dispatches in South Africa went unread and unheeded.[17]

The second penalty the NSC paid was that its policy options were, in the main, never implemented. The traditional failure of the bureaucracy to carry out the president's intentions had been a long-standing complaint. Surveying the past, Kissinger concluded that some of the most challenging and imaginative proposals had never been carried out because they had never commanded widespread understanding or support. By reconciling different bureaucratic interests, he hoped to forge a bureaucratic consensus. He forgot that the problem of bureaucratic politics involved bureaucratic procedures as well as conflicting interests, that simply because a particular policy had been agreed upon it did not follow that it would be automatically carried out.

A report prepared by the State Department in 1970 highlighted some of the difficulties with which officials often met in grasping the strategic objectives behind many of the tactical measures they were called upon to implement. Since its conclusions bear so profoundly on one of the main themes of this study, it is worth quoting at length:

> Specific decisions are generally communicated promptly and clearly to the implementing units. On occasion, however, the implementing unit is not specified precisely and the system suffers. More often the specific decision is transmitted without reference to the broader objectives which should guide the action office in carrying it out. Action offices thus must rely on rather rough and ready guidance of their own making, extrapolating from the specific decision and the very broad brush generalizations contained in public pronouncements by the President and the Secretary. The result can either be inconsistency in implementing or excessive caution. One reason for this lack of guidance is that departmental inputs to NSSMs are often not framed in such a way as to produce it. Also the Department usually does not participate in drafting NSDMs [National Security Decision Memoranda] it is required to implement.[18]

One should not be surprised that the Africa Bureau found some difficulty in implementing a policy it had played only a limited part in drafting. Instead of asking whether the United States could play a role in South Africa, the NSC might have asked whether the bureaucracy would be able to conduct it. Kissinger, who listened to George Kennan's advice on most matters, might have taken greater note of his warning that the administration required not only an occasional NSC paper but also intimate control over the day-to-day direction of policy.[19]

In time, Kissinger discovered this through experience. Some years later, in an interview with the *Washington Post* he dismissed the public's perception of how governments work: "The outsider believes a Presidential order is consistently followed out. Nonsense. I have to spend considerable time seeing that it is carried out and in the spirit the President intended."[20] That spirit was crucially important when everything depended on nuances of application. Moreover, a system that involved the president's chief aide or staff so directly consumed a good deal of their time, and by the time they had tackled the main policy matters—whether China, arms control, or détente—they had little energy left. Marshall Wright was not surprised to discover that most country program evaluations had been undertaken to keep whole areas of the world not of immediate concern off Kissinger's daily agenda.[21] In the eyes of his staff the main virtue of constructive engagement was that the policy was not expected to produce results for five to ten years, time enough for the NSC to tackle more immediate problems without having to attend to crises that had not yet broken out, or problems whose solution could be deferred almost indefinitely.[22]

This lack of oversight allowed policymakers who were opposed to closer links with South Africa more room for discretion than was desirable. Control by the White House had been exercised in the past by involving all branches of the administration in decision making. Kissinger, however, was so anxious to preserve the distinction between planning and operation, which he accused the Johnson administration of obscuring, that he often confused the relationship between the two.[23]

To his credit, he did not attempt to exclude the Africa Bureau from the drafting of NSSM 39. But he never succeeded in reconciling the bureau to his own preferred option. Newsom's deputy, Clyde Fergusson, writing some years after his retirement, expressed his profound dislike of closer contacts between the United States and South Africa. Like many of his colleagues, he would have preferred to apply penalties, not rewards: "No people throughout history has relinquished power without being required to do so. Only a combination of serious international and domestic pressure will bring home to the white South Africans the necessity of moving now rather than waiting until it is too late for any form of peaceful settlement."[24] Such a difference of opinion could not have been more profound.

At other times the Africa Bureau tried to obstruct the implementation of constructive engagement by calling for greater public interest and involvement. Beverley Carter urged American journalists who objected to their government's policy to bring pressure on the White House through their newspaper columns.[25] Newsom reminded the press that no administration could pursue a policy for very long that did not have public support.[26]

For many bureaucrats the chance of failure was always too high and its consequences too daunting to justify pursuing so controversial a policy. The higher reaches of the State Department could hardly fail to be conscious of the weight of public sentiment against apartheid. It was only to be expected that they should have seen and spoken of themselves as the representatives of public opinion. But their objections to engagement ran much deeper. They were unhappy that the NSC's responsibility stopped at long-range planning, leaving the State Department entirely responsible for the conduct of policy. As Morris later conceded, their original support for Option 3 had been informed by their understanding that it would have been the most easy to implement. Given that the department was better informed of its own limitations than the White House, the NSC might have taken greater note of its reservations about Option 2.[27]

The State Department also realized that the process of implementation involved lower-level officials, from desk officers to ambassadors, who labored under quite different constraints from their superiors. It was the middle-level officials who were called upon to interpret policy directives in the course of carrying them out, or communicating them to foreign governments. Their interpretation did not always correspond with the intentions of higher officials. To make matters worse, particular nuances in application were not always clear to officials in Washington, unless they were particularly conscientious in monitoring what was happening.

It was the South Africans who first realized that American policy rested not with Newsom or the White House, but with "low-to medium-level bureaucrats in the State Department"[28]—officials who, as Ken Owen later reported, saw nothing but "a vista of difficulties and dangers in which change would be painful and improvements in the general climate could, in the short term, be miniscule at best."[29] It was these middle-level officials who confounded Kissinger's attempt to put relations with South Africa on a better footing, and who bore the ultimate responsibility for the fact that in the end constructive engagement became only "a distillation" of Option 2.[30] It never represented more than a distillation because middle-level officials, field officers, and the like were in a position to choose the best available course. The NSC was not in a position to ascertain whether positive sanctions had been applied, whether political reforms had been introduced, or whether whatever progress had been made on the political front merited further concessions. Only the lower-level officials in the State Department were capable of undertaking such a review.

Accordingly, the scale of the administration's endeavors fell far short of Kissinger's original expectations. Because the White House had no control over the lower reaches of the government, it was unable to monitor its own policy. The extent to which the NSC could divorce planning from procedure in a way that the State Department could not explains why it so often made unreasonable demands on the bureaucratic process. It relied on the State Department not only to monitor the progress of constructive engagement but also to evaluate the significance of the political changes that might have been made in response. The difference between ends and means would not have been so important if South Africa had been brought into the process, or if it had been able to communicate with the White House directly, but the very secrecy in which it conducted its own operations ruled this out.

Ultimately, Kissinger is to be blamed for failing to come to terms with the bureaucratic process; for exaggerating the objectivity of his own staff and minimizing the subjective judgment on which policymakers have to rely; for neglecting the conflict in roles between the "objective" analyst and the policy advocate. To state this is to state the obvious. Constructive engagement depended for its success not only on the response it elicited from the South Africans but also the attitude of its own bureaucrats. If we want a single explanation for its failure we will find it in the alienation of the one officer who was in the best position to keep an eye on the behavior of middle-level officials: the assistant secretary of state.

In fairness to Morton Halperin, who drew up the revised NSC system during the transition from the Johnson to Nixon administrations, the assistant secretaries were originally going to be invested with responsibility for assigning the reviews, drawing up the terms of the agenda, and chairing the main committees.[31] Kissinger, however, used Halperin's blueprint to increase his own authority at the expense of that of the secretary of state. Although he had no wish to relegate the assistant secretaries to obscurity, he thought that it was only possible to reach a policy consensus by concentrating power in his own hands. By insisting that his own staff monitor every departmental position paper which came before the interdepartmental groups, he ensured that the assistant secretaries who chaired the meetings would have little opportunity to show any independent initiative of their own. The interdepartmental groups might well have been responsible for formulating policy choices, but the final decisions were taken by the Interagency Review Group, in which they were denied a voice. Kissinger's preference for chairing every important committee himself soon left him the only authority capable of distinguishing departmental opinion from fact, a development that became increasingly significant as meetings of the Interagency Review Group declined in frequency and committee discussions became the normal manner of conducting business.

In short, the NSC was powerful only in name. In retrospect it appears to have been an unaccountable body, not necessarily powerful for that, possessing great influence in principle but often unable to exploit it in practice; able to obstruct the State Department in small matters, but quite unable to pursue a consistent course in matters of higher strategy. It would have been better if Kissinger had recognized from the outset that the assistant secretary was the first official who could *commit* the government to act; that others merely issued orders.[32]

Had he done so he would have been well advised to have replaced David Newsom with one of his own creatures. It would have been more useful to have captured the Africa Bureau rather than fight a long and futile struggle against the obstruction of middle-ranking officials over whom he had no control. Curiously, he let the opportunity slip. Only one of the five regional bureau heads in the State Department owed his appointment to political patronage; the rest, including Newsom, were career officers who had made their way in the early 1960s. Newsom was one of Nixon's last appointments, a career diplomat who had been deputy director of the Office of African Affairs before becoming ambassador to Libya three years later. As he later confessed, the White House took so little interest in the continent that he was given sole responsibility for 90 percent of the administration's decisions.[33]

Nixon's indifference and Kissinger's preoccupation with more pressing matters left the bureau free to chart its own course. It is the more ironic, therefore, that the administration paid so little attention to the methods by which Kennedy with great success had foisted negative sanctions on a skeptical, not to say hostile, State Department. Kennedy's interest in African affairs had led him to appoint G.

Mennen Williams to the Africa Bureau even before choosing Dean Rusk to head the State Department. Williams was a powerful political figure in his own right, a former governor of Michigan and a prominent spokesman of the liberal wing of the Democratic party. Acting in concert in 1962, Kennedy and Williams were able to persuade the department to agree to an arms embargo in face of strong opposition from the secretary and under secretary of state.[34] The episode confirmed that, provided an assistant secretary had the ear of the president, policy decisions could be carried over the heads, if need be, of much higher officers who were too far removed to determine its implementation. Yet so anxious was Kissinger to maintain his own position after becoming secretary of state that he moved quickly to reduce the authority and influence of his own assistant secretaries by excluding them altogether from the Special Priorities Group that he set up in June 1975.[35]

The reverse, of course, also remained true. Unless a president, or his national security adviser, had access to officials below the rank of under secretary, the White House would exercise very little control over the implementation of policy.[36] Williams owed his appointment not to the fact that he represented a powerful constituency; he was appointed to create a constituency from scratch that would allow him in time to call upon an articulate lobby of academics, journalists, and black community leaders. By contrast, Nixon's preoccupation in the early 1970s with other matters of state reduced American policy in South Africa—in the words of one journalist at the time—to "a void, without knowledgeable leadership from either the President or the Secretary of State."[37]

One way of overcoming the objections of the professional diplomats might have been to appoint a team of officers with personal experience of South Africa. Kissinger's staff had no experience of Africa themselves;[38] yet they expected constructive engagement to be implemented by serving officers who had never served south of the Zambezi, a point to which Morris himself later drew attention.[39] No assistant secretary for African affairs had ever served as ambassador in South Africa, though William Satterthwaite had been appointed ambassador on resigning the post of assistant secretary in 1961. This may have been a poor option, given the marked differences of opinion between those who had served in South Africa and those who had not (as Satterthwaite's testimony before a congressional committee revealed in 1970). But it might have been worth trying. In 1973 Nixon actually offered Newsom's post to his ambassador in Pretoria, John Hurd. Hurd wisely declined the appointment, recognizing that without active presidential support his own position in the Africa Bureau would have been untenable.

The administration might also have defeated bureaucratic obstruction by throwing the whole question open to public discussion. Ironically, in its contempt for public opinion, the NSC may have misjudged the support on which it might have counted. Beverley Carter was convinced that the president's "tilt" toward the whites would have been more popular than the bureau's "tilt" against them. He admitted that the State Department would have preferred to discourage American investment in South Africa, but he conceded that on this issue as on several others it was in no position to move ahead of public opinion.[40]

For most of the 1970s opposition to corporate involvement was focused, in the main, on the corporations themselves rather than the government that provided them with credit guarantees and tax credits; for most of the period public disquiet—to the extent it existed at all—tended to be expressed at shareholders' meetings rather than in demonstrations in the streets. Constructive engagement might not have won much public support, but there was little evidence of any wish for tougher measures. The marked decline of the anti-apartheid movement in the late 1960s may have been due to America's preoccupation with the war in Vietnam, but for whatever reason the protesters chose to move the campaign into the boardrooms and university senates where they believed it would do the most good.

The final option open to the administration would have been to have subjected constructive engagement to congressional scrutiny. One of the special annexes to NSSM 39 had discussed the support which the NSC might be able to count upon in Congress. It had concluded that the majority of congressmen, although hostile to South Africa, did not favor American disengagement.[41] The administration had no real reason, in fact, to fear any substantial opposition. The executive continued to formulate policy and set out the framework in which it was discussed. This was particularly true in foreign policy.

It is true that after two years of mounting criticism in Congress the National Aeronautics and Space Administration (NASA) agreed to "phase out" its tracking station in Johannesburg. But the decision was taken in the end on administrative grounds that had very little to do with the fact that the NASA station had become the subject of a congressional inquiry.[42] Morris had recommended that the station should be retained only as long as it was required; its retention was never intended to be an incentive to good behavior. From the point of view of the South African government there was no reason why it should have been. Its eventual closure did not follow a congressional vote to terminate appropriations. Indeed, when NASA officials appeared before the House subcommittee on Africa during the 92nd congressional session, Congressman Charles Rangel failed to persuade either the Committee or the House to delete the costs of the Johannesburg station from the agency's annual budget.

Later in 1976 a vote in the House of Representatives challenged the administration's right to recognize the independence of the Transkei, even though it had denied any intention of doing so before the vote was taken. This was the first recorded vote in the House or the Senate in which a majority voted for a resolution critical of the South African government. Up to that time whatever congressional opposition there was owed much to the Watergate episode. It must also be remembered that by 1974 the collapse of the Portuguese empire had totally changed the situation in Southern Africa. By that time constructive engagement, as understood by Kissinger himself, had already disappeared down the highway of history with its baggage train of supporters following closely behind.

The absence of congressional scrutiny denied the government one of the few independent aids to monitoring the progress of its own policies: congressional hearings. As Newsom's successor at the Africa Bureau confirmed, every administration depended for the long-term success of its policies on public awareness of the issues.[43] Since Congress was not taken into its confidence, it was hardly in a position to review constructive engagement. Since the staff of the NSC were not publicly accountable, they could not be examined about its progress. Although members of the State Department were called upon to testify before a variety of subcommittees, often they were as ill-informed about the administration's intentions as the committee chairmen.

Congressman Diggs's subcommittee, the most active in Congress, was compelled to discuss economic issues—from American busi-

ness involvement in South Africa to the South African sugar quota
—until in the course of its hearings on the arms embargo in 1973 it
stumbled upon the first intimation that dual-purpose equipment
had been supplied to the republic on special terms. Roger Morris
himself was not called upon to testify until 1977, seven years after
resigning from the NSC in protest over the bombing of Cambodia. It
was during his testimony that the Nixon administration's attitude to
Congress was first revealed. Constructive engagement he claimed
had survived for four years "amid a somewhat justified contempt in
the executive . . . for the committees of the Congress and the Congress at large with respect to Africa. . . . No one seemed to really care
about serious policy on the Hill and those who made the pretense
were either quickly discovered to be ill-informed and thus no threat
to business as usual, or were simply co-opted in the habitual
manner."[44]

The upshot of all this is that the administration lost a useful ally.
The United States paid the price for Kissinger's preoccupation with
secrecy. Perhaps like many of his policies, constructive engagement
would have been too complicated for Congress, and too simplistic for
the real world. But until the Watergate scandal enabled Congress to
reassert its authority and to force the executive to provide the information necessary for the performance of its oversight and consultative functions, middle-level officials in the State Department were
able to interpret most policy guidelines as they wished, leaving the
White House free to authorize specific concessions to South Africa
that had no bearing on the letter or the spirit of constructive
engagement.[45] Had congressional hearings been held a few years
earlier, South Africa might even have learned of the new policy
through official channels rather than through the pages of the American press.

In April 1974 the Portuguese government was overthrown in a blood-
less military coup. The officers who were involved in the conspiracy
and who subsequently formed a ruling junta under the leadership of
Antonio de Spinola were not committed to transferring power in the
colonies immediately, although as it happened the transfer was rapid.
But all had taken to heart the message of Spinola's book *Portugal and
the Future*, which had cost him his army career; and most had taken
note of the demand by the junior officers in a document that had
been circulated much earlier in which they had called on the government to recognize "the irreversible and undeniable reality of African
nationalism."[1]

The intervention of the Portuguese army marked the closing chapter in the first attempt at constructive engagement. In Southern
Africa the Portuguese recessional opened up a 300-mile front on
Rhodesia's frontier with Mozambique, while depriving Salisbury of a
valuable ally. It also exposed Namibia's northern frontier at a point
where South Africa's control was at its weakest. As David Newsom's
successor reminded Congress, the collapse of Portuguese rule had
made the prospect of a military struggle in the region more attractive
than a negotiated settlement, and the management of the crisis much
more difficult.[2]

The Portuguese coup presented the United States with a direct
challenge to the central tenet of constructive engagement: that the
whites would maintain themselves in power for years and that they
would be only marginally threatened by the tide of nationalist feeling.
Long before the coup, however, the Nixon administration had begun

to entertain more profound doubts about the whole exercise. As Roger Morris later admitted, it had begun to question "the whole presumption of whether the United States could, or indeed should, by its own history, by diplomacy or any other means, try to influence the internal affairs of another society."[3]

In an interview with the *New York Times* in October 1974 Kissinger spoke despairingly of America's pragmatic but often self-defeating defense of the status quo, which had been thrown once again into relief by the coup in Lisbon: "One of the troubles of Western societies is that they are basically satisfied with the status quo so that . . . the tendency is not to change. I think this is a mistaken conception. But what comes after is so uncertain—and we really lack a philosophy for how to shape a new political evolution—that one tends to leave well enough alone." Whether constructive engagement offered a very plausible philosophy "for shaping a new political evolution" was a matter of serious doubt.

Toward the end of his term in office Kissinger came to recognize that American influence was strictly limited: "Our strength has become less predominant; our margin of error has narrowed; our choices more difficult and ambiguous."[4] In South Africa he came to question whether there was anything to gain from persuading the government that reform was for the best, when the United States itself was so uncertain about the outcome. In an article in the *New York Times* the veteran scholar George Kennan questioned whether it was right for any country to intervene: "whether outsiders, acting *from the background of their own concepts and experience* would be in a good position to decide what forms that change might usefully take."[5] By 1976 the United States had reconciled itself to a more limited role: that of an interlocutor, convinced that it had little control over events. Kissinger's dictum that the statesman should avoid being surprised by events was still the watchword of government policy, but a watchword that seemed increasingly to ring hollow as the months passed.

If constructive engagement had serious shortcomings, perhaps it would have been more sensible to have revealed rather than disguised them. The illusionist must retain his secrets or go out of business. The politician cannot afford to behave as an illusionist if no one trusts to his illusions. As David Newsom reminded an audience in 1972: "We are dealing in Southern Africa with governments which react strongly to outside pressures and are not easily susceptible to persuasion. . . . We are dealing with complex societies, not with the interests of one race but of many. . . . There are many real limitations on the extent to which we can influence the situation, both in terms of what might be supported domestically and of what we might be able to do in Africa."[6] The following year he was even more explicit and much less inclined to pass over some of the realities that he and his colleagues had come to appreciate in the intervening three years: "The influence of any nation, however powerful, in the internal affairs of another is severely limited. The idea that the United States . . . could bring about *fundamental* change in another society is without foundation. We certainly cannot do it in Southern Africa. If change comes it must come primarily from within."[7]

Such attitudes did not stem from any single event or set of events, but from the fact that several of Morris's a priori assumptions had been tested and found wanting. What had changed particularly between 1970 and 1973 was the gradual realization that constructive engagement had not brought change on the cheap, that the use of special incentives demanded far greater concessions than the United States could possibly meet. When the State Department attempted to describe the policy in August 1974, rewards or incentives were not even mentioned. Instead, it suggested that the United States had only intended to make clear "its abhorrence of South Africa's racial policies with a view to inducing the government to be more receptive to change, urging it to respect international standards and cautioning it on the dangers of its present course. It is hoped that this will gradually lead to the abandonment of South Africa's apartheid policies."[8]

In short, no one was really sure whether the United States had a role to play. Although much has been written about the scope of political influence, skepticism still tends to be the prerogative of the politician more than the political scientist. Politicians, more often than not, qualify, prevaricate, and point to the difficulties of predicting possible outcomes. Political scientists too often fall into the error of supposing that events might have taken a different course if other measures had been taken. The more often they rationalize, the more often they reduce complex events to single causes. Instead of defending it, even Roger Morris acknowledged several years later that "as a diplomatic concept . . . based on the premise that you could do something for constructive change," constructive engagement had demonstrated what should have been obvious from the very beginning, "that as a government we cannot conduct that kind of policy any more than we can conduct intervention in Southeast Asia."[9]

Not everyone, of course, believed that the policy had been bankrupt from the beginning. A report produced by the Senate Committee on Foreign Relations expressed the opinion that "Option 2 of the now famous NSSM 39, despite the frankness of its wording, remains the best policy for the future."[10] But the administration no longer shared that view, aware as it was of the disparity between its aims and attainments. Kissinger doubted the possibility of getting the South Africans to put their own house in order, while he solicited their assistance in persuading Rhodesia to do the same. In return for Pretoria's cooperation in bringing Ian Smith to the conference table, the United States was prepared to ease restrictions on Eximbank credits and dismantle some of the remaining restrictions on the sale of arms.

These measures were no longer held out as incentives for modifying the rules and regulations of apartheid. Their object was now quite different. Although Vorster denied that he had received anything for his assistance, his denials were not entirely convincing. The Americans may have promised a great deal more. It was rumored that Kissinger had given serious consideration to recognizing the Transkei as an independent state, and to supporting its application to join the United Nations.[11]

To all intents and purposes, therefore, constructive engagement passed into history in August 1974, until its revival six years later. Given Kissinger's temperament and determination to go for a quick success in Rhodesia and Namibia, it was inevitable that he would refuse to treat the separate problems of Southern Africa *d'une seule piece.* When he embarked on the first of two visits to the region in April 1976—almost two years to the day since the Portuguese coup —his first priority was to bring peace to the periphery of the *laager,* only secondly to bring peace within it. The Front Line States were told that they would have to allow South Africa time to dismantle apartheid if they wanted its support in Namibia and Rhodesia.[12] If the South Africans agreed to disentangle themselves from their commitments beyond the Limpopo, the Organization of African Unity

(OAU) would have to consider the whites as much a part of Africa as the republic's 21 million blacks, and accept that the South African problem could not be resolved around a conference table in Geneva.[13]

Constructive Engagement (1970–1974) in Retrospect

In looking back over the period, it is not at all difficult to explain why constructive engagement met with so little success. In some quarters of the administration it provoked measured skepticism, in others outright disbelief. Even its apologists lacked the confidence to persist in the face of such sustained opposition. But it is clear that these were not the only constraints or even the most telling under which the Nixon administration had to labor. Morris may have complained about the obstructionism he found in the State Department and the cynicism of those in the NSC who gave the policy their support only in the hope of keeping South Africa "on the back burner." His own conception of political change in South Africa, however, was deeply flawed, as was his idea of how one country might influence another.

We might begin by looking at the "autonomous probability" of events discussed by Karl Deutsch in his seminal analysis of political influence. For if we are to inquire why the United States failed to induce political change in South Africa in the early 1970s we must ask at the outset whether the time was auspicious for the application of positive sanctions. Fears of an immediate crisis, after all, did not weigh very heavily with most Americans either in or out of government. The NSC believed that the whites would remain in power in both the immediate and foreseeable future. It was an opinion shared by most South Africans as well. Their leaders had never felt more secure. They saw little reason to reform the institutions that had served them so well since Sharpeville. Some concessions were made, but on a scale which fell far short of what international opinion both demanded and expected. The most the government was prepared to contemplate was to strike a political bargain—to co-opt those black political leaders who would agree to accept the prevailing political order provided they themselves were given a role in it.

It is difficult to see how in these circumstances anything could ever have compensated the whites for surrendering the political power which underwrote their privileged economic position, or the economic privileges that underpinned white supremacy. The NSC may have held fast to a view of politics in which every actor is accessible to rational argument. However, it is one matter to recognize that an argument can reveal the existence of an interest; quite another to imagine that it can create it. Since the whites at this stage were not prepared to redistribute power or even share it, no incentives, however generous, would have proved effective; almost none *would* have appeared significant.

Possibly it would have been much wiser to have waited. In 1969 the whites were too confident, too given to wishful thinking, too attached to invented values and special interests. Acceptable solutions are not usually perceived prior to negotiation, but the possibility of a negotiated settlement was a proposition that both parties would have been prepared to entertain only after the costs of attaining their goals had required them to reassess their position. This is to say positive sanctions could have had some chance of success only in the context of concessions that the whites were already reconciled to making. But the contention that constructive engagement would prove successful if carried through to the letter could hardly be made on the understanding that it applied at all times and in all circumstances. Indeed, there was every reason to doubt the empirical truth of the contention, quite apart from the premise on which it was based.

In such circumstances, it was hardly very likely that the promise of rewards, few and insubstantial as they eventually proved to be, would have tipped the balance in favor of reform. Even the promise of substantial rewards would have had little effect. Morris was not entirely oblivious to these realities, but he imagined that the South African government would be brought to recognize at least that the force of nationalism could not be contained indefinitely, and that if reform were long delayed, it might be forced to respond to events not of its own making. Unfortunately, neither this perspective nor the conclusions that the United States drew from it were shared by the decision makers in Pretoria.

In addition, the Nixon administration was responsible for several other errors of judgment that compounded this mistake. It is true that it recognized very early on that unless constructive engagement produced substantial political concessions almost immediately after political and commercial relations between the two countries had been upgraded and unless some evidence could be cited to show that the whites *were* susceptible to forces other than violence, American policy might appear to be an overtly cynical betrayal of American ideals. Unless the United States could be shown to have provided "tactical encouragement for economic and social forces *already at work* within the white regimes," its own relations with Pretoria could be mistaken for accommodation.[14]

From the beginning the policy was fraught with difficulties. Because it would arouse controversy, it had to be conducted with excessive secrecy. Once that was the case the United States began to lose sight of its immediate objectives, while the whites for their part failed to recognize that any major policy shift was in the offing. Second, Morris's formula required Washington to assume a disproportionate share of the political costs. Although he expected the South Africans to embark upon what was somewhat obliquely termed "the tangible, albeit small and gradual moderation" of their policies,[15] the Americans would be required to provide sufficient incentives before the whites made any commitment of their own. The intention, though not unreasonable, exposed those responsible for it to a perennial dilemma. If the opportunity costs of intervening were not to outweigh the expected political returns, both parties would have to acquiesce in a larger role for the other. The preamble to Option 2 made this clear:

> This option accepts, at least over a three- to five-year period, the prospect of unrequited U.S. initiatives toward the whites and some opposition from the blacks in order to develop an atmosphere conducive to change in white attitudes through persuasion and erosion. To encourage this change . . . we would indicate our willingness to accept political arrangements short of guaranteed progress toward majority rule, provided that they assure broadened political participation in some form by the whole population.[16]

In short, there was every reason for Washington to have some say in what constituted "the tangible moderation" of minority rule. In accepting rewards for good behavior South Africa would be acquiescing by clear implication in America's right to intervene, to determine even in a minor key the South African political agenda. This was a point on which the two powers had never before reached agreement, a point that South Africa refused to concede.

It was doubtful whether this would have proved any more acceptable than in earlier years unless the United States had intended to make substantial and politically expensive concessions, and for this Option 2 made almost no provision. Morris proposed at most only broadening the scope of relations in response to the material improvement in the position of the nonwhite community. In pressing explicitly for changes "short of majority rule" the Nixon administration was in no position to offer any rewards of substance.

This dilemma called attention to a curious belief, which gained ground at the time, that the skillful use of positive sanctions would not only persuade Pretoria to respond to its representations but also help to determine the form of the response. Indeed, the promise of specific concessions to make more palatable the passage of specific legislation was an important, even implicit, part of the strategy. In practice, the situation was rather different. The fact that few of the sanctions discussed were related to any particular reform or set of measures rendered them largely irrelevant. When they amounted to the repeal of earlier negative sanctions, they merely confirmed the whites in their opinion that Washington had lost interest in the issue.

In the final analysis, the administration's problem was not that the sanctions it applied proved inappropriate; nor that the opportunity for applying them was peculiarly inauspicious; nor the fact that the whites would have been well-advised to have acted while there was still time, but the fact that the whites themselves did not believe any of these matters to be true. Rationality in assessing the costs and benefits of maintaining a government's policies is more often a goal to be sought than a premise to be assumed.

What should be stressed at the end of this brief survey of American policy, this critical but not entirely negative comment on constructive engagement, is that it is only part of the story. These years not only failed to turn South Africa upside down; they even failed to put it askew. It can be argued, of course, that it was more realistic than any of the other policies which had been pursued hitherto. Perhaps it might have been, but this was hardly high praise. If the implication of this argument is that the Nixon administration was highly astute, the evidence would hardly support it. There is little evidence that those who were called upon to execute American policy had any real understanding of what Morris had hoped to achieve—in the last resort not even Henry Kissinger. Even if they were obstructed time and again by the State Department, it can hardly be said that want of support at home was at the heart of their lack of success.

The Challenge from the Left:
The Carter Years (1977–1980)

The intellectual shortcomings of constructive engagement rendered it particularly susceptible to criticism. When it came, however, it arose from an unexpected source. The Carter administration took issue with the program on a number of points, the most trenchant of which (but also one of the least compelling) was its belief that South Africa's record on human rights made it next to impossible to deal as closely with Pretoria as Morris and Kissinger had required, or to hold out for anything less than immediate and unqualified majority rule.

In his inaugural address Jimmy Carter affirmed his commitment to making human rights the cornerstone of American policy with the solemn pledge "Because we are free, we can never be indifferent to the fate of freedom elsewhere." It was a message that marked a radical shift from the postwar program of containment, the latest version of which had been détente. The Democrat-controlled Congress of 1973 had already initialed this shift by requiring the State Department to submit annual reports on the state of human rights in more than one hundred countries, and by linking foreign assistance to human rights concerns. Even Kissinger had not been entirely oblivious to the issue, though he had never accorded it much importance. On becoming secretary of state he had instructed all embassy personnel to monitor the fate of political prisoners and refugees. Carter was not responsible for America's interest in human rights, only for the policy of "affirmative action." For when the first assistant secretary for human rights had begun work in 1977 she had found only two members of the State Department permanently assigned to the task.

Carter's own position was that human rights objectives must be linked to self-interest so that they could be effectively pursued with other foreign policy goals. For the new president America's extensive trade and investment ties with South Africa, not to mention its less publicized security interests, added to its obligations to seek the shortest route to majority rule. He rejected Kissinger's "linkage" argument that the promotion of human rights violations might be more costly than cost-effective. For much of the time he seemed to labor under the impression that virtue was its own reward. However, it would be wrong to suggest that the administration turned its back entirely on the Nixon years. Deputy Secretary of State Warren Christopher publicly recognized that while the United States would strive for consistency and evenhandedness in its approach to human rights violations, evaluations on a country-by-country basis might mean that pragmatism would occasionally override principle.[17]

Contrary to popular perception, the Carter administration did not come to power totally unaware of the difficulties it faced. There were many members, if not always the most vociferous, who asked whether outside intervention would promote human rights or make the situation far worse; whether public condemnation would actually achieve more than "quiet diplomacy"; whether American intervention would not render an impossible situation even more impossible still. Some even doubted whether Washington knew how to reshape the policies and institutions of other countries; whether it had the tools at its disposal to achieve particular goals in countries whose political, social, and cultural milieu was so at variance with America's own.

While the State Department struggled with defining a human rights initiative, the outgoing assistant secretary for African affairs, William Schaufele, soon to be replaced by Carter's own choice, Richard Moose, suggested a substantial revision of previous thinking. In a speech in April he appeared to apply the human rights rhetoric of the previous four months to Kissinger's communication policy of the previous eight years, an unbalanced dialectic that produced a rather confused approach—a synthesis that although repudiated by Carter toward the end of the year would ironically constitute the thrust of his policy toward Pretoria after 1979.

Schaufele's message was a variation of constructive engagement, shorn, to be sure, of its positive sanctions and accommodationist bias, but perfectly consistent with Morris's own understanding that the South Africans themselves would have to come to terms with the inequality of their own society; that without a measure of self-reflection aided if not abetted by the outside world, there would be no serious thinking at all, only an obstinate if self-defeating attachment to the old political values. In support of his thesis Schaufele believed that there were already clear signs of self-questioning on the part of many whites that deserved to be encouraged, not stifled at birth by gratuitous public criticism:

> Of all peoples we Americans should probably be chary about providing excessive and unsolicited advice to others about how they should solve their racial problems. . . . Our recent history provides testimony to the fact that change in the racial sphere came about gradually, unevenly, perhaps even grudgingly—not because outsiders . . . told us what was right but because the realization finally dawned on our people that . . . the status quo had to be changed for our own good.[18]

Because Schaufele detected "considerable soul searching on the part of the Afrikaner community," he contended that the Carter administration would have to "weigh carefully the relative merits of speaking out and of restraint."

Anthony Lake, the new director of policy planning, struck a rather different note, but one equally cautious in tone. It was clear from his earlier writings that he was no interventionist; indeed, he was deeply skeptical of the extent to which the United States should become directly involved in the region.[19] If he averred that it should not miss any opportunity to play a positive role in support of local challenges to white supremacy, he also considered that it would be quite wrong for Washington to become "blindly interventionist" in its approach.[20]

Schaufele also found an ally in the new director of the NSC, Zbigniew Brzezinski, who threw his full support behind a program designed to promote social change in South Africa on the explicit understanding that if it were pursued consistently it need not mark a radical turn of direction in American policy. In his memoirs, however, he records how the State Department plunged in without a coherent program. In the absence of a plan of action the Carter administration was bound on the one hand to antagonize the South African government, and on the other to raise expectations in the black community that no American government could possibly meet.[21]

Even before the first NSC meeting on Africa, during a briefing for congressmen in February 1977, Brzezinski and the new ambassador to the UN, the volatile and outspoken Andrew Young, had clashed over the issue of separate development. In hoping that South Africa would modify its policies, not abandon them altogether, Brzezinski did not depart significantly from Kissinger's hopes for "the modification of apartheid short of majority rule." Indeed, from the views that Brzezinski went on to express some years after leaving office, it was clear that the two men did not differ at all on the main premise of constructive engagement:

> We know from our own national experience that social rearrangements, particularly when they involve racial relations, are extremely difficult, extremely painful, and cannot be achieved overnight. We also know that if the process begins it is best to encourage it by praising, by approving what is being done and by encouraging it to become more rapid—rather than by either pointing the gun at somebody's head or condemning him because he hasn't transformed himself overnight.[22]

Brzezinski's views eventually struck a chord with Carter himself in the brief conservative phase at the end of his administration, when with Young sacked and Vance in retirement he came to recognize somewhat belatedly that a few ringing phrases, however sincerely delivered, would not bring down the edifice of apartheid, still less bring the South Africans to their senses. By then it was not at all clear whether reform would precipitate a revolution, or whether a revolution would necessarily follow if reform were long delayed. In the end, however, the approach advocated by Schaufele and others was deemed wrong and unworkable by the secretary of state, Cyrus Vance.[23] To ignore the situation in South Africa, the State Department believed, would mislead South Africans about America's real concerns and jeopardize the already slim prospects for a peaceful solution. Instead, the United States should press for a progressive transformation of South African society, an end to racial discrimination and the establishment of a new course toward full participation by all South Africans.

Vance's view that the United States should actively promote human rights in pursuit of majority rule through peaceful change and external pressure eventually prevailed. And yet, although the time may have been propitious for America to adopt a new approach to foreign policy, the human rights initiative was not well applied. In the aftermath of the Portuguese coup and the even more traumatic Soweto uprising, the only soul searching in the South African white community was about how to save their collective interests, how to modernize the apartheid system not how best to abandon it. To evaluate where Carter's human rights policy went wrong as well as the consequences for U.S.–South Africa relations, it is perhaps best to answer some of the questions Vance himself raised.[24] Did the United States understand the nature of the case at hand—the particular type and extent of human rights violations? Had it maintained a sense of perspective—by avoiding self-righteous indignation, by considering all aspects of the question, by looking at the context in which decisions and policies were made? These questions were to be centrally important in assessing why Carter's policy failed so completely, for upon its failure the Reagan administration was to base its own case for returning to constructive engagement. The reasons were many and varied, but perhaps Carter's most serious mistake was to have engaged in a spirited debate about constitutional matters before he had even defined what he meant by constitutional change.

On entering office Carter looked forward to immediate progress on the political front, perhaps because he was misled by the Soweto disturbances, as Kennedy had been misled by Sharpeville, into thinking that progress could not long be delayed. The meeting in Vienna between Vice-President Mondale and John Vorster promised as much. At a meeting in May 1977, just three months after the president's inauguration, the two men had a frank and often rancorous discussion of South Africa's domestic policies. Mondale soon discovered how impolitic it is in diplomatic negotiations to ask for too much at the negotiating table. The State Department's demands for "majority rule" and "free elections," if they had any meaning, were not modest goals. That is why the Vienna meeting broke up without agreement and plunged relations between the two countries into greater crisis than at any time in the previous ten years.

In fairness to Mondale, the Americans did not ask for immediate majority rule but instead stressed the need for equal social and political participation. While not specifying a blueprint or timetable for this "progressive transformation" of society, they did issue an ultimatum: if South Africa were not to take immediate steps toward the ultimate goal of a democratic multiracial state, it could expect no support from the United States. An angry Vorster had asked

Mondale if his interpretation of democracy meant "one man, one vote." Mondale responded that the American ideal included the equal right of every individual to vote in the understanding that all votes carried equal weight; later in a press conference he insisted that "one man, one vote" and "full political participation" by all citizens irrespective of race meant the same thing.[25] Winston Nagan later wrote of this crucial clarification:

> In the apartheid lexicon "full participation" might be not inconsistent with full participation in the blacks' own sphere of "separate" political and social development under the apartheid scheme. The policy clarifications made it explicit that the apartheid policies be halted but also that the institutions spawned by them be dismantled. The implications of such a policy are that the United States entertains the expectation that South Africa *ought* to move far and fast in the other direction."[26]

Unfortunately, the administration never really addressed the thorny question of black participation. If Nixon had been rather vague about the form that political change might take, Carter's fault was to be too specific. American policy seemed to totally ignore the growing debate on whether equal participation could successfully transform free men into responsible citizens, or whether it betokened no more than a ritual genuflection to majority rule. For many critics of the administration, including George Ball, the United States would have been better advised to have pressed for separate but equal privileges —for better educational opportunities and the speedy abolition of petty apartheid—and to have looked not for "the ultimate goal of a democratic social order" but at the process of getting there.[27]

The constitution proposed by the Progressive Federal party actually envisaged a federal government in which each race would have a minority veto under a system of proportional representation, and in which government by consensus rather than the majority would be the norm. But the Carter administration remained largely indifferent to such arguments. In an interview with the *Rand Daily Mail* Andrew Young criticized South Africa's human rights record for being worse than the Soviet Union's, where at least every citizen whether Russian, Uzbek, or Jew, was considered equal under the law.[28]

Young's comments highlighted a predicament that was unique to South Africa's black population. After the passage of the Transkei

Act, which effectively denationalized a million South Africans and made them overnight citizens of the first independent homeland, the Americans woke up to the fact that the claim to full South African citizenship was no less important than the claim to full participation in the political system. In these circumstances they might have taken greater note of counter-social rights—the claims of noncitizens in a society to be treated as equals even if denied political power or political rights.[29] Mondale's asking for equal participation in government—whether through majority rule or a more qualified political settlement—presumed a political society that did not exist and that could not be conjured into existence by legislation. Before reaching the stage of institutional dialogue, it was more important for the blacks to gain legal status as equal citizens, a fact to which Washington (apart from refusing to recognize Bophuthatswana) paid remarkably little heed.

Even without this dilemma the administration found itself out of step with black thinking, for all its claims to be in greater touch with black political movements than the previous administration. For most of the 1970s the blacks demanded a political dialogue, not the trappings of political responsibility. Steve Biko, the leader of the Black Consciousness Movement, admitted as much: "The simplest thing that needs to be done is to make negotiations possible. . . . Meaningful dialogue could begin an evolutionary bargaining process."[30] By refusing to vote in the elections for the government-sponsored community councils, the semi-executive bodies that had been introduced to replace the long-discredited urban Bantu councils, the blacks insisted on their right to be *consulted*. For many this was precisely what participation meant. In the Soweto elections of 1977 only 2 percent of the township's thirty wards were actually contested; only 6 percent of the voters actually bothered to turn out. At this stage most blacks wished only to be treated as equal citizens, rather than equal voters, since the vote itself would not necessarily mean very much, if it conceded merely formal rather than real responsibility for their own affairs. Indeed, this had been the main message of the education boycotts of 1976–1977 when black students in the thousands rejected a system of education that they considered inherently discriminatory because it promised to improve only their material condition rather than their political status. Only a third of those who were entitled to return to school actually did so.

If the United States had accepted the right of consultation, indeed the right to be petitioned and listened to, as a minimum counter-social right, there might have been some point in its representations. Until the necessity for an equal dialogue had been accepted, there was very little point in discussing political rights. The obstacles to discussion had to be removed before resorting to constitutional measures, if only to preempt the emergence of unrepresentative political authorities without support within the black community and without legitimacy in the eyes of the world.[31]

Moreover, even if the government had agreed to make political concessions or constitutional changes of a far-reaching nature, they would inevitably have been seen by the white voters as the beginning of a dangerous and irreversible slide to the one man, one vote system. A dialogue, by contrast, need not have necessitated immediate constitutional adjustments at all. The confidence of the white community might have been retained (and with it the government's credibility) by providing each community with an equal voice—not, it must be added, an equal vote, since the latter would have been tantamount to denying the whites an equal voice in their own future.[32] It is quite true, of course, that at Vienna Mondale was careful not to demand a one man, one vote system by name, but only equal participation, a goal that did not rule out at a later stage reserved votes for racial groups, or consensus voting in a national convention. After the meeting, however, the vice-president went on to clarify his remarks by repeating that every citizen should have the right to vote, and that every vote should carry equal weight. Yet if the principle of equal weight ruled out such procedural qualifications as reserved seats and separate cabinets, was this not actually tantamount to the one man, one vote system?

Even though the administration reacted in the strongest way possible to the further erosion of the dialogue that already obtained after the events of October 1977, it cannot be claimed that it acted with any real understanding of what those events really entailed for the other participants in the dialogue: the white community. Moreover, the *Declaration on South Africa*, which Washington drafted shortly afterward, still considered participation—this time with unequivocal reference to majority rule—as the end rather than the means: "Full and equal partnership of all individuals must find its expression through majority rule, which means that all, regardless of race, are entitled to participate in all phases of national life and to join in freely determining the political, economic, and social character of their society."[33]

These aims suffered a serious setback in Vorster's security clampdown in October, which seemed to deny the blacks any chance of participation at all. Under Sections 2 and 6 of the Internal Security Act, eighteen organizations and three publications were banned. Under Section 10(i) forty-seven black leaders were placed in preventative detention. Under Sections 9 and 10 seven whites were issued banning orders. Andrew Young's advice to the black community to boycott white businesses that were known to discriminate against black workers would have brought them into immediate conflict with Section 2(i) of the Terrorism Act, which made any attempt to cripple industry a criminal offense carrying a maximum sentence of five years in detention.[34] Certainly, the Carter administration identified the 1977 clampdown as the most serious setback to black participation seen since the post-Sharpeville repression. As Richard Moose concluded, even more serious than the individual measures was the collective message they carried: that in South Africa there was no prospect of a dialogue between ruler and ruled: "We did not lay a threat to the South African government, we posed a choice. Unfortunately, it chose to ignore it."[35]

Nevertheless, the administration failed to grasp the significance of these events. Although it recognized the importance of a free press and freedom of thought and Warren Christopher insisted that the banning of newspapers and the imprisonment of journalists were among the worst infringements of human rights,[36] it remained largely indifferent to the attack on the *white* press in 1977. It ignored the fact that two of the banned newspapers, *The World* and *Weekend World*, had been white-owned, and that one of the banned journalists had been the white editor of the *Daily Despatch*.

If the rights of a free press were essential, the white press was particularly important since a white regime was being asked to respond to American pressure. During the Security Council debate in November 1977 Andrew Young drew attention to the fact that "the South African government decided not to move in the direction of full political participation by all, but to break new ground by ending *all* political expression by *all* opponents of apartheid . . . black *and* white" (my emphasis).[37] The erosion of freedom of the press in the white community had been in train for fifty years. Since 1927, seventy-five separate laws had been passed that in various degrees had restricted press freedom.

It seems all the more surprising that the Carter administration paid so little attention to the threat to white political participation in this period, since the evidence of it accumulated in a relatively short space of time. The banning of *The World* in November 1977 was the first time that a major commercial newspaper had been forcibly closed since 1897, when the government of Paul Kruger had tried unsuccessfully to silence the Johannesburg *Star*. During Carter's term in office white journalists were forbidden to reveal the death of a citizen in police custody without the written consent of the minister of justice. Nor were they allowed to report attacks on government installations or industrial complexes, despite the fact that whites themselves might be employees of the institutions concerned. The government also set up the Steyn Commission to tighten press regulations even further. Its eventual report was to recommend the immediate closure of newspapers that in its eyes had "no place in journalism," as well as a system of compulsory registration which would have ensured that any journalist found guilty of "improper conduct" would have been struck off the list and prohibited from practicing his profession.[38]

As it was, "self-censorship" for newspapers became increasingly more severe. How far the press could continue to comply with the government's demands without surrendering its freedom altogether was a moot question, which the Carter administration declined to ask. The first serious attack by the government in 1973 had prompted the Newspaper Union to give itself the power to fine its own members. In 1977 it agreed to impose a more rigorous code, promising at the same time to exercise "due care and responsibility" when dealing with subjects that might give rise to racial enmity. In its attempt to appease the government and escape the full severity of legislation, the union gradually surrendered its freedom by installment.

In calling for greater black participation in the political system the State Department seemed largely oblivious to the decreasing participation of the *white* community. Indeed, it remained oblivious to the lessons of recent history. Although a considerable body of legislation had been drawn up in the first ten years of National party rule, its enactment had been delayed while it had been the subject of investigation by commissions of inquiry, many of which did not report for years. The introduction of apartheid, after all, had been accompanied by the denial of a whole series of rights that the white community had previously enjoyed, including the right to marry a person irrespective of color, to assemble with friends, to read publications of their choice, and to live in any part of the country without restriction.[39] In removing these rights the government had acted with great circumspection. Only after Sharpeville had many of these commissions of inquiry finally delivered their reports, confident in the knowledge that the white electorate would accept the denial of its own civil liberties as a necessary price for maintaining white supremacy.[40]

As in the past, however, the government acted with caution. The new commissions of inquiry set up to reform apartheid and extend the government's powers delivered their reports in the knowledge that they would not be enacted until the situation seemed right, until the government was certain that the white voters would be prepared to surrender the democratic institutions that had survived the years of National party rule, and to which the National party continued to point in claiming that South Africa differed markedly in its standards of political behavior from most other African countries.

After 1978 P. W. Botha set up a number of commissions: the Wiehahn Commission on labor relations; the Steyn Commission on the press; the Rieckert Commission on the pass laws, and the Rabbie Commission on security, all of which recommended further restrictions on *white* civil liberties. Throughout the period the United States made no representations and applied no pressure to reverse these developments. Instead, it complained that *black* participation in the system was inadequate; while true, this represented only part of the problem. If America's relationship with Pretoria had been closer, the South African government might have moved more cautiously in denying its own constituents a political voice.

A problem of another kind arose over the administration's understanding of racial discrimination. At Vienna Mondale insisted on the repeal of all discriminatory practices as a preliminary step toward creating a new and more equitable political order. There were many white voters, however—by no means all unqualified advocates of apartheid—who believed that the order should have been reversed. If as Mondale maintained "separateness is inherently discriminatory," was this an indictment of separateness, or a separateness denied the right of separation?

During a parliamentary debate in 1977 Vorster defended the principle that historical discrimination could only be redressed by pursuing separate development. In introducing a new set of constitutional proposals in September he insisted that if a Coloured parliament were to open its schools to white children, a white parliament could forbid them to attend.[41] In these circumstances would it not have been better to have reassured white opinion by recognizing the permissibility of the positive consciousness of a group—its *conscience historique*? Would Washington have been better advised to have abandoned support for the equal protection clause that outlaws discrimination, whatever the grounds, and to have substituted the group disadvantaged principle in its place?[42] Because these questions were never raised, Mondale's call for an end to discrimination was taken to be yet another sign of the administration's endorsement of the one man, one vote system.

Indeed, for a time the United States appeared to be demanding an end to discrimination without offering any guarantee of survival for the white community. Some years earlier Verwoerd had been the first to ask whether survival itself was not a human right, a question that came to be asked quite often in the years that followed.[43] Before leaving for Vienna the South African foreign minister told the press that the Carter administration appeared to be intent on forcing a liberal democratic system on his country in which the minority would be outvoted and destroyed.[44] Later Vorster insisted that his people would never commit racial suicide by conceding black majority rule.[45]

It was in this sphere most of all that Washington lost contact with popular fears, even as it remained fully alive to popular aspirations of the black community: "It may ultimately be that not much that we can do is really going to make any significant impact on the situation, but I still think it is very clear that we identify the U.S. government and the American people with the aspirations of the black majority," Moose reported to Congress.[46] Such principles, while no doubt worthy, were decidedly unhelpful if the main objective of the new administration was to work with the South African government in order to promote peaceful change. On reflection, even the South Africans admitted that if the defense of apartheid ever threatened the survival of the white community, they would have to look at it again "with meticulous honesty."[47] Unfortunately, Carter made little of these second thoughts because he gave so little thought to the outcome.

In seeking to explain this example of blinkered vision, we need look no further than the administration's unwavering belief in the applicability of America's own civil rights past to societies quite unlike the United States. It was fond of asserting that Americans could not divorce themselves from the struggle in South Africa, if only because it raised the question that was central to their own political development: whether people of different races could live together in plural societies such as the United States.[48] But the parallels drawn by Richard Moose and Cyrus Vance were absurdly naive and for the most part irrelevant. When Richard Hofstadter had described the civil rights struggle in the 1950s as a manifestation of "cultural politics" he had referred not to a clash of two bitterly opposed cultures, but to a political contest between two status groups whose historical divisions had been delineated in terms of economic status as well as social position.[49]

In South Africa cultural politics not only differed in degree; it involved considerably more than the struggle of an underprivileged group determined to achieve political power. The Soweto student leader Tebello Montapanyane warned Carter in this period that unless his administration understood the true position it would end up explaining South Africa's problems in terms of color when the real explanation was far more profound.[50] If South Africa's real tragedy, according to the opposition leader van Zyl Slabbert, was that both the white and black communities had come to define each other as the major obstacle to the realization of their own *national* potential, did not this provide some grounds for positive discrimination?[51] The United States itself had after all found it necessary to resort to positive discrimination to eliminate its negative manifestation — to impose equal practices on unequal historical conditions, to combat the worst effects of discrimination that had survived its legal proscription. These were questions that had begun to gain wide currency in Washington toward the end of Carter's period in office, and they set the scene for the Reagan administration's major policy review.

The Sullivan Principles and Sanctions

On another front—that of means rather than ends—the Carter years marked much less of a break with constructive engagement, although this was not to become apparent for some time. In its public censure of Pretoria's October crackdown the administration again conveyed its conviction that rapid and substantial change in the republic's racial policies was not only desirable in itself but necessary for true peace and stability in the region. Yet what effective action was Washington prepared to take, to what lengths was it prepared to go to achieve its stated aims?

Two weeks after the bannings and arrests of October, Young supported a Security Council resolution that called for a mandatory arms embargo, the first of its kind ever applied by the United Nations. This action, like Carter's decision to send a senior State Department official to Steve Biko's funeral and to withdraw (temporarily) the U.S. ambassador, a commercial officer, and a senior naval attaché, was largely symbolic. As Young himself admitted, "All we are trying to do in sanctions is say that we are prepared to help the more creative, conscientious, moderate leadership to develop immediately. . . . An arms embargo is more effective than a total economic blockade because it makes it uncomfortable for South Africans without forcing them to become completely independent."[52]

For the rest of the period the United States sought to move with greater caution. American participation in a multilateral sanctions effort was still out of the question, even though three separate African-sponsored resolutions confronted the American ambassador at the UN that autumn. Zbigniew Brzezinski pointed out that a major constraint which kept American policy from acceding to the logic of the sanctions argument lay in the reliance on Pretoria for assistance in procuring a Rhodesian settlement.[53] Such an assertion, which did not go entirely unchallenged from within the administration, tended to contradict Vance's own position that the United States should seek progress on the Namibian and Rhodesian questions while simultaneously pressing the South African government to concede some ground on apartheid.

The need for South African diplomatic support, however, did not entirely override the more profound goals of Carter's policy. All it did was to further enable the president and his senior advisers to understand that concerns other than human rights might dictate either a less intense pursuit of the policy, or at least a more prudent choice of means adopted on its behalf. Policymakers simply began to recall Warren Christopher's thoughts on blending pragmatism with principle: with limited means they had to settle for achieving what they could. Brzezinski's caveat signified only a change of emphasis, not a change of policy. His position revealed that the United States had decided by the end of 1977 to confront the region's problems seriatim: to bring about an internationally acceptable solution in Rhodesia, and then Namibia, before pressing ahead with the more intractable problem of persuading Pretoria to dismantle apartheid.

Nevertheless, the administration paid a high price for its pragmatic option. Because the United States and its Western allies had always refused to resort to comprehensive economic sanctions against the republic under Chapter VII of the UN Charter, Brzezinski's stance seemed a feeble excuse to most of its African signatories—especially since the pretext for imposing such measures had never been better. Delegates from the African states, as well as from other developing countries, had of course been raising their voices in various international forums for more than a decade on the subject of economic sanctions, but the United States found itself in a greater dilemma than usual. Public interest in the human rights initiative gave rise to increasing internal pressures as well as international demands for more positive actions that would not only express American disapproval but also punish—even effect significant changes in—South African society.

Just two days after the events of 19 October, for example, the congressional Black Caucus issued a twelve-point plan that urged legislative action for economic sanctions, a plan its members later discussed with President Carter.[54] The Black Caucus also sponsored a resolution denouncing the bannings and arrests. Strongly endorsed by Richard Moose, it gathered enough bipartisan support to breeze through the House of Representatives by a significant majority (347 to 54). Although the resolution called for effective measures against South Africa only in general rather than specific terms, and although it met with fairly lukewarm support in the Senate, it was the first resolution critical of apartheid to be adopted by either house.[55]

As the congressional Black Caucus lobbied congressional leaders, university students across the country conducted campus demonstrations for disinvestment. Franklin Williams, a former ambassador to Ghana, and other prominent black leaders formed a Coalition for Human Rights in South Africa, which presented Cyrus Vance with its own eleven-point program, including various proposals for disengagement, an oil embargo, and a requirement that American corporations based in South Africa vigorously apply the Sullivan code.[56]

There was no shortage of suggestions the following year. The spring issue of *Foreign Affairs* contained no fewer than forty-one graduated diplomatic, military, and economic options intended to generate change and minimize violence.[57] One of its authors was a former deputy assistant secretary for African affairs in the Nixon administration. Senator Dick Clark, the chairman of the Senate subcommittee on Africa, produced a report that, while rejecting the "more extreme measures" of disengagement and disinvestment, advocated a threefold strategy to discourage future American investment in the republic. It proposed, first, that the U.S. government should withdraw all facilities which promoted the flow of capital and credit to South Africa, secondly, that it should deny tax credits to any American firm that was found to be responsible for "unfair labor practices," and finally that it should "withhold official endorsement of private interest groups which organize in defense of U.S. corporate investment in South Africa unless they satisfactorily support the corporate guidelines and fair employment principles laid down by the U.S. government."[58]

Notwithstanding this abundance of unsolicited advice, the Carter administration remained excessively tentative on further substantive steps. Indeed, the years 1977 to 1979 might represent a brief interlude between the two phases of constructive engagement as far as means rather than ends are concerned, but for one important fact. In distancing itself from Pretoria the White House revoked many of the positive sanctions that had been adopted by the previous administration, a fact which made it all the more difficult for its own successor to reapply them four years later. Positive sanctions were dismantled, even if negative sanctions were not applied.

One example was that of Eximbank loans. In a memorandum to the congressional Black Caucus in March 1978 Brzezinski reported that the Bank's board of directors had become more circumspect about extending guarantees for long-term loans: "New procedures require that all EXIM approvals give careful consideration to human rights. This fact alone will ensure close scrutiny of new EXIM proposals affecting South Africa."[59] As it happened, the restrictions went much further. The United States had already adopted legislation restricting Eximbank support to South African importers whose conditions of employment met the standards prescribed by Washington. Public Law 95-630 prohibited the Bank from insuring any export commodity that might assist the South African government to maintain white supremacy, as well as any export to the government itself, unless it could be shown to have made some progress toward racial equality. It also prohibited exports of any kind unless the State Department could certify that the purchaser was an equal-opportunities employer. After September 1982 there were no new authorizations for Eximbank financing. As of March 1980 the Bank's exposure in the republic was $132.3 million ($95.5 million in financial guarantees, $13.5 million in commercial bank guarantees, and $23.3 million in short- and medium-term FCIA insurance).[60] This sum, while still large, compared markedly with the $265 million in 1976. It was a significant difference.

The modifications to the arms embargo that Nixon had also sanctioned inevitably fell victim to the 1977 mandatory review. Early in 1978 the administration extended the embargo to include such items as computers and fuel tanks. The Lockheed L-100, which had been previously sold to South Africa, was now catalogued with the C-130 military transport. Even before the November embargo, however, Carter had begun moving toward a total ban on the sale of arms. During congressional hearings in July Maurice Marcuss, the deputy assistant secretary of commerce, had intimated that NSDM 81 was under review.[61] In the end, the White House agreed to prohibit the sale, lease, or charter of all dual-purpose aircraft to the South African government or its agents. The embassy in Pretoria was entrusted with the task of vetting all future buyers. For their part, the latter had to certify that the aircraft in question would not be used in paramilitary activities, and that similar certification would be obtained from any subsequent purchaser in the event of resale. The embassy was given the job of monitoring these measures by random spot checks.[62]

These measures were significant only for the options they denied the Reagan administration a few years later. In themselves, they achieved remarkably little. Even the repeal of NSDM 81 was not as great a blow as Washington had imagined. ARMSCOR acknowledged that although it had been forced on occasions to pay more for American equipment, sometimes as much as twice the market price, American arms still managed to slip through the embargo quite apart from the fact that South Africa had become much less dependent on the United States as a supplier.

By 1979 none of this seemed to matter. By then the postwar goal of containing the Soviet Union had already reemerged as a priority, particularly on the African continent. In its first two years in office the Carter administration had cultivated a liberal tone and image, claiming that revolutionary transformations in the Third World should no longer be perceived as necessarily originating in the Kremlin. In his commencement address at the University of Notre Dame, Carter had vigorously declared, "We are now free of that inordinate fear of communism which once led us to embrace any dictator who joined us in that fear."[63] Nevertheless, as that fear reaffirmed itself, Washington moved increasingly toward a cold war stance. For Brzezinski, Soviet-Cuban support for Ethiopia in the conflict with neighboring Somalia, coming as it did in the wake of similar involvement in the Angolan civil war, suggested an ominous pattern.

Whether or not the Soviet leadership harbored ambitions to seek and exploit further opportunities for influence in Southern Africa, the United States acted as if those ambitions were undeniable, and real. It was a perception that enhanced its need to work more closely with South Africa in Rhodesia and Namibia. Conveniently, it found signs of progress in South Africa itself. Thus Brzezinski announced his discovery that "political change may be beginning to occur within South Africa," a fact that seemed to confirm him in his suspicion that the imposition of sanctions would be hasty, and certainly foolhardy.[64] Even the more liberal Cyrus Vance expressed the hope that "the beginning of basic progress will soon be seen."[65]

In addition to these regional and global restrictions on actions that would have effectively backed up the strident anti-apartheid rhetoric of Carter's first two years, some observers began to detect an even greater internal constraint: the belief that American corporations might serve as a useful political force for change instead of a bulwark for the status quo.[66] If the external constraints prompted American caution, this internal one marked a persistence of wishful thinking.

Liberal and conservative administrations since Eisenhower had adhered to the neutral policy of neither encouraging nor discouraging investment and trade. Carter merely steered the same course. The president's faith in economic engagement was not only demonstrated by his campaign remark to the *Financial Mail* that "economic development, investment commitment, and economic leverage . . . seems to me the only way to achieve racial justice,"[67] it was also affirmed when his administration spurned the recommendations of two interest groups that had played an important role in the presidential election. In January 1978 the NAACP board urged the withdrawal of American business from South Africa, and the following month the AFL-CIO executive council came out in support of the same position.[68]

Together with Andrew Young, however, Carter would continue to maintain that enlightened capitalism would bring interracial harmony and contribute to the eventual demise of apartheid in the same way that it had allegedly undermined entrenched racism in the American South.[69] Accordingly, Washington continued to encourage "the application of progressive employment practices" by American companies and committed its full support to the Sullivan code.[70] Significantly, however, it refused to make the code mandatory and in 1980 refused to tie Eximbank credits to formal observance of the main Sullivan principles.

At the end of the day, therefore, the administration had little to show for its endeavors. It could not even claim any credit for the reform program on which the South African government embarked, first hesitatingly and then with growing assurance in 1978; or for its decision—in the words of an editorial in the *Rand Daily Mail*— "to retreat into the future." This should have been a matter for concern among the policymakers in Washington. Precisely because the reform program was a retreat and not an advance, the United States needed to tread warily. Retreats, after all, often end in rearguard stands when one side presses the other too closely. For this reason the West needed to ensure that the whites were not provided with an excuse to mount a final, if futile, last stand.

8 The Reagan Administration and
Constructive Engagement, 1981–1985

When the Reagan administration once again took up constructive engagement, it was fitting that the move should have been welcomed by one of its original authors, Ken Owen. Writing in the immediate aftermath of the Carter years, Owen hailed the new policy as an example of "creative involvement" offering South Africa an opportunity it had ignored in the early 1970s and that it could not afford to ignore again.[1]

The author of the new attempt, Chester Crocker, had also been associated with the Nixon administration ten years earlier, as a staff officer on the NSC responsible for the coordination of all policy studies on Africa and the Indian Ocean. As assistant secretary for African affairs he brought with him a new understanding of what Kissinger and Morris had tried to achieve, and unlike them an unrivaled knowledge of the South African political scene, gained most recently as director of the Africa Studies Program at Georgetown University's Center for Strategic and International Studies.

Like Morris, Crocker took exception to the previous administration's abrasive rhetoric, its radical and allegedly unrealistic demands for a speedy transfer of power, and its many attempts, often half-hearted, to disassociate itself from the regime in Pretoria. Inevitably, he maintained, the South Africans had concluded that the United States had no real intention of assuming any responsibility for what happened.[2] Crocker himself had no qualms about the future and no hesitation in advocating purposeful American intervention:

> The many changes occurring in South Africa are inherently ambiguous. Nonetheless, it should be possible, at least, to agree

that black politics are characterized by an increasingly confident experimentation with various strategies for challenging white control while white politics are demonstrating a degree of fluidity and pragmatism that is without precedent in the past generation. The combination does not make meaningful evolutionary change certain, but it does make it possible for the first time in decades.[3]

Clearly, Crocker believed that it was in America's interest to foster and support reform and to recognize that in its absence the threat to American interests would inevitably gather momentum. The task, while difficult, was not impossible. Indeed, Crocker maintained that there was every reason to hope that it might meet with much greater success than it had in 1970.

Crocker's own policy of constructive engagement was based on three central premises, all of which touched upon South Africa's relationship with the outside world, and particularly the United States. The first was that evolutionary change was still more probable than revolutionary cataclysm, and that America could contribute to the first in a way that it could not to the second. Even if this were not the case, the option of disengaging hardly existed, except in the strictly limited sense of disassociating Washington from the policies of the Botha government. The alternative did exist: that of working with, rather than against, the government. In the process, of course, the Reagan administration would have to ensure that engagement did not become accommodation.

Second, the changes that the United States hoped would come about, preferably through government initiative rather than in response to the initiatives of others, were unlikely to obtain without some degree of outside intervention. External events and policies had always played a major role in South African history, often a significant one. This was likely to be the case more than ever as power began to ebb from the government into the hands of the non-white community. From that analysis it was but a short step to conclude that "what is needed is a clear Western readiness to recognize and support positive movement and engage credibly in addressing a complex political agenda."[4]

Crocker's third contention was that significant changes had already taken place for which the Botha government had received little international credit and to which the West had made little if any contribution. By turning its back on the internal dynamics of reform, Washington had recently forfeited what little influence it had once enjoyed. Earlier Crocker had developed this point by criticizing the Carter administration for profound tactical confusion, for giving every appearance of being uncertain in its own mind whether it wanted South Africa to find its own solutions or wanted to force South Africa to accept solutions of America's choosing—for being uncertain, in the final analysis, whether it wanted the South African problem to be internationalized or not.[5]

Given that the main objective of American policy was not to provoke South Africa into retreating into the *laager* but to help it find a way to break out, how could this best be done? Effective coercion was unrealistic. Effective direction even more so. Crocker went some way toward providing an answer by criticizing the Carter administration for focusing on the wrong issue—the ultimate goal, rather than the process of getting there. Probably change would only arise from hundreds of decisions, many drawn-out negotiations, and even a combination of violent and nonviolent action. The United States certainly did have a role, possibly a significant one, but it would deal itself out of the game if it refused to address the question of short-term or medium-term goals, if it refused to tarry "at the way stations along the road to majority rule."

Crocker's main message was that American policy urgently needed to transcend the fallacies and accepted opinions of the Carter years. A State Department committed to the same goals would have to accept that it could not accelerate the process of decay, or hasten apartheid's end; dying political systems often prove more resilient than originally imagined. At the same time it would be unrealistic to expect the system to collapse or change under the engine of economic development. Unlike Carter, with his fondness for enlightened capitalism, Crocker was honest enough to admit that although the transformation of apartheid through economic pressure was an attractive proposition, it also offered a dangerous form of escapism. It relieved the West of its responsibilities; worse than that, it could not be demonstrably proved. The thesis was not self-evident, though it might well be true.

In recommending constructive engagement, Crocker recognized in a way that the Nixon administration had not, that the United States would have to exert itself, to invest in change, to accept the political costs of cooperating with the South African government, and to be seen doing so in the full glare of publicity. Indeed, the pressure was unlikely to prove constructive unless it was accompanied by a clear readiness on the part of all Western governments to support reforms that had already been made: "Given the ferment within the country, change is unlikely to be constructive unless it is accompanied by a clear Western readiness to support positive steps; and the credibility of that support is as important as the credibility of the pressures applied."[6]

It says much for Crocker's honesty of purpose that he never tried to disguise the difficulty of the task. He even recognized that in some ways constructive engagement would be more difficult to implement in the early 1980s than ever before. The problem of fostering nonviolent change in any society was complex. As the bargaining positions of the two communities became more equalized over time, the distinction between basic change and uncontrolled upheaval might become much narrower, leaving even less room for maneuver for outside powers. At this juncture the timetables of the black nationalists might diverge considerably from that of the United States. In these circumstances the latter might find itself legitimizing by premature recognition movements that were denied such legitimacy in their own country. It could be argued, for example, that under Nixon the State Department had made too much of the homeland leaders; under Carter, too much of the Black Consciousness Movement. If such misunderstandings were to be avoided in the future, Washington would have to develop a much keener appreciation of the dynamics of internal change.[7]

Crocker also took issue with the Nixon administration's approach to constructive engagement on another count. He believed that the sources of Western pressure, as well as the resources at its disposal, were negligible. For that reason it was particularly important that the latter should not be wasted in largely symbolic gestures, for the most part triggered by transient domestic moods or ephemeral events. If the executive branch or Congress ever allowed domestic considerations to determine American policy, then the United States itself would become largely irrelevant to the future of South Africa.

The scope of external influence, of course, was determined not only by the principles on which the United States acted but also the ends to which it worked. From the strictly practical point of view,

Crocker had no doubt that it was worthwhile engaging in the contentious business of defining the political agenda. He was confirmed in this opinion by Botha's decision to press ahead with a policy of reform, a policy that he insisted could be supported with a clear conscience. For the first time in years the National party seemed to have produced a leadership that was prepared to arrest the slow decline into revolution, to contain the forces in its own ranks who wished to garrison the state against enemies internal and external alike, and to evolve a coherent and internally consistent domestic program to replace the discredited aspirations of the past.

From the outset Crocker hoped to establish links so close that Pretoria would have no objection to pressing ahead with its program. But he also recognized that such an understanding could not become the sheet anchor of American policy without a clear willingness on the part of the prime minister to press ahead more quickly than planned. In the figure of P. W. Botha, Crocker believed that he had found a leader who was committed to just such an approach if he were to be backed by the powers in the West. He was reluctant to condemn the regime untried; experience was to show that he may have been a little too trusting.

In the early years, however, Crocker remained firmly tied to the view that it would be grossly irresponsible of the West to allow the future direction of the reform program to be determined exclusively by the South Africans themselves or, more to the point, to leave the government hostage to its own back-bench MPs. If the government were able to look for support from outside, its hand might be strengthened considerably.

Such support, of course, meant a break with the secrecy and covert diplomacy of the Nixon years and a radical departure from the old attempts to mislead Congress and ignore public opinion. In calling for an open approach to constructive engagement Crocker was profoundly aware of the severe penalties Nixon had eventually incurred for what he termed "the executive hijacking" of policy. As he noted somewhat ruefully before coming into office, "Communication 'for the record' at home and abroad is a well-developed art form in U.S.–South Africa policy. Communication in the sense of actually transmitting ideas and signals about change is not."[8]

Taken separately or in the round, these ideas placed the assistant secretary well ahead of most of his predecessors. Obviously, the new administration was bound to be receptive to his ideas, presumably having less inducement to fight for opportunities when they could be secured at less cost, economically and politically, by persuasion rather than pressure. Yet his ideas were also attractive intellectually after the sterile years of public dispute that had gone before. It was therefore all the more unfortunate that as a political strategy constructive engagement was probably already an anachronism, fashioned for another age, irrelevant to Crocker's own. Considering the narrow margin of influence at his disposal and the unremitting pressures from his more conservative colleagues to enlist South African support in the second cold war, his new departures would probably have failed, even had this not been the case.

The Reagan Administration and South Africa, 1981–1985

After 1981 constructive engagement was no longer pursued out of the public gaze, or taken up by the NSC in the face of State Department opposition. This time it was adopted as official policy by the Africa Bureau itself, packaged for public consumption and sold publicly to Congress. It was also debated at the highest levels of the administration. In contrast to the 1970s, there were also open and extensive discussions with the South Africans themselves. Both sides were to work closely in the months that followed and, for the most part, in the open. Secrecy, even if it had been desirable, was no longer possible. The new administration was prepared to talk to the South Africans as often as necessary. Crocker had four meetings with Brand Fourie, the director general of the South African Ministry of Foreign Affairs before his appointment to the Washington embassy. Even President Reagan met with Prime Minister Botha within months of his own inauguration.

True to his first principles, however, Crocker went out of his way to signal to Pretoria that the United States had no intention of allowing constructive engagement to degenerate into accommodation or benign indifference. Although Reagan described South Africa as "a country that is strategically essential to the Free World" and mused over its friendship in the Korean and Second World wars, and Jeane Kirkpatrick, his outspoken ambassador at the United Nations complained that it had become "the victim of double standards," the United

States had no compunction about criticizing apartheid in the most unequivocal terms. Mrs. Kirkpatrick's deputy Kenneth Adelman described South Africa as pursuing the only system in the world "of denying its citizens natural rights which is openly and legally based on racism," a fact which bestowed upon apartheid "special distinction as the world's most condemned system."[9]

Crocker's own outspoken condemnation of apartheid earned him the abiding dislike of Senator Jesse Helms, who succeeded in blocking his nomination as assistant secretary of state for nine months. During his first visit to South Africa, the prime minister refused to see him. Two months later when he returned to the republic, this time as a member of a delegation headed by the deputy secretary of state, William Clark, an attempt was made to exclude him from at least some of the talks.

However, the conflicting statements that emanated from the administration at once encouraged the South Africans to hope for a substantial improvement in relations with Washington, while at the same time dampening their hopes. Crocker did not provide the full text of the terms of constructive engagement until a speech to the American Legion at Honolulu on 29 August 1981. On this occasion he pleased Pretoria by insisting that it would not serve U.S. interests to disengage from the region any more than it would to play down the seriousness of the situation. He made up a lot of lost diplomatic ground simply by refusing to prejudge the issue: "The Reagan administration recognizes that the future of Southern Africa has not yet been written. It would be an act of political irresponsibility and moral cowardice to conduct ourselves as though it had."[10] On the other hand, behind the scenes he was especially anxious to make clear that there could be no question of a close working relationship between the two countries until Pretoria had moved much farther along the road to political reform. As the newly appointed U.S. ambassador told a Senate committee the following spring, the future relations between the two states would depend largely "on the extent to which the policy of constructive engagement produces positive, measurable results."[11]

The South Africans were made aware of these conditions during a series of meetings between Pik Botha and Secretary of State Alexander Haig, which took place in May 1981. Several State Department briefing papers which were leaked shortly afterward revealed that the administration was anxious to convert South Africa from an international outcast into an important regional actor, a potential ally in America's never-ending attempt to contain Soviet expansionism. One of the most important papers, written by Crocker himself, made clear that "although we may continue to differ on apartheid and cannot condone a system of institutionalized racial differentiation, we *can* cooperate with a society undergoing constructive change."[12] The point of departure, therefore, for any major reappraisal of South Africa's position would have to be an explicit commitment to reform. The Reagan administration clearly believed three years into the reform program that this lesson had already been accepted by Botha, and the need to reform by all but his most intractable supporters. The National party, it seemed, had finally ceased to be led from behind in the name of consensus politics within the Afrikaner *volk* and was now being led from the front by an uncompromising advocate of change.

The essence of the problem for South Africa's leaders, by contrast, was not that they faced more political problems than at any other time in the past thirty years, but that the nature of these problems was far less susceptible to solution in at least two important respects. First, economic growth had begun to produce increasing demand for skilled labor faster than the market could meet it, and second the system could no longer solve the dilemma by the traditional means: restricting the influx of unskilled labor from the native reserves. What South Africa needed most was intensive not extensive sources of growth—high-quality labor and high productivity, neither of which could be met by the existing white labor pool. To increase the number of skilled black workers demanded profound political reforms, if the country was to escape the classical dilemma of frustrated rising expectations. The question remained: Could a state that was developing less quickly than at any other time in its postwar history afford them? Could the government forge new political constituencies loyal to the prevailing political order?

In the past, challenges to the political order had been met successfully by breaking up industrial strikes, arresting political leaders, even repatriating native laborers to their designated homelands. By establishing a coercive labor market in a country in which black workers had little or no political representation, the government had effectively stifled all opposition. For Vorster's successors these measures were no longer adequate, or in some cases even possible. For them the main threat to political stability came from an upwardly mobile black middle class that could not be co-opted and denied political representation indefinitely. It was in response to this problem that Botha had embarked upon what came to be known, perhaps euphemistically, as the reform program, for it became apparent quite early on that it involved really little more than the modernization of the existing apartheid system.

On every front it was clear that apartheid had been modernized, not abandoned. New legislation was passed that enabled the government—in principle at least, less often in practice—to co-opt a small, skilled section of the black work force, while denying the majority economic parity or social equality. By conceding economic privileges and security of residence to a minority, the government hoped to adapt and survive without having to abandon in the attempt any of the central tenets of separate development.

On the economic front, for example, it set out in 1978 with the clear intention of giving skilled laborers the right to form trade unions, but in such a way that their activities were highly circumscribed. The Wiehahn Commission, which was set up to look into the issue, was charged with responsibility for ensuring that "as many as possible of the worthy and effectively functioning institutions and practices of present system should be retained, and if need be, adapted, modernised, and brought into line with the needs of the day." In translating Wiehahn's recommendations into law, the government set out with the clear intention of enfranchising a minority of blacks by disenfranchising the rest, including some who had been unofficially represented for years, such as agricultural workers and miners. Its apparent tolerance of trade union activity may have been as unreal as many of its other concessions, but it was clearly consistent with the principle of divide and rule. To avoid confusion on this point, the commission actually recommended that the registrar, when deciding whether to allow a union to register or not, should not allow himself to be influenced by criteria such as majority representation.

On the social front, the Rickert Commission, the second to be set up by the government, was asked to review the influx control system that regulated the movement of black workers to and from the cities. Once again the government's commitment to reform was more apparent than real. Starting from the premise that the controlled move-

ment of population and controlled employment were the two principal pillars of sound community development, the commission
recommended the removal of restrictions on 1.5 million out of the
19 million urban blacks who enjoyed permanent status of residents.
Since 1945 most blacks had been banned from living in any urban
area unless they had been born there or had worked for more than ten
years for one employer, or for different employers for more than fifteen.

Finally, on the political front the government set out to accomplish two ends—first, to reach accommodation with the Coloureds
and Indians; second, to press ahead with the independence of the
homelands in the hope that the blacks could be discriminated against
on the basis of nationality rather than race. On neither count did it
meet with much success. More blacks continued to live in the
"white" cities than ever before. Many had neither roots nor relations
in the homelands. Fifty-seven percent had not even been born there.
The homelands themselves were by no manner of description economically viable, except for Bophuthatswana. The land purchased
under the terms of the 1936 Native Settlement Act had not even
been successfully transferred to the homeland authorities. Urging
that the entire policy be abandoned, the Bureau of Economic Research
recalled that twenty years earlier the Tomlinson Commission had
proposed a drastic reallocation of land only to have its recommendations rejected out of hand.

The only homeland which opted for independence in the period
1978–1981, the Ciskei, was a veritable postage stamp state with 50
percent of its population unemployed and 40 percent of its rural
population landless and dependent on imports for half its food—not
the most convincing criteria for statehood even in an African context.
The faster the government pressed ahead with the program, the more
it came up against its anomalies and limitations. Only by constantly
reformulating it could it be kept afloat.

One such life-saving device was Botha's 1979 scheme for a constellation of states, an idea that abandoned the old notion that the
border between white South Africa and the homelands should be
politically and economically indivisible. Plans were drawn up to give
the homelands extraterritorial jurisdiction over, and access to, the
urban Bantu councils and other semi-elected bodies that were responsible for regulating the lives of their own "nationals" in South Africa
proper, to divide the whole country into development regions admin-

istered by regional economic authorities whose membership would be made up of representatives of the homeland governments and the central government in Pretoria. "We have learned from experience," the prime minister told party supporters in November 1980, "that the scope for decentralisation of economic activity . . . is limited. To ignore the high degree of economic interdependence throughout South Africa would be foolish."[13] For many whites this was a price worth paying; for most blacks it was not worth the price of dividing their own community. It was they, not the whites, who would have to pay the bill. The government, after all, was merely shuffling the cards in the constitutional pack.

After 1977 South Africa was also engaged in a process of reshaping the political structures of apartheid in order to strengthen them in the face of mounting resistance. Specifically, the first three years of the Reagan administration saw the establishment of a new parliament, with separate white, Coloured, and Indian houses under a powerful state president and the unfolding of plans for the restructuring of government on strict apartheid lines and under strong central control.

The genesis of the new parliament went back to the proposals of a cabinet committee set up and chaired in the year of Soweto by the defense minister, P. W. Botha. Adopted by the National party in 1977, it went before Parliament in 1979, only to be withdrawn in the face of intense black opposition. Referred to the Schlebusch Commission, it was taken up the following year by the President's Council, a nominated advisory body of sixty people drawn from the white, Indian, and Coloured communities. The council effectively became the vehicle for the government's plans, presenting a report in 1982 that was much the same as the original cabinet committee proposal. The South African Constitution Act followed the next year, with the support of the Coloured Labour party and subsequently the majority party in the South African Indian Council. There were only two references in the Constitution Act to the African majority of the country: one stated that "the control and administration of black affairs" rested with the state president; the other specified that black affairs were a matter of common concern to all three houses of Parliament.

The new dispensation ranged far in scope. Its main features were a tricameral parliament with white, Coloured, and Indian chambers, each with exclusive authority to legislate on its own affairs; an executive president elected by a college of fifty white, twenty-five Coloured, and thirteen Indian members of Parliament; a mixed cabinet; joint standing committees composed of members of the three chambers; and a reconstituted President's Council to which deadlocked legislation would be referred.

Even more important than the new structure was the envisaged new political style. The government's main purpose seemed to be to break with the confrontation model of the Westminster system—to move away from institutionalized opposition to the executive, toward consultation, compromise, and accommodation. Negotiations in the standing tricameral committees on finance, justice, and foreign affairs were to be all-important, with the President's Council playing an advisory, mediating role.

In practice, however, even the power-sharing concept was more apparent than real. The power given to the three parliaments was so limited that the two nonwhite chambers were not able to repeal or amend the three laws that the nonwhite communities most abominated: the Race Classification Act, which rendered them second-class citizens; the Group Areas Act, which denied them the right to own and occupy property in white areas; and the Separate Amenities Act, which provided for the continued segregation of certain public facilities. Many Indian and Coloured leaders opposed the power-sharing scheme, not because the blacks were excluded from it but because they saw no sign that it would bring about any fundamental change in their own situation. The Reagan administration, by comparison, justified its support by claiming that there was a "hidden agenda" which when the time was right would include the 10 million urban blacks in the same way. Despite the fact that the government's plans made no overt provision for black representation, Crocker insisted that it would be foolish "to expect South Africa's would-be reformers to announce their game plan and their bottom line to the world at large."[14]

What the government itself had in mind was not a fourth chamber but an increase in local authority for townships such as Soweto and a stronger role for black local officials. That is all that the minister in charge of black affairs, Piet Kornhof, probably meant when he admitted that to pretend that the urban blacks did not exist amounted to "irresponsible and dangerous escapism." In these circumstances Washington might have asked itself whether the new constitutional dispensation opened up new options for dealing with the blacks, or actually limited them by finally closing off the path to participation in central government. Any upgrading of black powers in the localities would represent not a move toward direct representation but a move away from it. Here too neoapartheid meant just what it said—an adaption of the existing system, not a radical break with the past.

The United States found itself, therefore, committed to supporting a highly questionable program. Despite the need for a forward-looking debate in South Africa, the attitude of the government continued to be forged in the context of white supremacy. Botha's mind was not open to new possibilities, only tactical compromises. If public discussion of South Africa's future had intensified, the clarity of the debate had not improved.

Even if this had not been the case, there were three fundamental problems about America's support for the reforms of the period. The first and most worrying of these was that it had begun to produce sustained opposition within the civil service. Crucial decisions began to be delayed on the excuse that existing legislation had to be amended or repealed before new laws could be enacted. Other policies were legislated for, but were implemented only with difficulty. An aged and privileged elite proved to be too limited in numbers to carry out all the new policies, yet large enough to bar the path to black recruitment. Clientism and patronage pervaded the entire administration from the ministries to the courts of law. In short, it became increasingly difficult for the government to press ahead with the reform program, a problem that might have prompted Washington to question its open-ended commitment to government-initiated reform.

The main reason it did not was that the Reagan administration rapidly became enamored of the idea of reform by government fiat. For different reasons and with differing degrees of enthusiasm, many Americans had begun to express interest in the possibilities of centrally managed change. The idea of reform by diktat as an intellectual proposition exercized undoubted fascination for government and nongovernment spectators alike.

Models of authoritarian reform clearly fitted South Africa at the time more closely than they had in the period of the Nixon administration, when the survival of apartheid was rarely, if ever, a matter for discussion. In 1981 no less a scholar than Samuel Huntington, who had done much to shape American attitudes to Third World political developments in the 1960s, argued that in a multiethnic society is was "not inconceivable that narrowing the scope of political participation may be indispensable to eventually broadening that participation. The route from a limited uniracial democracy to a broader multiracial democracy could run through some form of autocracy."[15] Reforms conceded under pressure, he concluded, would only weaken the government, reduce its authority, and give rise to more extreme demands for power-sharing. If conceded too early, they might provoke a white counterrevolutionary backlash that might only with difficulty be contained.

Huntington's thesis aroused enormous interest in South Africa, in part because it already appeared that the government had begun to move along the path he had suggested. On coming to power, Botha had transformed the prime minister's office from a cabinet secretariat into a major planning body. After 1978 the State Security Council, instead of meeting several times every year, began to meet once a fortnight. The actual exercise of power became the responsibility not of elected representatives but of government nominees, both in the President's Council, which replaced the elected Senate, and the nominated bodies, which took the place of the provisional and divisional councils. Against this background, it was not surprising that the proponents of the new constitution began to talk of a "Gaullist option"—an authoritarian system dominated by a strong executive, powerful enough to carry the reform program over the most determined opposition from conservative-minded backbenchers.

At the same time the South Africans found in the Reagan administration a government in the West sympathetic to the concept of authoritarian reform. This was one reason why the administration remained relatively oblivious to the slow progress of the reform program, which should have raised doubts quite early on whether the government would ever be able to implement its major legislation. For the most part a predominantly Afrikaner bureaucracy whose numbers rose to 900,000 in this period and that accounted for no less than two-fifths of all government expenditure showed no inclination to act with speed; indeed, many government departments remained strikingly unresponsive to ministerial direction.

Stated simply, civil servants, 80 percent of whom were Afrikaners, many with twenty years or more in government service, could not be dismissed except on specified grounds and in accordance with a set of procedures in which they were entitled to full legal representation. The civil service may have been a creation of the apartheid state, but it was not its creature. In the opinion of Marinus Wiechers, the legal advisor to the government of Bophuthatswana, it had become virtually impossible for politicians to break through the bureaucratic barriers they themselves had created: "We have created a vast 'plural administration' to prove the fact that we are a plural society. In the long run this administration which should have been the servant of society has become its master."[16] Because every reform required the amendment of existing legislation and the enactment of new laws, the government delivered itself into the hands of its own bureaucrats. The legislation drafted to implement the proposals of the Rieckert Commission was a case in point. It required the repeal of no less than sixty-two statutes and comprised three separate bills. The Ministry of Cooperation and Development, which was responsible for the new legislation, drafted a bill that so conflicted with the government's intentions that it had to be withdrawn not once, but on three separate occasions when it came before Parliament. Finally, in an attempt to flush out the saboteurs, the prime minister ordered the department to reduce its staff. Unfortunately, this did not save the bills in question, two of which were referred back to a parliamentary commission under the minister of constitutional development. Nor did it save the career of the minister who lost his job.

Deliberate obstructionism, however, explains only half the story. Bureaucratic dissatisfaction reflected a more general crisis of morale. The existing 20 percent staff shortages could never be made good without black recruitment. As early as December 1981 Stephanus Botha, the minister of manpower utilization, warned of a complete breakdown if the situation were not remedied soon. The police force was understaffed by five thousand men. The Department of Justice found itself so short-staffed that the backlog of cases resulted in extended periods in detention—in some cases eight months in duration. High prosecution rates put a serious strain on the judicial system. In Pretoria only 57 percent of prosecution posts were actually filled, a serious problem in a country where 26 percent of all adult white labor was in the public service, the highest concentration of state employees outside the communist world.

Given the strains under which the existing system labored, the idea of extending it looked somewhat unconvincing, unless of course the government intended to recruit nonwhites, a point on which it could expect from the civil service unqualified opposition. The idea of employing black officials to push through reforms in the face of white, not to mention black, opposition defied imagination and suspended belief in a state where black policemen were not even allowed to issue parking tickets to white motorists. On this point, if on nothing else, the conservative Andries Treurnicht was undoubtedly right: "If one's standpoint is one of division or separation of power . . . then it goes without saying that this must be reflected in one's administration."[17]

Nor could the government be sure that the police would cooperate in implementing the reform program. Although police inquiries into pass law offenses had been significantly reduced, the reduction, far from demonstrating that the laws had been relaxed, revealed that they had been enforced at places of employment, if no longer on the streets. With police connivance, thousands of aid centers continued to process cases without benefit of a court hearing. The fact that in the space of one year alone (1982) all but 4,763 out of a total of 13,027 people processed in Pretoria were subsequently "endorsed out" to their respective homelands prompted one state prosecutor to resign in protest at police behavior.

Some months later a sixty-page report submitted to the attorney general reported that far from increasing labor mobility as originally intended, the aid centers had chosen to enforce the pass laws more ruthlessly than ever. On average, one in five blacks were repatriated to the homelands, often following cases that were conducted without judges' rules that allowed the accused to be silent under police interrogation. Its patience strained, the Johannesburg Chamber of Commerce was eventually prompted by the arbitrary behavior of the police to accuse them of failing to carry out the amendments to the pass laws recommended by the Rieckert Commission. Between 1982 and 1983 the police detained for interrogation twenty or so trade union leaders without apparent ministerial approval. Against none could they obtain a single conviction.[18]

Therefore, even if the government could preempt a white backlash, the case for authoritarian reform looked increasingly unconvincing. For far too long the discussion of the reform program had been based on a set of assumptions that were beginning to look demonstrably transparent. Those who exercised power, it had been argued, not only made policy but also carried it out. Often it might be formulated ineptly, or the government might run up against the hard facts of political life, but for good or ill it was assumed to be the main force influencing political change. These assumptions now looked decidedly suspect. In evaluating the future of the reform program, the Reagan administration should also have looked at the conflicts within government and between the executive and civil service at the level at which policy was actually implemented. The size and complexity of the administration and the tangle of conflicting interests it contained made the picture of an all-powerful government far removed from reality. Obstruction and confusion seemed to be the prevailing code of practice. The government's opponents had not lost the will to resist; they had merely been driven underground, where they were far harder to deal with and far more difficult to identify.

That the reform program should have met with the support of the Reagan administration was not in the circumstances very surprising. One of Henry Kissinger's favorite, if least profound, aphorisms was that there exist two kinds of realists—those who use facts and those who create them, the latter having a decisive advantage in the ceaseless battle to keep ahead of events.[19] Like Kissinger, Crocker imagined that a few initiatives taken in time might help the whites to come to terms with black nationalism and that in response to them the blacks would be forced to think of the future in less apocalyptic terms. He was not alone in imagining that South Africa faced a revolutionary future only because those initiatives had not been taken, that the government had delayed because it had not felt confident in the support of its own followers, and that the parliamentary system had left it with the will but not the power to act in time.

Perhaps the real problem, however, was that successive U.S. administrations should still have continued to believe this a plausible explanation of the predicament in which the government of South Africa found itself in 1981. In attempting to press ahead with the reform program Botha eventually discovered that government initiatives do not themselves always solve problems, that blueprints and grand strategies, however imaginative, often accomplish much less than first imagined, that far from action creating its own reality, reality frequently makes nonsense of the most far-reaching actions.

In its response to Botha's reforms the Reagan administration confronted a second problem, almost as intractable and profound as the first. Throughout this period Crocker was fully alive to the danger of pressing the South Africans to move faster than they were already doing, whatever criticism might have emanated from Washington about the disappointingly slow pace of reform. The erosion of support on the far right was taken very seriously, especially after the breakaway of seventeen Nationalist MPs under the leadership of the redoubtable Andries Treurnicht. As the new Conservative party began to make common cause with the Herstigte Nasionale party (HNP), and such political mavericks as John Vorster and Connie Mulder (both disgraced by the Information Ministry scandal), the threat of a split in Afrikanerdom became very real, a split that presented both an opportunity and a challenge: a challenge to the prime minister's authority and an opportunity to carve out a new base of support for the government among traditionally more liberal English-speaking voters.

For much of the time Crocker was far more preoccupied with the challenge than he was with the opportunities it presented, until it had become clear that the creation of the Conservative party marked more of a continuing fissure than a clean break, a fissure which was unlikely in the final analysis to undermine government support within Afrikaner circles.

This was not always the case. For several years it seemed that the prime minister had failed in his attempt to hold together the *verligt* and *verkrampte* wings of the party and in so doing had reopened the recurrent nightmare among Afrikaner leaders of presiding over a split in the National party of the kind that had been followed throughout South Africa's history by a radical shift to the right. Crocker, no less than Botha, was haunted by memories of the Hertzog/Botha split of 1914, the Malan/Hertzog breakaway in 1933, the rift between Smuts and Hertzog in 1939, and more recently still, the expulsion of the extreme right wing under Hertzog's son in 1969.

This was a development both governments wished to avoid. A repolarization of politics might indeed give Botha and his cabinet support from the English-speaking community and broaden the political base of the National party, creating thereby a more conventional political movement, structured along class rather than ethnic lines. But it might also deny the party the cohesion that had made it virtually unbeatable at the polls for thirty years and that in principle at least should have made it strong enough to dismantle apartheid by executive fiat with the same single-mindedness of purpose it had shown when introducing the system in the 1950s.

To Crocker the threat of a split in Afrikanerdom was not a matter to be taken lightly. In its existing form it represented a permanent parting of the ways between the reformist and reactionary wings, which had been held together previously simply by the overriding need to remain in power and preserve the unity of the *volk*. Until 1983 the question remained whether the threatened split would inspire Botha to press ahead even more decisively or frighten him into the same political paralysis that had afflicted Vorster in his last years in power, and accordingly deal the government out of the game as the initiator of change. Perhaps the United States had reason for concern in the early days of the new administration, if only because the August–October 1981 parliamentary session produced no legislative programs at all.

In any event the government did not lose its confidence but stood firm. In a referendum on the new constitutional dispensation in November 1983, Botha won an overwhelming two to one vote in favor of the proposed changes, a much larger margin than expected. In voting against Treurnicht and his supporters with their warnings of a "hidden agenda" for blacks and their opposition to power-sharing in any form, the white electorate also voted, of course, for an executive presidency through which a future government could challenge the power of the provincial party caucuses by devaluing the currency of the parliamentary system, and so bypassing the greatest obstacle to the reform program: an entrenched and unrepresentative majority in Parliament.

Not surprisingly, Washington reacted positively to the referendum result, pronouncing it a mandate for the government to move "decisively" along the road it was traveling.[20] Crocker himself welcomed the vote as "a new milestone in the modern history of white South Africa" which had revealed that "a clear majority of white South African voters had decided to take a step which opens the way to constructive evolutionary change."[21] Later, after admitting that it was impossible to predict where the government's policies might lead, he continued to insist that the referendum result had clearly revealed a new consensus in South Africa, a new understanding that it was no longer possible to "just toughen it out" with traditional apartheid policies.[22] The referendum came none too soon, for it was taken to be final confirmation that the government could still lead the country out of the political impasse into which Malan and Strijdom had led their followers, and for that reason alone deserved some political support. It was also taken to illustrate that South Africa was "moving again" at a time when constructive engagement had begun to come under increasing criticism at home.

If there was remarkably little to show for constructive engagement before 1983, this could always be put down to the government's need to move with circumspection. If America's influence had seemed much diminished, this could always be explained by the need to coax the government along, to steady its nerve, not undermine its confidence. The referendum victory changed all this overnight. The government now had a popular mandate to press ahead, or had it? For it could be argued with equal force that it had been given a vote of confidence in its attempts to reformulate apartheid, to bring it into the second half of the twentieth century—to adapt certainly, but to live by the same set of principles to which most white South Africans still subscribed.

By the end of 1984 it was possible to argue that there would be no radical changes over the next decade, only partial and often halfhearted tinkering with the system, that the reform program had in all essential respects been completed, leaving the government largely responsive to the initiatives of others. Faced with the total collapse of black local government, the government was forced to change direction. Confronted with six months of unrelenting rebellion in the urban black townships and the mounting threat of coordinated industrial action, the government was forced to accept the principle of a common South African citizenship for blacks in the nominally independent homelands, and the principle of power-sharing with blacks at the highest level of government, with only the precondition that individual and group interests should be constitutionally guaranteed. As the reform program collapsed around him, Botha found himself caught between mounting black rebellion, which finally forced a state of emergency in July 1985—the first for twenty-five years—and the erosion of his white political power base. By then it was difficult to see him as he had originally seen himself—the manager of change, a political puppet master who could get his players to play roles of his own choosing.

By 1985 South Africa was in a state of flux, with the about-face by nationalist Afrikanerdom reflected in specific policy changes that revealed the government had to proceed quickly merely to respond to events that were no longer of its own making. These included the scrapping of the act prohibiting multiracial political parties, the decision to abandon the planned removal of some 700,000 blacks living in white areas, the decision to amend the influx control and pass laws, and the promise to replace the all-white provincial councils (the second tier of government) with multiracial regional councils, including the representatives of black local authorities. These were, of course, important reforms, but they were not part of the reform program. Like constructive engagement, this passed into history in the riots of 1984–85. The government's power to initiate change passed away too.

Even if this had not been the case, the United States had begun to appreciate a third problem about its endorsement of the reform program. Huntington's authoritarian reform model had as its reverse side the need to act against white opposition, in effect to apply to the white community if necessary some of the draconian security measures that had been applied with great effect against those outside it. The influence of such thinking had been evident in Crocker's insistence long before coming to power that Pretoria should not be encouraged to scrap its security laws—in marked contrast to the usual demands made by American politicians.[23] It was also clearly evident in the State Department's 1981 human rights report, which in its discussion of South Africa vouchsafed the opinion that there could be little hope of political progress without the erosion of some of the civil rights the whites had long enjoyed: "While critics of the government at home and abroad tend to view repression as a negation of the existence of change, there is also reason to believe that the South African government regards tight security as a necessary condition of its reform efforts."[24]

Yet within a year the State Department had begun to sound a notably more ambivalent note. In its second human rights report it noted with alarm that one of the main developments of the year had been "the continued erosion of the rule of law and its replacement by administrative fiat."[25] It soon became clear that the threat to the press and the fact that white liberals had no effective redress against police harassment or detention without trial might soon create a more closed society in which there would be no effective restraints on government behavior. In a major speech the following autumn the under secretary of state Lawrence Eagleburger deplored the fact that the power of the courts continued to be circumscribed by executive action of a kind which had effectively denied them any control over government policy.[26]

What was particularly disappointing was that its much-improved relationship with Pretoria gave the White House remarkably little leverage over its actions. The Rabbie Commission, which had been set up ostensibly to liberalize the republic's security legislation, recommended only minor modifications of the provisions for detention without trial. By the end of 1982 the security police were still holding more than 180 people without charge, not to mention another 120 who were banned. All the commission recommended was that detainees should have the right of appeal every six months to a review board responsible to the minister of justice; that a special inspector of detainees be appointed; that the chief of police be required to apply to the minister of law and order for the extension of a detention order no less than once a month; and that the definition of communism be made more precise. However, the Internal Security Act, which embodied the commission's main proposals, did not require the minister to give effect to any recommendation by a board of review. In some three other instances the government actually tightened up the existing security laws.

The Intimidation bill appeared to have been designed to ensnare those responsible for promoting unrest among workers and students. The mere threat of assault that encouraged any person or group to "assume or abandon a particular standpoint" could now be punished with up to ten years' imprisonment. The Protection of Information bill, which provided equally long sentences for the unauthorized disclosure of information, made it more difficult than ever to monitor investment codes of conduct.[27] Had Clarence Mitchell been asked to draw up a review of South Africa's legal system in 1984, he might well have concluded that the situation had actually grown worse since the early 1970s, and that in its support for "authoritarian reform" the United States had turned a blind eye to the infringement of the few civil liberties that the white voters still enjoyed.

Yet when the Reagan administration chose to intervene decisively, its intervention was not entirely in vain. When it first came to office, more than one hundred laws already controlled the publication of news about all police and military activity. During the next four years journalism became one of the most harried professions in South African society. Four senior editors were questioned by the police for their allegedly "biased" reporting. One was brought to trial for exposing the prison conditions in which black detainees were held. Four journalists were sentenced between them to forty-two years' imprisonment; eighteen black writers were forced to flee the country. *The Post* and *Sunday Post*, two white-owned newspapers, with a substantial black readership, were closed down in January 1981.

Still dissatisfied with its powers, in 1980 the government appointed the Steyn Commission to ascertain what other restrictions might be introduced to safeguard "national security." Its eventual 1,400-page report made sobering reading. It concluded that the state could not permit absolute press freedom in the face of a "total onslaught" from the outside world; that the press must be required to operate within "a social responsibility framework"; and that reporters must be "professionalized" if they were to be permitted to write at all.[28]

The commissioners clearly wished to make it illegal for a newspaper to employ an unlicensed journalist or to publish an article by a reporter who had not been enrolled by a statutory body, to be appointed initially by the government. Their report made it plain that the major purpose of the proposals was to narrow the range of acceptable comment and to bring it into line with government thinking. To its own obvious satisfaction the commission concluded that the "professionalization" of the press would result in its "depoliticization," that journalists would be required to distinguish between "matters relating to the level of state craft" and matters suitable for partisan discussion. Had its report been adopted, the government would have been able to have effectively muzzled the press whenever matters of "national importance" were debated.

Under pressure from Washington, the government was forced to rethink its own position. Even at the time, American representations were acknowledged to have been an important, even decisive, factor in Pretoria's eventual decision.[29] Recognizing the political damage that would be done to South Africa's image by the further erosion of press freedom, Crocker prevailed upon Botha to allow the newspaper publishers to set up a media council of their own with the power to reprimand and fine newspapers found to be in breach of its own code of conduct. Although several editors expressed concern that this might open the way for an indirect system of control, they agreed for the moment that it was less disagreeable than the threatened licensing system.

On the whole, however, such instances were rare. American pressure did not produce many striking results, and seems to have been exercised infrequently, if at all, thereafter. Even constructive engagement could not alter certain cardinal facts. It may have lessened tensions, but in the last resort it could not erase long-held suspicions of American intentions. To that extent, the United States may have had fewer opportunities to influence events and government attitudes in particular than Crocker originally imagined. In a radio discussion three years into the president's first term, he insisted that "what has been done in the constitutional field provides a limited improvement in a limited area. We have never said ... that the reform package is a solution. We have said it is a step."[30] If so, it was a step toward which Washington contributed very little. Its policy from 1981 was shaped by the myth of a pragmatic and dynamic government pressing ahead with political change on a scale that could not have been imagined five years earlier. Like all myths, it contained a kernel of truth, but in time it became so magnified and embroidered that it became an identifiable and damaging misconception. The answers to the South African problem, of course, were few, but the reform program was not one of them.

It was perhaps a quixotic gesture on the part of history to have chosen so remote and quintessentially peripheral a country for so advanced an experiment in social engineering as apartheid. It was equally quixotic to imagine that South Africa of all countries would stumble upon the elusive grail of reforming a society out of a revolution in the manner of nineteenth-century Britain or more recently France under de Gaulle. De Gaulle had gone on to create in the Fifth Republic a constitutional hybrid, an absolute monarchy that practiced a ritual form of regicide every seven years, a despotism, to quote Mme de Stael, "tempered by assassination." In South Africa the political system brought to mind Thackeray's description of the British Raj: "a despotism of dispatch boxes tempered by the loss of the keys." South Africa was the absolute technocratic state, a state that had lost control over its own technocrats. In this case the keys were not lost; they remained firmly in the locks, but the government had found it increasingly difficult to persuade its own civil servants to turn them.

No less important than government-directed reform was the black
response to the reform program. The Reagan administration saw the
participation of black political leaders as the precursor of some form
of settlement by negotiation, a recognition in the first instance by
the whites themselves that definitive change, as opposed to unilateral adaptation, must be preceded by multiracial bargaining. It tended
to see the new municipal town councils and black trade unions as
institutions that, though imperfect, presented the black community
with an opportunity as well as a challenge. It was on the relationship
between these two themes—white-initiated reform and the black
response—that its hopes for constructive engagement largely turned.

In this respect, although Crocker may have looked to the early
1970s for inspiration and attempted to re-create the close working
relationship between Washington and Pretoria that Nixon had tried
to cultivate during those years, the past was not the only model that
influenced him. Ten years on, he was among the first to accept that it
was not enough to address the white community; that some account
had to be taken of the principal nonstate actors as well.

By 1981 many Americans had begun to see the solution to South
Africa's racial predicament in terms of black politics and the leverage
that black political groups could exercise—in short, the extent to
which the whites could not only initiate reforms but also respond to
the initiatives of others. It did not take long before the principal
themes and actors had been alotted their respective roles.

Unfortunately, the time for making such overtures to black political groups either at the center or the fringes of political life was not

especially propitious. Black politics had become so fragmented on tactical issues that it had become difficult for an outsider to negotiate the tangled web of political developments. At this stage it was not at all clear which of the numerous movements would eventually emerge victorious, or contribute most to the struggle for majority rule—the African National Congress (ANC), the United Democratic Front (UDF) formed to oppose Botha's constitutional reforms, the trade union movement, still in its infancy, or the student bodies that had articulated the message of black consciousness, indeed largely formulated it after 1972. As Crocker noted at the time, "a competitive race is under way among blacks to fill the many organizational vacuums (or seize the new opportunities) which exist (or are being created by the government) within the diverse black communities. Some of the sporadic violence reported to the outside world as a function of black-white confrontation is, in reality, a reflection of this competition."[1]

It followed from this analysis that it would be foolish to identify the "legitimate" representatives of black opinion and even more foolish to provide them with material support. On the other hand, the more material support Washington was prepared to provide the black community as a whole, the less likely it was to turn to externally funded armed struggle. By helping blacks in general to organize more effectively and to bargain on their own behalf without the intercession of outside parties, the United States imagined it could play a useful role. It chose the trade union movement as the group most deserving of its assistance, but channeled most of its funds into black education, a politically neutral forum, with the emphasis on long-term rather than immediate political bargaining. By helping young blacks to identify common interests and to recognize their common predicament, the Reagan administration hoped to provide them with the organizational power with which to demand more effectively a greater share of political responsibility.

Black Education and Political Change

The United States first announced its support for new educational programs in South Africa in a speech by its deputy ambassador at the UN, Kenneth Adelman, on 30 November 1981. Some time before that, however, it had begun developing its own initiatives, conscious that the lamentable state of education for black schoolchildren would not make the task any easier.

At the beginning of the decade all public, primary, and secondary schools were still racially segregated. Ninety percent of all black students at residential campuses attended exclusively black universities such as Fort Hare, the very first. Education for nonwhites was administered by thirteen separate departments in the white areas, six in the homelands, and four in the independent states. Within South Africa proper the government spent approximately ten times more per white student than it did per black, and five times more than it did per Coloured. For the average black student, high schools offered very few advanced courses, far fewer than for any other racial group. Of the 1,162 black secondary schools at the beginning of 1981, only 195 offered courses in mathematics, only 36 in accounting, and only 31 in business economics in the students' final year.

Not surprisingly, a congressional staff commission which went out to South Africa in August 1982 discovered an extraordinarily high wastage rate at both primary and secondary levels. Of the total number of students starting school in 1963 (who had completed at least twelve years of schooling), the whites numbered 60 percent, the blacks only 2 percent. Of the blacks who had attended school in white areas in 1967, only 1.25 percent had completed high school and gone on to pass the national matriculation examination.

From the time that Verwoerd had been education minister in the mid-1950s, the essential purpose of black education had been to prevent the social and political "absorption" of blacks into white society, to deny them qualifications for skilled jobs and to prepare the majority for more "fitting" social roles in their own national communities or homelands.[2] When the need to create more skilled candidates arose, these priorities were radically revised. The government decided to introduce compulsory education in black schools in 1974, but because of the school riots two years later and subsequent school boycotts, this decision was not implemented until 1981. Even then further political activism slowed down the expansion of compulsory education, with the number of primary school children involved rising from 45,000 when Reagan came to office to only 113,500 in 1984.

Despite these setbacks, spending on black education in white areas increased dramatically, doubling between 1980 and 1982. Dropout rates were reduced, sometimes substantially. By 1981 7 percent managed to finish high school, compared with 2 percent six years earlier, a marginal increase, perhaps, but one that served to illustrate a general trend. Apprenticeship training, once confined to the homelands, was offered in white areas for the first time. The Ministry of National Education also showed greater flexibility in granting permits to black students to study at "open" white universities if particular courses were not available at black institutions. During 1981, 4,034 blacks successfully enrolled at residential universities for whites, making 5 percent of the total enrollment.[3]

Yet these reforms, radical though they were in the light of Afrikaner tradition, did not disturb the basic rationale of apartheid—the formula of educating blacks for full participation only in their national communities rather than absorption into the national labor market. It was true that the government had significantly increased its spending on black education in white areas, but as a result of its own resettlement and influx-control programs it found it had direct responsibility for a declining proportion of black schoolchildren, two-thirds of whom came within the jurisdiction of the homelands, where their lot was so appalling that it gave rise to intermittent, but increasingly bitter, school boycotts, the most serious of which occurred in KwaZulu in 1982.

Overall per capita spending and teacher-pupil ratios for South Africa as a whole remained far less favorable to the black community than they had been in 1948 when the Nationalists took power.[4] The government had not even committed itself to a timetable for the movement toward full educational equality. Only 4.4 percent of South Africa's GNP was spent on education. According to some estimates, Pretoria would have had to have doubled its annual expenditure on education to have achieved racial parity within the next ten years.[5]

In these circumstances black discontent inevitably grew. Nearly half the black high school students who took their examinations in Soweto in November 1981 failed; many gained such poor pass grades that they found themselves ineligible for university entrance.[6] Bitterness about segregated education had sparked off serious nationwide disturbances in 1976, which had ended with seven hundred students dead. The blacks continued to argue that even by the system's own standards the situation was getting worse, not better. They were able to point to a dramatic drop in the number of black students who had graduated—of the total in their final year at high school 86 percent in 1976, 71 percent in 1979, and only 57 percent in 1981, the year the Reagan administration readopted constructive engagement.

During Reagan's first term, the situation barely improved. Less than 50 percent of black candidates passed the matriculation examinations of 1983. To the U.S. ambassador it seemed clear that the government intended to reduce, not increase, the number able to apply for university entrance, given that in 1983 only 11 percent of black matriculation candidates achieved an entrance pass, compared with 33 percent in 1978.[7] In the three-year period 1980–1983 more black schoolchildren may have matriculated than in the previous history of black education, but such statistics meant very little if they were not translated into university places.

Such excessively high failure rates inevitably accentuated discontent with the age restrictions that had been introduced in 1982 excluding all students over twenty from attending school and limiting the number of classes open to those between sixteen and twenty years, a measure that adversely affected those older, more politicized students who had missed school during the Soweto uprising, as well as those whose education had been interrupted through lack of funds.[8]

Clearly, then, there was a need for some external support if the students concerned were ever to benefit from the little the education system offered them. It was in order to discover the areas where money could produce the best return that a mission from the Agency for International Development (AID), led by its deputy assistant administrator for Africa, spent seventeen days in the republic in the closing months of 1981. In the course of their tour the members met officials from two of the three ministries responsible for the education of each racial group. Their final report devoted only minimal attention to the external scholarship program and focused attention instead on the views of those departments consulted. Later they were criticized for ignoring the opinions of black political leaders and dismissing the possibility of funding labor educational programs. Their final recommendation that an educational programs coordinator be assigned as a special assistant to the U.S. ambassador to provide "full-time professional advice and coordination with the black community" was never taken up.

By the time the AID team left for South Africa, the administration had already declared its opposition to any approach that would require the United States to play a role that was properly that of the South African government. It was careful not to indicate, however, which activities it believed would be most appropriate for each party, and equally careful not to discuss whether complementary or coordinated programs would be more desirable. In fact, the AID team excluded from the outset any direct assistance to or through the government, but did not rule out direct assistance to nonsegregated institutions which were in receipt of government funds. In this latter category it included teacher training colleges funded by the state, many of which ran nonsegregated upgrading programs for black teachers.[9]

Another concern of the administration was that it did not wish to alienate Pretoria by discriminating in favor of institutions that were known to be notoriously anti-apartheid. Crocker himself wished to encourage "a constructive process of change motivated by self-interest and not hindered by the continuing ideology of separation on the one hand, or the ideology of armed struggle as the only option on the other."[10] Inevitably, these considerations gave rise to the suspicion that the United States was not really prepared to underwrite any educational program that would bring it into direct conflict with Pretoria. Crocker admitted as much, conceding that "any approach which is interventionist in nature would be opposed by the South African government as it would by any sovereign state." Did this mean that Washington was prepared to give South Africa a veto over the assistance it was willing to provide? If, in the final analysis, South Africa continued to prohibit aid to change-oriented rather than government-sanctioned programs, would it have been more advisable to terminate all aid-related projects, rather than design programs that failed almost entirely to conform to the type of fundamental social and political change the United States ostensibly wished to see?

Change-oriented programs were not, in fact, uppermost in the administration's mind. It was reluctant to work with any black group directly. Even a small internal program that enabled U.S. consulates to prepare study guides for the Joint Matriculation Board examination, and that offered a direct input from community groups, although adopted in 1981 and budgeted for in fiscal year 1982 to the sum of $383,000, was later dropped for lack of community consultation.[11]

Another proposal to bring eighteen volunteer teachers to American universities for a two-months English teaching course highlighted a similar reluctance on the part of the administration to be identified with community initiatives. Although the candidates would have been selected by community-based organizations, most of their training would have taken place in the United States. The proposed course promised none of the political multiplier effects that might have resulted from building upon existing community capacity.

To judge from the confused nature of the U.S. embassy's self-help education projects, which totaled $94,000 in fiscal year 1982, the administration had no clearly defined objectives in mind, certainly none that appeared to be in the forefront of government thinking. The U.S. consulate in Durban allocated most of its funds to programs in government schools; the consulate in Cape Town tended to fund community-based initiatives. The field organization for monitoring and coordinating American aid reflected and contributed to the confusion. Since AID's Africa section was reluctant to become involved on the ground, given that its work was centered largely on black Africa, not the republic, most of the programs were run by U.S. Information Agency (USIA), which had experience in this field through administering the Fulbright scholarship scheme. Unfortunately, because the agency's main function was one of information exchange rather than internal development, it does not appear to have actively monitored internal activities; indeed, the contractors of the Joint Matriculation Board preparation program later complained about its lack of familiarity with the program.[12]

These concerns led many critics to suppose that the administration was engaged more in the breach than the observance, that it was clearly committed to increasing the quantity of education for black schoolchildren and students without challenging education's role in South Africa as an instrument of apartheid. They were confirmed in their own suspicions by Crocker's support for private-sector schemes such as a technical school in Soweto, which owed its creation to the U.S. Chamber of Commerce in South Africa. The school certainly provided much-needed basic clerical skills and professional business diplomas, but it hardly equipped its students for new economic and social roles in society at large. Indeed, the Chamber's own literature on the school placed it well within the traditional context of education, in its claim that the school would provide "a source of commercially well-trained blacks for employment within the South African business sector."[13]

Unfortunately, the Reagan administration left itself surprisingly open to such criticism, however unjustified, through the emphasis it continued to put on business initiatives, as well as its willingness to devise a tax policy that would offer American corporations a positive incentive to participate more fully in such educational programs. Altogether, U.S. companies spent $3 million in 1982 training their black employees, a 50 percent increase over the previous year. They also contributed a further $10.5 million on other socially related projects — a sum that represented slightly more than 2 percent of the total profits derived from U.S. direct investment in South Africa (at 1981 prices). Eight of the twenty-five largest American corporations contributed funds to the school that the U.S. Chamber of Commerce had established, in addition to several other commercial high schools in Soweto.[14]

Doubtless, such criticisms were distorted, and hardly portrayed the State Department in a fair or accurate light, but the administration had only itself to blame. Had it defined its terms of reference more carefully, the criticism might have been more muted. Equally trenchant remarks were made of its *direct* contribution. By the end of 1983 Washington was spending $4 million a year on a scholarship program that brought approximately one hundred black students to the United States for undergraduate and postgraduate degrees. By the end of 1984 over four hundred students had enrolled in campuses throughout the country. In South Africa itself it invested $2 million in the period 1983–1985 in a tutorial program designed to assist black high school students to prepare for their matriculation examinations, in a probably forlorn attempt to reduce the failure rates. Five million dollars was also set aside for an internal scholarship program that was intended to act as a counterpart to the scheme which brought black students to the United States.[15]

Despite these impressive figures and the extent of its investment, Washington appeared to shy away from funding black initiatives, even though the latter might have been considerably more effective in instilling black participants with a sense of confidence in their own abilities, fostering a willingness to take risks and rise to new challenges, and developing their ability to cope with setbacks. It hesitated, that is, to use education in the way that the director of the black South African Committee on Higher Education hoped it would be used, "to increase the black community's awareness of power."[16] The educational programs sponsored by the United States did not provide the average black student with a sense of responsibility to his community, any more than they helped facilitate community initiatives. Indeed, many in being flown to the United States for further training were uprooted from it. As a congressional staff commission was told by one of the educators attached to a community-based agency in Cape Town, formal education in the republic did not train blacks to become initiators of change, it merely equipped them with some of the basic skills necessary to earn a living.

Certainly, Crocker's priorities did not accord with those of the people he was trying to assist. To begin with, most blacks tended to look forward to more rapid political change than their white counterparts, and accordingly attached particular importance to the acquisition of scientific and technical skills that would be needed to run the country in a period of transition from minority rule. For many members of the black community, not all of whom were radical in inclination, the margin of time the United States imagined would precede fundamental change was far too long, and "optimistic."

For that reason its view of the government's reform program was largely negative. The blacks opposed constructive engagement for the same reason. They opposed it on the grounds that it would be read in South Africa as continued support for the existing pattern of nonwhite education. They were concerned that it might convey the impression that Washington was not opposed to assuming responsibility for what Pretoria itself should be doing, allowing the regime in the process to evade its moral obligations. On this latter point, their fear, though understandable, was clearly exaggerated. One reason, after all, for their lack of sympathy for business-sponsored projects such as the school sponsored by the U.S. Chamber of Commerce was that they lent themselves particularly well to the government's attempts "to co-opt a black middle class."[17]

Had the administration been more directly in contact with black opinion and the educational organizations that gave expression to their aspirations, it might have been more attentive to their concerns. As it was, to many blacks the Reagan team appeared to be compounding their problems. Rather than as a friend, it was seen as an enemy, an enemy cast in the role of an ingénue, unheeding before the fact, unprepared after it, unable to learn from its own experience of positive discrimination and equal opportunity programs.

The Reagan Administration and
the Trade Union Movement

In view of the emphasis the new administration put on trade union activity as an opportunity for learning basic bargaining skills that might in due course be translated and applied in the political arena, it is surprising that it did not channel more funds into the trade union movement. At the end of the period its contribution to black trade union support programs amounted to little more than $875,000, a marginal sum, even if it represented a substantial increase over the previous year (1983) when the sum had stood only at $190,000.

In South Africa itself many opportunities were lost to channel funds into some of the labor programs managed by the unions themselves. In 1981, for example, 400 of The Federation of South African Trade Unions' (FOSATU's) 1,500 shop stewards participated in the union's own training seminars. The Council of Unions of South Africa (CUSA) sent many of its rank-and-file members to similar weekly meetings. A number of its more senior officials even attended the urban training project administered by the University of the Witwatersrand. Many unaffiliated unions ran much less ambitious programs, in part because of manpower and financial shortages, in part because of government harassment, which might have been all the more reason for funding them.

In ignoring such schemes the administration was unable to forge tactical linkages between itself and the still incipient union movement. Suspicion accordingly dogged the administration's initiatives from the outset. One example was the American labor federation's program in South Africa, with a budget of $875,000 in 1985, run by the AFL-CIO's African-American Labor Center (AALC) in New York. Because it obtained 90 percent of its funds from the government, it invited suspicion of its motives, in this case quite unjustifiably. Many black leaders, many of them from CUSA, charged that the AALC Southern Africa program was intended to sow distrust among the various unions and thereby set back their ongoing unity negotiations. When its executive director Patrick O'Farrell visited South Africa in 1982, he was spurned as a suspected CIA agent by many of the men he had gone to see.[18]

Such distrust made it difficult for Washington to make any significant contribution in these early years to the development of those very bargaining skills its own corporations had played such a major part in encouraging. It is worth remembering that in 1979 the management at Ford's Uitenhage plant found that the work force was determined to put the political utility of industrial action to the test, with or without the government's sanction.[19] As the Allied Black Workers Union pointed out at the time, "Black workers' interests extend beyond the factory. They extend to the stringent, irksome and humiliating application of the influx control laws . . . to the lack of proper channels whereby people can equip themselves with basic skills, and to the lack of political power and the machinery to bring about a socio-economic and political system acceptable to all people."[20]

Clearly trade union activity could no longer be entirely divorced from politics even if its impact on political life was still indirect. In May 1981 the Allied Workers national union organizer made it clear that the context in which his members found themselves had become interlaced with political struggle all along the line. Everyday, he reminded the management, their workers came up against the six thousand regulations that regulated the private sector, rules that were described by the union's general secretary as "the building blocks" of apartheid.[21] In such circumstances it was small wonder that the strikers sought to articulate their political grievances by making contact with various organizations on the periphery of the labor market.

Although the government hoped that the Wiehahn reforms would keep the blacks out of politics, the unions quickly found that there was a growing demand among their members for them to play an active, even assertive role in local community affairs. They chose to do so by striking first in the subsidiaries of such American corporations as Ford and General Motors, confident that their political visibility would make it difficult for the management to ignore the aspirations of their own workers. Ford's decision to dismiss one of its own union officials in December 1979 for spending too much of his time on community activism triggered off a notable strike at its Struendale plant, which drew extensive support from the Port Elisabeth Civic Organisation (PEBCO) and prompted the eventual intervention of the U.S. consul general in Cape Town. At a nearby Goodyear works, not one of the seven representatives of the work force was elected from the apolitical United Auto and Rubber Workers Union. Everyone came from well-known and militant local community associations.[22]

American corporations were among the first to recognize that the workers had no wish to register under the 1979 legislation if, as a result, they were prevented from mobilizing support in the townships on such pertinent issues as rent increases and poor housing. The more prescient realized that many unions were not fighting for registration at all, but something more profound. In the run-up to the 1981 general election, hardly a week went by without a labor stoppage in one foreign-owned subsidiary or another. In the end, the Department of Manpower Utilization was forced to bring in several amendments to the Wiehahn legislation permitting registered unions to discuss local community issues without fear of legal reprisals.

In this retreat U.S. companies played an important role. It was management, after all, not the government, which first recognized that the unions could not be kept out of politics by registering them, but only by providing their members with other channels of political expression. It was the multinational corporations, even more than local business, who first lost patience with the government and began recognizing many unregistered unions. Faced with a wide variety of organizations, only a few of which had registered as the government had asked and many of which had refused to register at all, a growing number of companies felt they had no choice but to recognize unions that clearly represented their work force, even if they owed their popularity to their engagement in local community affairs.

In short, a good number of American companies played a role, even an important one, in persuading the government to rethink its position, to accept that the withdrawal of labor, either in the form of stay-away campaigns or formal work stoppages, was bound to be used for political ends. They also played a part, if a less significant one, in persuading some of their own workers that noncooperation was not their only option; that it was perfectly possible to use the institutions the government had given them to work within the system as well.

By 1982 the trade union movement had increased its membership from about 70,000 (1979) to 200,000, a dramatic rise of 200 percent.

As if to reflect the trend, labor unrest also rose sharply. There were 207 strikes in 1980, the year before constructive engagement was formally adopted; there were 342 in 1981, the number of workers involved in that year being the largest involved in strike action for twenty years. Clearly, a black union movement growing up outside official control might have significant implications for political change. It might create for itself and its leaders an independent black power base with which more established black groups might have to come to terms. More to the point, it might even succeed in scoring a number of victories, in some cases major concessions from the government, if not a major change in the direction of its policy.

Its earliest successes, however, were scored between 1979 and 1981. There were fewer successes to report after 1982 and far more setbacks. Between April 1981 and September 1983, 400 trade union leaders were detained by the police. In 1981 2,500 striking workers were deported to the homelands; 3,000 more in July 1982, in the space of a single month. During this period government restrictions actually increased. Mixed unions were outlawed, controls over registered unions were tightened up, trade unionists were prohibited from assisting political parties, and union federations from giving support to illegal strikes.[23]

As a result of these measures, the South African business community found itself in direct confrontation with the government. Business and government began to diverge to a degree unthinkable in the heady days of the Carlton conference (1979) when Botha hoped to co-opt the business community into his reform strategy. It was always an uneasy compromise, for having pushed for the Wiehahn reforms, most businessmen had no wish to see the leadership of the emerging union movement crushed in the name of national security. The first public cracks between government and business emerged in November 1984 when the Association of Chambers of Commerce, the South Africa Federated Chamber of Industries, and the Afrikaner Handels-instituut sharply criticized the arrest of twelve trade union leaders and two thousand others on the eve of delicate negotiations between business and black labor. The unprecedented joint statement by the three giants of organized industry was followed up two months later by a manifesto published not only in their own name but also in that of the Chamber of Mines of South Africa and the Steel and Engineering Industries Federation, collectively representing 80 percent of national employment. This amounted to a fundamental repudiation of government policies.

Yet apart from encouragement from the administration to its own multinationals to endorse the revised Sullivan principles of 1983, the authorities in Washington provided little direct assistance to the trade union movement. The new code itself merely required its signatories (134 U.S. companies in all, less than a fifth of the total) to use their influence to support the rights of black business to operate in urban areas; to influence other companies to follow equal-rights standards; to support the freedom of mobility of black workers and the scrapping of all apartheid laws. Even at this late stage the code was not made mandatory. The gap between America's professions of support and its actual policies grew wider every year.

The Reagan Administration and the ANC

This was all the more surprising since the administration put such a premium on fostering *internal* political change in opposition to externally funded revolution. It did not serve the interests of constructive engagement that the ANC was the fastest-growing black movement in the early 1980s, the one that most captured the imagination of the majority of young students and workers. The question remained: were they right to give the ANC their support?

On this point Crocker was quite unequivocal in his answer. Not all administration officials might have agreed that government-initiated change would meet with success, that the black groups it was attempting to buy off could be bribed and co-opted, and that at the end of the day Pretoria would find the money to finance the reform program. But did it necessarily follow that the ANC would remain the only relevant nationalist movement, the one with which the government would eventually have to come to terms? In a press interview in July 1984 Crocker went so far as to suggest that this was far from being the case, that what had been missed "in much of the public commentary in the West, particularly about the Nkomati agreement between South Africa and Mozambique, is that the illusion that armed struggle will solve South Africa's problems has been dealt a body blow . . . perhaps an irreversible one."[24] Events were to prove this a naively optimistic assessment.

In one sense, of course, this analysis was not entirely wide of the mark. Politics in South Africa had changed, and changed significantly some years before the Nkomati process that robbed the ANC of its bases in Swaziland and Mozambique. Long before 1984 the movement had been forced to come to terms with the reform program, and more particularly with those black groups that had been given a limited license to preach radical change. The constitutional initiatives by which the government hoped to devolve a range of powers to the blacks at the periphery of politics, while reserving power at the center for itself, were obviously not intended to be stages in the retreat from white supremacy, only adjustments in its method of retaining white control. The powers of the government at the center actually increased; it was only in the decentralized parts of the power apparatus—in the localities, and of course the homelands—that the blacks were given limited powers of self-rule.

Yet the constitutional initiatives seemed likely to prompt new responses to the prospects for cooperation and noncooperation alike, which could not be predicted until they had been made. Whether they chose to work the reforms or to press for further concessions, the blacks would have to take account of the new political dispensation almost as much as the new dispensation would have to take account of them. Whether they chose to work the reforms, to use the platforms they had been given, those platforms might make them relatively independent of externally based movements such as the ANC, if not entirely of the armed struggle.

Elsewhere in Southern Africa in the 1960s and 1970s there had been remarkably little scope for internal developments of this nature. In Rhodesia it had long been the hope of American conservatives that those Africans who qualified for the vote in the 1969 constitution (little more than ten thousand) would gain in number if sanctions were lifted, with the stimulus this would give to economic growth; and that in time the "qualified class" would increase in size until such time as it became possible for the white community to entertain without fear the prospect of "responsible" African rule.[25]

Throughout this period, however, the role of the blacks in such political exchanges as there were had been severely circumscribed by the fact that urban regulations, including entry permits and housing regulations, made it difficult if not impossible to mobilize the black work force, even if nationalist politicians had not been handicapped by the fact that approximately half of all employed males in the towns were nonresident.[26] Conservative black leaders like Abel Muzorewa may have hoped that the guerrilla struggle in Rhodesia would eventually be made redundant by the actions the workers took themselves, drawing inspiration in this respect from the strike in the Sahabani asbestos mines in the early 1960s, which had sparked off the first serious political violence in southern Rhodesia.[27] But even in the days of the Central African Federation the trade union movement had simply not been large enough to mobilize large-scale industrial action.

In Namibia so many blacks were part of the subsistence economy that when Pretoria decided to transfer power to groups other than the South West Africa People's Organization (SWAPO), it found it had to redistribute power to categories of its own making. Although this period saw political groups in the territory proliferate wildly, most represented only a handful of constituents, nearly all special interest groups and narrow lobbies that had almost no national following. When the United States first embarked on the first round of independence negotiations it was able to identify over thirteen national organizations and twenty-seven separate political parties, all of which claimed a share of political power.[28] Some may or may not have been creatures of South Africa's making, but Pretoria had clearly provided each with a role simply by permitting them to petition at all, and in each case to recognize the constituency they claimed to represent. When it came to linking them in a coalition government capable of mobilizing broad-based national support, the experiment immediately ran into difficulties. The collapse of the Democratic Turnhalle Alliance administration in 1981 revealed to a disbelieving government in Pretoria that political life for the great majority of the territory's inhabitants derived almost exclusively from their experience of the national liberation struggle.

The situation was rather different in South Africa, where years of industrialization, urbanization, and demographic pressure had resulted in the extensive integration of black workers into the wage economy. By 1980 over 70 percent of economically active blacks were to be found in wage-earning employment, compared with less than 25 percent in most other African countries. One obvious manifestation of this development was the ability of the workers to organize a trade union movement that after initial setbacks in the 1970s emerged sufficiently strongly to force itself on the attentions of the

ANC and the Black Consciousness groups, principally though not exclusively the Azanian People's Organization (AZAPO). For a time in Reagan's first term it even seemed that the trade unions had moved to the center of the debate which divided black opinion: whether to cooperate with the government or not.

Ten years earlier the ANC had tended to dismiss the trade union movement as a fledgling movement that would never fulfill its promise. The Black Consciousness Movement had, it is true, set out to capture it in 1972, but only in so doing to persuade the workers to see themselves as members of the black community, not as workers with specific interests and aspirations distinct from those of other economic groups. By the time Reagan came to power, even the ANC had been forced to accept that union politics was likely to make a distinct and possibly decisive contribution to political change. In short, several black organizations in South Africa were likely to enjoy real powers by the end of the 1980s that would make them much more responsive to local needs, and less preoccupied with national issues. The trade union movement already engaged in disputes over rents and inadequate housing and had become increasingly attentive to local political questions.

That was not to say that politics in South Africa would become balkanized, answering to the needs of the localities rather than the nation. Black consciousness would probably remain a national phenomenon, cutting across some of the spurious regional unities that might emerge. Nonetheless, it was most unlikely that local politics could be ignored completely; indeed, black politicians might find themselves at risk by focusing on all–South Africa political issues at the expense of their own grass-roots support. Even Buthelezi discovered that his multiracial Inkatha movement was more popular outside KwaZulu than it was within, where in the election of 1978 it scored less than 37 percent of the vote.

If black politics in the republic had been simply a response to Pretoria's initiatives, then balkanization might have been ignored, but this was not entirely the case, and had anyway become increasingly less so. And if the government was going to be forced with greater frequency to respond to black initiatives, the ANC and other national movements might find themselves having to strike unwelcome local deals and unpalatable political bargains with groups on the margins of political life. It might, in effect, have to redefine its role, as Crocker suggested would indeed be the case.

Yet the ANC, especially in the aftermath of Nkomati, did not conform to this comforting picture, comforting, that was, for the authors of the constructive engagement policy. Faced with an effective severing of its supply lines from the north and a sustained escalation of internal black resistance, the movement shifted at its 1985 congress, the first in sixteen years, from the twenty-five-year-old armed struggle to the promotion of general insurrection, a prospect which must have filled Washington with alarm. After the signing of the Nkomati accord between South Africa and Mozambique, the leadership came under pressure to review its strategy. Although it shifted its position on revolutionary violence from without, it did so only to call for the townships to be rendered "ungovernable" and turned into no-go areas, or liberated zones, where if any writ ruled it would be that of the army, not the police.

Flushed by the astonishing success of this strategy, which required the South African army to enter the townships for the first time since 1961, and paralyzed local administration, the ANC resolved to work toward a long-term work stoppage, to force the resignation of local black councils and in their place put more radical peoples' communities, and to assassinate or intimidate into resigning all blacks participating in government platforms. Collectively the new strategy represented a dramatic swing away from the armed struggle toward a popular uprising through civil disobedience, revolutionary tactics, and industrial action—hardly the climate in which constructive engagement could be pursued.

The local councils by which Crocker had set so much store in 1981 were the focus of some of the most intense struggles during 1984. Popular resistance became manifest immediately after the elections the previous November. The announcement of large rent increases (the only source of council finance) in the Vaal Triangle in September 1983 was met with refusal to pay and protests that, in the face of a repressive response by the government, developed into a sustained challenge to the administration of the townships. By November several councilors had been killed, many others forced to step down. By the end of the year only four out of twenty-two councils in the Pretoria-Witwatersrand-Vaal (PWV) area were still functioning.[29]

In the face of such protests, constructive communication could not be pursued. As the ANC moved to the center of the political stage in 1984–85 (with an admission by Botha for the first time that it might have to be allowed some role by the end of the decade), the Reagan administration found itself buffeted by events and unforeseen developments almost as much as the government it tacitly supported. By the end of the period the ANC had become the main protagonist in the eyes of both parties to the dispute.

In such circumstances the U.S. government had two alternatives: first, to come to terms with the ANC; second, to come out against it. That it chose to do neither suggested a remarkable indifference to developments within the black community, an indifference that became more marked and potentially more disconcerting during the political violence of 1984–85.

Living with a movement such as the ANC, even one committed to violence and some form of social democratic–socialist program, might have been less difficult for a Republican administration than its critics imagined given the remarkable spectacle in the summer of 1985 of South African businessmen flying to a Zambian game lodge to debate the respective merits of capitalism and socialism with the president of the exiled ANC. By the end of the period it had become patently clear that the government and the business community had diverged to a degree unthinkable in the heady days of the Carlton conference (1979) when the prime minister had hoped to co-opt the community into the reform process. It was always an uncomfortable compromise, particularly for some of the more farsighted business leaders who, having pushed for the Wiehahn labor reforms, had no wish to see the security forces crushing the leadership of the emerging black unions as they showed every sign of doing in November 1984 with the arrest of twelve leading trade unionists and two thousand others.

By then the business community had markedly shifted ground, having a better idea than the government itself of the risk of international sanctions and the danger of proceeding too slowly on the road to reform. While a sanctions program might well have a disastrous effect on employment, the value of the rand, and gross domestic investment, it would perhaps more seriously put an end to any hopes of consolidating the black middle class prior to any transfer or redistribution of power. If the existence of such a class was so important to the United States and South Africa alike, with whom did its future lie: with the government or the ANC?

The question was more than academic. By the mid-1980s wealth was being redistributed in South Africa at the rate of 7 percent a year—the most extensive redistribution in any country in the modern world that had not experienced a revolution, a fact not without irony for a country that many thought was about to pass through one. The whites' share of net disposable income was only 60 percent; by the end of the century (in terms of 1980 prices) the per capita disposable income of the black community was set to increase by 126 percent, making it the largest consumer group.

But sanctions were not the only Damoclean sword hanging over the heads of the community's more prosperous middle-class members. A far more potent threat came from within the community itself as the blacks struggled for advantage within their own ranks and as the riots in the townships revealed the depressing picture of a society at war with itself. By 1985 it had become clear to many business leaders that capitalism in South Africa had entered a fight for its survival. The business world faced the risk that unless it could distance itself from apartheid it might accompany it down the trap door of history. For the longer the impasse between black struggle and white repression continued, the more the blacks might see the destruction of capitalism as a precondition of their own freedom.

It was at this point that the business community's unqualified support for black consumerism might meet its nemesis if the situation did not improve. It was all very well drawing comfort from the fact that blacks now accounted for 46 percent of all food sales and half the television and radio market, but there was little comfort to draw from the township riots in which the most wealthy consumers themselves became the victims when embittered young blacks, many unemployed and with no immediate prospect of employment, began to equate affluence with apartheid.

As the government began to debate whether to allow upwardly mobile blacks to move out of the townships altogether into white residential areas where they would, of course, be much safer from attack, but also uprooted from the black community, some of the country's leading businessmen believed that in the ANC they had discovered a movement that was still committed to creating wealth as well as redistributing it, that had renounced out-and-out nationalization for a mixed economy on the Zimbabwean model, and that had finally eschewed, in a way that the Black Consciousness Movement had not, Nkrumah's fatal injunction to seek first the political kingdom on the understanding that all other things would be added unto it.

If this was indeed the situation, then the ANC was not really the problem; the problem was a government that seemed unable to move forward with dispatch. Debating with capitalists at a time when the townships were in flames was difficult for any party, however radical its credentials; debating the finer points of economics might hold dangers for a movement that had yet to win the political debate against more fundamentalist groups such as AZAPO.

On the other hand, if the Reagan administration really *did* believe its own propaganda, that the ANC was a Marxist front, that its leadership could not be trusted, that its leaders were committed to a violent revolution, that Marxism in the townships was a greater threat to Western capitalism than black fundamentalism, it might have been better advised to have identified much earlier with some of the other nationalist movements and to have ruled out any dialogue with the ANC. Such an initiative might have been unwise, even counterproductive, but in its absence its own policy could hardly be pursued with success. One of the interesting bylines to the subject is that there might even have been popular support at home for such a move among the very constituency that first challenged constructive engagement, which was not least of the ironies of a confused and complex political scene.

One of the most striking features of the early 1980s was the extent to which the American political right, dispossessed of its once overriding concern for South Africa's strategic importance, became markedly more critical of apartheid as an economic system, not as a political creed. Nancy Kassebaum, the chairman of the Senate subcommittee on Africa, regularly spoke out against the "Stalinist" principles on which the system was allegedly based: population control and influx-control programs that not only disrupted family life but also inhibited free opportunities and restricted home ownership in the townships—the very principles which were so dear to the neoconservative vote in the United States. With the support of neoconservative rather than liberal Republicans, Congress managed to pass an amendment to the Bretton Woods agreement in November 1983 that linked communism and apartheid by name as economic systems which imposed unwarranted constraints on labor and capital mobility.

Capturing this mood, Kassebaum was able to write: "It is ironic that those in South Africa who sound the most like republicans by demanding the right to private property, the right to be considered for jobs without regard to race, and freedom from government regulation and interference at home, in the schools, and at work, are described as 'radical left,' even Marxist."[30] The significance of Kassebaum's remarks was that they did not derive from a passing mood, an ephemeral commitment to personal liberty that might complicate the efforts of Washington and Pretoria to redress this very situation. Their significance derived from the set of beliefs that had brought Ronald Reagan to the White House and discredited the postwar liberal consensus with its emphasis on government subsidies and state regulation. It was not an argument that the president could ignore.

Yet, ironically, the same arguments might have worked for the administration rather than against it, if it had ever chosen to defend constructive engagement by reference to the unacceptable economic and political principles of the ANC. The apologists of private capitalism might not have liked what they saw in South Africa, but would a Marxist-Leninist government in the republic dismantle the public sector, or repeal all its security legislation? So closely allied to the ANC was the largely white-supported Communist party of South Africa, which was largely Stalinist in persuasion, that the question might have been used to outflank if not disarm Crocker's critics in his own party.

For, looked at in a particularly cynical light, apartheid was indeed what the critics claimed—an excellent case of state socialism. Its command economy was a central feature; the question of race a ridiculous aberration. Would a socialist government wish to deregulate the economy or, more to the point perhaps, repeal the pass laws? As an experiment in controlled urbanization it could well be argued that the influx-control legislation had prevented an even worse drift from the villages to the towns and the growth of the kind of shanty townships that had proliferated throughout the Third World. In the Soviet Union population control was an essential feature of central planning. Would a communist administration also wish to deny itself the most draconian set of security laws in the African continent, which provided a degree of popular control no other African state could ever match? Possibly many apartheid statutes would remain or be brought back, as Mugabe had kept Ian Smith's security legislation intact after 1980. The laws might merely be applied, on the basis of economic function rather than race, to different categories of people, but to the majority all the same.

In short, was it entirely fanciful to imagine that the United States might one day be faced with the prospect of a change of government which on the set of principles that Kassebaum and others wished to uphold could hardly be thought a change for the better? Fifteen years earlier Peter van den Berghe had been brave enough to pose such a question at a time when it was almost never asked: "I have little doubt that the first African government in South Africa will be better than the present government. It could scarcely be any worse. Unfortunately, I am not convinced that it would be enough of an improvement to want to fight for."[31] The Reagan administration, by contrast, never revealed that the question was ever in the forefront of its mind. If it was ever asked, it did not follow through to the answer. Perhaps it should have. It might have been a more plausible defense of constructive engagement than most of the others it produced, perhaps the only defense possible after 1984.

10 The Reagan Administration and the Use of Positive Sanctions

One of the most important points of contrast between the Nixon and Reagan administrations' understanding of constructive engagement was their attitude to the use of positive sanctions. By 1980 it was clear even to the most optimistic observer that the United States could hardly expect to purchase the political changes it wanted any more than it could obtain them through the threat of outright punishment. The record up to the early 1970s inspired little confidence in the use of sanctions of any kind, positive or not. It seemed equally undisputed that if the South Africans themselves were expected to draw up their own political agenda, if there was no role for the United States as a "planner" or "research agency," to use Crocker's own terms, there was no role for it as a banker either.[1]

Crocker's own view of positive sanctions was largely shaped by the experience of the Carter administration and the unfulfilled promise of its policies. "The underlying problem in Western policy" Crocker described some months before coming into office was "the natural desire to separate military ties, diplomatic relations, and economic links into three distinct categories."[2] Linking each, however, did not mean that Washington should take upon itself the responsibilities of power. It was not America's responsibility to provide payments for services rendered: "To the extent that we observed any reflection of our ideas in subsequent South African behavior or actions, we should say so. There would be no 'pay-off' except the obvious achievement of having communicated successfully with the United States—a relatively rare event and one that carries the implication of a continued relationship."[3]

As it happened, the Reagan administration went on to apply positive sanctions of a kind, although on a scale quite different from that of 1970. By now the Americans had come to recognize that their own resources, while still vast, were not of an order to fundamentally change a society, least of all one that was so impervious to external influence. Crocker also acknowledged that America's economic investment in constructive engagement in the 1970s had only yielded results comparable to those achieved by the other Western powers at much lower political cost.

In one of its first statements on export controls, the administration confirmed that it intended to maintain any controls which still served to disassociate the United States from the worst excesses of apartheid. At the same time it did not believe that coercion could bring about change. It was wholly opposed to any further extension of export controls or import restrictions; significantly, it made no mention of following Richard Nixon in relaxing them.[4] Indeed, according to the terms of constructive engagement outlined in a speech by Under Secretary of State Lawrence Eagleburger toward the end of the administration's first term, there would have been little point in applying positive sanctions anyway. If it was not America's intention to offer *tactical* advice to the South African government, then there was clearly no point in applying sanctions as an incentive or inducement to proceed faster on the road to political reform.[5]

Throughout this period it is difficult to find any evidence that the administration intended using America's export potential to influence political developments, despite the fact that the United States became South Africa's largest trading partner for the first time in 1980; and despite the fact that closer political ties between the two countries had encouraged some of South Africa's public sector corporations or parastatals to take a renewed interest in American suppliers. During the late 1970s, for example, American corporations had not even bothered to tender for large contracts from the Electricity Supply Commission (ESCOM), knowing they would not receive Eximbank support. Within months of Reagan's inauguration the situation changed dramatically. In August 1981 ESCOM awarded an American company a $735 million contract to supply boilers for a new power station.

Neither at this time nor subsequently did the administration debate whether influence could be generated by creating new sources of supply for the giant parastatals, or buying into them when—as part of a limited policy of privatization—some of their equity holding began to be sold on the stock exchange. If an opportunity existed, it was not taken up. Clearly, this was a notable oversight, for the rapid succession of events in South Africa required above all a coherent and considered response. The Reagan administration for the most part seems to have been far from agreed on the degree of political influence that might result from the kind of economic leverage which the Ford administration had hoped to generate at the time of the FLUOR debate.

Possibly, from arguing that cooperation in economic matters might be useful, one might have gone on to argue that it was essential if the promise of constructive engagement was ever to be fulfilled. If the United States and South Africa could not work together in a field that might one day have a direct bearing on the redistribution of economic power, was there much point in working together at all? This question not only applied to foreign investment; it also encompassed private bank loans. An analysis of U.S. bank loans to the public sector reveals that a slide from $1.2 billion to $350 million between 1977 and 1980 was transformed within two years into a rise of $623 million.[6] Nedbank, one of South Africa's major state-owned banks, raised no less than $200 million for the Treasury, much of which came from American banks. An examination of Federal Reserve Bank statistics on U.S. loans to South African banks, which the government had begun to use to raise foreign capital for public sector development, revealed a phenomenal rise in the years 1980–82. At the end of this period they amounted to 60 percent of the total volume of all U.S. bank loans to the republic.

Despite this remarkable growth in private bank activity, it is difficult to detect any clear encouragement or support by the administration. Its spokesmen were anxious enough to defeat any moves in Congress to restrict bank loans to South Africa, especially to the South African government and its many economic agencies. Why then did it not consider tying their continued availability to future political behavior? The limits imposed on America's margin of choice inevitably raised the question whether it could conduct a policy that appeared to consist entirely of passive responses rather than firmly held principles and long-term aims.

But was this also the case in three of the other areas in which

President Reagan relaxed existing controls: the sale of arms and nuclear-related material and the bountiful provision of IMF loans? The South Africans expressed a clear interest in the second of these during Pik Botha's trip to Washington in May 1981. In the others they clearly had an interest, if not an overriding one. What if anything did Washington make of this situation?

The Arms Embargo

The administration's justification for lifting some of the restrictions on the export of arms-related equipment made much less of the positive sanctions argument than the contention that the embargo had demonstrably failed to achieve its main objective. Over the past twenty years South Africa had developed the world's tenth largest arms industry. Because of its production capacity ARMSCOR had begun to look for foreign markets. With an asset value of $1.2 billion, it was already the second largest industrial corporation in the republic.[7] If this analysis did not lead the administration to conclude that all controls should be abolished, it did prompt it to question the effectiveness of the existing embargo. It also led it to question whether in some cases the restrictions might be modified, or even repealed, without doing irreparable harm to the embargo.

The first two items to come under review were dual-purpose aircraft and computers. In March 1982 the Commerce Department introduced a series of new guidelines which permitted the export under general license of five categories of goods to the military and police; the export of all other goods under a validated license was subject to the determination that export would not "contribute significantly to military and police functions." In addition it established two *de minimis* provisions: one allowing for the export of U.S. components constituting up to 20 percent by value of goods assembled overseas and sold to the military; the other permitting the reexport or resale to the military of minor items sold to purchasers other than the military, provided the former did not contribute significantly to military operations. In September these regulations were further modified to allow companies that had already sold equipment to the army under approved licenses to supply service manuals without a statutory requirement to submit a license for each application. It also agreed to allow the sale of air ambulances and the export without license of items falling under such miscellaneous categories as electronic products.

In the course of 1982 three companies applied for export licenses to sell air ambulances to South Africa—a contract which amounted to $15 million. The protest that arose over the sale of the six twin-engine aircraft turned on the fact that the twin-engine turbo-prop, the Super King Air 200C—supplied by the leading contender, the Beech Aircraft Corporation—had also been supplied to the USAF as the C-12A. Although the company subsequently denied that it could be converted for military use, the C-12A could be used as a naval reconnaissance aircraft[8]—exactly the equipment South Africa urgently needed to replace its own obsolescent maritime patrol planes, as P. W. Botha made clear during his tour of Western Europe in the summer of 1984.

More controversial still was the administration's decision to permit the sale of advanced computers. For although its spokesmen were undoubtedly right to point out that ARMSCOR had become a highly complex and sophisticated organization capable of producing combat aircraft, guided missiles, and an impressive range of electronic equipment, the expense of remaining in the technological forefront imposed very high opportunity costs that South Africa would clearly have preferred to offset by foreign purchases. One such weapon was the G5, the most modern 155mm field gun in the world, capable of firing projectiles up to 40 percent farther than any other comparable weapon.[9] Although ARMSCOR had originally purchased the gun on the black market in 1976 and thereafter began its own production, it could not duplicate the system's computer targeting, which had to be directly purchased from Canada and the United States.

The sale of computers, therefore, became a highly charged political issue. Between January 1981 and December 1982 the Commerce Department approved licenses for sales to South Africa valued at more than $162 million. In March 1982 it granted an export license to an American company to sell the Cyber 170/750 computer, and shortly afterward allowed the sale of Sperry Univac computers to the Atlas Corporation, a subsidiary of ARMSCOR. Together with the sale of IBM and Data General MV/8000 computers to the National Institute for Telecommunications Research—a subsidiary of the state-owned Council for Scientific and Industrial Research (CSIR)—these export licenses gave rise to the fear that South Africa might soon be able to break America's own cryptographic system. Such was their sensitivity that the State Department requested both the president and vice-president of the CSIR to plead their case in person. Discussions between Crocker and Under Secretary Richard Kennedy failed to resolve the internal debate. The case eventually had to be referred to the Secretary of State, who chose to grant a license in the end. Five months later an Amdahl computer with capabilities similar in all essential respects to the Cyber 170/750 was also approved for sale to the same institute.

The motivation which prompted the Reagan administration to reopen computer sales was partly understandable in the light of constructive engagement, and partly distinctive. Although it often seemed uncertain whether to tie such sales to specific policy changes on the part of the South African government, it obviously hoped that they would produce some political return. As the deputy secretary of commerce observed in February 1982, "We are taking small steps toward them; they should be taking small steps toward us."[10]

Clearly such cooperation had the support of those in the Pentagon who looked forward to amplifying South Africa's defense role in the region, and in turn its participation in the defense of interests common to both countries. In order to underline their *political* content, Crocker insisted that the United States could only have a productive relationship "with a society undergoing constructive change"; that there could be no "shortcut solutions to the question of the exercise of political power."[11] Both quotations, one from a report written for Alexander Haig, the other from a briefing paper prepared for Reagan's meeting with Pik Botha, were resonant with themes first heard in the early 1970s. If this was indeed the case, the modifications of the arms embargo paralleled NSSM 89 rather too closely. Both could be seen as halfhearted measures, more commercial than political in their impact, if not inspiration. Both could be taken as excellent examples of drift on the current of events rather than active and dynamic policies designed to direct those currents, as far as circumstances would permit, to America's own advantage.

Nuclear-related Exports

In the case of the export of nuclear-related equipment, the administration was forced to tread even more treacherous ground and was consequently all the more alive to the need to justify its decision. During congressional hearings in 1982 several government officials expressed the opinion that the approval of only a few licenses for nuclear sales might prove invaluable in maintaining a dialogue with South Africa, that Washington's ability to influence Pretoria depended on a willingness to consider favorably "a small carefully selected number of non-sensitive exports," and that the latter could make all the difference between whether the South Africans continued to ignore or listen to American advice.[12]

Here again, however, it must be questioned whether the United States actually derived any return from the modification of existing restrictions. On this occasion, of course, it had some grounds for hoping otherwise, since the South Africans themselves had requested American support. In a memorandum written in May 1981, Crocker clearly laid out what the U.S. actually wanted:

> —undertaking that U.S. will allow export permits to be issued for delivery of enriched uranium to France
> —if U.S. felt it couldn't supply enriched uranium via France, to make known to France it would *not* insist on conditions that imposed unilaterally on South Africa after signature of original supply contracts if France were to supply fuel
> —DOE agreed either to cancel the present contract for supply of enriched uranium to ESCOM at no cost or agreed to postpone execution of contract at no cost until time reached when deliveries to Koeberg from U.S. could be resumed.[13]

By March 1982 the South Africans needed American assistance rather urgently. The initial fuel loading of their French-supplied nuclear reactors at Koeberg was seriously delayed because of the absence of an adequate supply of enriched uranium. The U.S. Department of Commerce subsequently approved the export of two hydrogen recombiners for use at Koeberg, a sale that was later defended by the Arms Control and Disarmament Agency on the grounds that it would secure its own nonproliferation objectives.[14] There was particular interest at the time in persuading the South Africans to convert their research reactor at Safari to lower-enriched fuels in order to lower the proliferation risk that high-enriched uranium might be processed there.[15] However, Washington's efforts proved unavailing. South Africa doggedly refused to sign the Nonproliferation Treaty. The objective may have been set, but it was, alas, not fixed. The State Department was well aware that two American companies acting as brokers for South Africa had arranged for fuel sales to Koeberg through third-party contractors. Rather than exert pressure on Pretoria by making the transaction public, the administration chose to preserve its silence on the issue, later claiming to be shocked when the arrangement finally came to light.[16]

It may even have connived at much more. Among the nuclear-related items that were considered for export, one that figured prominently was the projected sale of ninety-five grams of helium-3, a product that could easily be converted into tritium and used to manufacture nuclear weapons. Even more controversial was the provisional export of a large hot-isostatic press, a sophisticated metallurgical device manufactured by only four companies in the world—three American and one Swedish. It was particularly unfortunate that the press was used in the American aerospace industry and reportedly in U.S. military programs, although such information continued to remain classified. In the end, the Department of Commerce prevailed upon the administration to reconsider its earlier deicision to ban the sale of the press, notwithstanding the fact that Sweden had been previously urged not to export the system to countries which might be in the process of developing nuclear weapons, a list that included countries as diverse as Israel, India, and Taiwan.[17]

Overall, it could hardly be said that the administration acted with great resourcefulness, that it made the most of its strengths, never conceding an issue of substance until it received a comparable concession. Nor could it be said that it prepared its hand particularly well keeping its trump cards to the end. For the most part it continued to act as if it did not possess any trump cards at all.

IMF Loans

The late 1970s marked a qualitative change in the nature of the South African economy as the high growth rates of previous years, which had been second only to Japan's, faded into history. Demandled inflation and spiraling public spending reduced economic expectations at the very time that the economy needed to grow at a faster rate than ever to absorb 350,000 blacks a year on the labor market. Like many countries in similar predicaments, South Africa was forced to resort to public borrowing to keep the economy going—one source being the International Monetary Fund.

In addition to relaxing some of the restrictions on trade between itself and South Africa, the United States also ensured that the IMF met South Africa's loan requests, the most important of which was made in 1982 for a $1 billion credit—the largest loan ever awarded from the Fund's Compensatory Financing Facility. On this occasion Washington certainly hoped for some tangible political return, a point that was actually made explicit during a UN debate when the American representative Gordon Luce defended the loan on the grounds that the republic was already making "constructive change in its racial policies."[18]

In essence, the economic problem which South Africa faced in 1982 was that, following several years of high growth on the back of a gold boom, the terms of trade had turned sharply against it. At the same time the government had failed signally to restrict imports, with the inevitable result that in only three years (1979–1981) the country's balance of payments turned from a surplus of almost $3 billion to a significant and serious deficit of $3.7 billion. By the end of August 1982 the country's foreign exchange reserves were barely large enough to cover a single week's imports.

When South Africa's application for a loan was first discussed by the IMF, the United States insisted that its lending rules must be applied impartially. Responding to criticism that the decision to grant a loan would be viewed as support for the prevailing political order, the State Department went to the extraordinary length of issuing a statement that "the U.S. position on the South African drawing indicates no change in our position on apartheid nor in our opposition to the use of force to resolve political differences in the region."[19] Clearly concerned about adverse publicity, Treasury Secretary Donald Regan insisted that South Africa's application must be considered on strictly economic criteria—that to oppose it on political grounds would violate the Fund's "apolitical nature."[20] Presumably this also applied to using the loan for more positive political purposes, for making it conditional on more radical reforms, or even endorsing South Africa's application to strengthen the hand of a reforming government, as Luce intimated in the UN. Which of these two spokesmen were to be believed? Did the decision to grant South Africa's request have any political content?

The financial assistance which South Africa eventually received fell under two categories—a standby arrangement which constituted approximately 40 percent of the total package and a loan under the so-called Compensatory Financing Facility. According to the IMF's own rules the circumstances warranting assistance under a standby arrangement had to arise from internal policies which had created serious balance of payments difficulties that were no longer sustainable. The Compensatory Finance Facility, on the other hand, was usually awarded when a country through no fault of its own experienced a temporary shortfall.

The facility carried much easier terms of conditionality than did assistance granted as a standby arrangement. The decision to apportion the loan as it was divided already constituted a decision as to what kinds of conditionality to impose. In other words, it was a decision as to what regulations, rules, and terms would be set for the IMF loan. In order to make that decision, there should have been a full analysis of the extent to which the government and its policies were responsible for the country's difficulties and the extent to which they were due to cyclical shortfalls beyond the government's control. That question was not addressed; it was simply ignored.[21]

The loan was even more questionable because South Africa clearly failed to meet the conditions on which the IMF actually insisted. Its dual exchange rate was not phased out as a precondition for the standby arrangements.[22] In September Pretoria even lowered the reserve requirement as a monetary policy. If anything, this was a signal for monetary expansion, not a measure of the government's determination to get the economy under control. The Fund also chose to view the country's import surcharge as a revenue-raising device when usually it regarded such instruments as protectionist acts on whose repeal it normally insisted.

Finally, as if this were not special pleading enough, the Fund's executive board did not deal with the main point at issue: the impact of apartheid on the labor market. This was especially surprising since the shortage of skilled labor was a persistent theme of IMF staff reports on South Africa, where the system was constantly portrayed as a quantitative restriction on the labor force and a qualitative hurdle that prevented the labor market from operating effectively.

These reports were taken so much to heart by the South Africans that their representatives on the Fund devoted four pages out of five of a reply to criticism of the loan agreement to a discussion of labor conditions.[23] Washington, however, did not seek to exploit South Africa's embarrassment. True, if it had been too demanding, Pretoria might have turned instead to the commercial market even if this would have meant borrowing money at double the 6 to 7 percent the IMF eventually charged. But the risk was not very great. Here was an excellent opportunity to tie the provision of a loan to a significant reform of South Africa's labor market, or at the very least to changes in the economics of apartheid; it was an opportunity, alas, which the administration passed up.

In looking back over the period it is clear that in attempting to sustain a working relationship with South Africa the United States had a range of tried and tested mechanisms. The problem was that there were no obvious guidelines as to which (singly or in combination) might work. Thus at times Washington was tempted to trade with Pretoria without qualification, at others to insist on prior guarantees or conditions, but rarely if ever to tie existing trade patterns to political behavior in the future. As an element of constructive engagement, positive sanctions seem to have passed into history, perhaps never to return.

By 1985 what had the Reagan administration to show for its commercial ventures? Although it is clear from table 6 that the overall trend toward higher exports to South Africa began well before the Reagan administration took office in 1981 and that in that sense the increased economic ties of the early years of the decade were a continuation rather than a reversal of former policies, three trends were clearly apparent. First, the Commerce Department issued 1,864 licenses in 1984, valued at $672.9 million—more than the Carter administration issued in three years. Even with all but the most sensitive items exempted from the licensing requirements by the administration's revision of the existing regulations, approvals were up by almost 80 percent over 1980, a figure that contrasted markedly with an average of only 15 percent for the rest of the world.

Second, a substantial proportion of the license approvals was for materials that could be used for nuclear weapons production or testing, although U.S. cooperation with South Africa technically remained prohibited because of the latter's refusal to sign the Nonproliferation Treaty. A General Accounting Office study covering the period of 1981 to 1982 found that South Africa was the second lead-

Table 6   Leading U.S. Exports to South Africa

Year	Computers	Aircraft	Total exports
1978	$ 52,753,000	$ 35,274,000	$1,079,600,000
1979	71,778,000	63,612,000	1,406,840,000
1980	111,883,000	264,119,000	2,452,543,000
1981	146,785,000	232,546,000	2,900,600,000
1982	170,738,000	266,709,000	2,359,891,000
1983	174,461,000	301,262,000	2,114,777,000
1984	184,662,000	145,223,000	2,463,215,000

SOURCE   Office of Export Administration, Department of Commerce.

ing purchaser of American "dual-purpose, nuclear-related" equipment. To compound this pattern, computers and aircraft were the consistent leaders in U.S. exports to South Africa, helping to make the U.S. trade balance with that country favorable in three of the administration's first five years. Computer sales continued to climb even as overall U.S. exports continued to fall, with some companies like Control Data deriving 50 percent of their financial returns from sales to the government or public sector corporations, including the government-run Council for Scientific and Industrial Research.

Inevitably, as the administration was forced onto the defensive in 1985, these three trading patterns began to excite particular controversy, and were taken by critics to be confirmation that the United States was aiding, if not abetting, the apartheid regime. Indeed, by the end of 1983 the administration found itself battling against a number of congressional initiatives to impose much harsher negative sanctions. In Reagan's first term four separate amendments aimed at outlawing future IMF loans, and prohibiting commercial bank loans to the South African government, as well as all future corporate investment, reached the floor of the House. The administration also faced an amendment to the Export Administration Act requiring the restoration of controls on arms exports, including "nonlethal" material such as computers and light aircraft. Only one of these amendments became law, but all were directly aimed at reversing recent modifications of trade controls.

In October 1984 matters came to a head when both the House and Senate conference committees agreed on an unprecedented ban on bank loans to the South African government and parastatals. The ban, along with stricter export regulations and a study of fair labor practices by American investors, was a compromise on a package of anti-apartheid measures the House had tried to attach to the Export Administration Act earlier in the session. Bank loan restrictions —part of an amendment sponsored by Representative Steven Solarz —and the restoration of strict controls on the sale of goods to the South African military sponsored by Representative Howard Berman had been adopted by the House of Representatives in October 1983. Solarz's amendment also banned the import of Krugerrand gold coins and required American companies to abide by a nondiscriminatory employment code, the 1983 modified Sullivan principles.

In any event, the House and Senate conference committees rejected both of these provisions as well as Representative William Gray's amendment banning *all* new investment in South Africa. An attempt by Gray to win conference committee backing for a weaker investment ban was also voted down. An amendment sponsored by the House Africa subcommittee chairman Howard Wolpe restricting the sale of nuclear-related equipment to signatories of the Nonproliferation Treaty was modified to include a limited number of items.

The following year Congress met with much greater success. The Senate Foreign Relations Committee, with the support of its Republican leadership, came out in strong support of selective sanctions. Other Republicans backed a host of tougher measures including a ban on all flights by South African Airways to the United States and a substantial reduction of South African consulates allowed to operate within the United States. In June the House formally adopted a resolution calling for sanctions to take immediate effect.

Quite separately from the moves in Congress, a nationwide campaign for the withdrawal of all American assets gained pace. Five states had already passed disinvestment laws barring the investment of pension and other state funds in companies doing business with South Africa. More than a dozen cities, including New York, Boston, Washington and Philadelphia, had done the same, and more soon followed. Perhaps the most important result of these protests was that they changed the climate of debate across the country into one in which the South Africans had few public defenders even among those who tried to fight back against disinvestment and withdrawal. Many congressmen who in all other respects would have been and were sympathetic did not wish to be publicly identified with the campaign for fear of being tarred with the apartheid brush.

In the face of such a sustained attack on constructive engagement and the positive sanctions that were expected to underwrite it, the administration did what it could to reassert its belief that international influence was unlikely to be increased by "pinpricks" such as restrictions on Krugerrand sales or landing rights for South African Airways. Crocker remained totally opposed to disinvestment—even, as he told the Senate Foreign Relations Committee in May, to making mandatory the Sullivan principles. He failed to see how waging an economic war against South Africa could advance U.S. goals. Four years on, the administration remained completely convinced that the best avenue for change in South Africa was to promote, not undermine, opportunites for the black majority. Increasingly besieged on all sides, the assistant secretary referred fittingly in 1984 to an "Orwellian perversity in proposing such measures in the name of liberal and humanitarian goals."[24] A few months later he went on to criticize the "ostrich approach" to politics that offered nothing by way of constructive change and which implicitly assumed that the South African problem would resolve itself.[25]

Lawrence Eagleburger went much further, claiming that were the congressional amendments to be adopted the United States would become entirely irrelevant to South Africa's future. He poured particular scorn on those who repeated "the slogans of liberation while denying us the ability to add an ounce of political will to solving the region's problems. At a time when we need all the leverage available to us, some argue for disinvestment and escape. They confuse the making of statements with the ability to influence events."[26] Eagleburger's criticisms might have been more trenchant if the administration had ever exhibited a clear understanding of what positive sanctions meant. They might even have carried the day had the administration ever acted with clearly defined ends in mind.

11 The United States, South Africa, and Regional Security, 1981–1985

So far the discussion of constructive engagement has been conducted in something of a vacuum. As Cantori and Spiegel have warned, by not considering the importance of regional relations those scholars who are preoccupied with the state as the only actor take too restrictive a view, while those who concern themselves with the international system as a whole adopt too broad a perspective.[1] American policy toward South Africa could never be entirely divorced from its regional context, much less so after 1978 than before. In the early 1970s the Nixon administration had not been especially influenced by regional developments, except for the hope that South Africa might be used as a Western proxy, like Iran in the Middle East—a thought in keeping with the Nixon Doctrine. Within ten years, however, the Reagan administration had become much more concerned, not with those elements of stability which American policymakers had retrospectively come to discern in the regional order, but with the destabilizing effects of war, the decline of the regional order, the disturbingly high level of violence beyond South Africa's borders.

By 1981 Southern Africa had become an increasingly contested arena in global politics, a potential point of conflict between the two superpowers. Despite the success of the Lancaster House conference and Zimbabwe's peaceful transition to independence, a combination of external pressures and internal stresses still prevailed. Six years after Angola's independence substantial Cuban forces remained behind as participants in a still unresolved and protracted civil war. The Warsaw Pact countries had concluded arms agreements with four countries in the region and boosted arms transfers by 250 percent.

Faced with the threat of an escalating guerrilla war and mounting instability on its borders, South Africa had significantly expanded its defense potential. Within a few years it had become a major regional power that had signaled its determination to resist guerrilla encroachment and strike directly at countries giving sanctuary to the ANC. The potential damage to Western interests in the area was enhanced by America's economic stake—$6 billion in trade and a dependence on minerals, from vanadium to platinum, which were vital to the industrial economies of North America and Western Europe.

Most members of the Reagan administration believed that the Soviet presence in Southern Africa required an understanding between South Africa and the West. There might be different views as to precisely what form such an understanding should take, but the picture of a more active American government on the one hand and a more committed and constructive South Africa on the other was one to which they all adhered. Involving South Africa in regional security, seeing off the Soviet challenge, and seducing Angola and Mozambique from the Marxist path became consuming obsessions in Washington—the shared aim of ostensibly opposed policymakers who might agree on little else and a major preoccupation of conservative writers who assigned South Africa a critical role.

Before discussing that role, however, we should perhaps look first at the nature of the Southern African region in which South Africa had been allotted its part. Defining the region's problems was one thing, defining its state system quite another. Southern Africa was for many nothing more than a geographical expression whose coherence as a region derived from the definitions provided by economists and political scientists. Although an extensive literature has emerged on its regional identity, there is still divergent opinion both on its economic constituents and the criteria for membership.[2]

The region, in fact, has been constantly redefined and redrawn in the light of contemporary attitudes, anxieties, and interests, somewhat loosely described as the preoccupations of the moment. Thus in the early 1960s it was fashionable to speak of the emergence of a regional order based on a "white redoubt"—on South Africa itself, Rhodesia after UDI, and the Portuguese colonies where the whites consolidated their position in response to the nationalist challenge. The South Africans were in the forefront of attempts to forge closer links. For them there was an obvious appeal in working more closely with other minority rule regimes. In 1965 Pretoria gave a loan to the Smith government for the Chiredzi-Mbizi rail link and the Chiredzi dam. In the aftermath of UDI the giant South African company, Anglo-American, was responsible for expanding Rhodesia's mining industry, opening up a new nickel mine at Bindura, and extending the existing phosphate mine at Dorowa.[3]

For economists brought up in a geopolitical tradition, it came as no surprise that South Africa agreed to finance a rail link between Nacala and Malawi, furthering the latter's dependence on Portuguese East Africa for its outlet to the sea. South Africa's exclusion in the 1960s from such international organizations as the Economic Commission for Africa (ECA) persuaded Pretoria to finance such regional schemes as the Kunene and Cabora Bassa dams. Both were originally planned as vast white settlement programs which would strengthen the whites' hold and legitimize their presence. This wider design foundered, however, when Western companies, largely in response to international pressure, pulled out of the largest scheme of all: the Zambezi Valley Program between 1969 and 1971.

Until the end of the Johnson administration, nevertheless, there was sustained interest in Washington in the prospect, however remote or unlikely, of the extension of this white regional order to include South Africa's more dependent black neighbors. In establishing an office for the U.S. Agency for International Development (USAID) in Lusaka in 1968 it signaled its intention to abandon bilateral aid programs in favor of programs that would encourage regional cooperation—which in the case of Zambia meant largely cooperation with its white neighbors.[4]

The renegotiated customs union between South Africa and the BSL states (Botswana, Swaziland, and Lesotho) consolidated South Africa's influence by removing the residual British presence in the form of grants-in-aid, which prior to 1970 had helped to subsidize their budgets.[5] Some observers even saw American aid in the form of an international loan for the Selibe-Phikwe mining industry as tacit support for this process, an instrument that increased Botswana's regional integration, while simultaneously reducing its contact with the outside world.[6] Botswana's state of dependency was quite evidently extensive. It relied so heavily on the rail link with Rhodesia that it was reduced in 1972 to lobbying the U.S. government to sell new rolling stock to Rhodesian railways in defiance of UN sanctions.[7]

However, even at the time general pessimism about the eventual prospects of black majority rule was further darkened by the vicissitudes in which countries like Botswana were placed by sanctions against Rhodesia. Botswana was among the first black African states to try to escape South Africa's orbit.[8] With the opening in 1968 of the Ndola-Dar-es-Salaam oil pipeline, followed some years later by the Tanzara railway, Zambia also initiated steps to disengage from the white system. The nationalization of its mines in the early 1970s provided it with further funds for new infrastructure programs all looking to trade with the east, not the south, and at one time even appeared to offer the prospect of alternative sources of development aid from the Eastern bloc.[9] Indeed, Pretoria's attempts to create a Southern African "common market" or economic commission came to nothing. In an article on the prospects for an Economic Commission for Southern Africa, one South African economist highlighted South Africa's recent trade agreement with the Malagasy Republic (1970); yet it was the revolution in Madagascar the following year that put an end to such dreams, and with them hopes of a more general dialogue with Pretoria.[10]

The model that gained ground throughout Nixon's term in office and even beyond, was a modified version of the first—a regional order under white control. The second was focused not on a crumbling white redoubt but on hopes of building a new and more constructive relationship with its neighbors. It was a relationship the South Africans hoped would be based not on hegemonic but "systemic" cooperation, a relationship between equals (with South Africa being primus inter pares as befitted its predominant economic position) that would provide an alternative, on the one hand, to isolation, and on the other, to full integration. Interdependence, not integration, was the key word, although those like Kenneth Kaunda who felt threatened by the program rapidly reached the disturbing conclusion that the "Boer trek was still on."[11]

The collapse of the white redoubt between 1974 and 1979 did not set the program back; indeed, it appeared to enhance it (although the outward policy—as a phrase—was soon abandoned). The weakness of states such as Mozambique made them more susceptible, not less, to South Africa's economic influence and the political leverage that came with it. After Mozambique's independence the new regime found itself reliant on South African assistance to help run the port of Maputo and to keep open the railway to the south, as well as the old arrangements for migrant workers who received 60 percent of their wages at the old official gold price. The assistance provided by the South Africans ranged from the loan of train locomotives to the installation of a new signaling system, and even the construction of a loop line to increase the capacity of the rail link between Komatipoort and Maputo.

The centrality of communications (most of them dating to the 1930s or earlier) to regional integration and South Africa's economic pull was emphasized, or symbolized, by two diplomatic events in this period. The brief period of détente between South Africa and Lusaka was initiated in the compartment of a train owned by South African Railways on the bridge over the Victoria Falls. Nine years later in February 1984 Samora Machel and P. W. Botha met at Komatipoort to sign a nonaggression pact, an arrangement which also institutionalized and extended economic cooperation between two countries who were in all other respects violently at odds.

It was always inevitable, however, that the revised model for South Africa's regional role would be rejected and found to be as unappealing as the original. At no time in the 1970s did it ever look as though the black members of the Southern African state system would voluntarily accept a regional order in which South Africa remained the dominant power. The outward policy, moreover, as Timothy Shaw observed at the time, offered a conservative not a radical future. Ultimately it was "another attempt to divert support . . . toward collaboration with South Africa, to achieve regional coexistence without a significant redistribution of resources."[12]

In time the outward policy was narrowed to South Africa and the independent homelands, and the peripheral countries in the Southern African Customs Union and Rand Monetary Area. South Africans soon began talking about a "constellation of states," economic cooperation that stopped short at the Limpopo not the Zambezi. Zambia and its immediate neighbors began to think in terms of a third economic model, an alternative future, to reduce their dependence on South Africa, to escape from what Joseph Nye and Robert Keohane call "asymmetrical interdependence," to create through cooperation among themselves a new economic regime.[13]

The reality which the Reagan administration faced was the Southern African Development Coordination Conference (SADCC), a collection of nine regional powers committed through the Lusaka Declaration of 1980 to forge "genuine and equitable regional integration" with particular emphasis on self-reliance and independence. Yet the first five years of SADCC's existence were characterized by growing dependence on South Africa by the majority of the nine states. South Africa remained the largest trading partner of seven of its members; indeed SADCC's trade with the republic was seven times higher than that between the member states themselves. Nearly all of them discovered that their import-export trade would grind to a halt were they to be deprived of the South African rail network. On an average day in January 1985, 7,200 South African wagons could be found carrying goods on the lines of SADCC countries, compared with only 900 wagons from the latter countries on South African rail lines. So important had South Africa become to the transport sector of the region that five years after SADCC set the severance of transport links with the republic as its primary objective special arrangements had to be made for transport officials of all nine SADCC countries, including Angola and Tanzania, to meet more frequently with South African officials to discuss the sub-continent's transport problems.[14]

This brief discussion of the three models of regional relations surely shows that the dominant model that prevailed at any one time was never more than a partial view of a very complex situation. In that it drew attention to some important aspects of the subject and especially to South Africa's dominant position, it was never wholly wrong, but in that it gave a disproportionate emphasis to a limited number of considerations, none of the models was wholly right either.

The three models were also the creation of demand as well as supply. In the early 1960s the pessimistic picture of a white-dominated state system seemed more appropriately to mirror contemporary experience. Not until white rule began to crumble first in the Portuguese colonies and then in Rhodesia, the most beleaguered state of all, did South Africa's outward strategy which had been talked about by Verwoerd in the late 1950s,[15] become popular for the first time. Similarly, if the aims of SADCC gained wide currency after 1979 that was because they seemed to be attuned to the prevailing mood after Zimbabwe's independence. To this extent the economic history of Southern Africa, which every generation seems to rewrite, may be more a creation of the audience than the authors.

This should also make us very cautious in our approach to the literature of the subordinate state systems which began to gain ground after 1968 with the publication of an article by Lawrence Bowman.[16] Bowman's intention was to show "that this system can be described as an entity; that it operates quite independently of the dominant world power blocs; and most importantly, that it can best be analyzed and understood in terms of its own interrelations." Having stated his premises, Bowman reached the conclusion that "the overwhelming structural characteristic of Southern Africa and the one that more than anything else makes the system unified is the domination of the area by South Africa's economic wealth and economic demands."[17]

A few years later Kenneth Grundy objected to Bowman's use of the word *subordinate* to describe the state system on the grounds that although the Great Powers might *appear* to exercise greater power than the subsystemic actors, there were numerous instances when global conditions did not permit the strongest states to dictate policies within the region. Writing in 1973 he was also more pessimistic than Bowman about the system's fundamental stability. Indeed, he opined that it was essentially unstable despite its amazing staying power.[18] Grundy's thesis has survived the passing of time. By 1981—when the Reagan administration came to look at Southern Africa—it should have been clear that it was dealing with an essentially unstable system, made more unstable still by South African military intervention, over which neither the United States nor the Soviet Union exercised any control, either as a deterrent or a mitigating influence.

Indeed, if we compare the situation in 1981 with Grundy's predictions we can see how the latter were born out by events. Grundy got the answer right; most others did not. The situation in the early 1980s did not bear out, for example, the predictions of another state systems writer, Christian Potholm. Writing in 1972 he surmised nine future scenarios, in two of which he predicted that South Africa would withdraw into a garrison state able to prevent large-scale insurgency but not able to maintain the entire system against attack; and that the South African–centered subsystem of the early 1970s would soon be reduced in size and scope.[19] Neither of these pessimistic scenarios came true. South Africa instead succeeded in sustaining a systemic role by the unqualified use of its military power. The United

States even came to place its hopes in the fact that the role seemed to be a permanent one, and that the republic's military power afforded the best hope of containing the Soviet threat.

Events were very soon to show, however, that South Africa was not—what so many of the state systems writers supposed—a client state of the West, a subimperial power, a Western surrogate in all but name. Subimperialism was a favorite theme of the 1970s. As Timothy Shaw concluded: "A subimperial state exists at the center of the periphery; it is a client state that is able to exert dominance in one region of the Third World. Thus it can exploit the process of regional integration while at the same time remaining dependent on a greater metropolitan power."[20] Subimperial states, Shaw argued, promote economic growth and acquire military domination through their association with major powers. Some writers saw in the appearance of Marxist-Leninist states in the region the chance that the Soviet Union might promote subimperial powers of its own.[21]

Even at the time, however, it was a doubtful formulation. South Africa's association with the Western state system came to an end with its own withdrawal from the Commonwealth in 1961 and with the West's obvious reluctance to enter into military pacts like the much-discussed South Atlantic Treaty Association (SATO), even its unwillingness to honor existing military understandings such as the Simonstown agreement, which was finally terminated at Britain's request in 1974. By the end of the 1970s South Africa was very much a regional power with strictly regional interests, a fate which seemed to confirm the contention of Cantori and Spiegel that "every nation state . . . is a member of only one subordinate system."[22]

The event that did more than anything else to reconcile the South Africans to their independent status and that should have ended any speculation about a subimperial role, was the dismal story of the South African Defense Force's intervention in Angola in the wake of Portuguese decolonization. After Angola it became difficult for the republic to entertain hopes of an alliance with the Western powers, now that it had become unequivocally clear that being pro-West no longer meant being Western. As the United States admitted at the time, there could be no question of ever supplying arms to Pretoria in a conflict in which its own forces were not themselves engaged.[23] This in effect meant that South Africa might be used as a proxy but would have only itself to rely on if it found itself committed to an open-ended conflict.

The increasingly independent use of South African military power after 1978 reflected a growing awareness of this conclusion. As Vorster told the nation in a New Year message in 1977, the West had not only lost the initiative but had gone onto the defensive not only in Southern Africa but everywhere else.[24] Thereafter Pretoria intervened on its own account, revealing something that Washington chose to ignore for far too long, that the position had begun to change, and in changing to reveal starkly the irreconcilability of the West's needs and South Africa's aspirations.

Confirmation of this change of status—from erstwhile proxy to independent (even neutral) power—came with the dramatic contraction of the South African Navy (SAN), now starved of new equipment by the arms embargo and denied the minimum that would have been needed to make it a useful antisubmarine force. Once the proud possessor of a flotilla of frigates, by 1981 it had only one left. After 1979 the SAN became a glorified coastal patrol force, able with its new Israeli Resheff-class missile boats and thirty fast harbor-patrol craft to protect shipping in inshore waters, but unable to patrol the waters off Mozambique and Angola or to observe more than 60 percent of shipping movements out at sea, certainly unable to conduct antisubmarine missions in the face of a putative Soviet threat. In November 1984 even its Shackleton patrol aircraft were finally withdrawn from service. With their demise the SAN became a full-fledged African force whose sole responsibility was surveillance of the country's coastline against smuggling and guerrilla incursions. Like most other African navies, it chose to forgo the purchase of expensive and potentially unusable frigates and corvettes in favor of more appropriate but less sophisticated technology.

But the South Africans went beyond merely reorganizing force structures in the face of the West's apparent indifference to their fate. They threatened to use their naval vessels for a very different purpose than the protection of Western shipping. In the late 1970s the government imposed strict new controls on international shipping in transit past the Cape. In 1981 it gave the SAN extra powers to stop or search any vessel suspected of carrying arms to guerrilla movements in neighboring countries. These measures were supplemented by occasional demonstrations of military power—such as the buzzing of U.S. aircraft carriers in 1980 as they rounded the Cape at a time of particular tension between Pretoria and Washington.[25] Incidents such as these should have served to illustrate that Pretoria was now its own master, no longer beholden to the West, certainly no longer in awe of it.

Yet it was the United States' belief that its interests and South Africa's were very similar, together with its belief—based on a quite inadequate understanding of the Southern Africa state system—that South Africa's military power might be a factor making for stability rather than instability in the region, that led the United States in 1981 to work toward a division of responsibilities in the elusive quest for regional security. Grundy's original analysis went unheeded. It was to be another five years before the dissenting heresies of one generation became the entrenched orthodoxies of the next.

The Reagan Administration and the New Strategic Relationship

In the course of a series of talks held between Pik Botha and Alexander Haig in May 1981 the Reagan administration intimated that it hoped for "a more positive and reciprocal relationship between the two countries based upon shared strategic concerns in southern Africa."[26] In Crocker's memorandum to Haig before the May 14 meeting he advised that the United States should insist that it also had a role in rebuilding stability in the region, that it was a shared goal which could not be reached without American participation, and that in the last resort the United States could not afford to give Pretoria a blank check.

At the same time Crocker began a series of discussions with all the major actors in the region, not just the government of South Africa, to identify the extent to which their own priorities and concerns fitted in with the Reagan administration's objectives. The three priorities that were eventually identified were regional security, independence for Namibia, and, only last, peaceful change within South Africa itself.[27]

Both reviews illustrated two new features which the Reagan administration brought to constructive engagement: an avowed interest in cooperating with South Africa to meet a Soviet threat which often appeared more imaginary than real and an equally strong wish to press ahead with Namibia's independence in the hope the rest of

Africa might be reconciled to constructive engagement. Crocker's recognition that relations with Pretoria would be greatly influenced by its relations with its immediate neighbors merely echoed the views of Hilgaard Muller thirteen years earlier: "To the extent to which the West is becoming aware of our fruitful cooperation with other countries in Africa its attitude and disposition toward us are improving and I believe that this will happen to an increasing degree. We must simply accept that our relations with the rest of the world are largely determined by our relations with other African states."[28]

The question remains whether those relations were quite as constructive as the United States imagined, or whether they contributed in any constructive way to regional stability. By 1983 it appeared to many observers that the South Africans had indeed been given a blank check. By then Washington was dealing with a country that seemed to be largely oblivious to, or independent of, American influence or restraint, able and willing to advance interests of its own that did not always correspond to the interests of its superpower patron.

At a conference in Harare in January 1983 America's critics admitted that it might indeed still be the main hope for peace in the region, but that it had shown no inclination to promote it by bringing South Africa into line. Howard Wolpe, the chairman of the House subcommittee on Africa, added his own voice to the chorus of protest, claiming that nothing of substance had been achieved over the past three years—that Washington had compounded an already unstable situation by making it clear that whatever course of action South Africa wished to pursue would meet with Washington's tacit acquiescence, if not its overt support.[29]

In the very month of President Reagan's inauguration South Africa's forces conducted their first cross-border raid into Mozambique against the ANC bases. It was the beginning of a more aggressive program of destabilization which reached a peak in 1983. It was a program that promised stability of a kind, but not quite the stability Crocker had in mind in drafting his famous memorandum to Haig in May 1981. It was a stability for which America eventually paid a high price, and which contributed not a little to the eventual demise of constructive engagement.

South Africa's Policy of Destabilization
(1981–1985)

In keeping with its declared objective of putting the Front Line States on a defensive footing while the reform program was implemented at home, the SADF carried out a broad policy of destabilizing any country which aided or abetted the ANC. Acts of sabotage and economic disruption ensured that its neighbors remained economically weak, increasingly dependent on outside aid or South African assistance. Destabilization was a high-risk policy, for it exacerbated suspicion and heightened tensions in the region, but it was also quite a sophisticated policy in that it obviated any need to remove the governments affected. Since it was in Pretoria's interest that there should be no successful black government in Southern Africa, it was enough to impede their success.

Looked at historically the policy had an inherent logic of its own. Vorster had been the first South African leader to warn of such attacks in 1967 when Zambia had allowed itself to be used by SWAPO guerrillas as a base of operations. The first attack took the form of a small raid into the Western Province in 1971. From the very first the threat of escalation was implicit. Writing in 1973 Kenneth Grundy had warned that only a thin dividing line existed between military penetration and political intervention.[30] That line was eventually crossed in 1978 when the SADF launched Operation Reindeer and engaged the Angolan army for the first time in the first of many pitched battles near Cassinga and Chetequera. Reindeer was followed in March 1979 by two smaller raids against Angola and Zambia respectively, neither of which did much damage. During Operation Skeptic in June 1980 the SADF penetrated more than 120 kilometers into Angola, killing more than 360 SWAPO insurgents and eliminating a major SWAPO base. Operation Smokeshell which followed was the largest operation to date, involving three squadrons of Mirage IIIs and Buccaneer bombers and requiring the largest mobilization of South African forces since the Second World War.

The United States largely remained silent in the face of these ever-escalating raids, a term that was itself something of a euphemism. The year 1981 saw three successive invasions, Carnation, Protea, and Daisy, the second the most extensive of all, involving over 11,000 men and 250 armored vehicles. In the eighteen days of Operation Daisy the SADF advanced an unprecedented 250 kilometers inland. The increasing use of heavy equipment, including ninety Centurion tanks, was made necessary by the fact that South Africa's forces were no longer engaging a guerrilla army but a highly trained if somewhat unpredictable modern force that had begun to sustain an increasing number of casualties. Sixty percent of the casualties during Operation Protea were incurred by the Angolan army.[31]

The escalating scope of the fighting was reflected in the increasing share of the defense budget required to fund actual combat operations — 66 percent in 1982–83, 72 percent the following year. January 1982 saw Operation Super, a small-scale incursion into north Kaokoland that resulted in the destruction of a SWAPO transit camp for the loss of only three South African soldiers. In August Pretoria launched its most ambitious raid to date, Operation Mebos, which left the SADF in occupation of a large span of countryside in the south until the winter of 1984–85. Occasionally, however, the pressure was kept up, with Operation Askari in December 1983 being the largest for three years and also, as it turned out, the most costly. Indeed, mounting losses of hardware and men forced a strategic withdrawal a few days ahead of schedule.

The Reagan administration's silence in the face of these attacks seemed somewhat at odds with its initial objectives. Questioned by the House Committee on Foreign Affairs, Crocker insisted that regional security ran in both directions across international borders. Instead of condemning each transgression of sovereignty, the United States had chosen instead the less gratifying but more important task of keeping in touch with both sides: "In Southern Africa as in the Middle East it is not by choosing sides that we shape events or resolve conflicts."[32] The Middle East seemed to be a favorite analogy with administration spokesmen. A few months later Lawrence Eagleburger warned that the tragedies of the Middle East could be repeated in Southern Africa and the interests of the West put at risk unless the cycle of violence was reversed. He even went on to blame the Soviet Union (not South Africa) for turning the southern part of the African continent into an enlarged version of Lebanon.[33]

To America's European allies, however, the analogy was a little too precise. South Africa like Israel seemed to be a client state that had long escaped from the control of its patron. America's inability to prevent a thousand Israeli tanks from besieging Beirut in the summer of 1982 seemed at one with its manifest inability to prevent the South Africans from attacking Angola, producing over $7 billion worth of damage and creating a refugee problem that after Somalia's was the worst in Africa. Since 1975 half a million Angolans had been made homeless by the fighting; Operation Protea added 80,000 more in the space of three weeks. Forced to abandon their fields and cattle, thousands of peasant farmers were reduced to a permanent state of economic dependency; many more became refugees in their own country. Comparisons with Israeli policy in southern Lebanon suggested themselves to a visiting UN delegation, among whose members was a former U.S. attorney general, Ramsey Clark.

As with Israel, Washington found its influence over Pretoria much more muted in time of crisis than it did in more tranquil times. When the Reagan administration finally attempted to mediate between Angola and Pretoria it met with behavior that could only be described as gratuitously insulting. In June 1982 the president's special roving ambassador General Vernon Walters, traveled to Luanda with a firm understanding from the South Africans that there would be no invasion of the country that summer. Within hours of his embarking for Washington the SADF crossed the frontier, this time to stay for the next two years.[34] The administration soon found that it had even less leverage over South Africa than it did over Israel. There were no arms shipments that could be suspended, no military sanctions which could be taken. Thus, the claim that constructive engagement had won the Americans much greater influence in Pretoria than they had enjoyed during the Carter years was not easy to support.

The fact that the policy did not endear the United States to Angola was not in this respect very important. It is precisely the powers that can act as intermediaries which have the most influence, the best intermediaries being those not with the least bias, but the most leverage.[35] But it was precisely because this was the case that the United States should not have deluded itself for so long that it could "build bridges and explore avenues of agreement" with both parties, as it had in the Middle East with the Israelis and the Arabs.[36] It was not the Reagan administration's bias which told against it, but the fact that the arms embargo had robbed it of any control over the use of force by South Africa then or in the future.

Unfortunately, if constructive engagement was by character bilateral, South Africa's *machtpolitik* was entirely unilateral. Far from providing a means by which the two countries could work together in producing a more durable security system for the region, engagement provided a framework in which South Africa could act largely independently of the United States, and even in defiance of U.S. interests. The government of P. W. Botha was first and last unilateralist, firmly committed to a policy of maneuver at home and abroad to offset the country's narrowing security options, wedded to using America as long as it could for its own tactical purposes.

Instead of asking how long South Africa could serve Western interests in the area, the United States contributed to the emergence of a regional power that was, for the most part, unaccountable to either of the superpowers. Instead of prevailing upon Pretoria to leave Namibia as soon as possible, it connived at its continued presence by developing the fiction that the Cuban presence in Angola was the real stumbling block. Had Washington grown so accustomed to its own impotence that it had lost the will to assert itself? Only by dispersing the fog of wishful thinking created by constructive engagement could it ever hope to comprehend the fundamental question (much less the answer): could it by close association with Pretoria effectively transform an apartheid state into a responsible and respected member of the international community?

This question was raised not only by South Africa's threatening behavior in Angola but also by its actions in Mozambique. The conflict Pretoria contributed to there was quite different from that in its other Marxist-Leninist neighbor. It was a hidden war, with few pitched battles and no fixed front lines. No regular South African soldiers operated in the country; instead, the army operated through the Mozambique National Resistance (MNR), a movement almost totally dependent on outside supplies. In supporting the rebels, originally a hodgepodge of dissidents and criminals put together by the Rhodesian security forces and then handed over to the South Africans on the eve of Lancaster House, Botha and his cabinet had two aims in view—first, to so destabilize the government of Samora Machel that it would be forced to divert manpower and money to a costly and protracted conflict; second, to deny the ANC sanctuary in a country that was only three hundred miles from the republic's industrial heartland.

It was also able to inflict far more damage on Mozambique's economy through indirect means than proved possible in Angola. South

African traffic through Maputo tailed off sharply. Chrome, manganese, and other ferro-alloy exports were among those diverted to Durban and Richards Bay. The number of rail trucks moving across the frontier fell from 3,547 in December 1980 to 1,284 two years later, to a mere 736 a year after that.[37] The port of Beira, historically Zimbabwe's major international outlet, suffered the most. In 1983 Zimbabwe exported only 55,000 tons through the port, a mere fraction of pre-sanctions trade.

The implications and consequences of this policy of destabilization should not have been lost on the United States. In 1982 P. W. Botha explicitly compared his country's role in Southern Africa to that of the United States in the Western Hemisphere, citing a "special responsibility" similar to the Monroe Doctrine in "the promotion of stability and the strengthening of democratic forces against communist subversion."[38] It was not an analogy that should have inspired the Reagan administration with much confidence that Pretoria would be amenable to American influence, given the little credence it put in European representations about its own policy in Central America.

As defined by its own under secretary of state, Lawrence Eagleburger, the administration's concept of regional security rested on three key premises, none of which was in keeping with South Africa's own security interests. It could hardly be said that Pretoria had satisfied the first: respect for all international boundaries and renunciation of the use of force across them, any more than it had observed the second — that states had a duty not to acquiesce in planned acts of violence by guerrilla groups based in their territory. South Africa had trained and equipped Muzorewa's auxiliaries in the Transvaal and allowed the rebel movement in Lesotho free passage through the Orange Free State, not to mention its support for the MNR. Eagleburger's third premise — that the United States should serve as an honest broker with all the regional actors, and not just South Africa alone, had been belied by its persistent refusal to condemn any of South Africa's actions in the Security Council, despite the intercession of its own European allies.

Instead, the United States tacitly acquiesced in a kind of *pax Pretoriana* that left Pretoria unchallenged at home and easily dominant in the region. The argument offered in justification was that South Africa needed time to move toward a political solution to its own affairs, but it could equally be said that it seemed to have no particular end in sight. No government spokesman appeared to have any answer for the country's future beyond such vague formulas as "consociation" or "constellation of states." Destabilization was a strategy without a goal.

South African propaganda made much of the "total onslaught" of Marxist forces against the West and the Soviet threat in the region, but when pushed for details nobody seemed to take that threat very seriously, except Washington. Its own military operations did more to discredit the West and the United States by association than any Soviet policies. Added up, overt and covert South African military action and the absence of any credible explanation for its policies made the neighboring states' analysis look increasingly plausible — that the impact of South Africa's own domestic dilemma had begun to engulf Southern Africa, engaging the United States in turn in a broadening, increasingly destructive conflict—the opposite of what constructive engagement was intended to achieve.

The second part of their analysis also seemed true: that Pretoria would not have succeeded in its policy of destabilization, or certainly not so effectively, but for two factors. First there was the Reagan administration's tacit policy of collusion, which represented a failure of nerve, possibly a lack of real interest in the region, but certainly an introspective withdrawal of faith in the scope of its own influence. This was accompanied by an unhealthy preoccupation with a Soviet threat, which was, to say the least, a little unreal. Both tendencies reinforced a profound pessimism that without South Africa's support the West would not be able to contain the Soviet Union. Thus although from time to time the administration continued to insist that the conflicts of Southern Africa could only be solved by political, not military, solutions,[40] it seemed ready enough to acquiesce in South Africa's interventionist policy, largely one suspects because it knew it had very little alternative.

Much to its surprise the United States found that its working relationship with Pretoria was not a very close one. As time went on the South Africans became increasingly less receptive to American ideas, increasingly reluctant to listen to American advice, increasingly impervious to American appeals. In Namibia they continued to drag their feet. It was remarkable, for example, that despite much time and effort and at least fifteen high-level meetings between American and Angolan officials between April 1981 and October 1983 no real progress was made on Namibia. The Angolans made concession after concession; South Africa made none.

The United States' limited influence was even more evident in Mozambique. Long before Machel's refusal of Soviet assistance after South Africa's last raid against the ANC in May 1983, Washington had been convinced that Mozambique was a "responsible" power deserving of some support from the West. The United States did not, for example, extend the same recognition to the MNR as it did to the União Nacional para a Independeñcia Total (UNITA): indeed it publicly recognized it as a South African creature.[41] Even more surprisingly, it went on to acknowledge that it would be difficult for Machel not to acquiesce in some ANC presence on its soil given his revolutionary past.[42]

These professions of support, unexpected as they were welcome, encouraged Machel to request American military assistance, a request that appears to have been taken seriously by some sections of the administration, especially with regard to the strategically vital Beira-Mutare corridor. By 1983 the United States appeared to be much less concerned about the presence of the ANC in neighboring countries than the two-way flow of guerrillas and military operations across South Africa's frontiers, a point of issue in the discussions between the director of the CIA William Casey and his South African hosts.[43]

But when it came to the point of serious negotiation the United States was either unable or unwilling to do very much. It tried at one stage to convince Pretoria that its assessment of the Soviet threat was deeply flawed—during a secret briefing in Washington between members of South Africa's State Security Council and the CIA early in 1983. It failed, however, to carry the day or to persuade the South Africans that their raids into neighboring countries were unnecessary or ill-advised.[44]

Given so little support by the West and very little by the Soviet Union, it is not altogether surprising that by the end of the year most of the neighboring states had decided to come to terms with the situation. The conclusion of a nonaggression pact between South Africa and Mozambique in the spring of 1984 caught the world by surprise. Pretoria's sudden switch from aggression to détente was as puzzling to many South Africans as it was to many outsiders more used to news of guerrilla attacks and military reprisals.

The United States played a part in the transition process. The nonaggression pact had its distant origins in a meeting between Machel and the new American secretary of state, George Shultz, at the United Nations in the summer of 1982. It also could be traced to a little-noticed meeting between Chester Crocker and Pik Botha in Rome in the final quarter of 1983. The agreement that was eventually signed bound Mozambique to prevent the ANC from launching attacks against South Africa in return for a similar undertaking by Pretoria to discontinue support for the MNR. The wording of the treaty was much tougher than expected. It suggested that the ANC, which had used Mozambique as its main planning and logistics base, would have severe problems in the future in operating in South Africa at any level.

On the other side of the continent an agreement was also patched up between South Africa and Angola by which the former agreed to pull out its troops in the south, where they had been in occupation for the past eighteen months. By the end of the year a joint monitoring commission had been established in the Namibian border town of Oshikango while further efforts were made to conclude talks on Namibia's independence.

Four months before the agreement with Mozambique, Lesotho, having also felt the cost of South African raids and support for its own dissident guerrillas, not to mention the semi-blockade of its landlocked borders, had begun to evacuate members of the ANC in compliance with Pretoria's demands. Swaziland, always the most nervous of South Africa's neighbors, had been the first to act by expelling all known ANC supporters at the beginning of 1983.

What did the United States gain from these agreements? Was Southern Africa more stable, and its own regional interests more secure? In one sense South Africa itself appeared to be more secure than ever. It appeared to have come close to its original objective of creating a *cordon sanitaire*—a buffer zone around its frontiers. The ANC had been the standard bearer of black liberation since 1912. Now it seemed it would be unable to stage attacks outside the country and would have to focus instead on its underground bases with much greater risk of its activists being captured. All in all, the events of 1984 represented a personal triumph for P. W. Botha and seemed to mark the success of his policy of *machtpolitik*, which he had pursued with extraordinary consistency since first coming to power.

Obviously, South Africa would remain for many years yet the main determinant of the region's future. Divide and rule had been the guiding principle of its subjugation of its own black population, helped in no small measure by the inability of the blacks themselves to unite. To some extent, this was also true of its relations with its black neighbors. Their histories, economic circumstances, and differing degrees of dependence on the republic, as well as the very different political preferences of their leaders, varied widely, making it difficult for them to provide a common front. Until such time as radical reform in South Africa itself made possible normal diplomatic relations, they had little option but to strike individual bargains with Pretoria. Insurance is seldom glorious, but it is usually prudent.

But not all the Front Line States found themselves in the same predicament as Mozambique. Their reaction to the nonaggression pact signed between the two countries was distinctly cool. Only one government leader, the prime minister of Swaziland, accepted an invitation to attend the signing at Komatipoort. There was, indeed, a danger that the South Africans might react overconfidently. Machel agreed to negotiate under pressure of economic disaster and serious internal revolt, both of which had raised doubts about the survival of his regime. It did not follow that the other regional governments would feel similarly compelled to sign such pacts or accept a *pax Pretoriana*.

Second, the United States was wrong to imagine that the accord with Mozambique and Angola would bring their own internal troubles to an end. Far from it. Machel's handling of the negotiations left the impression that the pact was a balanced quid pro quo in the security field. It was nothing of the kind. Despite the pact, MNR attacks actually increased and moved nearer to the capital than ever before. In the north the movement mounted operations for the first time on the main road and rail links between Nampula and the port of Nacala, disrupting in the process life in the country's two most populous provinces.

The nonaggression pact was, in fact, a highly one-sided agreement which stopped South Africa only from providing the MNR with further supplies and equipment, but did not stop it from supplying the MNR beforehand with enough arms and ammunition to last more than a year. Clearly, Pretoria intended to keep open the option of destabilizing Maputo, and indeed continued to airlift supplies to the MNR as late as December.

Nor was it altogether clear what the Angolans had won by signing a disengagement pact in February. After the Lusaka meeting the Americans described the agreement as "an important step along the road to a settlement in Southern Africa."[45] But the South Africans did not leave until the following spring and continued to engage in hostile activities, one of the most blatant of which was an attempt in May 1985 to sabotage the Cabinda oil refineries, an attack which had it met with success might have cost the country $450 million in repairs and lost production.[46]

The South Africans, for their part, continued to supply UNITA with equipment and to press on Washington its right to be taken into account in any negotiations on Namibia. Prior to the Lusaka accord the South African Air Force had begun to slip through the country's air defenses to supply UNITA units as far north as Malange province. The bombing of the town of Congamba in August 1983 probably marked a turning point, an operation that together with Askari in December was clearly designed to make it easier for UNITA to move up the eastern corridor to the frontier with Zaire along the so-called Savimbi trail—named after the movement's leader Jonas Savimbi.

By the beginning of 1985 even the Americans were beginning to wake up to the fact that the Nkomati process promised very little, indeed, that it might even be a dead end. Slowly the policymakers in Washington began to suspect that the strategy the South Africans had been pursuing for the last five years had become an end in itself, not a means to an end. Somewhat to its own surprise Pretoria discovered that its military power could not be translated into political influence, certainly not an influence that was very durable. Rather ominously, military spending, which had actually fallen at the height of the policy of destabilization, rose by 21 percent in the year after the signing of the Nkomati agreement. To that extent the *pax Pretoriana* was not a peace at all, but a permanent state of insecurity both for the "imperial" power itself as well as its neighbors.

Unfortunately the strategy was highly dysfunctional. The United States had hoped, of course, that South Africa's military might could be put to good use; as Vice-President Bush put it in a speech in November 1982 (before the Nkomati accord), "to help establish a framework for restraint and broad rules of conduct which [would] discourage the use of outside force in African conflicts and encourage the peaceful settlement of conflicts in the entire region."[47] But

South Africa's military intervention had gone far beyond even the much disputed right of hot pursuit, or the search and destroy missions which the Rhodesian security forces had conducted in Mozambique between 1976 and 1979, much to South Africa's initial displeasure.

The fact that South Africa's own raids into Angola, Mozambique (1981–83), and Lesotho (1982) had not dragged in the Soviet Union owed little to crisis management on the part of Pretoria, and much more to the Soviet Union's own self-restraint, informed no doubt by a reluctance to become involved in yet another open-ended conflict in the Third World at a time when its forces were already overextended. Threats were made to intervene on Angola's behalf, but they were not very convincing.

Even when Moscow delivered a warning in January 1984 in the wake of Operation Askari, the Russians were careful to explain that it should not be regarded as a threat, only a forecast of the "logical and reasonable consequences of its conduct."[48] Significantly, the consequences were not spelled out. That situation, however, was not necessarily immutable. There was always the possibility that at some future date South Africa's actions might compound the risk of escalation. The Soviet Union might one day take the view that its prestige was at stake and step up military aid. Since this was precisely what Washington wished to avoid, it could hardly have been very happy when the South African defense minister Magnus Malan threatened after Nkomati to take firm action in the future "regardless of the consequences,"[49] for it was with the consequences that great powers like the United States had to live.

Suspecting such an outcome, some officials were far from unqualified in their support of South Africa. The U.S. ambassador for one voiced his concern in a speech he delivered in 1983:

> We do not believe that lasting regional security can be based on one power using its superior military strength to impose its will on its neighbors. As Henry Kissinger once pointed out, under such circumstances the total security of one power entails insecurity for its neighbors. It is precisely such a sense of insecurity which provides the Soviet Union with the best opening to establish and expand its influence.[50]

These concerns came to the fore in the first months of the administration's second term, when it became clear that while the SADF might be strong enough to force its neighbors into Nkomati-style accords, it could not enforce them. Even had they wished, the South Africans could not maintain local regimes in power against movements such as the MNR and UNITA, which they had helped to sustain, and in the case of the former even brought into being. In brief, Pretoria—for all its vaunted military power, could not decide the extent to which local governments could absorb their own insecurity. By concluding the Nkomati accord with Mozambique it actually lost control of the MNR, which split into semi- or wholly autonomous armed units, largely self-sufficient and accountable to no one. Despite its equivocal attitude to Machel, the republic was clearly appalled at the prospect of Mozambique degenerating into a state of armed anarchy that proved beyond the capacity of any regional power to control.

Most ironical of all, the SADF found it could not even defend South Africa's own economic interests against MNR attack or sabotage. In May 1985 the rail link between Maputo and the border was severed by guerrilla action for the fourth time since the beginning of the year. Since Nkomati the movement had continued to blow up pylons supplying South Africa with electricity from the Cabora Bassa dam, as many as twenty-nine by the end of 1984, often within a day or two of being repaired. When it was originally built the dam was meant to supply 10 percent of South Africa's energy requirements; in 1984–85 it supplied almost none.

In a vain attempt to salvage the Nkomati process the two governments agreed to set up a joint operational center in April 1985. Yet the South Africans were unable to assist in the only way that might have mattered. They did not have the money to fund Mozambique's counterinsurgency operations as they had those of Rhodesia in the closing years of the war. By 1979 Pretoria was subsidizing up to 40 percent of military operations and sustaining Rhodesia's beleaguered economy to the amount of 16 percent of its GNP.[51] Nor had it the troops to launch a large-scale military sweep in Manicaland on Samora Machel's behalf. It was clear that the white South African electorate, which already suffered a large number of national servicemen to be more or less permanently deployed in Angola and Namibia, would not have allowed another open-ended military commitment

on behalf of a government that until 1984 was considered to be outside the pale of civilized conduct.

In a sense, therefore, the challenge of South Africa's military power
was one-dimensional, focused on economic sectors that could be
attacked or sabotaged, but not defended. South Africa looked increasingly like a military giant that was also a political dwarf, quite incapable of reshaping a regional order, and therefore quite unable to play
the role the United States had hoped it might when it first embarked
on its policy of constructive engagement. The SADF's inability to
promote regional security soon became a central feature of the setting within which the separate nations of Southern Africa continued
to struggle to survive.

In the end, as some observers had long expected, the South Africans were driven back on destabilization, whether its neighbors were
party to nonaggression pacts or not. The central watchword for the
members of the state system, if no longer *e luta continua* (the
struggle continues) was *primeira a defesa* (the first priority is defense).
Washington finally woke up to this fact after a raid on Gaberone in
June 1985 which served to bring home another reality that had been
missed in all the false euphoria over the original Nkomati treaty
—that the ANC had not been eliminated and that nothing in South
Africa itself had changed or improved for the better.

Botswana was an easy enough target—a landlocked country of
meager resources, with no adequate means of protecting itself or
indeed effectively controlling the activities of guerrillas across its
borders. Botswana was the last convenient infiltration route for the
ANC, and Pretoria attributed the sharp rise in the number of guerrilla
"incidents" (more in the first six months of 1985 than the whole of
1984) to the Botswana connection.

The plight of besieged Gaberone drew an immediate and sympathetic response from the West, with the United States recalling its
ambassador for consultations for the first time in the period of the
Reagan administration. Coming as it did after the Cabinda raid and
Pretoria's decision to install a new government in Namibia in defiance
of Western policy, the raid signified a more aggressive South African
policy, a policy that was dictated very largely by the bankruptcy of
the Nkomati process.

For nothing in the recent agreements had changed the situation in
South Africa itself, which erupted into widespread violence in

1984–85, finally putting pay to Botha's extraordinary hope that Pretoria could have normal diplomatic relations with its neighbors without undertaking serious internal reforms. It was appropriate that Kenneth Kaunda, who had so often been pilloried in the past for advocating a dialogue with Pretoria, was the first leader to warn against complacency—and to remind the United States that the problem was "not Mozambique, it is not Zambia, it is not Angola, or even SWAPO. The problem is the philosophy of apartheid."[52]

Nor had the ANC's defeat eliminated the nationalist challenge. Far from it. It had merely caused the black movements inside South Africa to reassess their own political strategies. As Dr. Alan Boesak, the main force behind the United Democratic Front, told a rally in Johannesburg, "The first thing South Africans will have to do is to forget that others will liberate them. If you want freedom you will have to do it yourself."[53] That is not quite what Crocker had in mind. Yet it was the lesson most black leaders drew from the apparent "collusion" between Washington and Pretoria. Reflecting on American policy in this period, Bishop Desmond Tutu, the secretary of the South African Council of Churches, was moved to ask: "Can they show us anything that they can say is a gain for their constructive engagement? I can show several things on the debit side. One is the scuttling of the Geneva talks on Namibia last January. Two is South Africa's brazenness in her incursions into Angola making it even more unlikely that the Cubans will leave, thus going contrary to the Reagan administration's aspirations of containing Soviet expansionism."[54]

The feeling of being ill-served by American diplomacy threatened to increase the blacks' sense of isolation and to induce greater unanimity among them and—to that extent—made Pretoria's position more tenuous, rather than more secure. Despite the considerable euphoria, therefore, there was no evidence to support Crocker's conclusion that the Nkomati accords represented "a historic watershed" for Southern Africa.[55] Nor, to cite the Portuguese foreign minister, did it appear that the region was about to enter "an era of prosperity unprecedented in its history." The real era of prosperity was in the late 1960s when South Africa embarked on an "outward policy"—an economic offensive born of a feeling of security and self-confidence after the post-Rivonia trials and the crushing of dissent, a period presided over by John Vorster in two separate incarnations—that of minister of justice and prime minister.

In 1983, by contrast, South Africa's trade with black Africa fell for the third successive year. Appropriately, the military offensive that followed swiftly on the collapse of the "outward policy" was the work of a former defense minister, P. W. Botha. At home apartheid came under challenge, and even contracted, though not always in ways that were immediately recognizable to the outside world.

By the end of 1984, therefore, all the problems combined, and all to South Africa's disadvantage. What is so surprising is that constructive engagement staggered on for so long, for in reality it passed away in the riots in the eastern Cape, and was effectively bankrupt after the attack on Gaberone. South Africa now faced the greatest challenge to apartheid since it had first taken shape forty years before, as well as the most significant threat to the reform program by which the government hoped to transit with reasonable success the next quarter century. At the same time that the reform program became more uncertain and/or more unacceptable, constructive engagement became less convincing as a philosophy and less credible as a policy. The failure of South Africa's forward policy at about the same time contributed in no small part to American disillusionment, revealing what many writers in the late 1960s had long maintained, that events in the region and events at home were intimately, even directly, connected.

South-West Africa had been the subject of international controversy since 1946 when the future of South Africa's mandate was first discussed. Entrusted to the League of Nations after the First World War, the terms of South Africa's trusteeship were never made explicit. The powers of the mandatory authority were considered to be coextensive with its rule and continued to remain so long after the League passed into history. Therefore South Africa's unwillingness to surrender the territory was not really surprising. Its mandate was the only one of its kind to share a common frontier with the protecting power, the only mandate whose security was of corresponding interest to the trustee. After the League's demise South Africa resisted every attempt by the United Nations to change the territory's status from the time that the International Court of Justice (ICJ), while affirming that the mandate had survived the League's passing, nonetheless gave the General Assembly the right to be informed of the actions of the trustee. During the period 1950–1965 the Assembly passed seventy-three different resolutions calling on Pretoria to surrender its authority and place the territory directly under UN trusteeship. All of them without exception met with a negative response.

Indeed, with the victory of the National party in 1948 events seemed to run in a quite different direction. Within a year legislation was passed giving the territory direct representation in the Union Parliament. A few years later in 1954 native affairs were placed under the jurisdiction of South Africa's minister of native affairs. In the early 1960s the Odenall Commission, recognizing that separate development could be used to advance more general aims, recommended the division of South-West Africa into separate homelands, each to become in time an independent state. These events prompted Ethiopia and Liberia to take the issue to the ICJ in 1966 in the hope of obtaining a ruling that would find South Africa in violation of its internationally mandated obligations. As soon as it appeared that the original charge could not be proved, the claimants appealed to the judges on quite separate grounds: namely, that the trusteeship principle had been rendered anachronistic by the egalitarian principles of the UN Charter. These arguments in turn met with no success; in the end, the court failed to reach a verdict.

As in the case of South Africa itself after Sharpeville, the events of 1966 were an example of a crisis that had disappeared. At the height of the dispute the United States had prepared for the worst. In a memorandum to the president the State Department had warned in July 1964 that if the International Court ruled against Pretoria "we may be in a serious crisis with South Africa next year."[1] Events moved in a different direction, but not quite as the Johnson administration had expected or hoped.

Frustrated in international law, the African countries turned the ICJ's indecisive judgment to good account in the General Assembly. They were helped by South Africa's decision to assume direct control of the territory's mining, taxation, and labor offices, changes in its international status which were in direct contravention of the International Court's judgment that any revision in status must first obtain the prior approval of the United Nations.

The United States, acting on this principle, did not oppose a General Assembly resolution to terminate the mandate (indeed the initiative came from the U.S. ambassador himself). Nor did it oppose the setting up of an ad hoc committee, later renamed the Council for Namibia, after the territory was renamed by the General Assembly in 1968. The council spent the next few months lobbying support in the Security Council for terminating South Africa's mandate, an objective which met with success on 20 March 1969 when the Security Council ordered Pretoria to withdraw from the territory within the next twelve months.

The African bloc in the United Nations had also hoped that the council would find South Africa's continued presence a threat to international peace, so that the provisions of Chapter VII of the Charter might come into force as soon as possible. In this they were disappointed. They had to be content instead with paragraph 8 of Resolution 264, in which the council had agreed to reassess its position should the South Africans fail to comply with its order.[2]

Compared with its record on most other Southern African issues, Washington rather surprisingly kept well ahead of African demands in these critical years. Its record on Namibia was blameless, and difficult even for its most outspoken critics to fault. It rejected South Africa's original argument that South-West Africa be placed under the Chapter XII trusteeship arrangement; it had also submitted during the ICJ's first set of hearings in 1950 an opinion that the territory's status should continue as before; in 1966 it remained consistent with its earlier position by voting in favor of disallowing the mandate even though the International Court had declined to issue a verdict.

Throughout this period Washington had been guided by one central need: to resolve rather than intensify the dispute. For that reason it had resisted all attempts to turn the process of decolonization in this, one of its most intractable problems, into yet another test of the UN's credibility and purpose. Side by side with this positive record, therefore, was also to be found a record of abstentions and vetoes that altered the way in which the United States saw its own role and the role of its critics. Although it submitted a statement to the ICJ in 1950 arguing that South Africa must be considered accountable in law under the provisions of Chapter XI of the Charter, it did not accept the contention that the mandate should therefore be placed under the trusteeship arrangements contained in Chapter XII.

While it supported the Assembly's decision to terminate the mandate in 1966 and establish an ad hoc committee, it refused to join the council for Namibia. When it eventually submitted its opinion to the International Court in 1970 in the hope of resolving once and for all the question whether the Security Council was actually obliged to expedite its own rulings, it did so with the proviso that the final verdict could have no bearing on its trade with Namibia, and none on the validity of the licenses and commercial concessions that had been awarded to American companies.

By the time Richard Nixon came to power it was clear that progress was not going to be made at a very fast pace. South Africa had failed to comply with Resolution 264. The situation was uncertain. Neither side seemed sure how best to proceed. Long before the U.S.

mission at the United Nations had begun to argue the merits of seeking another court opinion, Kissinger had come to recognize that the clarification of the legal implications of Resolution 264 might be useful. In a confidential memorandum he proposed that the United States should support, but not propose, such a step.[3] William Rogers had already come out in strong support of the more extensive use of Article 96 of the Charter, which provided for recourse to the ICJ on the grounds that advisory opinions were important in building confidence, if only because legal obligations were less contentious than their political counterparts.[4] Like many others in the State Department, Rogers tended to gloss over the fact that whether the legality of an issue was resolved or not, and whether advisory opinions might or might not have jurisprudential value,[5] once the court had come to a decision on Namibia the matter would no longer be a subject of legal speculation but of political debate; it would no longer be a cause célèbre but a diplomatic problem.

The International Court delivered its verdict in June 1971. Nothing in its terms conflicted with Nixon's own priorities for constructive engagement; indeed the two complemented each other rather well. The court's verdict did not discharge South Africa from keeping the United Nations informed of all developments. Indeed, the judges insisted that as long as it remained in occupation of the territory South Africa must *work with* the Security Council in the task of helping the people of South-West Africa to exercise their right to self-determination.

In that respect, if in that respect alone, the opinion confirmed the United States in the belief that any bridges which might be built across the divide separating the protagonists would have to pass through Pretoria. Only the previous year, Charles Yost had outlined his own understanding of the UN's responsibilities in the matter: to be informed of events and to act on them "by all peaceful and practicable means."[6] These aims, which were neither exceptional nor very remarkable, conformed with the original aims of NSSM 39, which had opined that without challenging the illegality of South Africa's continued presence, it was in America's best interests to play down the issue and reach some kind of modus operandi with the occupying power.

Perhaps this explains why when the court finally concluded that the General Assembly had acted within its competence in revoking the mandate and by eleven votes to four declared South Africa's continued occupation of Namibia to be illegal, the United States was the only Western member of the Security Council to accept the judgment without reservation. Its reasons for doing so were many, one being that the verdict was not incompatible with the spirit of constructive engagement, or what Judge Dillard described in his final summing up as "a negative duty of restraint, not a positive duty of action."

In drawing up its brief the United States had not once addressed the original question upon which the court had originally been asked to comment—what if any were the legal consequences of South Africa's decision to defy the General Assembly's revocation of the mandate? Instead the American representatives had argued that Pretoria must continue to honor its obligations so long as it was responsible for Namibia's administration. The court's final ruling concurred in almost every respect with this stance, a fact that did not go unremarked in Washington:

> The fact that South Africa no longer has any title to administer the territory does not release it from its obligations and responsibilities under international law towards other states in respect of the exercise of its powers in relation to this territory. Physical control of a territory and not sovereign legitimacy of title is the basis of state liability for acts affecting other states.[7]

By obtaining a watertight judgment in favor of continued communication, the Nixon administration found itself in a strong position to resist all further pressures for negative sanctions. In his speech to the General Assembly on 4 October Rogers maintained that the court's opinion represented a vote for peaceful negotiation, not violence.[8] It could even be construed as another link in the chain of engagement, one which inflicted little permanent damage on America's existing links with South Africa, which continued to be the main medium of American influence. The court's verdict only affected visa, air transport, and extradition agreements as well as the convention on double taxation. All other links were left intact.

Nixon, NSSM 89, and Political Change
in Namibia (1969–1972)

Even so, the administration's policy toward Namibia did differ quite
markedly from its policy toward South Africa. Its first concern following the Security Council vote in March 1969 and its subsequent
decision to seek a final judgment from the ICJ was to seize the initiative as it had done so tellingly in 1962 when it had anticipated the
UN arms embargo by adopting one of its own. On the State Department's behalf William Rogers was personally involved in lobbying
the White House against any further investment in Namibia, since
he judged that once the court had delivered its verdict foreign investment would come under direct attack in the UN.[9] For his part,
Kissinger was prepared to give Rogers what he wanted in return for
the State Department's tacit acquiescence in some of the other measures Nixon had already approved in NSDM 55.

The measures presented for discussion in its sister memorandum
NSSM 89 went largely with the grain of State Department opinion,
not against it. After much debate Nixon agreed to a package of five
proposals, four of which differed from those he had already endorsed
with regard to South Africa itself:

> The United States will officially discourage investment by U.S.
> nationals in South-West Africa.

> Export-Import Bank credit guarantees and other facilities shall
> not be made available for trade.

> U.S. nationals who invest in South-West Africa on the basis of
> rights acquired through the South African government since adop-
> tion of UN General-Assembly Resolution 2145 (1966) shall not
> receive U.S. government assistance in protection of such invest-
> ments against claims of a future lawful government of South-
> West Africa.

> The United States will encourage other nations to take actions
> similar to the above, but will not exert pressure on them to this
> either in the United Nations or in our bilateral relations.

> . . . the President intends that the foregoing decisions be regarded
> as concerned solely with South-West Africa. They are not to be

regarded as a precedent for the application of similar restrictions and policies to South Africa.[10]

These measures notwithstanding, the Africa Bureau had also hoped for a blanket ban on all further investment, together with an official warning that sanctions might well be applied to South Africa itself if it persisted in flouting international opinion.[11] The White House refused to countenance either proposal. It was not prepared to engage in a damaging confrontation with South Africa merely to enforce a UN resolution that in its heart it was convinced would serve no useful purpose.

It also believed that it had done just enough to satisfy African and international opinion—companies that had invested in Namibia since 1966 found their deeds of title now in question, without much hope of appeal in American courts. On several occasions the Securities and Exchange Commission (SEC) intervened directly to discourage further investment, most notably in 1972 when it successfully prevented Gemstone Miners from selling securities to finance the exploitation of an amethyst concession in the northern part of Namibia.[12] On the whole, however, such direct intervention was fairly infrequent. Active discouragement amounted to little more than the transmission of three documents: a letter of support of the UN Declaration on Human Rights; a statement requesting all employers to provide adequate means of subsistence for their black employees; and a set of guidelines on the terms and conditions of employment, which from 1973 were sent to all American corporations in South Africa as a matter of course.[13]

Within the administration, as so often in the past, communications broke down from the outset. Neither the Commerce Department nor the Small Business Administration was ever informed of the existence of NSSM 89, or the administration's deliberations; both institutions first learned of the NSC study through reports in the press. The Internal Revenue Service also continued to remit credits to companies to offset taxes paid to the South African government. It consistently refused to accept that double taxation agreements had been declared illegal by the ICJ and continued to resist every attempt by the UN secretariat to remove them from its register of international treaties. When the State Department finally agreed to suspend the system in 1973, it insisted that the UN should not construe from its decision any admission that the legality of such transactions had ever been in doubt.[14]

Few companies, in fact, were discouraged from investing. Of the fifteen corporations active in Namibia in 1972, all but three had begun their operations after 1970. Commenting on Bethlehem Steel's new concession at Grootfontein, one South African newspaper remarked that the investment was significant not because of the size of the company's initial outlay, but because of the management's decision to invest at all, considering the fact that it so clearly ran counter to official policy.[15]

None of this might have mattered very much had the corporations concerned not been seen as a medium of American influence, as Kissinger and Morris hoped they would be used in South Africa itself. When an occasion eventually arose that demanded decisive action—as it did during the Owambo strike of 1971—the administration failed to act at all, even though U.S. corporations were in the front line. Washington's lackluster response to the strike challenged David Newsom's somewhat inflated claim that the new guidelines on investment in the territory had made the United States "more responsive and relevant" to the aspirations of the black community.[16] The Owambo strike found Washington neither responsive nor particularly relevant to African needs.

Throughout the 1970s Namibia seemed to many outside observers to be a typical example of a colonial economy, with a third of its GNP expatriated every year in corporate profits, with two-thirds of its GDP earned in the export and exploitation of nonfuel minerals, and with over half of all foreign investment in its mining sector contributing 75 percent of the territory's taxable revenue. South-West Africa was not only an export-oriented economy; it was an economy almost exclusively geared to the large-scale and highly profitable exploitation of natural resources.

In explaining the expansion of Namibia's mineral industry it was not really necessary to look much further than investment by foreign corporations, among whom U.S. companies stood out. Between them American Metal Climax (AMAX) and Newmont owned the controlling share of the giant Tsumeb corporation, whose earnings each year accounted for no less than 20 percent of Namibia's export earnings, as well as 80 percent of mining revenue. Unlike most American companies, both AMAX and Newmont earned a considerable percentage of their overseas profits from Namibia: 30 percent and 39 percent, respectively. Newmont's original shareholding in Tsumeb had actually turned it into a multinational corporation.[17]

It was particularly significant, therefore, that the Tsumeb corporation found itself at the center of a political storm in 1971. With 5,000 employees on its payroll, the corporation was by far the largest employer of contract labor in the territory. Under the contract labor system a single authority—the South-West Africa Native Labour Association (SWANLA)—acted as the employers' agent in hiring African labor. Workers were then farmed out among the different companies according to local demand. The result, as the workers themselves pointed out, was to rule out any possibility of free contact between worker and employer. The Owambo workers had many grievances against the system. They maintained that the contract labor system denied them rights which even their counterparts in South Africa enjoyed: the right to choose their own occupation, to remain with the same employer, and to enjoy continuous occupation of the same job, without which they could never negotiate for higher wages.

These grievances provoked a massive strike in December 1971, which, starting in Walvis Bay, spread in no time at all to the Tsumeb mine, where 3,700 workers chose voluntary dismissal and asked to be repatriated to their homelands. Within weeks the strike had closed all but one of the corporation's mines. The following March, Newmont reported that production had fallen by 25 percent. By the end of the month it had been curtailed drastically. Only after the Owambo workers formed their own committee and won the grudging support of the Owambo Legislative Council did the government agree to negotiate directly with the strike leaders. Under pressure it agreed to close down SWANLA and to set up in its place labor employment bureaus in each of the territory's separate regions, permitting employer and employee direct contact for the first time. In addition, both sides agreed that breach of contract would no longer be a criminal offense, but a matter of civil action.

Nevertheless, for all the breaking of new ground, these gains were more apparent than real. South Africa's capacity for improvising as well as policing ever more stringent security legislation detracted from all three concessions. As long as freedom of movement continued to be restricted, companies such as Newmont and AMAX were in no position to act as brokers between the government bureaus and their own employees. As long as the workers still needed the permission of the authorities to work outside their own homelands, new job opportunities meant very little anyway. As long as the employers of labor continued to recruit as a group rather than on an individual basis, freedom of association meant very little.[18] The Owambo strike may have forced the government into a tactical retreat, but it managed to retreat in good order.

Most disturbing of all, perhaps, the strike failed to elicit a consistent or immediate American response. If attempts to get the blacks themselves to bargain with the government on their own behalf were central to the strategy of constructive engagement, the issue received little attention in Namibia despite the fact that the contact forged between the Owambo workers and the Owambo Legislative Council offered the first opportunity for political action since the proscription of SWAPO's internal wing in 1969. In the face of government repression both during the strike and in its aftermath, the Nixon administration achieved remarkably little. When the strike leaders were arrested it confined its public disapproval to issuing official pleas on behalf of the 130 workers involved, later claiming, with little evidence to show for it, that they largely owed their suspended jail sentences to its own diplomatic intervention.[19] Had it done more on their behalf it might have boosted the confidence of the strike committee. Had it condemned the contract labor system in a more forthright fashion it might even have persuaded its own corporations of the justice of the workers' cause.

Since it was the contract labor system that was at fault in preventing employers and employees from talking to one another and in regulating the free association and movement of workers, the system as well as the laws under which the striking workers were first brought to book should have been a major subject of discussion between the American and South African governments in the winter of 1971. The legal codes in operation in Namibia, after all, had already been condemned. In 1968 the United States had strongly criticized the extension of the Terrorism and Suppression of Communism Acts to South-West Africa and the trial of thirty-seven Namibian citizens that had followed. All thirty-seven had been charged with engaging in terrorist acts, in this particular instance, membership of the banned movement SWAPO, even though at the time of their arrest the movement had not yet been proscribed. Thirty-one were found guilty, three of offenses under the Suppression of Communism Act. Only two were acquitted; one died during the trial.

The introduction of this legislation in 1968 was important precisely because it reduced the opportunities for bargaining with the government and at the same time increased the political costs of attempting to do so. It drove many Africans who would have preferred to have worked within constitutional channels into the arms of militant groups who had long given up the struggle and turned to violence. One of Yost's first statements in the Security Council was directed at the adoption of Clauses 10 and 29 of South Africa's General Law Amendment Act by the territorial administration in Namibia that further reduced the possibility of negotiation and peaceful change.[20] The State Department was at a loss to see how the situation would ever improve if the blacks were denied the right to register their grievances, or even to communicate them.

Recognizing this problem the department continued to make strong representations whenever political trials were held. In November 1973 the American ambassador complained about the spate of public floggings and the arrest of fifteen members of SWAPO's nonmilitary wing. Officials from the embassy in South Africa later attended the trial of five of the detainees. Eight such visits were made in the course of 1972, including one by the ambassador and another by a senior official from the State Department.[21] Nevertheless, in the higher reaches of the Nixon administration few conclusions of general significance were drawn from this experience. Washington seemed to be totally oblivious to any connection between the legal restrictions of 1968–69 and the outcome of the Owambo strike three years later, and certainly either unprepared or unwilling to assist black workers to negotiate on their own behalf rather than through the labor bureaus that emerged in 1972. In the absence of such assistance the people of Namibia had only SWAPO to turn to.

The United States and the Quest for an Internal Settlement (1978–85)

It is not within the scope of this study to follow the evolution of American policy after 1972, by which time the State Department was firmly of the opinion that negotiations would be better handled either through the UN secretariat or through an ad hoc committee of the Security Council with a mandate from the General Assembly. Mostly as a result of the collapse of Portuguese power, Pretoria had also come to the conclusion, reluctantly to be sure, that power would have to be transferred eventually. Since it remained as opposed as ever to a SWAPO government, it had no option but to build up a coalition of disparate black groups in the hope of finding a formula for an internal settlement acceptable to Western, if not international, opinion.

Its very first attempt to win some support from the West, principally from the United Kingdom and the United States, had come in 1968 with the implementation of the Odenaal Commission, which although extending South Africa's legislative authority over the territory—a move which brought it into immediate conflict with the UN—also meant speeding up the independence of the homelands. Vorster's decision to press ahead with the commission's report reflected a wish to accommodate the West, not antagonize it: "We have deliberately tried to act in a more positive way and to move away from the negative and formalistic attitude which very sound reasons compelled us to adopt in the past."[22] In moving ahead with the creation of legislative councils in the homelands at the same time as proscribing SWAPO, South Africa proceeded from its own particular understanding of what was, and was not, acceptable to Western opinion.

By 1974, when it became clear that this initiative had been rendered increasingly transparent by the radical turn of events on Namibia's border, Pretoria chose to investigate the chances of bringing to power a government that would be more willing than SWAPO to guarantee its own interests. The following September it convened a conference at the Turnhalle building in Windhoek, which was attended by the representatives of eleven separate population groups, plus a white delegation under the leadership of Dirk Mudge. The government claimed, of course, that the conference was open to all, but only those who had accepted the racial and ethnic divisions it had imposed were invited to attend or allowed to participate.

The Turnhalle conference dragged on for two years, during which time hundreds of SWAPO members and supporters were arrested and detained without trial. In March 1977 the conferees finally produced a draft constitution that made provision for eleven ethnic authorities, a fifty-member national assembly, and a council of ministers. The

Turnhalle group simultaneously petitioned Pretoria to recognize an interim administration based on the new settlement.

By the time the Reagan administration came to office, two matters had been resolved. First, in response to a request by the five Western members of the Security Council in 1977 (who went on to form a permanent ad hoc group known as the Contact Group), the South Africans had agreed, not without reservations, not to transfer power to an interim government, but to await the results of internationally supervised elections in which swapo for one would be allowed to participate. The Turnhalle conference was disbanded in 1977, its petitions ignored. Although elections for an internal government were held toward the end of 1978, they did not lead—in the first instance—to the setting up of an internal administration. Similarly, although the constituent assembly that was formed after those elections transformed itself into a national assembly in May 1979, Pretoria continued to maintain overall veto over the council of ministers, to make laws by proclamation, and even to repeal legislation drafted by the assembly. Such restrictions guaranteed that there would be no internal settlement independent of the United Nations as long as negotiations with the Contact Group continued, even if they failed to produce immediate results.

Second, South Africa committed itself to un-supervised elections from at the very latest April 1978. The terms of un participation were not so easily agreed. Between 1978 and 1980 the Contact Group met with persistent evasions on this score, and persistent South African objections, even though it found itself progressively conceding most of Pretoria's demands. It agreed, for example, that South Africa should remain in occupation of the territory until independence; that it would not be required to dismantle the homelands until elections had been held; and that the elections would even be run by South African officials who would have general responsibility for choosing the electoral system, maintaining a register of voters, and even counting the number of votes. swapo failed to persuade the Contact Group that the secretary-general's special representative should be given at least a veto over the South African administrator-general.

In addition the Contact Group agreed that the elections would be held before power was transferred, that a un peacekeeping force and the 1,500-strong South African army would be jointly responsible for monitoring the peace, and that SWAPO would be given only four months, not seven, in which to contest the elections. Finally, the Contact Group also agreed that although the SADF would be allowed to operate in "selected locations" where demilitarization would not apply, SWAPO would be required to remove its forces behind a fifty-mile demilitarized zone on both sides of the border within the first fourteen days of a settlement. Clearly, it no longer believed it possible to "corral" the South African army as Andrew Young had once hoped.

By August 1980 South Africa had only two remaining objections to the UN plan: the question of UN impartiality, given that the Security Council still recognized SWAPO as the "sole" representative of Namibian opinion; and the Contact Group's alleged lack of consultation with the territory's "internal parties." In response the Western powers proposed an all-party conference in Geneva at which they hoped both issues would be resolved. The Geneva conference marked the culmination of the Contact Group's four-year effort to produce a settlement acceptable to international opinion. Its collapse confirmed two sobering conclusions—first, that Pretoria still doubted the capacity of the Democratic Turnhalle Alliance to win an election against SWAPO, despite its thirty-seat majority in the National Assembly; second, that it hoped for even more concessions from the new American administration.

For a brief moment, it appeared those concessions would be forthcoming. Throughout the spring of 1981 the Reagan administration was tempted on more than one occasion to disengage from the talks—to withdraw from the Contact Group and attempt through bilateral diplomacy to resolve the outstanding problems where multilateral diplomacy had so demonstrably failed. Under pressure from the other members, the United States decided to persevere for the time being, but it warned the international community at the same time that it would not continue to be involved if it felt the prospects for success were bleak; that it would "not permit its energies, time and credibility to be frittered away in a drawn-out and fruitless diplomatic charade."[23] The fact that the charade continued, that it was France in the end, not America, which withdrew from the Contact Group in December 1983 in protest at the lack of progress that had been made, illustrated one of the principal contentions of the administration's critics: that constructive engagement could hardly be described as a two-way street. To a large extent Washington as much as Pretoria was to blame for the charade that the Namibia negotiations were to become over the next few years.

Although the administration's original intention had been to pull out of the talks, Crocker later argued that while America's leadership role in the Contact Group was not one it had sought, it was one that it was "uniquely qualified to fill." As he told the Council for Foreign Relations later in the year, "All parties shared our view that South Africa held the key to a settlement and agreed further that the new American administration was uniquely positioned to explore with the South Africans conditions under which they would be prepared to turn that key."[24] The United States embarked on a fairly exhaustive review process quite early on in its first year in office. Talks with the other members of the Contact Group, the Front Line States, and the government of Nigeria culminated in a meeting in Cape Town and Windhoek in June between Judge Clark and senior South African officials. The Clark mission in Windhoek met with all the internal parties to the dispute, including the Democratic Turnhalle Alliance (DTA), SWANU (South-West Africa National Union), NIP (Namibia Independence party), the Federal party, the CDP (Christian Democratic party), and SWAPO's internal wing. The central purpose of the review was to determine whether enough common ground existed to warrant renewed efforts by the West to reach an internationally acceptable settlement.

Before taking office Crocker had already sketched out the three essential elements of any future American initiative, elements that he maintained had been notably absent from the Carter administration's approach to the problem. First, despite its willingness to talk to the internal parties, he was quite clear in his belief that it would be foolish for the United States to recognize any proposed internal settlement. Such an arrangement could at best make sense only as an interim step toward an international settlement.[25] It was significant, however, that the Clark mission had flown to Windhoek at all. Traditionally, the Contact Group had avoided direct contact with the Namibian political parties except for SWAPO. Even at Geneva it had insisted on treating them as part of the South African delegation. By entering into direct negotiation with, among others, the DTA, the administration consciously or unconsciously conferred legitimacy on the parties for the first time.

Second, Crocker had argued that the United States would have to strive as much as it could to allay Pretoria's concern about the impartiality of its own proposals, and in particular the impartiality of the proposed UN peacekeeping force. In his Pretoria talks with Magnus Malan in April he had insisted that the United States could not scrap Resolution 435 without great difficulty. It wished to supplement it rather than discard it entirely. Central to his thinking, however, was the need to recognize that South Africa alone held the key to the success or failure of the talks. The message came out clearly in a memorandum on his conversations in South Africa: "USG believes it would be possible to improve U.S./S.A. relations if Namibia were no longer an issue. We seek a settlement, but one in our interest, based on democratic principles. Our view is that South Africa is under no early military pressure to leave Namibia. The decision belongs to SAG and ways must be found to address its concerns."[26] In doing so Crocker stressed the need to retain maximum flexibility about the form of an eventual agreement. He wished above all to avoid being boxed into his own proposals if they appeared unlikely to bridge the gulf that divided the respective parties. Inevitably, this meant looking again, if not at Resolution 435, then at least at the Contact Group's original proposals.[27]

Unfortunately, none of these three elements were either very realistic or even desirable. To begin with, South Africa remained committed throughout the period under discussion to finding an internal administration that would be able to win elections against SWAPO, and thereby deny its leader Sam Nujoma any real share of political power. It was precisely because he intended to press ahead with reforms on the home front that P. W. Botha could not be seen relinquishing power in Namibia to a movement whose Marxist-Leninist sympathies were widely known. In a sense constructive engagement in South Africa precluded any settlement in South-West Africa, especially when most opinion polls in the republic clearly showed that up to 75 percent of the white electorate saw little or no necessity to concede power at all.

When the DTA had first been hatched in 1978 Pretoria had been sufficiently confident of the alliance's electoral prospects to subscribe to an agreement on a cease-fire. Its optimism soon faded when the potential for radical black politics became clear with Robert Mugabe's landslide victory in Zimbabwe's preindependence elections two years later. The negotiations on Namibia then turned into a circular exercise, with effects that were particularly devastating for the DTA, which began to lose support among both its black and white constituents at an alarming rate. The whites resented its attempts to attract black support by erasing the last vestiges of apartheid. For their part, most blacks were distinctly unimpressed by these efforts, many of which were blocked by South African officials in their exaggerated concern to avoid a right-wing backlash.

Recognizing that the DTA's popularity had almost slipped beyond recall, South African military intelligence attempted in 1982 to fashion a new coalition of the territory's ethnic groups that might serve the purpose for which the DTA had been designed. On this occasion the leadership under Mudge successfully fought back, but it could only be a matter of time before the alliance forfeited South African support entirely. Botha's decision in 1984 to end Namibia's four-year experience of internal self-government did not add any new cards to South Africa's hand; it merely prolonged the game somewhat longer. The resignation of the council of ministers in January and the immediate reimposition of direct rule from Pretoria ended for the time being an attempt that was probably always doomed to failure: the attempt to build the alliance into a moderate, popular multiracial coalition.

Throughout 1984 the South African government procrastinated and prevaricated until it had had time to put together another internal administration. In the spring of 1985 it strained America's patience to the utmost when it installed a new regime in the territory, thereby exciting the not unjustified suspicion that Botha's real intention was to abandon international plans for Namibia's independence in favor of his own. The Reagan administration felt especially aggrieved. For more than four years it had invested much time and energy endeavoring to persuade the South Africans of the merits of the UN plan. Now it all seemed to have come to nothing, shrugged off by the South Africans themselves and under increasing fire from an impatient Congress.

Outwardly, it is true, little changed when the new government took office. South Africa decided to hand over only limited powers to a coalition of internal Namibian parties, retaining for itself such important portfolios as foreign relations, defense, and internal security. Its administrator-general remained in office, holding the power of veto over legislation and control of the police. In effect, Namibia had been granted a form of government similar to that which had existed from 1979 to 1983. But the implications this time were more profound. The main task of the interim government was to draft an independence constitution and to win approval for it in a referendum. Botha's clear purpose was to help pro-South African parties in their efforts to gain ground over SWAPO. This internal strategy clearly took precedence—as in a sense it always had threatened to—over any international attempt to achieve a settlement.

The risks to South Africa in pursuing such a strategy were considerable, not just so far as its dealings with the West were concerned, but internationally as well. The new Namibian government was led by lackluster politicians with little popular appeal. On the most optimistic assessment internal parties in the multiparty conference in Windhoek could claim a following of no more than 15 percent of the population. The rest supported either SWAPO or those parties who were equally unwilling to acquiesce in Pretoria's internal strategy.

Four years after the United States first embarked on constructive engagement, it had little to show for its efforts. To slap the Reagan administration in the face with Namibia at a time when it was under increasing pressure from Congress to revise if not reverse the policy altogether might seem a singularly perverse gesture, but it was not entirely unexpected from a country that had been given every benefit of the doubt, and every encouragement, from an ally whose friendship was largely unrequited. Similarly, the second element of Crocker's program—his attempts, not entirely unavailing, to guarantee the "impartiality" of a UN peacekeeping force—actually delayed rather than advanced the prospects for peace by alienating SWAPO in almost exact measure as they reassured the South Africans. If the latter were genuinely concerned about the putative UN force's partiality, SWAPO was equally concerned about its effectiveness. If impartiality could only be guaranteed at the expense of its effectiveness, the whole peacekeeping exercise might have disastrous consequences.

In Angola the Portuguese army had not only looked on as the white settlers evacuated the country—it had also permitted them to take almost everything of value with them, including most of the colony's transport, office equipment, and machinery. It is true that in principle a peacekeeping force should serve both sides without using force except in self-defense against either, but can it allow a country to be pillaged before its very eyes without courting the charge of collusion? Most of the whites who fled from Angola seemed determined to guarantee their long-standing forecast that the Africans would never be able to govern Angola by themselves.[28] The Movimento Popular de Libertação de Angola (MPLA) had been especially critical of Lisbon's role in the closing months of the colonial administration for "its confused attitude toward events," for the decision of the authorities to stand on the sidelines rather than adopt a more constructive, if less "dispassionate" stand.[29]

It is not necessary to take SWAPO's arguments at face value to recognize that the Contact Group's decision to allow South Africa to monitor the peace and the South African army to remain in occupation at the same time the guerrillas were required to retire behind the official demilitarized zone might have had unacceptable political implications. In his seminal study of low-intensity operations, Frank Kitson remarks that it is vitally important that those engaged in countering subversion should distinguish their activities from those of peacekeeping, even if their outward form might be the same. Conversely, it is distinctly unhelpful if the two very different operations are ever associated in the minds of the very parties involved.[30] SWAPO could hardly be blamed for linking the two, once the United States and its allies agreed that the South African army should be given a fairly free rein. The price of bringing Pretoria into line was the price it paid in lost credibility.

Perhaps, the Reagan administration's most serious error, however, was doing what Crocker had originally hoped to avoid—becoming boxed into its own proposals, in particular through its decision to link South Africa's withdrawal from Namibia with the Cuban withdrawal from Angola. In a news release dated 21 June 1982 the South African prime minister insisted that his government could not "enter into the third phase (actual implementation) of the agreement with the Western Five unless the Cubans are withdrawn from Angola."[31] This was to be a determining theme of the talks from that moment on.

Yet the linkage question had actually been raised much earlier in a speech by Secretary of State Alexander Haig, in which he had gone on to argue that there was an "empirical relationship" between the independence of Namibia and the Cuban presence in Angola. "Although we intend to proceed unilaterally along the line for Namibian independence, we cannot ignore that empirical relationship."[32] Even the South Africans, who had never once mentioned linkage during the Carter years, seemed surprised by this development. The idea of linking the two issues seems to have been first raised by Crocker and Clark during their visit to Cape Town in June 1981; the South African leaders did not publicly insist on linkage as a sine qua non of a settlement until more than a year later, when all the other major obstacles had been overcome.[33] If their insistence proved the rock on which further progress foundered, it was the Americans who gave them the opening.

Certainly, Crocker became an unquestioning advocate of linkage in the months that followed, in this respect more royalist than the king. In a midterm assessment of administration policy in April 1983 he reiterated that the Cuban issue was not a diplomatic device but an objective reality, one that the South Africans had repeatedly made clear was fundamental to their security concerns.[34] Ambassador Nickel talked of an objective reality as well:

> We have recently heard much rhetoric about the alleged "evils" of linking Namibian independence to the withdrawal of Cuban troops from Angola. We listen to this public criticism philosophically because we know that privately most of these critics admit that they have no practical alternative. After all, the need for parallel progress is rooted in political reality and much as one may dislike reality there is no way to escape it.[35]

Yet the reality seemed always to be changing almost as fast as the United States caught up with it. Commenting on a recent speech in which Crocker had insisted that there was an "intimate" relationship between the conflicts in Angola and Namibia and that a satisfactory outcome could be based only on a parallel movement to resolve both issues, a State Department official continued to maintain that the United States had no wish to create a *formal* link between the two problems, only to ensure that discussion of both should be a "precondition" of any general agreement.[36]

Linkage was given a further twist in June 1982 when the administration began to consider the inclusion of UNITA in the talks, again without any apparent prompting from South Africa. At a press briefing another State Department official concluded that there could be no successful *regional* solution to the Namibian problem without taking into account the interests of all the parties, including those in conflict with the MPLA.[37] Before very long the administration began to speak of a "parallel move on the two questions," arguing that a settlement in Namibia agreeable to international opinion would create "ideal circumstances" for national reconciliation in Angola, then in its seventh year of civil war.

From the outset, of course, America's allies on the Contact Group were critical of linkage because Namibia's independence was an *unqualified* obligation mandated by the ICJ; the withdrawal of the Cubans was not. They also maintained that the Cubans might have withdrawn some years earlier but for the MPLA's reliance on external assistance as a protection (if not a deterrent) against South African raids. A communiqué between Castro and President dos Santos on 20 March 1984 renewing the offer to disengage the bulk of Cuban forces aroused especially hostile comment in the Soviet press, a fact which gave rise to the suspicion that the communiqué may have been intended to prepare both Cuban and Angolan opinion for an eventual pullout. Until Pretoria stopped its raids, however, the promise of the communiqué could not be fulfilled. Indeed, the last major deployment of Cuban forces—the airlift in March 1983 of 7,000 men—had been in response to the most recent South African incursion.

The real reason for America's continually shifting justification for linkage may have been concealed in Crocker's speech to the American Legion in August 1981, in which in an unguarded moment he had asked "how a young government in the fragile new state of Namibia can be expected to survive and prosper with a seemingly endless civil war on its northern border, with a substantial Soviet-Cuban presence nearby, and with the *consequent prospect of a new sequence of intervention involving both South African and communist forces*" (my emphasis).[38] Such remarks, though not often expressed in public, were highly revealing because they were the first recognition that linkage worked both ways. If it was in America's strategic interest to persuade the Cubans to withdraw their forces from Angola, once they had departed the problem of South African intervention would still remain. The remarks made by Pik Botha during Crocker's first visit to South Africa suggested that the SADF might well prefer a low-level conflict on the Angola-Namibian frontier to a Namibia in which the ANC would be able to operate without let or hindrance.[39]

In that respect, Angola and Namibia had both become battlefields in which both the Soviet Union and South Africa had come to develop surprisingly similar objectives. Both countries seemed to expect political gains from a continuation, even intensification of hostilities; both seemed lukewarm, if not openly hostile to America's attempts to find a permanent solution to regional problems that had preoccupied the respective parties for the better part of five years.

In 1981 the United States had set out with the noble intention of encouraging more effective communication between South Africa and its neighbors as a first step to bringing peace to the region. The dialogue, however, had been intended—in Crocker's own words—to be a "two-way street" in which the United States would not be maneuvered into providing "a smokescreen for actions which excite the fear of other states in the region."[40] Within a few years, however, it had become clear that the trap had not been avoided. To Nancy Kassebaum, constructive engagement could in no way be described as "a two-way street. A missing ingredient has been the recognition that 'sticks' as well as 'carrots' may be needed to make South Africa reach a settlement in accord with UN Resolution 435."[41]

The only occasion on which the United States came near to applying pressure was in the early days of the administration when Crocker had shown himself predisposed to treating SWAPO as an "authentic" movement, rather than a Soviet client. In an interview given in Harare he claimed that it was a gross "oversimplification" to paint the movement as a Soviet mouthpiece and from the support it received from Moscow to conclude "that this by itself accounts for what SWAPO does or what SWAPO would do if it were to win the election."[42] During his follow-on visit to South Africa a few days later he strenuously contested during five hours of discussion South Africa's caricature of SWAPO as a Soviet puppet. Two months later he met SWAPO's representative at the UN, in the first official contact between the administration and a senior SWAPO spokesman.[43]

Thereafter, however, the administration preferred to defer to South African sensibilities. If it ever thought of applying "sticks," it never did so, despite urging on one occasion from of all people Dirk Mudge, who expressed his "concern" after the talks in Zurich in September

1981 between Crocker and Pik Botha that the Americans would allow themselves to be kicked around indefinitely.[44] These comments probably said more about the DTA's fast-eroding support than the concerns of the South African government.

If the Zurich talks produced a degree of accommodation on the part of South Africa that had not been seen beforehand, was this the result of American pressure, or appeasement? It was rumored immediately afterward that Washington had been ready to provide Botha with a formidable list of guarantees in return for a promise to press ahead with the negotiations, including an agreement to prevent the ANC from using Namibia as a future base of operations and a tacit understanding that the United States would not oppose any attempt by Pretoria to mount a land and sea blockade of Namibia to prevent the influx of Soviet arms.[45] In fact, it is most unlikely that the United States would have agreed to such a package, given its far-reaching scope, but the rumors may well have reflected desperation in the American camp, and possibly a willingness on the part of some officials to concede a great deal more in order to patch together an agreement.

In questioning American policy, Senator Kassebaum had gone on to argue that it was surely time to broaden the scope of American diplomacy, to concede that quiet diplomacy had failed and to remind Pretoria that it too had responsibilities which it had failed signally to discharge, or even acknowledge. In Namibia as elsewhere in the region the United States derived very little from constructive engagement, the South Africans a great deal. In claiming otherwise, the administration deceived only itself.

13 Toward a Conclusion: The Reagan Administration and Political Change in South Africa

How much more difficult it is to imagine a revolution that is to come—to space it properly through a long period of time, to conceive what it will be like to the people who live through it. Almost all social prediction is catastrophic and absurdly simplified.
—Walter Lippmann, *A Preface to Politics*

Thus there are innumerable intersecting forces, an infinite series of parallelograms of forces which give rise to one result—the historical event. This may again itself be viewed as the product of a power which works as a whole unconsciously and without volition. For what each individual wills is obstructed by everyone else and what emerges is something that no one willed.—Friedrich Engels to J. Bloch, Königsberg, 21 September 1890

By the end of 1985 America's second attempt to apply constructive engagement had run into serious trouble. The Eastern Cape, a once sleepy rural hinterland with an industrial coastal fringe, had been in intermittent turmoil for more than a year. The U.S. press reported almost daily outbreaks of arson, school boycotts, and deaths, numbering more than 770 in all. The well-attested brutality of the police was matched by a popular backlash of increasing savagery against the most easily accessible symbols of state oppression—those blacks holding positions in the apparatus of government and law enforcement.

Prime targets were black policemen, who accounted for half the force, and black town councilors—especially the latter. The township councils, seen by Pretoria as offering a form of local self-government, were scorned by most blacks as no more than agents for transmitting decrees on such matters as rents and electricity charges, and as insultingly inadequate substitutes for real political rights. 1984 was also the worst year for strikes in South Africa's history, with more workers involved in industrial unrest than the previous worst year—1982. Up to a million schoolchildren also refused to attend school. The view from Washington was that the state could face cycles of ever-lengthening periods of disruption and civil disobedience—a kind of low-level political war of attrition, the outcome of which could not be predicted with any certainty.

By April 1985 the Reagan administration had come under attack from within its own party. Backed by the Republican majority, the Senate approved by 89 to 4 a resolution condemning "the violence of apartheid" and demanding that Secretary Shultz conduct an independent investigation into the police shootings at Uitenhage on the twenty-fifth anniversary of the Sharpeville massacre. The pressure on the administration sparked off by Bishop Tutu's visit to Washington at the end of the previous year en route to receive his Nobel Peace Prize forced the president to admit that "quiet diplomacy" was no longer sufficient. The damage, however, went much deeper than South African charges in the weeks that followed that the United States had once again misunderstood their efforts and betrayed constructive engagement to appease a vociferous but visible minority. Reagan found himself under attack not only from the likes of Congressman Solarz and the congressional Black Caucus but also from his most vocal supporters—conservative Republicans who wished to mold the party into the natural governing party of the 1990s.

Thirty-five of them wrote an open letter to the South African ambassador condemning the Uitenhage killings and disassociating themselves from Crocker's policies. One of the letter's authors, Congressman Vin Weber of Minnesota, a staunch Reagan loyalist and member of the Republican National Committee, wrote an article in the *Washington Post* stating in fairly categorical terms why the United States could no longer afford to be identified with the South African government:

> Under conservative guidance America must clearly define the moral basis for its leadership to the world. . . . Domestically, we have succeeded in challenging the moral dominance of redistributionist economics with an economic philosophy based on growth and opportunity. Internationally, however, we have been reluctant to face the same challenge. Therein lies the great challenge inherent in the question of South Africa.[1]

Weber went on to argue that by failing to reject apartheid more force-fully the Reagan administration had effectively blocked its own efforts to wean the Third World from the discredited liberal and socialist orthodoxies of the previous decade.

To justify sanctions against Nicaragua, the United States would have to apply sanctions against South Africa. To command the politi-cal heights in the developing world, it would have to sacrifice South Africa to the Third World majority. These were the sentiments of a rising number of Republican ideologues, not content to spend the rest of their careers in opposition. Wishing to construct a new, more profoundly appealing image for their party, they were prepared to do so if necessary at Pretoria's expense. Together with the universal call for sanctions these developments represented a significant, even ter-minal setback for constructive engagement as a realistic political program that could command the support of a substantial number of congressmen and politicians. The congressional campaign in particu-lar was a major turning point.

When one describes the events of 1984–85 as a turning point, one is implying that at the very least a decisive shift of some kind took place—that the decisions taken and the choices made were absolute in a particular way—that they foreclosed options which had pre-viously been open. In the first and simpler sense, the sanctions initiative marked a turning point in a number of ways. It was the moment when the balance of political power within the United States shifted decisively in favor of the anti-apartheid lobbies. Even conservative senators and congressmen began to turn their attention to coercion to force the pace of political reform. American policy changed from a focus on the reform program inspired largely by South African ideas to a less narrow focus on more fundamental political change inspired by America's example. In the second sense also it can be argued that the sight of an administration under siege from its own supporters marked another turning point in the sense of a point of no return, a foreclosing of the positive sanctions option, less cer-tainly a break on any future partnership or "accommodation." The option of working with Pretoria on a program that both countries could agree on seemed to have passed forever.

In retrospect, perhaps it is surprising that the administration escaped censure for as long as it did. For it seemed clear from the outset that the South Africans had still not come to terms with the need for change. None of the government's reforms seemed to have undermined white supremacy. Indeed, they were so ambiguous that in 1980 Buthelezi had been moved to call for a complete moratorium on further discussions with the government until it had become clear in which direction it intended to go.[2] If this was of great concern to Washington, it did not express its misgivings in public. In the final analysis Crocker's endorsement of constructive engagement was based on his strongly held view that the blacks could not hope to challenge white supremacy directly. The ingredients of a revolution might well be present, but the necessary catalyst was probably not. In 1981 as in 1970 the whites looked as though they would survive for years.

That was not to say, of course, that the South African government was invulnerable, it was only to note that the balance of coercive power still remained overwhelmingly in its favor. There might be every reason to anticipate continued political conflict ranging from mass demonstrations to strikes. Violence and political reform might well go hand in hand, but for the foreseeable future the initiative still lay with Pretoria. On this score, if nothing else, Crocker was adamant: "It is misleading to speak in terms of a simple choice between peaceful and violent change and wrong to assert that it is too late to forestall mass revolutionary violence. The still enormous disparity in the kinds of physical power in the hands of the white and black communities provides a margin of time and a firm check on sudden political disintegration."[3] His perception may not have been entirely wrong, but the conclusions he drew from the premise were highly questionable. It was especially unfortunate to have imagined that the whites themselves, if properly organized and directed, could control the pace of change any more than they could in 1970. If it was Crocker's firm belief that the United States could not manage the process on its own, it was also his firm conviction that the pace of change could still be controlled and channeled and that by the time the blacks had acquired tangible bargaining power they would not have lost interest in power-sharing.[4]

In this respect he shared almost the same perspective as Roger Morris: that the ruling elite accepted the need for reform but did not know how to control it; that the blacks knew that change was on the way but did not know how to exploit it; that the United States still had time to provide both parties with tangible assistance.[5] The administration may not have put its faith entirely in government initiatives, but it still looked to coalitions and power bases within the National party and increasingly to the army and policy technocrats who had concentrated power in five working commissions and cabinet committees, of which by far the most important was the State Security Council. Clearly, it still believed that the government could control the situation, that its power stemmed from the fact that it could not be forced to share power, let alone transfer it; and that "autocratically and imposed reform could become part of a process leading at a future stage to compromise and accommodation."[6] Such, after all, was the central premise of constructive engagement. It was also the central argument of its critics, who contended that unless Botha was prepared to move faster, the United States might soon find that its policy was neither "constructive" nor "engaged."[7]

Perhaps, however, both sides would have been better advised to have asked whether the government could still play a role, whether change without revolution was still realistic. In a midterm assessment the American ambassador Herman Nickel went some way to questioning some of the assumptions on which his country's policy was based:

> We cannot dictate policy to any state in the region, nor would we want to. We can influence, we can suggest, we can act as the honest broker, but in the final analysis we must deal in the realm of the possible. . . . We are not *deus ex machina*. What we can do is add our voice and influence to forces that are already at work here. If we carefully husband our [resources] for cases in which it can make a difference, there is a chance it can tip the scales.[8]

In part, this was an almost faithful refrain of Newsom's more cautionary speeches ten years earlier. But if the position had not changed substantially since then, if the United States was still as "powerless" as it had been before, might the corollary not hold true as well? Was the South African government any more powerful or independent an agent as an initiator of change than it had been in 1972? And if this was indeed the case, what did this entail for the reform program by which the Reagan administration set so much store?

The South African Government
and Political Reform

By the early 1970s, under very little pressure or prompting from the West, the National party had begun to move away from the stock formulas that had served it so well since 1948. All but the most diehard politicians had begun to realize that apartheid would have to be modernized, if it were not to be abandoned. The United States was not oblivious to this development, but it made the mistake of assuming that the government was more powerful as an instrument of change than in fact was the case.

The mistake was an understandable one. In the 1960s many of South Africa's most prominent critics had argued that the government was quite incapable of initiating change at all. It was a viewpoint trenchantly described only to be debunked by the German sociologist Heribert Adam:

> The opposing blocs of African and Afrikaner nationalism have become increasingly polarized and both display readiness to use force. An end to communication between the antagonists parallels a refusal to compromise and negotiate; a lack of consensus about the rules of the game accompany the mutual denial of legitimate right to power; gradual reform instead of revolution is thus ruled out by the South African political system.[9]

The advocates of constructive engagement, like Adam himself, assumed that the political system could be reformed without undermining the political order. In one sense, of course, the evidence bore out such a contention. Change was possible. There was no reason to think that the irrationality of racial beliefs influenced the implementation of racial discrimination. Indeed, there was every reason to endorse Adam's description of the South African government as a "pragmatic racial oligarchy" sensitive in the end to its own survival, as well as the propagation of its own ideology.

Since the United States believed that the government had it within its power to avert a revolution, there seemed every reason to hope that constructive engagement might bring Pretoria to its senses much sooner. Unfortunately, the Nixon and Reagan administrations fell into the trap Heribert Adam had avoided: imagining that white initiatives were enough. If Crocker was less blameworthy than Morris in this respect, even he placed too much emphasis on government actions and too little on what the blacks might do to help themselves.

The government, of course, *was* immensely powerful. It had maintained itself in power for forty years, often in the face of sustained opposition. The whites alone exercised power, and only they could distribute it according to categories of their own devising. Often they listened to petitions from groups that they alone chose to recognize; frequently they recognized many that would never have existed but for the fact of their recognition.

Yet by the beginning of the 1980s it had already become apparent that the government was no longer quite as powerful as the United States imagined. The sheer size and complexity of the administration and the tangled web of conflicting interests involved made the picture of an all-powerful machine a long way removed from reality. Obstruction and confusion seriously set back the reform program. The right wing, which was strongly entrenched in the bureaucracy, had far from lost the will to argue or resist. The government had merely succeeded in driving the opposition underground, where it was far harder to deal with, and where of course it was far harder for political scientists to follow. Moreover, limits had clearly been reached in the manipulation of black politics. In the past the government had intervened to define the terms of the public debate. Politics had been reduced to the status of petition rather than negotiation. A number of black groups had petitioned the whites in the hope of winning concessions. By conceding some of their demands the government hoped to divide the black community.

Yet by the time Reagan entered office it had already become clear that the explanation for the rise and fall of many black movements, the reason why some had become more prominent and assertive than others, and why some were in receipt of much broader support, no longer rested on government recognition alone, but their willingness to work with or boycott government-created institutions. Where the precise balance lay between the government and the black community had not yet been determined—though, given the nature of any society in flux, it was probably to be located in the middle ground rather than at either extreme. But there was no reason to imagine that the whites would retain the initiative indefinitely, or that the blacks would not one day turn the institutions they had been given to their own advantage. Indeed, it might not matter in the end whether the government succeeded in directing the reform strategy from above, but whether it would be able to respond to initiatives from below. In short, the reform program might actually produce rather than preempt a revolution of rising expectations, a concern that does not appear to have been in the forefront of American thinking until rather late in the day.

In the 1970s the government had created a situation in which black participation in politics had become possible for the first time. The year 1971 had seen the first meetings between the cabinet and homeland leaders, which from time to time were boycotted or allowed to lapse whenever the latter thought it advisable. One of the few political rights of which they could not be deprived was the right to refuse to cooperate with the government in any initiatives they thought detrimental to their own position. Boycotts nevertheless were limited in scope and of uncertain political value. The self-denying ordinance of refusing to participate in white-sponsored institutions was inevitably self-defeating. Many black leaders found themselves in a political no-man's-land without an opportunity to articulate the demands of their own followers. In time the majority expressed a wish to move away from the politics of protest to the politics of power, to escape from the hierarchical relationship in which they had been forced hitherto to petition the government for redress of their grievances rather than to negotiate with it on equal terms.

For the first time the reform program gave those leaders an opportunity to make their participation conditional upon their demands being met. The government may not have been surprised that critics such as Nthano Motlana, the chairman of the Soweto Ten, continually claimed that its proposals to extend local powers in the cities would be worthless unless black councillors were given financial control, but it was undoubtedly disappointed when the members of its own sponsored organizations, including the president of the Urban Councillors' Association, argued that it was not enough to allow the blacks to run their own affairs in the localities unless in the process they were given an opportunity to administer power at the center.[10] Given such lukewarm support, it is not surprising that the first community elections produced only a 6 percent turnout.

In December 1983 the voters once again turned their backs on the township council elections, with less than 20 percent bothering to vote, less than 10 percent in Soweto. In view of the fact that the new councils were supposed to have as much power as their white counterparts (except for the denial of tax-raising authority) this appeared to confirm Treurnicht in the view that the black voters would be satisfied with nothing less than majority rule and that in attempting to appease them the government would slowly whittle away its own position until finally recognizing that it had inadvertently conceded most of their demands.

To its dismay, Pretoria found that its "collaborators" would not collaborate. Many refused to accept that their economic interests could be divorced from political power in a country where their subordinate economic position was considered to be a reflection of their devalued political status. Many believed they were involved in a total struggle to overthrow the main foundations of the apartheid system—the pass laws, the Group Area Act, and the battery of legislation administered by the Ministry of Co-operation and Development. The boycott of government institutions revealed the reluctance of the nonwhite majority to accept any concessions that stopped short of a transfer of political power. As the leaders of the Coloured school boycott explained in 1980, "The whole educational system against which we are rebelling stems from the fact that we are denied basic political rights and thus political power."[11]

At the base of the township revolts lay mass poverty, hunger, and suffering. South Africa's postwar history showed that every time employment fell abruptly, periods of widespread unrest could be expected. This was true at the time of Sharpeville and again during the Soweto riots of 1976. It occurred again in the autumn of 1984 with the interval between each cycle growing ever briefer, a fact which illustrated that the downturn in the economy was not cyclical, but structural, and therefore endemic.

With it went the central plinth of the reform program: the co-optation of nonwhite leaders. Political co-option in the form of separate parliamentary chambers for Coloureds and Indians, and local authorities for the country's ten million urban blacks, could only succeed if there was enough prosperity for brown and black elites to dispense patronage and for the subsistence expectations of their own supporters to be met. Otherwise the wrath of the community would be turned on those who profited from the system, which is precisely what happened in 1984–85 when the principal victims were black councilors, men who for the most part found themselves in the position of generals without troops, and even without quartermasters, for they had been denied the power to tax local businesses.

Failing to provide these authorities with real resources, the government had, in fact, asked the nonwhite communities to administer their own poverty. The results were predictable, even if they were not actually predicted. The new Coloured and Indian assemblies were not able to demonstrate to the voters that they had made any real difference either in the political process or in redistributing "the spoils of modernity"—jobs, houses, and above all education where the government's insistence on segregated schools remained a major source of conflict. The elected representatives of Coloured and Indian opinion failed, in short, to set their own reform agenda or to project themselves as an indispensable part of the reform program.

If there was every prospect of the new constitutional settlement coming unstuck in the 1989 elections, the attempt to devolve power to black local authorities collapsed almost as soon as it began. The intention was to have 103 elected councils operational at the beginning of 1985. Yet as the death toll mounted that summer, the South African Council of Churches knew of only three councils that were still functioning, the Urban Foundation knew of only six. There was no real ground for the hope that the structures of black participation could be built up from the base of local government. There was no foundation on which to build.

In short, the whites appeared to have reached the stage where they could only sustain white control by shifting the basis of their rule, dropping one set of collaborators and taking up another. In principle, this process could have continued indefinitely from local government to the twenty-one regional service committees that Pretoria planned to introduce as the next step in devolving political power. But in practice, recent events had taken the game out of the croupier's hands. There was now a shortage of groups ready to place bets at the government's table, while the economic crisis had given the house remarkably few bargaining chips of its own. The economic recession had knocked P. W. Botha's calculations askew, depriving him of willing collaborators, bringing into question at the same time the quest for what could only half-facetiously be called "sharing power without losing control." If that was the only vision of the future, there might be precious little point in devising unworkable new constitutions, or running fictional representative councils, or carrying representatives who represented only themselves. This would not be so much an endgame, as a refusal to play the game any longer.

From this analysis two conclusions seemed to follow: that it was highly unlikely that the government could control the pace of change as Crocker imagined; and worse, that the reform program might well stimulate precisely those revolutionary expectations it was designed to scotch. The efficacy of boycotts can seldom have been so impressively demonstrated as it was in the two elections for the tricameral Parliament in 1984, in which only 30 percent and 20 percent, respectively, of the Coloured and Indian voters bothered to turn out. In short, the government may have had a central role to play, but not quite the role it imagined. In 1951 Malan had written to the ANC leadership informing it that his government had no objection to Bantu initiatives provided they were restricted to the Bantu community.[12] Clearly, by 1980 this was no longer the case. Bantu initiatives were bound to determine changes in the white dispensation as well. The pace of change was likely to be determined not only by whether the whites acted in time, but whether South Africa's nonwhite population chose to cooperate or boycott the institutions it had been given; whether black initiatives met with a rather different response than they had thirty years earlier.

A second conclusion that it was possible to draw was that the reform program had not only failed in its main purpose of creating a black middle class with a vested interest in the prevailing political system, but had also raised expectations that it could not meet, and thus stimulated revolutionary aspirations that the government was ill-positioned to contain. If that was the case, was constructive engagement self-defeating rather than collusive, as its critics continued to maintain? This would appear to have been the case. It would seem that the Reagan administration made a fatal mistake in imagining that reform could preempt a revolution, an understandable mistake, of course, on the popular reading of such historical examples as the three reform acts in nineteenth-century Britain that had broadened the political base of politics with conspicuous success.

In Britain the success of the First Reform Act of 1832 was that the newly enfranchised voters soon identified with the ruling elite, an unforeseen development that made possible the further extension of the vote beyond the middle class. After winning the vote from a

Whig government, many of the newly enfranchised middle class immediately transferred their loyalty to the party of the landed gentry, which had fought the passing of the act and which immediately afterward had set its face against any further reform of the electoral system.

The success of the experiment, however, as one historian reminds us, was not comprehensive. In Ireland the new voters did not identify with the elite—the Anglo-Irish Ascendancy. For the most part they spurned it, as they had done before the vote had been extended. In Ireland there was no homogeneous population as there was on the mainland but a deeply divided community characterized by significant ethnic, racial, and religious differences. In the rest of the United Kingdom, by comparison, there were few social barriers other than class to assimilating with the ruling elite, and class differences could be overcome by wealth in the matter of a single generation.

Across the Irish Sea this was not the case.

> In Ireland as in England there was a rising middle class in 1832. But unlike its English counterpart the Irish Catholic middle class did not become conservative; it became revolutionary. The English middle class held no brief for those who remained outside the political process. The Irish Catholic middle class did . . . because they regarded themselves as Irish first, and middle class only very secondarily. The reforms may even have intensified their revolutionary zeal by raising their expectations, and so increasing their disaffection.[13]

This thesis seems to hold a key to understanding political change in a country as ethnically diversified as South Africa. This is particularly true if one goes beyond the First Reform Act and looks at the remaining two—the acts of 1867 and 1885, which set the seal on what the first had achieved. Neither the second nor third acts, by the way, produced majority voting. Even as late as 1900 four out of ten U.K. citizens were still denied the vote.[14] When all adult males were enfranchised after the First World War, together with women over the age of thirty, the situation at last changed dramatically. In the election of 1923 three quarters of those entitled to vote did so the *first* time.[15] It may well be true that in Britain power eventually passed from the few to the many, but we can no longer account for this by reference to the reform acts alone. The process took much longer and had still to go far after the passage of the Third Reform Act in 1885. The implications of the analogy for a country like South Africa should be strikingly clear. At the most obvious level the republic will not be able to engage in quite such a leisurely progress. Indeed, it may well have to proceed much more quickly than any country in a similar situation has ever done in the past. Whether the government can hope to control, or even influence, the pace of change is not at all clear.

That political power was in the end transferred in Britain also owed a great deal to the Benthamite confidence that men would perceive and pursue their own interests regardless of class. On this reading the vote was a useful instrument of enlightened self-interest, the very fulcrum of the debate during the nineteenth century on the value and future of democracy. In South Africa's case the government clearly hoped that a black middle class would eventually be given the vote as an interest group and identify thereafter with its white counterpart. What Pretoria set out to achieve in the early 1980s was not the *embourgeoisement* of the black community, however, as the British had understood it a hundred and fifty years earlier. Far from attempting to carve out a cohesive class of owners of the productive means, or a group with a monopoly of economic power in its own ethnic constituency, the politics of decentralization and homeland development was an attempt to ensure that whatever capitalist class emerged would be bound to white interests, a process that Sam Nolutsunghu argues can better be described as one of *encadrement*, "a chapter in the story of the further expansion of white capital, of the deepening of its use of black labor—now hierarchically differentiated and pressed for greater productivity both economically and in the extended reproduction of existing political relations."[16]

Encadrement is a much better term than *embourgeoisement* because the process by which both were achieved or attempted in the two very different societies explains why the first was necessarily more limited in scope than the second. It was equally clear that arithmetical equations applied much more directly in nineteenth-century Britain than they could ever hope to do in late-twentieth-century South Africa. In the former, as long as the Liberal party believed that only 7 percent of the borough inhabitants were artisans, there seemed to be a good reason for expanding the franchise because there were so few. When it was discovered that the true figure was as high as 26 percent, the fact that there were so many seemed an excellent reason for enfranchising more.[17]

Liberal politicians may have talked about the franchise in terms of its political value, but the party's political agents were firmly convinced of the wisdom of extending the vote *because of the numbers involved*. For the great majority of men in political life it had become abundantly clear by the 1860s, if not before, that the artisans as a class might in time become receptive to the same cultural influences as the enfranchised middle class, and that the interests of labor, although distinctly separate, were not necessarily antagonistic to the prevailing political culture. It was even possible to point to the divisions within the labor movement that induced such despair among more radical politicians, among the labor aristocracy, even among those outside it who occasionally identified with the landed interest—a phenomenon that helped to convert the established political parties into mass political movements as the century drew to a close.

In South Africa the situation faced by the government in 1981 was very different. If class had been entirely a question of wealth or social status, it might have had a chance of creating a specific class interest among skilled black workers, particularly those who were already to be found in managerial positions or at the head of small businesses. Frequently, however, class is derived from common values and normative beliefs, which partly draw their definition from comparison with the values and beliefs of other "reference groups," especially those in the ascendant. If the comparison is unfavorable, it usually leads to feelings of relative deprivation; if the comparison is favorable, deprivation should not be an important issue.[18]

Relative deprivation, however, can also arise in circumstances where material conditions may be similar but where beliefs may differ quite significantly, and where a society reflecting only the normative beliefs of the dominant group may close ranks against outsiders. When Pareto speaks of class he also speaks of "elite derivations," of a closely related set of ideas which members of a group accept regardless of the truth because those ideas serve to justify their material interests.

Derivations, unlike ideologies, do not serve to justify the pursuit of class interests. They spring instead from "instincts" that correspond to general theories. When Pareto speaks of actions sustained by derivations he does not maintain that the people concerned share consistent purposes and come together in order to achieve them; he speaks of them being drawn together by the need to give effect to "instincts" of which they may well be unconscious. Their actions may, of course, be an outlet for their "instincts," but the theories used to justify their actions merely provide excuses for acts of whose hidden springs they are not always aware.[19]

In a context almost exclusively derived from the interaction of different cultures, the instincts of a reference group whatever its provenance are more likely than not to be influenced by race. Men may well belong to several different reference groups, but what will make a group *politically* significant is its salience in a political context. In South Africa race rather than class is bound to remain the most salient issue.

The government may have embarked upon the reform program in the hope of co-opting a specific reference group—the black skilled worker—with whom the white middle class could identify and vice versa. It may have hoped—in Marxist terminology—that the black middle class would eventually come to represent a subculture, consumed with a form of "false consciousness" that would prevent it from mobilizing mass support or providing the masses with political leaders.

If this was its aim, however, it could hardly be said to have succeeded. Indeed, in one respect the position was worse than it had been *before* the reform program. Back in 1971 Adam had argued that collective black action had failed in the 1950s because in the absence of the conscious homogeneity of nonwhite interests they had been inspired by no common sense of purpose or political vision: "In Marx's categories they constitute a class 'in itself' but they are further away than the European proletariat ever has been from a consciousness with which they form a class 'for itself'."[20] This was no longer true by 1981. Much had changed in the course of the 1970s, including the rise of black consciousness, which inspired by the experience of the Afrikaners, set out to transform the black community into a political nation. In the face of the strong ideological pull that race exerted in South Africa, it became increasingly questionable whether a black middle class would ever see its social situation in the same terms as its white counterpart.

It is worth remembering that Max Weber placed almost as much emphasis on status as he did on class and in contradistinction to the other insisted that status was entirely a matter of consciousness, and that status groups were communities held together by common values.[21] For Weber class politics was primarily concerned with material interests; status politics was not. In South Africa the government's own reforms appeared to have consolidated a status group certainly better off materially than the black proletariat but apparently quite prepared to mobilize mass support in its own interests when presented with an opportunity.

Perhaps most disturbing of all for the government was the mounting evidence that its hopes of cutting off such avenues had come to nothing. Indeed, during the Port Elizabeth and East London strikes, which brought out 50,000 workers in the summer of 1980, their leaders were found almost without exception to be white-collar employees rather than shop-floor activists. Militancy in the mines was also largely sponsored by a union (NON) whose leadership was made up of clerks and surface workers, not workers underground. If that event was any guide, it seemed that the more prosperous black workers might try to press for greater concessions by articulating the aspirations of the unskilled workers more effectively than they could hope to do themselves.

In this respect the government found itself looking in vain for "moderates" with whom it could work, much less form an alliance. As Nolutsunghu argues, the Black Consciousness Movement in the early 1970s should have been the ideal candidate, a movement without communist links, operating solely in South Africa with little if any outside support or understanding, at the time of reform-mindedness on the part of Pretoria. Could it have been turned into a political agent with whom the government could establish some form of relationship, however unlikely? We will never know because it was the government's own actions that radicalized the BCM leadership up to the point of its bloody confrontation with the state in the streets of Soweto. For this, if for no other reason, Nolutsunghu writes:

> The story of the Black Consciousness Movement . . . is of overwhelming importance and relevance to any consideration of change by incorporation or "accommodation." It shows most poignantly that the counter-insurgency approach of tolerating and giving scope only to "nationalists" whom the ruling class

considers "moderate" necessitates an escalation of repression against the ever-growing number who are not so esteemed. It is therefore a strategy of violence and no portent of peaceful change.[22]

It was of course the violence that the reform program eventually promoted in 1984–85 which brought to an end the program and with it constructive engagement.

It remains to challenge the final premise of engagement—the claim that economic growth might bring in its train political emancipation. The National party had clearly failed to come to grips with the dilemma of economic expansion—the ever-pressing demand for skilled black labor that the government could only meet by allowing blacks into jobs previously reserved for whites. Did it follow, however, that this situation could be controlled or that it was strictly compatible with the evolutionary rather than revolutionary model?

Stated simply, there were more job vacancies by the late 1970s than there were skilled laborers to fill them. Faced with this reality the government had been forced to abandon some of its most cherished ideological tenets that had served it so well since 1948. The outcome was not without irony given the fact that the National party had won the 1948 election partly on the fears of white voters that the United party's economic program might lead to the eventual erosion of white supremacy. Smuts had warned the electorate that the country would have to make maximum use of its manpower if it wished to continue its economic expansion. He had also spelled out what this might mean: a speeding up of the urban black housing program; the transfer of executive and financial powers to the Native Representative Council; and the legalization of black trade unions. Smuts's belated liberal conversion did nothing to help his party's cause, yet looked at thirty years later the situation led many to believe that in the intervening period South Africa had merely been marking time.

The debate about the political consequences of economic growth has a long history and this is certainly not the place to go into it at any length. It *is* the place however to question the Reagan administration's understanding of it, in particular its argument that different stages of growth would automatically lead to different stages of political development. If as one of Nixon's favorite economists Michael O'Dowd maintained, the blacks would be accommodated "on the right side of the economic fence"—by which he meant that political rights would follow upon, not precede, an improvement in their economic status—the situation looked rather perilous.

Writing in 1978 O'Dowd had postulated that South Africa had just reached the stage of economic development that the United Kingdom had attained in the 1860s—the period of the Second Reform Act.[23] Unfortunately, the pace of political developments in the age of P. W. Botha promised to be much less leisurely than it had in the age of Anthony Trollope.

Indeed, the United States might have asked whether, far from promoting positive political change, growth might merely fuel discontent and disaffection. In 1965 the talented black journalist Nat Nakasa had predicted that as the blacks grew richer so they would grow more discontented: "Africans have tasted enough to make them realize what they are being deprived of by apartheid, and it is this which in the long run will make them transcend their present preoccupations and awaken their political fervor."[24] This was especially likely to be the case if economic growth failed, if it failed to meet popular expectations, if it provided too little in the way of resources for the government to fund a reform program, or to fund it as adequately as it would have liked.

Some economists, notably Lawrence Schlemmer and Edward Webster, foresaw three possible outcomes on the economic front, the most critical of which was likely to arise from economic failure rather than success:

1. Change toward a more stable but highly unequal society in which there is sufficient improvement of material conditions for blacks to prevent their sense of relative deprivation from rising to a threatening level;
2. Change toward a materially more prosperous society but one in which class tensions increase in spite of improved standards of living and in which the increasing preponderance of black workers within the economy puts them in a position to force a radical restructuring of society;
3. A situation in which, owing to continued white intransigence, there is relatively slow overall growth, little or no improvement or even a decline in the standard of living of blacks, leading to increasing social tension and perhaps, with outside aid, a rapid

restructuring of society either in the direction of socialism or black capitalism.[25]

The Reagan administration did not really address any of these problems or try to prepare alternative policies for alternative outcomes. There was a tendency instead in its initial treatment of South Africa only to examine the aspect of the problem that interested it most —the O'Dowd thesis—and to neglect other interpretations. Naturally, the future was unpredictable; there were too many variables whose implications were not clear, and too many new factors that were neither foreseen nor foreseeable. But Washington did not spend enough time asking if its own predications could be validated either.

Even more surprising, it seems to have hardly addressed the immediate issue—whether in a period of international recession South Africa could afford an adequate reform program, whether it had the resources to buy off its opponents, to invest in new constituencies, to divide the blacks by carving out new interest groups and underwriting them. Even using O'Dowd's statistics for the 1970s—a decade of growth rather than economic contraction, a decade when the republic had moved from the stage of initial rapid growth under a harsh government to one of growth coupled with social reform—the position seems to have deteriorated, not improved. Between 1970 and 1973, white:black average real wage ratios either narrowed or widened depending on which deflation index one chooses to use. In the 1960s per capita ratios actually rose because of the high growth rate of the black population. The same trend was true in education, where the proportion of black students in secondary schools increased by less than 2 percent.[26]

During Reagan's first term the situation grew more acute. Black unemployment continued to rise as high as 8 percent in the cities, probably twice that in the rural areas. The government hoped to use the rise in unemployment to empty the black urban areas of "contract" workers, but landlessness and poverty in the homelands made pressure toward the urbanization of marginal black workers much greater.

In the cities the average annual earnings of black wage earners did not increase very fast. The white:black wage ratio, it is true, contracted from 1:7 in 1970 to 1:4, but Pretoria openly admitted that it was beginning to find it increasingly difficult to narrow the gap any further. The dramatic rise in labor militancy revealed the full extent to which expectations had become increasingly frustrated. Particularly worrying were wage disputes in traditional high-wage black sectors such as the gold industry, where workers went on strike because wage increases proved lower than expected despite the fall in gold prices to almost half the record rates of 1980. The automobile industry could not meet demands for a 75 percent increase in the minimum wage in 1981 because of declining consumer demand. The following year the engineering workers demanded a 100 percent increase in their minimum hourly wage despite finding themselves and their employers in a period of unremitting recession.

By the end of 1984 the government's strategy of relying on economic growth to alleviate political frustration was already beginning to look increasingly unconvincing. Not surprisingly many began to question whether Pretoria could fund a reform program at a time when it was already relying on the building societies to meet the targets of its own housing program, when it was taxing business at higher rates than ever to build black schools, when the full cost of reform, from providing separate parliaments and the salaries of their respective MPs to developing fifty-four new townships instead of repatriating 700,000 more workers to the homelands, was finally beginning to come home.

There were a number of indications that the government could no longer fund its own program, but every sign that the Reagan administration expected it could. The agonizing self-appraisals that affected the one do not seem to have influenced the other.

By the end of 1985, therefore, the administration for all its good intentions and the boldness of its original strategy had very little to show for its endeavors. In South Africa it faced a government locked into a posture of strategic indecision, obviously unwilling to embrace thoroughgoing reform for fear of losing what remained of its traditional support, yet equally unable to fall back on unmitigated repression for fear of completely alienating groups it had previously been able to ignore—the Coloured and Indian communities, white liberals, businessmen worried by labor militancy, even international opinion as the prospect of sanctions crept nearer.

For the majority of whites life had become a holding operation filled with suspense. The government appeared to be unable to retreat or to advance, fascinated with its own inability to control events. Most civil servants appeared to be an increasingly solipsistic caste more concerned with the future of their own jobs than with reforming political society. In a country in which the government apparently could not reform, or change direction, or contain violence at an acceptable level, or even depoliticize black unrest by meeting economic expectations, it was not surprising that every change was seen by rulers and opposition alike as cracks in a crumbling edifice. Among the white community as a whole there was a sense of weariness, half fearful and half expectant. The moral certainties of the Malan and Strijdom eras had passed into history, leaving few if any hopes of white renewal.

In the United States the Reagan administration seemed equally beset by enemies, equally caught in a mood of indecision, poised between endeavor and inertia. Conservatives, if not already engulfed in despair, continued to look to internal reform, liberals to dream of a process of political evolution that would stop short of armed conflict or revolution. More radical men believed in more radical solutions, but radicalism was not in vogue in the 1980s and the climate of opinion in America on the whole discouraged more speculative thinking. For all of them, observers and participants alike, there was still a long way to go across regions as yet uncharted. What might lie on the other side was, as Lippmann had maintained, still unknown.

Was this all that five years of constructive engagement had accomplished? If so, it held out little promise for the future. Indecision may be understandable, even endearingly honest, but it is not a political virtue. As a famous philosopher once warned, the difference between leading a crowd and being pursued by it can often be disconcertingly slight.

Bibliography

I. Primary Sources

A. Congressional Hearings, 1969–1983

Congress and foreign policy, 1976. Report of the Committee on International Relations, House of Representatives, 95th Congress, 1977.

Control on exports to South Africa. Hearings before the Committee on Foreign Affairs, Subcommittee on Africa and International Economic Policy and Trade, House of Representatives, 97th Congress, 2nd Session, December 1982.

Controls on the export of nuclear-related goods and technology. Hearings before the Committee on Foreign Affairs, Subcommittee on International Security, House of Representatives, 97th Congress, 2nd Session, June 1982.

Critical developments in Namibia. Hearings before the Committee on Foreign Affairs, Subcommittee on Africa, House of Representatives, 93rd Congress, 2nd Session, April 1974.

Enforcement of the U.S. arms embargo against South Africa. Hearings before the Committee on Foreign Affairs, House of Representatives, 97th Congress, 2nd Session, March 1982.

Faces of Africa: Diversity and progress; repression and struggle. Report of Special Study mission to Africa, 1971–1972, Committee on Foreign Affairs, Subcommittee on Africa, House of Representatives, 92nd Congress, 2nd Session, 1972.

Foreign policy choices for the 1970s and 1980s. Hearings before the Committee on Foreign Relations, Senate, 94th Congress, 1st and 2nd Sessions, 1976.

Implementation of the U.S. arms embargo (against Portugal, South Africa, and related issues). Hearings before the Committee on Foreign Affairs, Subcommittee on Africa, House of Representatives, 93rd Congress, 1st Session, March 1973.

International protection of human rights. Hearings before the Committee on Foreign Affairs, Subcommittee on International Organizations and Movements, House of Representatives, 93rd Congress, 1973.

Namibia and regional destabilization in Southern Africa. Hearings before the Committee on Foreign Affairs, House of Representatives, 98th Congress, 1st Session,

February 1983.

Nomination of Henry A. Kissinger to be Secretary of State. Hearings before the Committee on Foreign Relations, Senate, 93rd Congress, 1973.

Policy toward Africa for the 1970s. Hearings before the Committee on Foreign Affairs, Subcommittee on Africa, House of Representatives, 91st Congress, 2nd Session, 1970.

Proposed expansion of U.S. military facilities in the Indian Ocean. Hearings before the Committee on Foreign Affairs, Subcommittee on the Near East and South Asia, House of Representatives, 93rd Congress, 2nd Session, 1972.

Resource Development in South Africa and U.S. policy. Hearings before the Committee on International Relations, Subcommittee on International Resources, Food, and Energy, House of Representatives, 94th Congress, 2nd Session, May 1976.

Resources in Namibia: Implications for U.S. policy. Hearings before the Committee on International Relations, Subcommittee on International Resources, Food, and Energy, House of Representatives, 94th Congress, 2nd Session, June 1975/May 1976.

Review of State Department trip throughout southern and central Africa. Hearings before the Committee on Foreign Relations, Subcommittee on Africa, Senate, 92nd Congress, December 1974.

South Africa. Hearings before the Committee on Foreign Relations, Subcommittee on African Affairs, Senate, 94th Congress, 2nd Session, 1976.

South African restrictions. Hearings before the Committee on Banking, Finance, and Urban Affairs, Subcommittee on financial institutions, House of Representatives, 98th Congress, 1st Session, June 1983.

To increase the U.S. quota in the IMF and related matters. Hearings before the Committee on International Trade, Subcommittee on International Trade, Investment, and Monetary Policy, Senate, 98th Congress, 2nd Session, May 1983.

U.S. business involvement in Southern Africa, Part 1. Hearings before the Committee on Foreign Affairs, Subcommittee on Africa, House of Representatives, 92nd Congress, 1st Session, 1971.

U.S. business involvement in Southern Africa, Part 2. Hearings before the Committee on Foreign Affairs, Subcommittee on Africa, House of Representatives, 92nd Congress, 1st Session, 1972.

U.S. business involvement in Southern Africa, Part 3. Hearings before the Committee on Foreign Affairs, Subcommittee on Africa, House of Representatives, 93rd Congress, 1st Session, 1973.

U.S. corporate interests in South Africa. Report to the Senate Committee on Foreign Relations, January 1978.

U.S. policy toward Africa. Hearings before the Committee on Foreign Affairs, Subcommittee for Africa, House of Representatives, 94th Congress, 2nd Session, May 1976.

U.S. policy toward South Africa. Hearings before the Committee on International Relations, Subcommittee on Africa, House of Representatives, 95th Congress, 1st Session, March 1977.

U.S. policy toward South Africa. Hearings before the Committee on Foreign Affairs, Subcommittee on Africa, Senate, 96th Congress, 2nd Session, March 1980.

U.S. policy toward Southern Africa. Hearings before the Committee on Foreign Relations, Subcommittee on African Affairs, Senate, 94th Congress, 1st Session, 1975.

U.S. policy toward Southern Africa. Hearings before the Committee on International Relations, Subcommittee on Africa, Senate, 96th Congress, July 1977.

U.S. security agreements and commitments abroad. Hearings before the Committee on Foreign Relations, Subcommittee on U.S. Security Agreements, Senate, 91st Congress, 1st Session, July 1970.

U.S. and Southern Africa: A report. Study mission to Southern Africa. Committee on Foreign Relations, Senate, April 1976.

B. U.S. Government Statements

Adelman, K. Official Statement by U.S. ambassador . . . during the plenary debate on apartheid, 30 November 1981. *Southern Africa Record* 25/26 (December 1981).

Adelman, K. Statement on the subject of apartheid by the U.S. ambassador . . . to the General Assembly, 17 December 1981. *Southern Africa Record* 27 (June 1982).

Bush, G. "United States and Southern Africa: Extracts from an address by the Vice-President . . . to the Kenya Chamber of Commerce," 19 November 1982. *Southern Africa Record* 29 (December 1982).

Christopher, W. "Human rights: An important concern of U.S. foreign policy." *Department of State Bulletin* 76:1970 (28 March 1977).

———. "Human rights: The diplomacy of the first year." Address before the American Bar Association, New Orleans, 13 February 1978. *Department of State Bulletin* 78:2012 (March 1978).

Crocker, C. Extracts from statements and answers to questions by the U.S. designate at a national foreign policy conference for representatives of the media, 2 June 1981. *Southern Africa Record* 24 (August 1981).

———. "Regional strategy for Southern Africa." Address before the American Legion in Honolulu, 29 August 1981. *Department of State Bulletin* 81:2055 (October 1981).

———. "United States and Southern Africa." Address to Council on Foreign Relations, New York, 5 October 1981. *Southern Africa Record* 27 (June 1982).

———. Speech concerning U.S. assistance in the education of black South Africans by Assistant Secretary at Georgetown University. *Southern Africa Record* 27 (June 1982).

———. "The Reagan administration's African policy: A progress report." Address before the Fourth Annual Conference on International Affairs, University of Kansas, 10 November 1983. *Department of State Bulletin* 84:2082 (January 1984).

Derian, P. "Human Rights and South Africa." *Department of State Bulletin* 80:2043 (October 1980).

Diggs, C. "Action Manifesto." *Issue* 2:1 (Spring 1972).

———. *Assessment of your report on the implementation of Security Council Resolution 309 concerning the question of Namibia.* Memorandum to Dr. Kurt Waldheim, UN Secretary-General, 1972.

Dunfey, W. "U.S. policy on apartheid." *Department of State Bulletin* 80:2037 (April 1980).

Bibliography 289

Eagleburger, L. "Southern Africa: America's responsibility for peace and change." Address before the National Convention of Editorial Writers, San Francisco, 23 June 1983. *Department of State Bulletin* 83:2077 (August 1983).

Easum, D. "Southern Africa: Five years after the Lusaka Manifesto." Address at Symposium, Patterson School of Diplomacy and International Commerce, University of Kentucky, Lexington, 26 November 1974. *Department of State Bulletin* 61:1581 (16 December 1974).

———. Interview. *Africa Report* 20:1 (January/February 1975).

Finger, S. Statement to Committee of 24, April 1969. *Department of State Bulletin* 60:1561 (26 May 1969).

———. Statement to Committee of 24, April 1970. *Department of State Bulletin* 62:1609 (27 April 1970).

Fletcher, J. "U.S. discusses action to combat racism and discrimination." Statement of U.S. representative to Committee of 3 (Social, Humanitarian, and Cultural), 3 November 1971. *Department of State Bulletin* 65:1692 (29 November 1971).

Goldberg, A. "Peace and justice among nations: Agenda for the international community." Address before the Economic Club, 2 May 1966. *Department of State Bulletin* 54:1404 (23 May 1966).

Kissinger, H. Address before the St. Louis World Affairs Council, 12 May 1975. *Department of State Bulletin* 82:1875 (2 June 1975).

———. "Building an enduring foreign policy." Speech before the Economic Club of Detroit, 24 November 1975. *Department of State Bulletin* 73:1903 (15 December 1975).

———. Interview with the press, 24 June 1976. *Department of State Bulletin* 75:1933 (6 July 1976).

———. "The challenge of Africa." Address before the Convention of Opportunities Industrialization Center, 31 July 1976. *Department of State Bulletin* 75:1943 (20 September 1976).

———. "The U.S. and Africa: Strengthened ties for an era of challenge." Address to annual conference, National Urban League, Boston. *Department of State Bulletin* 65:1939 (23 August 1976).

———. Address before the Permanent Representatives of the United Nations, 8 October 1976. *South Africa Newsletter* 8:3 (1976).

Lake, A. "Africa in Global Perspective." Christian Herter Lecture, Washington, D.C., 27 October 1977. *Department of State Bulletin* 77:2007 (12 December 1977).

McGee, G. Speech before the Foreign Policy Association, Oklahoma City, 8 May 1950. *Department of State Bulletin* 22:572 (19 June 1950).

Mitchell, C. Statement, Special Political Committee, UN General Assembly, 23 October 1975. *Department of State Bulletin* 73:1899 (17 November 1975).

———. "U.S. discusses human rights in South Africa." Address to Special Political Committee, UN, 28 November 1975. *Department of State Bulletin* 73:1905 (29 December 1975).

Moose, R. "U.S. policy toward South Africa." *Department of State Bulletin* 80:2040 (July 1980).

———. "Southern Africa: Four years later." *Department of State Bulletin* 81:2046 (January 1981).

Newsom, D. "The U.S., UN, and Africa." Address before the Chicago Committee of Council on Foreign Relations, 17 September 1970. *Department of State Bulletin* 62 (October 1970).

———. "U.S. options in Southern Africa." Address at Northwestern University, 8 December 1970. *Department of State Bulletin* 64:1647 (7 January 1971).

———. "A look at African issues at the UN." Address to Atlanta Press Club, 21 September 1971. *Department of State Bulletin* 65:1685 (11 October 1971).

———. "U.S. government and business: Parties in African development." Address to African-American Chamber of Commerce, New York, 16 February 1972. *Department of State Bulletin* 66:1708 (20 March 1972).

———. Interview. *Africa Report* 17:3 (March 1972).

———. "Southern Africa: Constant themes in U.S. policy." Address to mid-American Committee at Chicago, 28 June 1972. *Department of State Bulletin* 72:1726 (24 July 1972).

———. "U.S.-African Interests: A frank appraisal." Speech to Royal Commonwealth Society, 14 March 1973. *Department of State Bulletin* 68:1764 (16 April 1973).

Nixon, R. *U.S. foreign policy for the 1970s: A new strategy for peace.* (Washington, D.C., 1970).

———. "U.S. foreign policy for the 1970's: Building for peace." Report to U.S. Congress, 25 February 1971. *Department of State Bulletin* 64:1656 (22 March 1971).

———. "U.S. foreign policy for the 1970s: The emerging structure of peace." *Department of State Bulletin* 66:1707 (13 March 1972).

———. "U.S. foreign policy for the 1970s: Shaping a durable peace." *Department of State Bulletin* 68:1771 (4 June 1973).

Phillips, C. Statement to Committee of 4. *Department of State Bulletin* 61:1587 (24 November 1969).

———. Statement before the Security Council, 29 December 1972. *Department of State Bulletin* 67:1741 (6 November 1972).

Rogers, W. Interview with Hearst Newspapers, 29 January 1970. *Department of State Bulletin* 62:1601 (2 March 1970).

———. Report on African tour to Congress. *Department of State Bulletin* 62:1608 (20 April 1970).

———. "The rule of law and the settlement of international disputes." Address before the American Society of International Law, 25 April 1970. *Department of State Bulletin* 62:1612 (18 May 1970).

———. "U.S. foreign policy." Report to Congress, 26 March 1971. *Department of State Bulletin* 64:1658 (1971).

———. "Relating our national idealism to international realities." Address to Council for Foreign Relations, New York. *Department of State Bulletin* 63:1669 (21 June 1971).

———. "A legacy of peace: Our responsibility to future generations." Address before the 26th UN General Assembly. *Department of State Bulletin* 65:1687 (25 October 1971).

———. "Seeking a peaceful world." Address at Commonwealth Club, San Francisco, 18 July 1972. *Department of State Bulletin* 67:1729 (14 August 1972).

Schaufele, W. "U.S. relations in Southern Africa." Address before the American Academy of Political and Social Science, Philadelphia, 16 April 1977. *Department of State Bulletin* 76:1976 (7 May 1977).

Shultz, G. Extract from an address entitled "The U.S. and Africa in the 1980s," by U.S. Secretary of State to the Boston World Affairs Council, 15 February 1984. *Southern Africa Record* 35 (April 1984).

Smith, R. "The dilemma of foreign investment in South Africa." Address before the American Society of International Law, 30 April 1971. *Department of State Bulletin* 64:1670 (28 June 1971).

Vance, C. "Human rights and foreign policy." *Department of State Bulletin* 76:1978 (23 May 1977).

———. "The United States and Africa: Building positive relations." *Department of State Bulletin* 77:1989 (8 August 1977).

Williams, M. "U.S. policy toward South Africa." *Department of State Bulletin* 54:1395 (21 March 1966).

Yost, C. "U.S. deplores minority rule in Southern Africa." *Department of State Bulletin* 61:1568 (July 1969).

———. Statement to Security Council, 13 June 1969. *Department of State Bulletin* 61:1669 (21 July 1969).

———. Statement before the Security Council, 20 June 1969. *Department of State Bulletin* 61:1569 (21 July 1969).

———. "U.S. stake in an effective UN." Address before the National Convention, 19 May 1970. *Department of State Bulletin* 62:8 (8 June 1970).

Young, A. "Developments concerning apartheid." *Department of State Bulletin* 77:1997 (3 October 1977).

C. Government Publications

Answers to clarifications on questions posed by AID about the University Preparation Program. San Diego, Calif.: Consulting Group, Inc., 30 October 1981.

Automating apartheid: U.S. computer exports to South Africa. Philadelphia: American Friends Service Committee, 1982.

Establishing a business in South Africa, OBR 70-50. Department of Commerce, September 1970.

International transfer of conventional arms. Washington, D.C.: U.S. Arms Control and Disarmament Agency, 1973.

Investing in apartheid: U.S. corporations in South Africa. Philadelphia: American Friends Service Committee, 1982.

Market profiles for South Africa, OBR 70-40//National Security Study Memorandum 39 (NSSM 39), AF/NSC 69–68, 9 December 1969.

Military exports to South Africa. Philadelphia: American Friends Service Committee, 1984.

National Security Decision Memorandum 81 (NSDM 81), NSC, 17 August 1970.

Survey of Current Business (issues 1969–1974), Department of Commerce.

U.S. educational assistance in South Africa: Critical policy choices. Report of a Staff Mission to South Africa, August 1982, Committee on Foreign Affairs, House of Representatives, 30 December 1982.

D. UN Publications

Activities of transnational corporations in South Africa. UN Center against Apartheid, Department of Political and Security Council Affairs, 9/78, May 1978.
Bank loans to South Africa 1979–mid 1982. UN Center against Apartheid, December 1982.
Conference paper 7. UN Center against Apartheid, Department of Political and Security Council Affairs, November 1977.
Foreign investment in apartheid. UN Unit on Apartheid, Department of Political and Security Council Affairs, 1972.
Industrialization, foreign capital, and forced labor in South Africa. UN Department of Political and Security Council Affairs AS/10, 1970.
International Conference of Experts for the Support of Victims of Colonialism and Apartheid in Southern Africa, Oslo, 9–14 April 1973. *Objective Justice* 5/3 (July–September 1973).

E. Memoirs, etc.

Acheson, D. *Present at the creation.* New York: W. W. Norton, 1969.
———. *This vast external realm.* New York: W. W. Norton, 1973.
Attwood, W. *The reds and the blacks.* London: Hutchinson, 1967.
Ball, G. *The discipline of power.* Boston: Little, Brown, 1968.
Bowles, C. *Promise to keep: My years in public life.* New York: Harper and Row, 1971.
Brzezinski, Z. *Power and principle.* London: Weidenfeld and Nicolson, 1983.
Crocker, C. "A mid-term assessment of the Carter administration's policies in Africa." *International Affairs Bulletin* 3 (1 June 1979).
———. "South Africa: Strategy for change." *Foreign Affairs* 59:2 (Winter 1980).
———. "A U.S. Policy for the 1980s." *Africa Report* 26:1 (January-February 1981).
Diggs, C. "My visit to South Africa." *Africa Report* 16:8 (November-December 1971).
Fergusson, C. "South Africa: What is to be done?" *Foreign Affairs* 56:2 (January 1978).
Finger, S. "A new approach to colonial problems at the UN." *International Organization* 26:1 (Winter 1972).
Humphreys, H. "It's time to build a new relationship." *Africa Report* 18:4 (July-August 1973).
Kennedy, E. "What America should do." *Africa Report* 20:6 (November-December 1975).
Kissinger, H. *The White House years.* London: Weidenfeld and Nicholson, 1979.
McGee, G. "U.S. Congress and the Rhodesian chrome issue." *Issue* 2:2 (Summer 1972).
Moynihan, D. *A dangerous place.* London: Secker and Warburg, 1979.
Yost, C. "World order and the American responsibility." *Foreign Affairs* 47:1 (October 1968).
———. *The conduct and misconduct of foreign affairs.* New York: Random House, 1972.

F. Newspapers and Journals 1969–1983

Africa
Africa Confidential
Africa Contemporary Record
Africa Report
Africa Today
African Development
African Index
Congressional Record
Issue
New York Times
The Star (Johannesburg)
Washington Post

II. Secondary Sources

A. Books and Dissertations

Adam, H. *Ethnic power mobilized.* New Haven: Yale University Press, 1979.

Arnheim, M. *South Africa after Vorster.* Cape Town: Howard Timmins, 1980.

Beichman, A. *The other state department: The U.S. mission to the United Nations.* New York: Basic Books, 1968.

Bissell, R. *South Africa and the United States: The erosion of an influence relationship.* New York: Praeger, 1982.

Bowman, L. *Politics in Rhodesia: White power in an African state.* Cambridge, Mass.: Harvard University Press, 1973.

Butler, J., R. Rotberg, and J. Adams. *The black homelands of South Africa.* Berkeley: University of California Press, 1977.

Cantori, L. *The international politics of regions.* Englewood Cliffs, N.J.: Prentice-Hall, 1970.

Doxey, M. *Economic sanctions and international enforcement.* New York: Oxford University Press, 1971.

Dugard, J. *Human rights and the South African legal order.* Princeton: Princeton University Press, 1978.

Emerson, R. *The U.S. and Africa: Background papers and final report of 13th American Assembly.* New York: Columbia University Press, 1958.

Gerhart, E. *Black power in South Africa: The evolution of an ideology.* Berkeley: University of California Press, 1978.

Gonze, C. *South Africa: Crisis and U.S. policy.* New York: American Committee on Africa, 1962.

Grundy, K. *Confrontation and accommodation in Southern Africa: The limits of independence.* Berkeley: University of California Press, 1973.

Hance, W. *Southern Africa and the United States.* New York: Columbia University Press, 1968.

Jackson, R. *The multinational company and social policy.* New York: Praeger, 1974.

Jaros, D. *Political behaviour: Choices and perspectives.* Oxford: Basil Blackwell, 1974.

Kadish, M. *Discretion to disobey: A study of lawful departures from legal rules.* Stanford: Stanford University Press, 1978.

Kissinger, H. *A world restored: Metternich, Castlereagh, and the problem of peace, 1812–22.* London: Weidenfeld and Nicolson, 1957.

———. *Nuclear weapons and foreign policy.* New York: Doubleday, 1957.

———. *The necessity for choice: Prospects of American foreign policy.* London: Chatto and Windus, 1960.

———. *American foreign policy: Three essays.* New York: W. W. Norton, 1969.

Kotze, D. *African politics in South Africa, 1964–74: Parties and issues.* London: Hurst, 1975.

Lake, A. *Caution and concern: The making of American policy toward South Africa, 1946–71.* Ph.D. diss., Princeton University, 1974.

———. *The tar baby option: American policy toward southern Africa.* New York: Columbia University Press, 1976.

Liss, A. *Apartheid and the UN: Collective measures, an analysis.* New York: Carnegie Endowment for International Peace, 1965.

Mathews, A. S. *Law, order, and liberty in South Africa.* Berkeley: University of California Press, 1972.

Mazrui, A., ed. *Africa: The next thirty years.* London: Friedmann Julian, 1974.

Morris, R. *Uncertain greatness: Henry Kissinger and American foreign policy.* New York: Quartet Books, 1977.

Nielsen, W. *African battleline.* New York: Council on Foreign Relations, 1965.

———. *The Great Powers and Africa.* London: Pall Mall Press, 1969.

Nolutshungu, S. *South Africa in Africa: A study in ideology and foreign policy.* Manchester, Eng.: Manchester University Press, 1975.

———. *Changing South Africa: Political considerations.* Manchester, Eng.: Manchester University Press, 1982.

Razis, V. *Swords or ploughshares: South Africa and political change.* Johannesburg: Raven Press, 1978.

Renwick, R. *Economic sanctions.* Cambridge, Mass.: Harvard University Press, 1981.

Rhoodie, E. *The third Africa.* Cape Town: Twin Circle, 1968.

Rostow, W. *The U.S. in the world arena: An essay in recent history.* New York: Harper and Row, 1960.

Schlemmer, L. *Change, reform, and economic growth.* Johannesburg: Raven Press, 1978.

Schlesinger, A. *A thousand days in the White House.* New York: Andre Deutsch, 1965.

Seiler, J. *The formulation of U.S. policy toward Africa 1957–76: The failure of good intentions.* Ph.D. diss., University of Connecticut, 1976.

Shepherd, G. *The U.S. and non-aligned Africa.* Occasional Paper I, University of Denver, 1970.

Spring, M. *Confrontation.* Johannesburg: Valiant, 1977.

Stockholm Institute of Peace Research. *Southern Africa: The escalation of conflict.* Stockholm: Stockholm Institute of Peace Research, 1976.

B. Articles

Abernathy, D. "The major foreign policy positions of the Reagan administration: Implications for U.S.-South African relations." *International Affairs Bulletin* 5:2 (1981).

Baldwin, D. "Interstate influence re-visited." *Journal of Conflict Resolution* 15 (December 1971).

———. "Power analysis and world politics." *World Politics* 31:2 (January 1979).

———. "The power of positive sanctions." *World Politics* 24:1 (1971).

Ball, G. "Asking for trouble in South Africa." *Atlantic Monthly* (October 1977).

Barber, J. "Economic sanctions as a policy instrument." *International Affairs* 55:3 (July 1979).

Bowman, L. "The sub-state system of Southern Africa." *International Studies Quarterly* 11:1 (1968).

Brotz, H. "Constitutional change in South Africa: Utopian and political." *South Africa International* 9:2 (October 1978).

Chettle, J. "The evolution of U.S. policy toward South Africa." *Modern Age* (Summer 1972).

———. "The politicisation of the International Monetary Fund." *Southern Africa International* 14:2 (October 1983).

Clough, M. "Why carrots alone won't work." *African Index* 4:10 (30 June 1981).

Doxey, M. "Alignments and coalitions in Southern Africa." *International Journal* 10, No. 3 (Summer 1975).

Eidelberg, J. "U.S.–South African relations—a rejoinder." *Africa Insight* 11:12 (1981).

Fergusson, C., and W. Cotter. "South Africa: What is to be done?" *Foreign Affairs* 56:2 (January 1978), 253–78.

Galtung, J. "On the meaning of non-violence." *Journal of Peace Research* 3 (1965).

———. "On the effects of international economic sanctions: With examples from the case of Rhodesia." *World Politics* 19:3 (April 1967).

Gann, L. "What should the Reagan administration do about South Africa?" *South Africa International* 13:3 (January 1982).

Gappert, G. "The emerging political economy of the Indian Ocean." *Current Bibliography on African Affairs* 4:6 (November 1971).

Greenberg, S. "Economic growth and political change." *Journal of Modern African Studies* 19:4 (1981).

Harshorne, K. "The unfinished business: Education for South Africa's black people." *Optima*, 30 July 1981.

Huntington, S. "Reform and stability in South Africa." *International Security* 6:4 (Spring 1981).

Isaacs, M. "Tilting toward South Africa." *Africa Report* 21:2 (March/April 1976).

Javits, J. "The congressional presence in foreign relations." *Foreign Affairs* 48:2 (January 1970).

Johnson, R. "An examination of the U.S. Congress's treatment of Southern African issues between 1971 and 1976." Paper presented to Southern Africanist Association / Southern Political Science Association, 4 November 1976, Atlanta (unpublished).

Johnson, W. "U.S. foreign policy toward Africa." *Africa Today* 20:1 (1973).

Kiewiet, C. "The revolution that disappeared." *Virginia Quarterly Review* 46:2 (Spring 1970).

Kennan, G. "Hazardous courses in Southern Africa." *Foreign Affairs* 49:2 (January 1971).

Kornegay, F. "Africa and presidential politics." *Africa Report* 21:4 (July/August 1976).

Macrae, N. "The green bay tree." *The Economist*, 29 June 1968.

McHenry, D. "Captive of no group." *Foreign Policy* (Summer 1974).

McKeon, N. "After the election." *Africa Report* 17:9 (1972).

Morris, R. "Race war diplomacy." *New Republic*, 26 June 1976.

O'Dowd, M. "South Africa in the light of the economic growth." *South Africa: Economic growth and political change*, edited by Adrian Leftwich. London: Allison and Busby, 1974.

Oudes, B. "Africa and the Watergate mentality." *Africa Report* 18:3 (May/June 1973).

———. "Observations on America's policy problems." *Issue* 3:4 (Winter 1973).

Pogrund, B. "Reagan's shift: The view from Pretoria." *Washington Quarterly* 5:1 (Winter 1982).

Reisman, M. "Polaroid power: Taxing business for human rights." *Foreign Policy* (Fall 1971).

Sadie, J. "An economic commission for Southern Africa." *South Africa International* 1:4 (April 1971).

Savage, M. "Costs of enforcing apartheid and the problems of change." *African Affairs* 76:304 (July 1977).

Seiler, J. "The failure of U.S. Southern Africa policy." *Issue* 2:1 (1972).

———. "Has constructive engagement failed? An assessment of Reagan's Southern African Policy." *South Africa International* 13:3 (January 1982).

———. "South Africa in Namibia: Persistence, misperception, and ultimate failure." *Journal of Modern African Studies* 20:4 (December 1982).

Shaw, T. "Southern Africa: Co-operation and conflict in the international subsystem." *Journal of Modern African Studies* 12:4 (1973).

———. "International organisations and the politics of Southern Africa: Towards regional integration or liberation?" *Journal of Southern African Studies* 3:1 (October 1976).

Shepherd, G. "The U.N. arms embargo on South Africa and the Cape route." Paper presented to 16th annual convention of the International Studies Association, Washington, D.C., 1975.

Wallerstein, P. "Characteristics of economic sanctions." *Journal of Peace Research* 5:3 (1968).

Yoder, S. "Does America have a policy?" *Africa Report* 20:3 (May/June 1975).

Young, O. "Interdependences in world politics." *International Journal* 24 (Autumn 1969).

Zartman, W. "Africa as a sub-state system." *International Organisation* 21 (1967).

Notes

Preface

1   Cited in Kenneth Adelman, *African Realities* (New York: Crane, Russak, 1980), 154.

1   The United States and South Africa, 1960–1968

1   Eschel Rhoodie, *The third Africa* (Cape Town: Twin Circle, 1968).

2   Statement of Adlai Stevenson 2 August 1963, reprinted Annex 10 National Security Study Memorandum 39 (NSSM 39) AF/NSC IG 69–8 (9 December 1969).

3   It would be wrong, however, to suggest that the National party's program in 1948 marked a total break with the past. In fact, the second Smuts administration had continued the steady drift toward white supremacy. The Native Urban Areas Consolidation Act systematized further the provisions of the Native Urban Areas Act of 1923 and 1930. The Apprenticeship Act of 1944 further secured skilled jobs for the Europeans. His anti-Indian legislation was extensive. To quote Pierre van den Berghe, "When the Nationalists won in 1948 they only had to extend and systematize an already imposing structure." *South Africa: A study in conflict* (Berkeley: University of California Press, 1965), 127.

4   Cited in Amy Vandenbosch, *South Africa and the world: The foreign policy of apartheid* (Lexington: University of Kentucky Press, 1970), 235.

5   Cited in Rupert Emerson, *The United States and Africa: Background papers and final report of the 13th American Assembly* (New York: Columbia University Press, 1958), 100.

6   James Barber, *South Africa's foreign policy, 1945–1970* (London: Oxford University Press, 1973), 66.

7   Cited in Colin Gonze, *South Africa: Crisis and U.S. policy* (Berkeley: University of California Press, 1965), 178. Not everyone agreed. Secretary of State Christian Herter was unhappy with the language of a statement put out by the State Department after the Sharpeville massacre. He warned Eisenhower that the United States might be accused of inciting revolution. See George Noble, *Christian*

Herter (New York: Cooper, 1970), 169.

8   Barber, *South Africa's foreign policy*, 191.

9   Harold Macmillan referred to the "winds of change" during a speech before the South African House of Assembly in 1960. During his New Year address in 1977 John Vorster told the South African people, "The storm has not yet struck. We are only experiencing the whirlwinds that go before."

10   Chester Bowles, *Promise to keep: My years in public life* (New York: Harper and Row, 1971), 428.

11   John Chettle, "The evolution of U.S. policy toward South Africa," *Modern Age* (Summer 1972), 260.

12   Statement by Joseph Satterthwaite, *Policy toward Africa for the 1970s*, Hearings before the Committee on Foreign Affairs, Subcommittee on Africa, House of Representatives, 91st Congress, 2nd Session, 1970, 37.

13   Cornelis de Kiewiet, "The revolution that disappeared," *Virginia Quarterly Review* 46:2 (Spring 1970).

14   Van den Berghe, *South Africa: A study in conflict*, 262.

15   D. E. Russell, *Rebellion, revolution, and armed force* (New York: Academia Press, 1974), 53–54.

16   "Department of State National Strategy Series—South Africa." Intermediate draft prepared by William R. Duggan and Waldemar B. Campbell, 28 October 1963.

17   Report SCN 10059/636 (CIA: Office of Current Intelligence), 10 May 1963.

18   Statement of Mennen Williams, Assistant Secretary for African Affairs, *United States–South Africa relations*, Hearings before the Committee on Foreign Affairs, House of Representatives, 89th Congress, 2nd Session 1966, 2–5.

19   See Mortimer Kadish, *Discretion to disobey: A study of lawful departures from legal rules* (Stanford: Stanford University Press, 1973), 93–140.

20   Arthur Schlesinger, *A thousand days in the White House* (New York: André Deutsch, 1965).

21   Cited in Bruce Oudes, "Evolving American views of South Africa," in Richard Bissell and Chester Crocker, *South Africa into the 1980s* (Boulder, Colo.: Westview Press, 1979), 185.

22   Memo SP 21880/410 (Department of State, 28 October 1963).

23   *National Security Study Memorandum (NSSM) 39*, Washington, D.C., 15 August 1969, AF/NSC10 69.

24   Seretse Khama, "African-American relations in the 1970s: Prospects and progress," address at the third annual conference, African-American Dialogue, 8 March 1971.

25   "Charles Yost supports UN Security Council resolution on Namibia," *Department of State Bulletin (DSB)* 60:1554 (7 April 1969), 301.

26   George W. Shepherd, *The United States and non-aligned Africa* (Optional Paper No. 1, University of Denver, 1970).

27   Williams's statement, *United States–South African relations*, 4.

28   George Ball, *The discipline of power* (Boston: Little, Brown, 1968), 254.

29   George Kennan, "Hazardous courses in Southern Africa," *Foreign Affairs* 49:2 (January 1971), 222.

30   Ball, *The discipline of power*, 246.

2   National Security Study Memorandum 39

1   Richard Nixon, *U.S. foreign policy for the 1970s: A new strategy for peace* (Washington D.C.: GPO, 1970), 15.

2   Henry A. Kissinger, *The necessity for choice: Prospects for American foreign policy* (London: Chatto and Windus, 1960), 341.

3   Cited in Roger Morris, *Uncertain greatness: Henry Kissinger and American foreign policy* (New York: Quartet Books, 1977), 111.

4   Ibid., 112.

5   Patrick Duncan, "Toward a world policy for South Africa," *Foreign Affairs* 42 (October 1963), 43.

6   Richard Bissell, *South Africa and the United States: The erosion of an influence relationship* (New York: Praeger, 1982), 25.

7   Morris, *Uncertain greatness*, 114.

8   Ibid., 113.

9   Seretse Khama, "African-American relations in the 1970s: Prospects and progress," address at the Third Annual Conference, African-American Dialogue, 8 March 1971.

10 *National Security Study Memorandum 39* (NSSM 39), 66.

11 Ibid., 64.

12 Ibid., 50.

13 Ibid., 70.

14 Ibid., 74.

15 Ibid., 73.

16 Ibid., 69.

17 See in particular Robert A. Packenham, *Liberal America and the Third World* (Princeton: Princeton University Press, 1973), and John L. S. Girling, *America and the Third World: Revolution and intervention* (London: Routledge and Kegan Paul, 1980).

18 Chester Bowles, *Promise to keep: My years in public life* (New York: Harper and Row, 1971), 428–29.

19 Statement by Henry A. Kissinger, Secretary of State, *U.S. policy toward Africa*, Hearings before the Committee on Foreign Relations, Subcommittee on African Affairs and Subcommittee on Arms Control, International Organizations, and Security Agreements, U.S. Senate, 94th Congress, 2nd Session, May 1976, 397.

20 January 1970, *Department of State Bulletin* 62:1601 (2 March 1970), 220.

21 Cited in Sam Nolutshungu, *South Africa in Africa: A study in ideology and foreign policy* (Manchester, Eng.: Manchester University Press, 1975), 75.

22 See Stephen Krasner, *Defending the national interest: Raw material investment and U.S. foreign policy* (Princeton: Princeton University Press, 1978).

23 Statement of James Blake, Deputy Assistant Secretary for African Affairs, *Resource Development in South Africa and U.S. policy*, Hearings, Committee on International Relations, Subcommittee on International Resources, Food, and Energy, House of Representatives, 94th Congress, 2nd Session, May–June 1976, 13.

24 Statement of Stanley Katz, Deputy Assistant Secretary for International Economic Policy and Research, Department of Commerce, ibid., 189.

25 Blake statement, ibid., 15.

26 Cited in Tex Bosson and Benson Varon, *The mining industry and the developing countries* (London: Oxford University Press, 1977), 32.

27 Statement of Charles Yost, U.S. Ambassador to the United Nations, *Policy toward Africa for the 1970s*, Hearings before the Committee on Foreign Affairs, Subcommittee on Africa, House of Representatives, 91st Congress, 2nd Session, 1970, 301.

28 Charles Yost, *The conduct and misconduct of foreign affairs* (New York: Random House, 1972), 134.

29 Interview, Washington D.C., 15 October 1979.

30 See George Ball, *The discipline of power: Essentials of a modern world structure* (Boston: Little, Brown, 1968), 245. Testimony of Dean Acheson, *Rhodesia and U.S. foreign policy*, Hearings before Committee on Foreign Affairs, Subcommittee on Africa, House of Representatives, 91st Congress, 1st Session, 1969, 124–73.

3   Negative and Positive Sanctions

1   Johann Galtung, "On the effects of international economic sanctions: With examples from the case of Rhodesia," *World Politics* 19:3 (April 1967), 412.

2   Peter Wallenstein, "Characteristics of economic sanctions," *Journal of Peace Research* 5:3 (1968), 262.

3   Margaret Doxey, "International sanctions: A framework for analysis with special reference to the UN and Southern Africa," *International Organization* 26:3 (Summer 1972), 547.

4   Klaus E. Knorr, *Power and wealth: The political economy of international power* (New York: Basic Books, 1973), 156, 197.

5   Margaret Doxey, *Economic sanctions and international enforcement* (London: Oxford University Press, 1971), 14.

6   Ibid., 26.

7   Galtung, "On the effects of international economic sanctions," 8407.

8   George Ball, *The discipline of power*, (Boston: Little, Brown, 1968), 245.

9   Cited in Doxey, *Economic sanctions*, 41.

10 James Barber, "Economic sanctions as a policy instrument," *International Affairs* 55:3 (July 1979), 370–73.

11 Doxey, *Economic sanctions*, 140.

12 Robin Renwick, *Economic sanctions* (Cambridge, Mass.: Harvard University Press, 1981), 92.

13 Galtung, "On the effects of international sanctions," 407.

14 G. Shepherd, *Anti-apartheid: Transnational conflict and Western policy in the liberation of South Africa* (Westport, Conn: Greenwood Press, 1977), 4.

15 Harold and Margaret Sprout, *Man-milieu relationship hypotheses in the context of international politics* (Princeton: Princeton University Press, 1956), 39–49.

16 William Gutteridge, "The strategic implications of sanctions against South Africa," in R. Segal (ed.), *Sanctions against South Africa* (London: Penguin, 1964), 115.

17 Oran R. Young, "Interdependencies in world politics," *International Journal* 24 (Autumn 1969), 746–47.

18 David Baldwin, "Power analysis and world politics," *World Politics* 31:2 (January 1979), 176.

19 Stephen Krasner, "State power and the structure of international trade," *World Politics* 28 (April 1976), 320.

20 Renwick, *Economic sanctions*, 80.

21 Amitai Etzioni, *A comparative analysis of complex organizations* (New York: Glencoe Free Press, 1961), 313.

22 Eric Partridge, *Usage and abusage* (London: Penguin, 1973), 354.

23 D. Jaros and L. Grant, *Political behaviour: Choices and perspectives* (Oxford: Basil Blackwell, 1974), 275.

24 See David Baldwin, "The power of positive sanctions," *World Politics* 24:1 (1971); J. Tedeschi, "Threats and promises," in P. Swingler (ed.), *The structure of conflict* (New York: Academic Press, 1970); B. Schlenker, "Reactions to coercive and reward power: The effects of switching influence modes on target compliance," *Sociometry* 39:4 (1976); Tedeschi, "Social power and the credibility of promises," *Journal of Personality and Social Psychology* 78 (1968); Tedeschi, "The exercise of power and influence: The source of influence," in J. Tedeschi (ed.), *The social influence process* (Chicago: 1972). There is only one discussion of positive sanctions in a specific policy context, Richard Smoke and Alexander George, *Deterrence in American foreign policy* (New York: Columbia University Press, 1974), but it is largely confined to a few pages.

25 D. Easton, *The political system* (New York: Knopf, 1953), 143–44; R. Dahl, *Modern political analysis* (Englewood Cliffs, N.J.: Prentice-Hall, 1970), 32–33.

26 Felix Oppenheim, *Dimensions of freedom* (New York: Random House, 1961), 45.

27 Robert Dahl, *Modern political analysis* (Englewood Cliffs, N.J.: Prentice-Hall, 1963), 50–51. This passage does not appear in the revised edition.

28 Baldwin, "The power of positive sanctions," 26.

29 J. Rosenau, "Foreign policy as adaptive behavior," *Comparative Politics* 2 (1970), 365–87.

30 D. Vital, *The inequality of states* (London: Oxford University Press, 1967), 90.

31 J. Nelson, *Aid, influence, and foreign policy* (London: Macmillan, 1968), 67.

32 S. Huntington, "Foreign aid: For what and for whom?" *Foreign Policy* 1 (1970–1), 188.

33 Cited in Melvin Gurtov, *The United States versus the Third World* (New York: 1972), 162.

34 Cited in R. Walton, *Cold war and counter-revolution* (New York: Viking Press, 1972).

35 Baldwin, "The power of positive sanctions," 29.

36 T. Schelling, *Strategy of conflict* (Cambridge, Mass.: Harvard University Press, 1960), 131–34.

37 Gil Fernandes, "The Azores over Africa," *Africa Today* 19:1 (1972), 5.

38 John Marcum, "The politics of indifference: Portugal and Africa, a case study in American foreign policy" (Eduardo Mondlane Lecture, Syracuse University, 1972).

39 Cited in *Congressional Record* 118:12, pp. S9643–44.

40　J. Burton, *Systems, states, diplomacy, and rules* (Cambridge: Cambridge University Press, 1968).

41　Karl Deutsch, *The analysis of international relations*, (Englewood Cliffs, N.J.: Prentice-Hall, 1978), 26.

42　Regis Debray, *A critique of arms* (London: Harmondsworth, 1977), 67.

43　Talcott Parsons, "On the concept of political power," *Proceedings of the American Philosophical Society* 108 (1963), 239–40.

44　See T. Milburn, "What constitutes effective deterrence?" *Journal of Conflict Resolution* 3 (1959), 138–45.

45　J. Lieberman, "Threat and assurance in the conduct of conflict," in R. Fischer (ed.), *International conflict and behavioral science* (New York: Basic Books, 1964), 110–22.

46　M. Legassick, "Legislation, ideology, and economy in post-1948 South Africa," *Journal of Southern African Studies* 1:1 (1974), 5–35

47　D. Easton, *A systems analysis of political life* (New York: Wiley, 1965), 170–73.

48　Harry Strack, *Sanctions: The case of Rhodesia* (Syracuse, N.Y.: Syracuse University Press, 1978), 27.

49　Galtung, "On the effects of international economic sanctions," 393.

50　D. Baldwin, "The costs of power," *Journal of Conflict Resolution* 15:2 (1971), 147.

51　Interview with Fannie Botha, Pretoria, June 1978.

52　Cited in J. Day, "The Rhodesian African nationalists and the Commonwealth African states," *Journal of Commonwealth Political Studies* 7:2 (1969), 141.

53　J. Harsanyi, "Measurement of social power, opportunity costs, and the theory of two-person bargaining games," *Behavioral Science* 7 (1962), 67–80.

54　W. Gamson, *Power and discontent* (Homewood, Ill.: Dorsey, 1968), 74–75.

55　Karl Deutsch, *The nerves of government* (New York: Free Press, 1963), 116.

56　J. Galtung, "On the meaning of non-violence," *Journal of Peace Research* 3 (1965), 247.

57　J. Race, *War comes to Long An: Revolutionary conflict in a Vietnamese village* (Berkeley: University of California Press, 1972). See also Robert Sanson, *The economics of insurgency in the Mekong Delta* (Cambridge, Mass.: MIT Press, 1970).

58　M. Ball, "Issue for the Americas: Non-intervention against human rights and the preservation of democratic institutions," *International Organization* 25:2 (1961), 21–23.

59　Galtung, "On the meaning of non-violence," 249.

60　M. Heilman, "Threats and promises: Reputational consequences and the transfer of credibility," *Journal of Experimental Social Psychology* 10 (1974), 310–24. See also S. Lindskold and J. Tedeschi, "Reward, power, and attraction in inter-personal conflict," *Psychnomic Science* 22 (1971), 211–13.

61　L. Fouraker and S. Siegel, *Bargaining behavior* (New York: McGraw-Hill, 1963).

62　Tedeschi, "The exercise of power and influence," 315; F. Stech, "The effectiveness of the carrot and stick in increasing dyadic outcomes during duopolistic bargaining," *Behavioral Science* 29:2 (1984), 11.

63　David Newsom, "A look at African issues at the UN," address at the Atlanta Press Club, 21 September 1971, *Department of State Bulletin (DSB)*, 65:1685

(11 October 1971).

64 Franco Nogueira, *Salazar*, Vol. 5, *A resistencia, 1958– 64* (Porto: Livraria Civilizacao Editora, 1984), 210. I am grateful to Gillian Gunn for the translation of this and other passages that follow.

65 Arthur Schlesinger, *A thousand days in the White House* (New York: André Deutsch, 1965), 489.

66 Dean Acheson, *Present at the creation* (New York: W. W. Norton, 1969), 729.

67 Schlesinger, *A thousand days*, 490.

68 Security Council S/PV 1045, 26 July 1963.

69 Memo to the president from Walt Rostow, deputy special assistant to National Security Affairs, 14 July 1961.

70 Enclosure 1 to dispatch, Lisbon 310, 7 March 1961.

71 Chester Bowles, "Proposals for a breakthrough in U.S.-Portuguese relations in regard to Africa," White House memorandum for the secretary of state, 10 January 1963.

72 Enclosure to dispatch, Lisbon 279, 3 Feburary 1963.

73 Instructions to Lisbon, Department of State airgram, CA-2167.

74 Letter from Franco Nogueira to George Anderson, September 1965, enclosure 2 to airgram, Lisbon A-131, 6 October 1965.

75 Enclosure 1 to Airgram A-328, 14 March 1966.

76 Letter from Salazar to George Ball, under secretary of state, 27 February 1964.

77 Statement of George Anderson, *Policy toward Africa for the 1970s*, Hearings before the Committee on Foreign Affairs, Subcommittee on African Affairs, House of Representatives, 91st Congress, 2nd Session, 1970, 124.

78 Ibid., 132.

79 Ibid., 121.

4   The Nixon Administration and South Africa, 1969–1974

1 Statements of Roger Morris, *South Africa*, Hearings before the Committee on Foreign Relations, Subcommittee on African Affairs, U.S. Senate, 94th Congress, 2nd Session, 1977, 237.

2 Statement of David Newsom, Assistant Secretary for African Affairs, *Policy toward Africa for the 1970s*, Hearings before the Committee on Foreign Affairs, Subcommittee on Africa, House of Representatives, 91st Congress, 2nd Session, 1970, 324.

3 William Rogers, "Report on African tour to Congress," *Department of State Bulletin (DSB)* 62:1608 (20 April 1970), 9.

4 David Newsom, "A look at African issues at the UN," address to the Atlanta Press Club, 21 September 1971, *DSB* 65:1685 (11 October 1971), 377. The Lusaka Manifesto was signed by the Front Line States in 1969. On the whole, it was a conciliatory statement that offered South Africa a reasonable timetable for majority rule providing she publicly committed herself to introducing it.

5 *The Star* (Johannesburg), 20 March 1976.

6 Embtel 37828, U.S. Embassy, Cape Town, 3 February 1976.

7 Richard Nixon, "U.S. foreign policy for the 1970s: The emerging structure of

peace," State of the World Address, 9 February 1972, *DSB* 66:1707, 366.

8 Cited in David Davis, *African workers and apartheid* (London: International Defence and Aid Fund, 1978), 6.

9 NSSM 39, 79.

10 Newsom statement, *Policy toward Africa for the 1970s*, 336.

11 The exceptions were Swazi, whose status was that of a territorial authority, and South Ndebele, that of a regional authority.

12 Cited in Willard Johnson, "U.S. foreign policy toward Africa," *Africa Today* 20:1 (1973), 210.

13 *The Star*, 11 March 1972.

14 See D. A. Kotze, *African politics in South Africa, 1964–74* (London: Hurst, 1975).

15 Colin Legum, "Political leadership in the Bantustans," *Third World* 2 (1973), 17.

16 Interview in Washington, D.C., October 1979.

17 Clarence Mitchell, "U.S. discusses human rights in South Africa," address to Social Political Committee, United Nations, 28 November 1975, *DSB* 73:1905 (29 December 1975), 926.

18 Daniel Moynihan, *A dangerous place* (London: Secker and Warburg, 1975), 242.

19 Mitchell, "U.S. discusses human rights," 928.

20 Ibid.

21 John Dugard, *Human rights and the South African legal order* (Princeton: Princeton University Press, 1978).

22 Statement of Beverley Carter, Deputy Assistant Secretary for African Affairs, *Policy toward Africa for the 1970s*, 329.

23 When the United States acted at all, it did so covertly. The CIA continued to fund the American Lawyers Committee for Civil Rights, which had been set up in the early 1960s under a John F. Kennedy Trust "for the defense of persons charged with crimes under undemocratic legal systems." The committee was involved in a number of cases including the trial of twenty-one suspected terrorists in 1970, the trial of thirteen members of the Unity Movement in 1971, the trial of SASO in 1972, and Robert Sobukwe's action against the minister of justice two years later. See Aida Parker, *Secret U.S. war against South Africa* (1977).

24 Nixon, "U.S. foreign policy for the 1970s" (Cape Town), 366.

25 *New York Times*, 10 November 1971.

26 Newsom statement, *Policy toward Africa for the 1970s*, 323.

27 Ibid., 325.

28 Newsom, interview with *Africa Report*, 13.

29 NSSM 39, 79.

30 The team comprised Dr. Chester Marcus, Dr. Wesley McCain, Dr. Edwin Munger, and Dr. Harriet Murphy.

31 *The Star*, 7 October 1972.

32 Statement by Edwin Munger, *U.S. policy toward Southern Africa*, Hearings before the Committee on Foreign Affairs, Subcommittee on African Affairs, U.S. Senate, 94th Congress, 1st Session, 1975, 271.

33 Statement of Donald M. Irwin, *U.S. business involvement in Southern Africa*, Hearings before the Committee on Foreign Affairs, Subcommittee on Africa,

House of Representatives, 92nd Congress, 1st Session, 1972, 167.

34   Statement of Nathaniel Davis, Assistant Secretary for African Affairs, ibid., 367.

35   Interview in Washington, D.C., October 1979; Interview in Pretoria, July 1978.

36   *The Star*, 12 August 1972.

37   Gatsha Buthelezi, "White and black nationalism: Ethnicity and the future of the homelands," Alfred and Winifred Hoernle Memorial Lecture, South African Institute of Race Relations, January 1974 (mimeo).

38   Jeffrey Butler, Robert Rotberg, and John Adams, *The black homelands of South Africa* (Berkeley: University of California Press, 1977), 224. On becoming assistant secretary in 1974, Nathaniel Davis insisted that the homeland leaders would have to organize themselves on a national level if they ever wanted international recognition. Statement of Nathaniel Davis, *U.S. policy toward Southern Africa*, 360.

39   Ibid., 227.

40   *The Star*, 14 August 1972.

41   Statement of David Newsom, *DSB* 68:1767 (7 May 1973), 580.

42   Department of State reply to Charles Diggs's Action Manifesto (18 February 1972), in *Faces of Africa: Diversity and progress; repression and struggle*, Report of the Special Study Mission to Africa, 1971–72, Subcommittee on Africa, House of Representatives, 92nd Congress, 2nd Session, Appendix 29.

43   Two other options were to buy investment rands, which would sell 40 percent below the exchange value of the rand, or to buy American nonresident bonds, which on low rate of interest would last three years.

44   *Foreign Investment in Apartheid* (UN Unit on Apartheid, 1972).

45   Robert Smith, "The dilemma of foreign investment in South Africa," address before the American Society of International Law, 30 April 1971, *DSB* 64:1670 (28 June 1971), 827.

46   Statement by John Fletcher to Committee of Three (Social, Humanitarian, and Cultural), UN General Assembly, 3 November 1971, *DSB* 65:1692 (29 November 1971), 637.

47   Department of State reply, *Faces of Africa*, 425.

48   David Newsom, "U.S. aid and investment in Africa," speech before World Affairs Council, Rochester, N.Y., 27 May 1970, *DSB* 62:1617 (22 June 1970), 781.

49   Cited in D. Hobart Houghton and J. Bagut, *Source material on the South African economy*, vol. 3 (1920–70) (London: Oxford University Press, 1971), 251.

50   Norman Macrae, "The green bay tree," *The Economist* 29 (June 1968). John Sackur wrote in *The Times*, 26 April 1971, of Macrae's thesis, "The idea of economic forces overcoming the political power structure as it were by internal subversion is immensely attractive It offers the prospect of change in the satisfaction of moral qualms at absolutely no cost to anybody."

51   Michael O'Dowd, "The stages of economic growth and the future of South Africa" (Johannesburg, n.d.) (mimeo.).

52   Richard Nixon, "U.S. foreign policy for the 1970s," 366.

53   Newsom statement, *Policy toward Africa for the 1970s*, 335.

54   Although South Africa was omitted altogether from the country market surveys produced by the Department of Commerce, one of its publications (OBR 70-40,

Market profiles for South Africa) cited the double taxation agreement with the
United States as an investment incentive, while another (OBR 68-12, *Selling in
the Republic of South Africa*) advised companies to set up sales offices in South
Africa to expand their operations.

55   For Chrysler's contribution see *Washington Post*, 11 May 1972.

56   See statement of W. B. Ewald, African-American Institute, Africa Policy Information Center, 29 March 1972, and E. N. Estes (General Motors), South Africa
seminar paper presented by the executive general manager to the Council of
Religion and International Affairs, 16 October 1972. Mobil published a paper in
the summer of 1972 that made its own position clear: "What is most needed to
the continued improvement of the material well-being of nonwhites in South
Africa is not disinvestment, but greater investment. Over the long term only
economic growth can create additional jobs, more job mobility, and greater opportunities for human advancement. And capital investment is a catalyst of economic growth." Cited in *Church investment, corporations, and Southern Africa*
(Corporate Information Center: National Council of Churches, 1973), 129.

57   Smith, "The dilemma of foreign investment," 826.

58   *New York Times*, 3 May 1971.

59   *The Times* (London), 10 July 1971.

60   Fletcher, address to the Committee of Three.

61   Statement of Harold B. Scott, Deputy Assistant Secretary and Director of the
Bureau of International Commerce, Department of Commerce, *U.S. business
involvement in South Africa*, Part I, Hearings before the Committee on Foreign
Affairs, Subcommittee on Africa, House of Representatives, 92nd Congress, 1st
Session, 1971, 236.

62   Anthony Lake, *Caution and concern: The making of American policy toward
South Africa, 1946–71* (Ph.D. dissertation, Princeton University, 1974). See also
Charles Diggs, "My visit to South Africa," *Africa Report* 16:8 (November 1971),
17.

63   Morris statement, *South Africa*, 236.

64   *U.S. business involvement in Southern Africa*, Part 3, Hearings before the Committee on Foreign Affairs, Subcommittee on Africa, House of Representatives,
93rd Congress, 1st Session, 1973, Appendix 1.

65   David Newsom, "U.S. government and business: Partners in African development,"
address to African-American Chamber of Commerce, New York, 16 February
1972, *DSB* 66:1708 (20 March 1972), 444.

66   Ibid., 13.

67   *U.S. policy toward South Africa*, Hearings before the Committee on International
Relations, Subcommittee on Africa, House of Representatives, 95th Congress,
1st Session, 3 March 1977, 38.

68   *U.S. business involvement in Southern Africa*, Part 3, 12.

69   See Lawrence Schlemmer and Tim Muil, "Social and political change in the
African areas: A case study of KwaZulu," in Leonard Thompson and Jeffrey
Butler (eds.), *Change in contemporary South Africa* (Berkeley: University of Cali-
fornia Press, 1975), 107–38.

70   *The Times*, 9 May 1974.

71   David Newsom, "U.S. options in Southern Africa," address at Northwestern
     University, Evanston, Ill., 8 December 1970, *DSB* 54:1647 (11 October 1971), 84.
72   David Newsom, "U.S.-African interests: A frank appraisal, speech to Royal Com-
     monwealth Society, 14 March 1973, *DSB* 68:1764 (16 April 1973), 106.
73   Interview with David Newsom, Assistant Secretary for African Affairs, *Africa
     Report* 17:3 (1972), 16.
74   *The role of popular participation in developing countries* (Cambridge, Mass.:
     MIT Press, 1968), 16.
75   Ball, *The discipline of power*, 259.
76   G. Mennen Williams, action memorandum to Dean Rusk, 29 April 1964.
77   A. S. Mathews *Law, order, and liberty in South Africa* (Berkeley: University of
     California Press, 1972), 299.
78   Morris statement, *South Africa*, 238.
79   Henry Kissinger, "The challenge of Africa," address before the Convention of
     Opportunities Industrialization Center, 31 July 1976, *DSB* 75:1943 (20 Septem-
     ber 1976), 350.
80   Mitchell statement, *Policy toward Africa for the 1970s*, 265.

5   Two Case Studies of Positive Sanctions

1   *Washington Post*, 8 November 1970.
2   Memorandum from Maurice Stans, Secretary of Commerce, to Richard Nixon,
     May 1969.
3   Memorandum from Theodore Eliot, Department of State, to Henry Kissinger, 14
     March 1971.
4   The deficit was $250 million in 1970 (although according to some interpretations
     the loss may have been as little as $25 million). See *Resources of South Africa*,
     Hearings before the Committee on Foreign Relations, Subcommittee on African
     Affairs, Senate, 94th Congress, 2nd Session, 1976, Appendix 3, p. 254.
5   Statement by Stephen Minikes, Vice-President Export-Import Bank, *U.S. policy
     toward South Africa*, Hearings before the Committee of Foreign Relations, Sub-
     committee on Africa, House of Representatives, 94th Congress, 2nd Session,
     1976, 599.
6   David Abshire to Congressman Charles Diggs, 18 February 1972, *Faces of Africa:
     Diversity and progress; repression and struggle*, Report of the Special Study Mis-
     sion to Africa, 1971–72, Subcommittee on Africa, House of Representatives,
     92nd Congress, 2nd Session, Appendix 29, 424.
7   Memorandum from Fred Bergsten to Henry Kissinger, 22 March 1971.
8   Memorandum from Marshall Wright to Henry Kissinger, 29 March 1971.
9   Charles Diggs, *Action Manifesto*, reprinted in *Issue* 2:1 (Spring 1972), 53.
10   Statement by Stephen Minikes, *Resource development in South Africa and U.S.
     policy*, Hearings before the Committee on International Relations, Subcommit-
     tee on International Resources, Food, and Energy, House of Representatives, 94th
     Congress, 1st Session, May 1976, 383.
11   Ibid.
12   *U.S. policy toward South Africa*, Hearings before the Committee on International

Relations, Subcommittee on Africa, House of Representatives, 95th Congress, 1st Session, March 1977, 604.

13   *New York Times*, 13 March 1976. Eximbank increased its limit in South Africa in 1971 so that General Electric could tender for a contract from South African Railways, thus breaching its own rules. *Washington Post*, 15 January 1972.

14   Statement by Myron Kratzer, Deputy Assistant Secretary, Bureau of International, Environmental, and Scientific Affairs, *U.S. policy toward Africa*, Hearings before the Committee on Foreign Affairs, Subcommittee on Africa, House of Representatives, 94th Congress, 2nd Session, May 1976, 297.

15   Statement by Nelson Sievering, Assistant Administrator for International Affairs, Energy, Research, and Development Assistance, *Resource development in South Africa*, 58.

16   Statement by James Blake, Deputy Assistant Secretary for African Affairs, *U.S. policy toward Africa*, 308.

17   *New York Times*, 31 January 1976.

18   The letter is cited at length in Maxine Isaacs, "Tilting towards South Africa," *Africa Report* 21:2 (March/April 1976), p. 7.

19   Ibid.

20   Statement by the Director of Export/Import Control, Department of Commerce, *Implementation of the U.S. arms embargo (against Portugal, South Africa, and related issues)*, Hearings before the Committee on Foreign Affairs, Subcommittee on Africa, House of Representatives, 93rd Congress, 1st Session, May 1973, 273.

21   Ibid., 3.

22   Ibid., 148.

23   Ibid., 53.

24   *National Security Decision Memorandum 81* (NSDM 81), National Security Council, 17 August 1970.

25   NSSM 39, 83.

26   Interview in Washington, D.C., October 1979.

27   In their testimony to the House subcommittee on national security, the director of the State Department's bureau of politico-military affairs and the deputy assistant secretary of defense both volunteered an opinion that South Africa had a role to play in Western security; but when they were pressed to define it, their evasive answers revealed that they had not given the matter much thought. Statements of Ronald Spiers and Robert Pranger, *The Indian Ocean: Political and strategic future*, Hearings before the Committee on Foreign Affairs, Subcommittee on National Security Policy and Scientific Developments, House of Representatives, 1st Session, July 1971, 166, 171.

28   *New York Times*, 12 July 1970. Interview with William Rogers. See also David Newsom, "The UN, U.S., and Africa," address before the Chicago Committee of the Council for Foreign Relations, 17 September 1970, *DSB* 63:1633 (12 October 1970), 503.

29   *U.S. business involvement in Southern Africa*, Part 1, Hearings before the Committee on Foreign Affairs, Subcommittee on Africa, House of Representatives, 92nd Congress, 1st Session, 1971, 291.

30   *Implementation of the U.S. arms embargo*, Hearings before the Committee on

Foreign Affairs, Subcommittee on Africa, House of Representatives, 93rd Congress, 1st Session, March 1973, 53.

31 Statement by Rauer Meyer, director, Office of Export Control, ibid., 35.

32 Ibid., 27.

33 NSDM 81, 6.

34 *The military balance 1976–77* (London: International Institute for Strategic Studies, 1977).

35 *International transfer of conventional arms* (Washington D.C.: U.S. Arms Control and Disarmament Agency, 1973).

36 *Africa Contemporary Record, 1974–1975* (London: Rex Collings, 1975), A94. Even then the administration insisted only on minor modifications. SAFAIR agreed not to employ South African air force pilots, or to allow military personnel in their planes, or to park them in military hangers.

37 Compare *The military balance* with *Southern Africa: The escalation of conflict* (Stockholm Institute of Peace Research, 1976); *International military aircraft and aviation directory* (New York: Aviation Advisory Services, 1977); Statement of Sean Gervasi, *U.S. policy toward Southern Africa,* Hearings before the Committee on International Relations, Subcommittee on Africa, House of Representatives, 96th Congress, 1st Session, 14 July 1977.

38 In December 1977 the State Department recommended the sale of 6 Cessna crop dusters, which were entirely modeled on the Cessna 185.

39 *The Times,* 25 April 1978.

40 Lake, "Caution and concern: The Making of U.S. policy toward South Africa, 1966–1972" (Ph.D. dissertation, Princeton University, 1976).

41 *Implementation of the U.S. Arms embargo,* 123.

42 Cited in *Far Eastern Review* 71:5 (30 January 1971), 6.

43 *Washington Post,* 16 January 1977.

44 Geoffrey Kemp, "South Africa's defence program," *Survival* 14:4 (July/August 1972).

45 *Conference Paper 7* (UN: Center Against Apartheid, Department of Political and Security Council Affairs, November 1977).

46 NSSM 39, 69.

47 *The Star,* 6 January 1973.

48 *The Guardian,* 5 December 1973.

49 Statement of John Reed, Director, Africa Regional Office, Department of Defense, *Disaster assistance to Angola,* Hearings before the Committee on International Relations, 94th Congress, 2nd Session, 1976, 56.

6 Constructive Engagement

1 Cited in Bruce Oudes, "The United States year in Africa," *Africa Contemporary Record 1974–1975* (London: Rex Collings, 1975), A93–94.

2 David Newsom, "Southern Africa: Constant themes in U.S. policy," address to mid-American Committee at Chicago, 28 June 1972, *DSB* 72:1726, (24 July 1972), 120.

3 Statement of Roger Morris, *South Africa,* Hearings before the Committee on

Foreign Relations, Subcommittee on African Affairs, Senate, 94th Congress, 2nd Session, 1976, 189.

4   Statement of Paul O'Neil, *Complex of Portuguese-U.S. relations*, Hearings before the Committee on Foreign Relations, Subcommittee on Africa, House of Representatives, 93rd Congress, 2nd Session, 20.

5   Anthony Lake, "Caution and concern: The making of U.S. policy toward South Africa, 1966–1972," (Ph.D. dissertation, Princeton University, 1976).

6   John Seiler, "The formulation of U.S. policy toward Southern Africa, 1957–76: The failure of good intentions" (Ph.D. thesis, University of Connecticut, 1976), p. 344.

7   Interview, Washington, D.C., March 1980.

8   *Washington Post*, 17 September 1973.

9   Henry Kissinger, *The White House years* (London: Weidenfeld and Nicolson, 1979), 47.

10   *The Star*, 24 February 1972.

11   Henry A. Kissinger, *American foreign policy: Three essays* (New York: Norton and Co., 1969), 20.

12   John Chettle, Washington letter, *South Africa International* 1:3 (January 1971), 160.

13   Cited in Gary Gappert, "The emerging political economy of the Indian Ocean," *Current Bibliography on African Affairs* 4:6 (November 1971).

14   *New York Times*, 2 May 1971.

15   Cited in Gail Cockran, *Vorster's foreign policy* (Pretoria: Academia, 1970), 193.

16   Interview, Washington, D.C., October 1979.

17   Interview, Pretoria, July 1978. The first newspaper article to discuss NSSM 39 appeared in the *New York Times* on 2 April 1972. Terence Smith wrote a dispatch which revealed that the Nixon administration was pursuing a policy "of deliberately expanding contacts and communication with the white governments of Southern Africa." The content of Option 2, however, was not leaked until April 1974. All that the *Washington Post* (8 November) discovered in 1970 was that the White House had decided to opt "where useful [for] small but increasing accommodation with white minority governments."

18   William Macomber, *Diplomacy for the 1970s: A program of management reform for the Department of State* (Washington, D.C., 1970), 556–57. There is, of course, a vast literature on the subject of bureaucratic politics. Two of the most useful books are by the men who were responsible for revamping the NSC system in 1969. Henry Kissinger, "Bureaucracy and policy making," in Morton Halperin and Edward Kanter (eds.), *Readings in American foreign policy: A bureaucratic perspective* (Boston: Little, Brown, 1973); and Morton Halperin, *Bureaucratic politics and foreign policy* (Washington D.C.: Brookings Institution, 1974).

19   Cited in I. M. Destler, *Presidents, bureaucrats, and foreign policy* (Princeton: Princeton University Press, 1972), 139.

20   *Washington Post*, 23 August 1970.

21   Interview, Washington, D.C., March 1980.

22   One of the ironies of constructive engagement was that it made few demands on the bureaucracy's time. Only in 1976 did events in Southern Africa appear at the

top of Kissinger's agenda, meriting two shuttle tours of the region by Kissinger himself and many months of discussions. In this case a crisis created time, rather than compressed it.

23 Ian Dextler, "Can one man do?" *Foreign Policy* 5 (Winter 1971–72), 30.

24 Clyde Fergusson and William Cotter, "South Africa: What is to be done?" *Foreign Affairs* 56:2 (January 1978), 266–67.

25 *The Star*, 15 September 1970.

26 Cited in Oudes, "The U.S. year in Africa," A54.

27 Roger Morris, "Race war diplomacy," *New Republic*, (26 June 1976).

28 Statement of Nathaniel Davis, Assistant Secretary for African Affairs, *U.S. policy toward Southern Africa*, Hearings before the Committee on Foreign Relations, Subcommittee on Africa, Senate, 94th Congress, 1st Session, 1975, 353.

29 *The Star*, 1 April 1970.

30 *The Star*, 15 September 1970.

31 Roger Morris, *Uncertain greatness: Henry Kissinger and American foreign policy* (New York: Quartet Books, 1977), 79.

32 Roger Hilsman, *The politics of policymaking in defense and foreign affairs* (New York: Columbia University Press, 1971), 34.

33 Interview with David Newsom, *Africa Report* 17:3 (March 1972), 15.

34 Lake, "Caution and concern," 144.

35 *Washington Post*, 29 June 1975.

36 Kissinger thought he had solved the problem by establishing informal meetings with Under Secretary of State Eliot Richardson without William Rogers's knowledge. But he discovered quite soon that he really needed access to bureaucrats much lower down in the State Department. See John Learcos, "Kissinger's apparat," *Foreign Policy* 5 (Winter 1971–72), 33.

37 *Africa* 53 (January 1976).

38 None of Kissinger's staff in 1969 had experience of Africa. Morris was a former Soviet analyst. Marshall Wright had never been to Africa before his appointment and never visited the continent while he was at the NSC. His successor, Fernando Rondon, had at least been chief political officer in the U.S. embassy in Malagasy before diplomatic relations were broken off in 1971.

39 Morris, "Race war diplomacy," 12.

40 *The Star*, 15 September 1970.

41 NSSM 39 Annex 6: Subject: Growing congressional interest in Southern Africa.

42 *The Star*, 12 July 1973.

43 Statement of Donald Easum, Assistant Secretary for African Affairs, *Review of State Department trip throughout Southern and Central Africa*, Hearings before the Committee on Foreign Relations, Subcommittee on Africa, Senate, 92nd Congress, December 1974, 15. Public indifference continued until recently. Senator Dick Clark, the chairman of the Senate's Africa subcommittee, confided in 1978 that his committee had not received a single representation from a black group asking it to hold hearings on South Africa.

44 Statement of Roger Morris, *South Africa*, Hearings before the Committee on Foreign Relations, Subcommittee on African Affairs, Senate, 94th Congress, 2nd Session, 1976, 190–91.

45   For Congress's position in this period, see Edward Kennedy "What America should do," *Africa Report* 10:6 (November–December 1975); Jacob Javits, "The congressional presence in foreign relations," *Foreign Affairs* 48:2 (January 1970), 233.

7   The Challenge to Constructive Engagement

1   *The Guardian*, 23 March 1974.
2   Statement of Donald Easum, Assistant Secretary for African Affairs, *Review of State Department trip through Southern and Central Africa*, Hearings before the Committee on Foreign Affairs, Subcommittee on Africa, House of Representatives, 93rd Congress, 2nd Session, December 1974, 28.
3   Statement of Roger Morris, *South Africa*, Hearings before the Committee on Foreign Relations, Subcommittee on African Affairs, Senate, 94th Congress, 2nd Session, 1976.
4   Henry Kissinger, "The U.S. and Africa: Strengthened ties for an era of challenge," address to annual conference, National Urban League, Boston, *DSB*, 65:1939 (23 August 1976), 261.
5   *New York Times*, 2 May 1976.
6   David Newsom, "Southern Africa: Constant themes in U.S. policy," address to the mid-American Committee at Chicago, 28 June 1972, *DSB*, 72:1726 (24 July 1972), 120.
7   David Newsom, "U.S.-African interests: A frank appraisal," address to the Royal Commonwealth Society, 14 March 1973, *DSB*, 68:1764 (16 April 1973), 460.
8   Cited in *U.S. policy toward Southern Africa*, Hearings before the Committee on Foreign Relations, Subcommittee on African Affairs, U.S. Senate, 94th Congress, 1st session, 1975, 370.
9   Morris statement, *South Africa*, 238.
10   *Disaster assistance in Angola*, Hearings before the Committee on International Relations, Subcommittee on International Resources, Food, and Energy, House of Representatives, 94th Congress, 2nd Session, 1976, 154.
11   *New York Times*, 25 June 1976.
12   *The Star*, 8 May 1976.
13   *African Development*, August 1976. At the twelfth OAU summit in Dar-es-Salaam, Nyerere maintained that Africa's real quarrel was not with Salisbury but Pretoria, as the colonial power in Namibia, as Rhodesia's patron, and as an apologist for racial discrimination. Cited in Stanley Yoder, "Does America have a policy?" *Africa Report* 20:3 (May/June 1975), 17. Kaunda also considered that South Africa was "almost a colonial power" in Rhodesia. *The Star* 2 April 1976.
14   NSSM 39, 52.
15   Ibid., 66.
16   Ibid., 67.
17   Warren Christopher, "Human Rights: An important concern for U.S. foreign policy," *DSB* 76:1970 (25 March 1977), 289.
18   William Schaufele, "U.S. relations in Southern Africa," address before the American Academy of Political and Social Science, *DSB* 76:1976 (9 May 1977), 468.
19   Anthony Lake, "Caution and concern: The making of U.S. policy toward South

Africa, 1966–1972" (Ph.D. dissertation, Princeton University, 1976).

20 Anthony Lake, "Africa in global perspective," Christian Herter Lecture, Johns Hopkins University, *DSB* 77:2007 (12 December 1977), 844.

21 Zbigniew Brzezinski, *Power and principle* (London: Weiderfeld and Nicolson, 1983), 140.

22 Cited in Martin Spring, *Confrontation* (Johannesburg: Valiant, 1977), 23.

23 Cyrus Vance, "The United States and Africa: Building positive relations," *DSB* 77:1989 (8 August 1977), 168.

24 Cyrus Vance, "Human rights and foreign policy," *DSB* 76:1978 (23 May 1977), 506.

25 "Vice-President Mondale visits Europe and meets with South African Prime Minister Vorster," *DSB* 76:1997 (20 June 1977), 666.

26 Winston Nagan, "The U.S. and South Africa: The limits of peaceful change," in René Lamarchand (ed.), *American policy in Southern Africa* (Washington, D.C., 1981), 232–33.

27 George Ball, "Asking for trouble in South Africa," *Atlantic Monthly* (October 1977), 43–51.

28 *The Times*, 7 May 1978.

29 R. G. Ranchod, "Political rights and majority rule," in John Beynon (ed.), *Constitutional change in South Africa* (Pietermaritzberg: University of Natal, 1978), 44.

30 Cited in Lake, "Africa in a global perspective," 844.

31 When Andrew Young visited Cape Town in April 1977, the Black Peoples Convention refused to meet him in protest at his willingness to talk to allegedly "unrepresentative" black leaders.

32 Howard Brotz, *The politics of South Africa: Democracy and racial diversity* (London: Oxford University Press, 1977), 150.

33 The text appears in Colin Legum (ed.), *Africa contemporary record, 1977–1978* (London: Rex Collings, 1978), B871–72.

34 See Andrew Young's speech to South African business leaders, *Race Relations News* (Johannesburg, Institute of Race Relations, July 1977).

35 Statement of Richard Moose, Assistant Secretary for African Affairs, *U.S. policy toward South Africa*, Hearings before the Committee on Foreign Affairs, Senate, 99th Congress, 2nd Session, March 1980, 107.

36 Warren Christopher, "Human rights: Principle and realism," address before the American Bar Association, *DSB* 77:1992 (27 August 1977), 76.

37 *Washington Post*, 5 November 1977.

38 For a lengthier discussion of the episode, see Chapter 9.

39 For some of the other liberties that the white community deliberately denied itself, see Julian Friedmann, *Basic facts on the Republic of South Africa and the policy of apartheid* (New York: UN Center against Apartheid, Department of Political and Security Council Affairs, 1977).

40 For the 1960s see Martin Legassick, "Legislation, ideology, and economy in post-1948 South Africa," *Journal of Modern African Studies* 1:1 (October 1974), 5–35.

41 Cited in Matthew Midlane, "The crisis facing South Africa," *Round Table* 274

(April 1979), 116.

42   Oliver Fiss, "Groups and the equal protection clause," *Philosophy and Public Affairs* 5 (Winter 1976), 157.

43   Hugh Tinker, *Race, conflict, and international order* (London: Oxford University Press, 1977), 47.

44   *The Star*, 10 May 1977.

45   *International Herald Tribune*, 10 September 1977.

46   Moose statement, *U.S. policy toward South Africa*, 13.

47   Cited in Heribert Adam, "Survival politics: Afrikanerdom in search of a new ideology," *Journal of Modern African Studies*, 16:4 (December 1978), 662.

48   Statement of Philip Habib to House Subcommittee on African Affairs, 3 March 1977, *DSB* 76:1970 (28 March 1977), 289.

49   Richard Hofstadter, *The paranoid style in American politics and other essays* (New York: Knopf 1965).

50   *New Africa*, December 1977, 1188.

51   *The Times*, 5 September 1977.

52   *Washington Post*, 8 November 1977.

53   Clyde Fergusson and William Cotter, "South Africa—what is to be done?" *Foreign Affairs* 56:2 (January 1978), 263.

54   Thomas Karis, "United States policy toward South Africa," in Gwendolen Carter and Patrick O'Meara (eds.), *Southern Africa: The continuing crisis* (London: Macmillan, 1979), 352.

55   Ibid.

56   Ibid.

57   Fergusson and Cotter, "South Africa," 269–73.

58   Dick Clark, *U.S. corporate interests in South Africa*, Report to the Subcommittee on African Affairs of the Committee on Foreign Relations, U.S. Senate, January 1978, 13–14.

59   Cited in Dean Prinsloo, *U.S. foreign policy and the Republic of South Africa* (Pretoria: Foreign Affairs Association, 1978), 79.

60   The Carter administration did not go as far as the Senate Subcommittee on Africa, which urged the withdrawal of all Eximbank credits. See *Africa Research Bulletin*, (January 1978), 4563.

61   *The Star*, 21 July 1977.

62   Prinsloo, *U.S. foreign policy and the Republic of South Africa*, 59.

63   "Address by President Carter at Commencement, Notre Dame," *DSB* 76:1981 (13 June 1977), 622.

64   Karis, "United States policy toward South Africa," 354.

65   Ibid.

66   Ibid.

67   Cited in Jennifer Seymour Whitaker, *Africa and the United States: Vital interests* (New York: New York University Press, 1978) 203.

68   Karis, "United States policy toward South Africa," 355.

69   "Developments concerning apartheid—a statement by Ambassador Young," *DSB* 77:1997 (3 October 1977), 446–48.

70   "Employment practices in South Africa," *DSB* 77:2003 (14 November 1977), 685–86.

8 The Reagan Administration and Constructive Engagement, 1981–1985

1 J. Eidelberg, "U.S.–South Africa relations—a rejoinder," *Africa Insight* 11:2 (1981), 60.

2 Chester A. Crocker, "A mid-term assessment of the Carter administration's policies in Africa," *International Affairs Bulletin* 3:1 (June 1979), 21.

3 Chester A. Crocker, "South Africa: Strategy for change," *Foreign Affairs* 59:2 (Winter 1980), 324.

4 Ibid., 325.

5 Crocker, "A mid-term assessment," 24.

6 Crocker, "South Africa: Strategy for change," 325.

7 Statement of Chester A. Crocker, *U.S. policy toward South Africa*, Hearings before the Committee on Foreign Affairs, Subcommittee on Africa, Senate, 99th Congress, 2nd Session, March 1980, 677.

8 Crocker, "South Africa: Strategy for change," 350.

9 Kenneth Adelman, Official statement by U.S. ambassador during the plenary debate, 30 November 1981, UN General Assembly, *Southern Africa Record* 25/26 (December 1981), 59.

10 Chester A. Crocker, "Regional strategy for Southern Africa," address before the American Legion in Honolulu, 29 August 1981, *DSB* 81: 2055 (October 1981), 26.

11 Cited in *Africa contemporary record, 1981–1982*, edited by Colin Legum (London: Rex Collings, 1982), B778.

12 Scope Paper: U.S.–South Africa relations. Memorandum from Chester Crocker to secretary of state, State Department, 14 May 1981.

13 *International Herald Tribune*, 2 September 1980.

14 Chester A. Crocker, "The Reagan administration's Africa policy: A progress report," address before the Fourth Annual Conference on International Affairs—University of Kansas, 10 November 1983, *DSB*, 84:2082 (January 1984), 43.

15 Samuel Huntington, "Reform and stability in South Africa," *International Security* 6:4 (Spring 1981), 3–25, reprinted from address at the biennial conference of the Political Science Association of South Africa, Rand Afrikaans University, 17 September 1981.

16 Cited in Heribert Adam and Hermann Giliomee, *Ethnic power mobilized: Can South Africa change?* (New Haven: Yale University Press, 1979), 61.

17 *South Africa comment and opinion*, 12 May 1978.

18 *Financial Times*, 15 March 1982.

19 Henry A. Kissinger, *The troubled partnership* (New York: Harper and Row, 1965), 251.

20 Crocker, "The Reagan administration's Africa policy," 44.

21 Ibid.

22 *Africa News*, 14 November 1983.

23 Crocker, "South Africa: Strategy for change," 344.

24 *Wall Street Journal*, 14 September 1982.

25 *Christian Science Monitor*, 9 February 1983.

26 Lawrence Eagleburger, "Southern Africa: America's responsibility for peace and

change," address before the National Convention of Editorial Writers, San Francisco, 23 June 1983, *DSB* 83:2077 (August 1983), 12.

27 *New York Times*, 15 May 1982.
28 *Washington Post*, 2 February 1982.
29 *The Observer* (London), 27 June 1982.
30 Cited in *Africa contemporary record, 1982–1983*, A149–50.

9   The United States and the State of Black Politics, 1981–1985

1   Chester A. Crocker "South Africa: Strategy for change," *Foreign Affairs* 59:2 (Winter 1980), 342.
2   See Mokunbung Nkomo, "The contradictions of Bantu education," *Harvard Educational Review* 51 (February 1981), 127.
3   Muriel Hurrell (ed.), *Survey of race relations in South Africa in 1981* (Johannesburg: Institute of Race Relations, 1982), 380.
4   Kenneth Harshorne, "The unfinished business: Education for South Africa's black people," *Optima* 30 (July 1981), 24.
5   *U.S. educational assistance in South Africa: Critical policy choices*, report of a staff study mission to South Africa, 21–28 August 1982, Committee on Foreign Affairs, House of Representatives, 30 December 1982, 11.
6   *Focus on political repression in Southern Africa* (London: International Defence and Aid Fund), 53 (July–August 1984).
7   Herman Nickel, "Constructive engagement at mid-term," *Southern Africa Record* 31 (April 1983), 23.
8   *Focus* 53 (July–August 1984).
9   AID Fact-Finding Team, *South Africa educational report*, November–December, 1981, passim.
10 *U.S. educational assistance*, 15.
11 "Answers to clarifications on questions posed by AID about the University Preparation program," Consulting Group Inc., San Diego, Calif., 30 October 1981.
12 *U.S. educational assistance*, 32.
13 American Chamber of Commerce in South Africa, *PACE Bulletin* 2:11.
14 Ibid.
15 Lawrence Eagleburger, "Southern Africa: America's responsibility for peace and change," address before the National Convention of Editorial Writers, San Francisco, 23 June 1983, *DSB* 83:2077 (August 1983).
16 *U.S. educational assistance*, 15.
17 Ibid., 20.
18 *Africa News*, 28 January 1985, 11–12.
19 See David Hauck, *Black trade unions in South Africa*, (Washington D.C., Investor Responsibility Research Center, 1982), 27.
20 Statement issued by the Black Allied Workers Union (SA), London, 14 June 1979.
21 *Financial Times*, 26 May 1981.
22 *New York Times*, 28 December 1980.
23 *Focus* 49 (November–December 1983).
24 *The Guardian*, 20 July 1984.

25 Statement of E. F. Andrews and Allegheny Ludlum, *U.S. policy toward Southern Africa*, Hearings before the Committee on Foreign Relations, Subcommittee on Africa, Senate, 94th Congress, 1st Session, 1975, 471.

26 Lawrence Bowman, *Politics in Rhodesia: White power in an African state* (Cambridge, Mass.: Harvard University Press, 1973), 52.

27 Marcelle Roy, "The contract labor system and the Owambo strike," *African Studies Review* 16:1 (April 1973), 101.

28 Statement of William Schaufele, Assistant Secretary for African Affairs, *U.S. policy toward Africa*, Hearings before the Committee on Foreign Affairs, Subcommittee on Africa, Senate, 94th Congress, 2nd Session, May 1976, 306.

29 *South Africa Report*, 26 April 1985, 7.

30 *Washington Star*, 10 June 1981.

31 Pierre van den Berghe, "A reply to Matthew Nkoana," *New African* 53 (November 1969), 42.

10 The Reagan Administration and the Use of Positive Sanctions

1 Statement of Chester Crocker, *U.S. policy toward South Africa*, Hearings before the Committee on International Relations, Subcommittee on Africa, House of Representatives, 95th Congress, 1st Session, March 1977.

2 Chester A. Crocker, *South Africa's defense posture: Coping with vulnerability* (Beverley Hills: Sage, 1981), 83.

3 Crocker statement, *U.S. policy toward South Africa*, 703.

4 Statement by Princeton Lyman, Deputy Assistant Secretary for African Affairs, before the Committee on Foreign Affairs, Subcommittee on Africa and International Economic Policy and Trade, House of Representatives, 2 December 1982, in *DSB* 83:2074 (May 1983), 27.

5 Lawrence Eagleburger, "Southern Africa: America's responsibility for peace," address before the National Convention of Editorial Writers, San Francisco, 23 June 1983, *DSB* 83:2077 (August 1983).

6 Statement of Randall Robinson, Executive Director, Transafrica, *South African restrictions*, Hearings before the Committee on Banking, Finance, and Urban Affairs, Subcommittee on Financial Institutions, House of Representatives, 98th Congress, 1st Session, 8 June 1983, 95.

7 *U.S. implementation of the arms embargo against South Africa: A review of national legislation and enforcement procedures*, (New York: Special Committee against apartheid, 1–3 April 1981, 18.

8 *Business Week*, 26 April 1982.

9 See *Enforcement of the U.S. arms embargo against South Africa*, Hearings before the Committee on Foreign Affairs, House of Representatives, 97th Congress, 2nd Session, March 1982, 123.

10 *Washington Post*, 27 February 1982.

11 *Washington Post*, 5 June 1981.

12 Statement of Harry Marshall, Principal Deputy Assistant Secretary, Bureau of Oceans and International Environmental and Scientific Affairs, *Control on exports to South Africa*, Hearings before the Committee on Foreign Affairs, Sub-

committee on Africa and International Economic Policy and Trade, House of Representatives, 97th Congress, 2nd Session, 9 February/2 December 1982, 192.

13   *U.S.–South Africa nuclear relations*, Washington, D.C., 14 May 1981, reprinted in Richard Leonard, *South Africa at war: White power and the crisis in Southern Africa* (Westport, Conn.: Lawrence Hill, 1983), 254.

14   Statement of Archelaus Turrentines, Deputy Assistant Director for Nuclear Weapons Control, Arms Control, and Disarmament Agency, *Controls on export of nuclear-related goods and technology*, Hearings before the Committee on Foreign Affairs, Subcommittees on International Security and International Economic Policy, 97th Congress, 2nd Session, 24 June 1982, 30.

15   Ibid., 32.

16   Ibid., 53–54.

17   *Africa* 134 (October 1982), 51.

18   *New York Times*, 15 October 1982.

19   Ibid.

20   Ibid.

21   Statement of Richard Eckaus, *To increase the U.S. quota in the IMF and related matters*, Hearings before the Committee on International Trade, Subcommittee on International Trade, Investment, and Monetary policy, Senate, 98th Congress, 2nd Session, 3 May 1983, 641.

22   Ibid., 644.

23   John Chettle, "The politicization of the International Monetary Fund," *South Africa International* 14:2 (October 1983), 377.

24   Chester A. Crocker, "An update of constructive engagement in South Africa," statement before the Committee on Foreign Relations, Subcommittee on African Affairs, Senate, 99th Congress, 1st Session, 26 September 1984, 6.

25   Chester A. Crocker, "Reagan administration's Africa policy: A progress report," *DSB* 84:2082 (January 1984), 42.

26   Eagleburger, "Southern Africa: America's responsibility for peace," 8–9.

11   The United States, South Africa, and Regional Security, 1981–1985

1   Louis Cantori and Steven Spiegel, *The international politics of regions* (Englewood Cliffs, N.J.: Prentice-Hall, 1970).

2   See, for example, Timothy Shaw, "Southern Africa: Cooperation and conflict in the international subsystem," *Journal of Modern African Studies* 12:4 (1973), 633–55; William Zartman, "Africa as a sub-state system," *International Organization* 21 (1967), 545–64; Lawrence Bowman, "The substate system of Southern Africa," *International Studies Quarterly* 11:1 (1968), 231–61.

3   V. M. Nyathi, "South African imperialism in Southern Africa," *African Review* 5:4 (1975), 460.

4   Kenneth Grundy, *Confrontation and accommodation in Southern Africa: The limits of independence* (Berkeley: University of California Press, 1973), 71.

5   Christian Potholm, "The effects on South Africa of changes in contiguous territories," in Leonard Thompson (ed.), *Change in contemporary South Africa*

(Berkeley: University of California Press, 1975), 333.

6   P. Smit, "Botswana: Resources for development" (Pretoria: Africa Institute, 1973).
7   Potholm, "Effects on South Africa," 336n.
8   Seretse Khama used to refer in this period to Botswana's "outward policy, a policy which although it has attracted less international attention than that of a neighbour country . . . is not without its own significance for the future peaceful development of our region." Speech delivered at a dinner given by the chairman of Botswana RST and Bamangwato concessions, cited in William Henderson, "Independent Botswana: A reappraisal of foreign policy options," *African Affairs* 73 (1974), 44.
9   Henry L. Bretton, *Power and politics in Africa* (London: Longmans, 1973), 87.
10 J. L. Sadie, "An economic commission for Southern Africa," *South Africa International* 1:4 (April 1971), 167–75.
11 Cited in Gail Cockram, *Vorster's foreign policy* (Pretoria: Academic, 1970), 126. For a discussion of this model by three contemporary South African economists, see J. A. Lombard, P. J. van der Merwe, and J. J. Stadler, *The concept of economic cooperation in Southern Africa* (Pretoria: Econburo, 1968), 34.
12 Timothy M. Shaw, "International organizations and the politics of Southern Africa: Toward regional integration or liberation?" *Journal of Southern African Studies* 3:1 (October 1976), 5.
13 Joseph Nye and Robert O. Keohane, *Power and interdependence: World politics in transition* (Boston: Little, Brown, 1970).
14 "SADDC: Plans for and obstacles to equitable regional integration," *Southern African Facts Sheet* 72 (June 1985), 4.
15 F. R. Metrowich, *South Africa's new frontiers* (Johannesburg: Valiant, 1977), 9.
16 L. Bowman, "The substate system," *International Studies Quarterly* 11:1 (1968). See also Margaret Doxey, "Alignments and coalitions in Southern Africa," *International Journal* 10:3 (Summer 1975); Richard Dale, "Southern Africa: Research frontiers in political science," in Christian Potholm and Richard Dale (eds.), *Southern Africa in perspective* (New York: Free Press, 1972).
17 Bowman, "The substate system," 20.
18 Grundy, *Confrontation and accommodation*, 301.
19 Potholm, "Toward the millennium," 325.
20 Timothy Shaw, "Kenya and South Africa: Subimperialist states," *Orbis* 21:2 (Summer 1977), 376.
21 V. M. Nyathi, "South African imperialism in Southern Africa," *African Review* 5:4 (1975), 394.
22 Cantori and Spiegel, *The international politics of regions*, 5.
23 Statement of John Reed, Director of Africa Regional Office of the Assistant Secretary of Defense, *Disaster assistance to Angola*, Hearings before the Committee on International Relations, Subcommittee on Resources, Food, and Energy, House of Representatives, 94th Congress, 2nd Session, 1976, 56.
24 B. J. Vorster, "Our house is not built on sand," *South Africa Panorama*, February 1977, 30.
25 Richard Bissell, *South Africa and the United States: The erosion of an influence relationship* (New York: Praeger, 1982), 65.

26 Scope paper memorandum from Chester A. Crocker to Secretary of State Alexander Haig in preparation for Haig's meeting with Foreign Minister Pik Botha, 14 May 1981.

27 Statement of Chester A. Crocker, Assistant Secretary for African Affairs, *Namibia and regional destabilization in Southern Africa*, Hearings before the Committee on Foreign Affairs, House of Representatives, 98th Congress, 1st Session, 15 February 1983, 21.

28 Cited in Grundy, *Confrontation and accommodation*, 297.

29 *Washington Post*, 18 January 1983.

30 Grundy, *Confrontation and accommodation*, 297.

31 *The Times*, 9 September 1981.

32 Crocker statement, *Namibia and regional destabilization*, 51–52.

33 Lawrence Eagleburger, "Southern Africa: America's responsibility for peace and change," address before the National Conference of Editorial Writers, 23 June 1983, *DSB* 83:2077 (August 1983).

34 Gerald Bender, "The Reagan administration and Southern Africa," *Atlantic Quarterly* 2:3 (Autumn 1984), 239.

35 Pierre Hassner, "Superpower rivalries: Conflict and cooperation," Diffusion of Power Part 2—Control and conflict, Adelphi Paper 134 (London: International Institute for Strategic Studies, 1977).

36 Chester A. Crocker, "The Reagan administration's Africa policy: A progress report," address before the Fourth Annual Conference on International Affairs, U.S.–Africa relations since 1960, University of Kansas, 10 November 1983, *DSB* 84:2082 (January 1984).

37 *Financial Times*, 13 January 1984.

38 *The Star*, 27 November 1982.

39 Eagleburger, "Southern Africa: America's responsibility," 10–12.

40 Frank Wisner, Interview with *Seminario* (Lisbon), 17 December 1983.

41 U.S.–Mozambique: The State Department perspective," *Africa Report* 28:1 (January/February 1983), 46.

42 Ibid.

43 Bernard Weimer, "U.S. and the Front Line States of Southern Africa: The case for closer cooperation," *Atlantic Quarterly* 2:1 (Spring 1984).

44 When Washington was prepared to exert pressure, the results could be quite dramatic. In January 1982 South Africa was persuaded to rearrest forty-five mercenaries who had taken part in an abortive hijacking and attempted overthrow of the government of the Seychelles. Although Pretoria was not directly involved in the attempt, there was evidence to show that it had been discussed with the security services and that the government may even have provided logistical support and arms (*New York Times*, 22 April 1982). Finding its reluctance to prosecute the mercenaries unacceptable, the United States hinted at the possible severance of air links under the terms of the Bonn Declaration against terrorism in the air unless the ringleaders were brought to trial. In a further move the U.S. Embassy sent a group at counselor level to the Foreign Ministry to convey Crocker's deep concern (*Washington Post*, 6 January 1982). This was an area, of course, in which South Africa was highly vulnerable. If the seven major Western powers had

banned all flights to and from the republic, South Africa's isolation would have been complete.

45 Cited in *Africa contemporary record, 1983–1984*, edited by Colin Legum (New York: Africana, 1985), A11.

46 *West Africa*, 3 June 1985.

47 George Bush, "A new partnership with Africa," extracts from an address to the Kenya Chamber of Commerce, Nairobi, 19 November 1982, *Southern Africa Record* 29 (December 1982), 35.

48 Cited in Colin Legum, "The continuing crisis in Southern Africa," in *Africa contemporary record, 1983–1984*, A45.

49 *Financial Times*, 9 January 1984.

50 Herman W. Nickel, "Constructive engagement at mid-term," 28 February 1983, published in *Southern Africa Record* 31 (April 1983), 22–23.

51 *New York Times*, 17 December 1979.

52 *The Times*, 16 March 1984.

53 *The Observer*, 18 March 1984.

54 Cited in Benjamin Pogrund, "Reagan's shift: The view from Pretoria," *Washington Quarterly* 5:1 (Winter 1982), 182.

55 *Los Angeles Times*, 24 April 1984.

12 The Namibia Issue, 1970–1985

1 Memo to President Johnson from William Brubeck, 29 July 1964.

2 UN Security Council Resolution 264, 20 March 1969. See also the secretary-general's report on the implementation of Resolution 264 in UN Doc S/9204.

3 National Security Decision Memorandum 55 (Subject—South-West Africa), 17 April 1970 (revised 22 May 1970).

4 William Rogers, "The rule of law and the settlement of international disputes," address before the American Society of International Law, 25 April 1970, *DSB* 62:1612 (18 May 1970), 623–27.

5 Some authorities believed it had none. See Solomon Slonim, *South-West Africa and the United Nations: An international mandate in dispute* (Baltimore: Johns Hopkins University Press, 1973), 351.

6 Charles Yost, "U.S. supports Security Council resolution on Namibia," *DSB* 60: 1554 (7 April 1969), 301–03.

7 *Legal consequences for states of the continued presence of South Africa in Namibia (South-West Africa) notwithstanding Security Council Resolution 276* (The Hague: ICJ, 1971).

8 William Rogers, "A legacy of peace: Our responsibility to future generations," address to the 26th session of the General Assembly, *DSB* 65:1687 (25 October 1971).

9 *New York Times*, 21 May 1970.

10 NSDM 55.

11 Interview with Charles Yost, U.S. ambassador to the United Nations 1969–1970, Washington D.C., October 1979.

12 Statement of Ralph S. Hocker, Associate Director, Division of Corporation on

Finance, Security, and Exchange Commission, *Critical developments in Namibia*, Hearings before the Committee on International Relations, Subcommittee on Africa, House of Representatives, 93rd Congress, 2nd Session (February/April 1974), 48.

13   Statement of Nathaniel Davis, Assistant Secretary for African Affairs, *Resources in Namibia: Implications for U.S. policy*, Hearings before the Committee on International Resources, Food, and Energy, House of Representatives, 94th Congress, 1st Session (June 1975/May 1976), 19.

14   Ibid.

15   *The Star*, 14 November 1970.

16   Interview with David Newsom, *Africa Report* 17:3 (March 1973).

17   *Tsumeb: A profile of U.S. contribution to underdevelopment in Namibia* (New York: Corporate Information Center of National Council of Churches, April 1973).

18   John Kane-Berman, *Contract labour in South-West Africa* (Johannesburg: South Africa Institute of Race Relations, 1972).

19   Statement of Robert Smith, *U.S. business involvement in Southern Africa*, Part 3, Hearings before the Committee on Foreign Affairs, Subcommittee on Africa, House of Representatives, 93rd Congress, 1st Session, 1973, 64.

20   Charles Yost, "U.S. supports UN Security Council resolution on Namibia," *DSB* 60:1554 (7 April 1970).

21   Smith statement, *Business involvement*, 57.

22   Cited in Michael Arnheim, *South Africa after Vorster* (Cape Town: Howard Timmins, 1979), 95.

23   Statement before the Committee on Foreign Affairs, Subcommittee on Africa, House of Representatives, 96th Congress, 1st Session (17 June 1981), *DSB* 81:2053 (August 1981).

24   Chester Crocker, "U.S. interests in Africa," address before the Council for Foreign Relations, New York, 5 October 1981, *DSB* 82:2058 (January 1982), 26.

25   Chester Crocker, "A U.S. policy for the '80s," *Africa Report* 26:1 (January/February 1981), 10.

26   Memo of conversation April 15/16 1981 Pretoria AF-10 McElhaney S/P Keyes AF/S.

27   Crocker, "U.S. policy for the '80s."

28   Gerald J. Bender, "Angola, the Cubans, and American anxieties," *Foreign Policy* 31 (1978), 8.

29   *Africa* 50 (1975).

30   Frank Kitson, *Low-intensity operations: Subversion, insurgency, and peacekeeping* (London: Faber, 1971), 144.

31   Cited in *Namibia and regional destabilization in Southern Africa*, Hearings before the Committee on Foreign Affairs, House of Representatives, 98th Congress, 1st Session, February 1983, 90.

32   Cited in Colin Legum, "The Southern Africa crisis," in *Africa contemporary record 1981–1982*, edited by C. Legum (London: Rex Collings, 1982), A17.

33   John de St. Jorre, "Africa—crisis of confidence," *Foreign Affairs* 61:3 (1983), 685.

34   Chester A. Crocker, "A mid-term assessment of constructive engagement," House

of Representatives, 13 February 1983. See *Southern Africa Record*, April 1983, 18.
35   Ibid., 22.
36   *The Times*, 19 September 1981.
37   Cited in Legum, "The Southern Africa crisis," A31. (See note 32.)
38   Chester Crocker, address to the American Legion, Honolulu 29 August 1981, reprinted in *Africa Report* 26:6 (November/December 1981), 10.
39   *Washington Post*, 12 September 1981.
40   *Washington Post*, 20 March 1981.
41   Cited in Statement of Gray, *Namibia and regional destabilization*, 6.
42   *The Star*, 14 April 1981.
43   *New York Times*, 25 July 1981.
44   *The Times*, 22 September 1981.
45   Legum, "The Southern African crisis," A23.

13   Toward a Conclusion

1   *Washington Post*, 9 December 1984.
2   *The Times*, 19 August 1980.
3   Crocker, "Strategy for change," *Foreign Affairs* 59:2 (Winter 1980), 344.
4   Chester A. Crocker, "U.S. policy for the '80s," *Africa Report* 26:1 (January/February 1981), 14.
5   B. Pogrund, "Reagan's shift: The view from Pretoria," *Washington Quarterly* 5:1 (Winter 1982).
6   Crocker, "Strategy for change," 344.
7   John de St. Jorre, "South Africa: Is change coming?" *Foreign Affairs* 60:1 (Fall 1981), 106–22.
8   Hermann Nickel, U.S. Ambassador, *A mid-term assessment of American policy*, address before the American Chamber of Commerce in South Africa, 16 February 1983, reprinted in *Southern Africa Record* 32 (April 1983), 21.
9   Heribert Adam, *Modernizing racial domination* (Berkeley: University of California Press, 1971), 13.
10   *Financial Times*, 1 November 1980.
11   *The importance of a method in our struggle*, pamphlet issued at a meeting of the Committee of 61 on 19 April 1980.
12   Cited in D. Kotze, *African politics in South Africa, 1964–74* (London: Hurst, 1975), 209.
13   Michael Arnheim, *South Africa after Vorster* (Cape Town: Howard Timmins, 1979), 90.
14   Neal Blewett, "The franchise in the United Kingdom, 1885–1913," *Past and Present* 32 (December 1965), 31.
15   M. Kinnear, *The fall of Lloyd George: The political crisis of 1922* (London: Macmillan, 1973), 21.
16   Sam Nolutshungu, *Changing South Africa: Political considerations* (Manchester, Eng.: Manchester University Press, 1982), 90.
17   Charles Seymour, *Electoral reform in England and Wales* (London: David and Charles, 1970), 254.

18   Robert Merton, *Social theory and social structure* (Glencoe, Ill.: Free Press, 1968), 279.

19   John Plamenatz, *Ideology* (London: Macmillan, 1970), 125.

20   Adam, *Racial domination*, 71–72.

21   Raymond Aron, *Main currents in sociological thought*, vol. 2 (London: Weidenfeld and Nicolson, 1968), 179–252.

22   Nolutshungu, *Changing South Africa*, 143.

23   Lawrence Schlemmer and Edward Webster, *Change, reform, and economic growth* (Johannesburg: Raven Press, 1978), 40.

24   Cited in E. Patel, *The world of Nat Nakasa* (Johannesburg, 1975), 68.

25   Cited in Vincent Razis, *Swords or ploughshares: South Africa and political change* (Johannesburg: Raven Press, 1978), 142–43.

26   Mark Orkin, "Review of change, reform, and economic growth in South Africa," *Social Dynamics* 4:1 (1978), 69–70.

Index

Christopher Coker is lecturer in international relations at the London School of Economics and editor of *The Atlantic Quarterly.* His publications include *U.S. Military Power in the 1980s* (1983), *The Soviet Union, Eastern Europe, and the New International Economic Order* (1984), and *The Future of the Atlantic Alliance* (1984).

Library of Congress Cataloging-in-Publication Data
Coker, Christopher.
The United States and South Africa, 1968–1985.
Bibliography: p.
Includes index.
1. United States—Foreign relations—South Africa.
2. South Africa—Foreign relations—United States.
I. Title.
E183.8.S6C65 1986   327.73068   86-2203
ISBN 0-8223-0665-4